Enabling Public Service Innovation in the 21st Century

E-GOVERNMENT
in ASIA

Enabling Public Service Innovation in the 21st Century

E-GOVERNMENT in ASIA

Compiled & Edited by

James SL Yong

TIMES EDITIONS

© 2003 Times Media Private Limited

Published by Times Editions
An imprint of Times Media Private Limited
A member of Times International Publishing
Times Centre, 1 New Industrial Road
Singapore 536196
Tel: (65) 6 2139288
Fax: (65) 6 2854871
Email: te@tpl.com.sg
Online bookstore: http://www.timesone.com.sg/te

Times Subang
Lot 46, Subang Hi-Tech Industrial Park
Batu Tiga, 40000 Shah Alam
Selangor Darul Ehsan, Malaysia
Fax & Tel: (603) 56363517
Email: cchong@tpg.com.my

National Library Board (Singapore) Cataloguing in Publication Data

E-government in Asia : enabling public service innovation in the 21st
   century / compiled & edited by James S.L. Yong. – Singapore :
   Times Editions, 2003.
   p. cm.
   ISBN : 981-232-591-3 (pbk.)

     1.   Internet in public administration – Asia. 2. Electronic government
       information – Asia. 3. Administrative agencies – Asia – Data
       processing. I. Yong, James S. L., 1959-

JQ24
351.5957 – dc21   SLS2003019669

Printed in Singapore

PREFACE

The Rise of e-Government

The years around 1993 until 1996 were the exploratory years for the popular Internet. That was when the novelty of e-mail, websites and online forums captured the attention of people from all walks of life. It was a time of pioneers and of experimentation. Personal and company websites sprouted everywhere. The subsequent years of 1997 to 1999 were the days of e-Commerce and e-Business. Recognised successes like Amazon.com, Yahoo! and eBay motivated millions of entrepreneurs to jump onto the online commerce bandwagon. That was accompanied by an unrelenting search for the new business model that would excite venture capitalists and attract millions in funding — the dot com era was born. The mood was one of unbridled exuberance. Conventional management thinking was turned on its head. Youthful millionaires were put on pedestals as poster children of the new economy. Then came 2000 and the bursting of the bubble. It started slowly at first, then picked up momentum and once-revered start-ups began to fall like dominoes in quick succession. This continued through much of 2001. The pendulum swung to the other extreme. Financiers, who just eighteen months previously had been throwing millions at startup ventures, were now screening business projections and asking for near guarantees before they would even consider a project. In short, funding practically dried up.

While all this was happening, the potential of the Internet and new technologies was not going unnoticed by another sector. The government or public sector had been observing and experimenting with their own online presence. Technology was nothing new to governments. Public administrations have always been heavy users of information technology. However, for the past few decades, the focus of their attention was largely on "back-room" automation — introducing data processing machines to inject more efficiency into internal procedures and processes. Led by early initiatives in some Western developed nations, the projects became more extensive and ambitious. These initiatives began to come under a new category called "electronic government", popularised as "e-Government" probably around mid 2000.

The whole idea was to use the technologies not only to enhance internal processes, but to re-conceptualise and deploy services that would better meet public needs. In fact, many e-Government initiatives effectively created an alternative new channel for citizens and businesses to engage with government administrations at a faster pace, more conveniently and at a lower cost.

Why this Book?

I have often been asked: why develop a book on e-Government? Why e-Government in Asia? There are several driving factors for this book.

The first factor is personal interest. Governments touch more lives than any other institution in the world. The potential impact that e-Governments can have on society will only increase in significance. Asia, home to more than 60 percent of humanity, is arguably subject to even more transformation than some of the developed nations in the Western hemisphere. Asia is a heterogeneous mix of races, languages, religions and cultures. The nations may be at differing stages of their economic development, and some of them concurrently span the agricultural, industrial and information economies. This book is the product of a dynamic and fascinating study of an increasingly pervasive phenomenon.

The second factor is my professional involvement in e-Government. Over the past two decades of my career, I have had the opportunity to engage with and consult for a variety of organisations, both in the commercial and government arena, in several countries within Asia. For the past five years, I am privileged to have been a member of National Computer Systems Pte Ltd (NCS), an organisation that has been closely involved in government ICT[1] design and deployment in Singapore, Hong Kong and other countries in the Asia-Pacific region. The work of NCS in the public sector over the past 22 years has involved envisioning, architecting and implementing complex IT solutions for governments.

The third and possibly most compelling driving factor for this book is a belief that such a book can play a role in opening up more cross-sharing of knowledge and experiences among the countries in Asia. The journey of e-Government is one that most nations deeply believe is key to their progress, and rather than each nation reinventing the wheel, the chapters of this book may point to avenues for cross-sharing and collaboration. If we can achieve, even in a small part, this objective, we would have made our contribution to the brotherhood of Asian nations.

We have chosen to focus specifically on e-Government programmes in Asia, as opposed to extending the coverage worldwide, because we believe that Asian nations have unique needs for e-Government, driven by their social and cultural heritage, and they also face different challenges along their journey. This is borne out by some of the case examples discussed in the chapters. A practical reason is that focusing on Asia also gives us the opportunity to delve deeper into the subject matter. Further, being Asians ourselves, the authors have a greater familiarity with Asian customs and practices, and can better relate to the environment and needs.

Who will Find this Book Useful

We believe the contents of this book will be useful for several audiences.

The first group are the public sector executives who are themselves involved either in directing, developing or deploying e-Government programmes. They will,

---

[1]   Information and Communications Technology.

hopefully, find it beneficial to learn what their contemporaries in other nations are doing.

The second group include those working in the private sector or non-governmental organisations that engage with government administrations. Such engagement may be linked to the provision of products and services to government ministries or agencies, and it will be invaluable for them to get a better understanding of e-Government directions and priorities.

This book will also be of relevance to students and academics who may be interested in management of technology and change. The arena of e-Government is arguably even more impactful than that of e-Business.

Structure of this Book

This book is divided into three parts.

* The first part, entitled "Scope", offers our understanding of what e-Government is. Ever since the term evolved, there have been many perspectives rendered and many frameworks developed. We review some of these and explore what it means to be on the e-Government journey.
* The second part is entitled "Vision". The individual chapters in this section deal with different economies in Asia — focusing on their overall vision, strategies and focus areas, as well as on the key challenges and lessons they have gained in the process. It is not possible within the scope of this publication to cover every economy in Asia. The selection covered (Brunei Darussalam, China, Hong Kong SAR, India, South Korea, Malaysia, Singapore, Taiwan and Thailand) hopefully gives a fair reflection of the e-Government scene in Asia.
* The third and final part is entitled "Perspectives". Here, we focus on several disparate areas — some service, some infrastructures, some practices — where the authors share their views on what is happening and key areas of e-Government solutions, services or challenges. The concluding chapter offers some perspectives of what may be in store in the forthcoming years.

This book contains the views of many co-authors with deep and varied experiences in e-Government. While individual perspectives may vary in details, I have found that the overall sentiments and key objectives are common to all.

James SL Yong
Senior Director
Institute for Insights & Innovation
National Computer Systems Pte Ltd
Singapore

jslyong@singnet.com.sg

15 June 2003

ACKNOWLEDGEMENTS

It has been my privilege to edit and author this book. This has been an intellectually stimulating exercise and a wonderful opportunity to meet and share ideas with many individuals who are in the forefront of the exciting e-Government programmes in their countries. It is a revelation to uncover the wealth of ideas and innovations that have been conceived to meet the needs of different nations and to overcome some of the challenges faced.

Profound gratitude must first go to Mr Lee Kwok Cheong, CEO of NCS, without whose leadership and encouragement, this book would never have been realised. Without the commitment and support of NCS, it would not have been possible to carry out the interviews and necessary research.

It is "natural" that this book on e-Government should have been born from within NCS. Thousands of professionals within NCS have for the last 20 years been deeply involved in envisioning, architecting and implementing IT solutions for Government — beginning way before the term "e-Government" was popularised. First as part of the National Computer Board (NCB) in Singapore, NCS were the key implementers of the Civil Service Computerisation Programme. They have been involved in government strategic IT master planning not only for Singapore, but for other countries, such as Mauritius. After NCS corporatised in 1996 and became a commercial entity, our consultants have been involved in projects for the governments of Singapore, Hong Kong and other Asian countries.

If developing a book can be compared to a journey, I cannot adequately thank all those along the winding road, who provided invaluable assistance in one form or another. In addition to the authors, who will be mentioned later, let me attempt to list some of the individuals and organisations involved in the development of this book. If I should inadvertently miss out anyone, please accept my advance apologies.

My sincere appreciation goes to individuals from various government or government-related agencies across the region. In the spirit of cross-border knowledge sharing, they have generously shared their experiences and contributed to the overall body of knowledge on e-Government in Asia. In particular, I would like to mention: the Information Technology and State Stores Department (ITSSD) in Brunei Darussalam, the Commerce, Industry and Technology Bureau (CITB) in Hong Kong SAR, the Malaysian Administrative Modernisation and Management Planning Unit (MAMPU) and Multimedia Development Corporation (MDC) in Malaysia, the Infocomm Development Authority (IDA) and Ministry of Finance (MOF) in Singapore, the Research, Development and Evaluation Commission (RDEC) in Taiwan, and the National Electronic and Computer Technology Centre (NECTEC) in Thailand.

I would like to acknowledge various individuals within the NCS Group in Singapore and its overseas offices: Evan Cheah, Eunice Chew, Murie Chow, David Chua, Foo Hooi Ling, Goh Gek Noi, Robin Hu, Tony Lau (in Malaysia), Lee Kang Yam, John Li (in China), Lim Boon Guan (in Brunei), Christopher Lim, Ng Beng Lim, Rita Ong, Zoe Tan, Derry Tung, Wee Teck Hin, Yip Kong Ban, Yong Teck Thong and Vanessa Zehnder. They were involved at different stages of the project, sharing their expertise and experiences, helping in research, proposing sources of information and reviewing content. Thanks also to Hamidah Abdullah for her tireless administrative support throughout the entire project.

Much generous assistance has been received from other parties such as Professor Xiong Chengyu of Tsinghua University, Beijing, Dr Vincent Ming and Ms Grace Kuo in Taipei, Vishwanath Ramachandran in Hyderabad, Dr Alvin Mah and Alex Yong in Kuala Lumpur, Perry Chou and Yap Yean Teo in Singapore.

The quality of this book has been considerably enhanced by the superb advice and editorial efforts of Times Media staff, especially Ms Anita Teo-Russell.

Finally, loving thanks to my parents for all their support, and to my wife Jacqueline and daughter Jemima for bearing with this somewhat cranky writer for the past year.

ABOUT THE AUTHORS

Editor and Author

James SL Yong is the Senior Director, heading the Institute for Insights & Innovation (I^3), a research & strategic consulting arm of National Computer Systems Pte Ltd (NCS). James has been with NCS for five years, and in that time has headed both the business consulting and technology consulting groups. He has also provided consulting to public and private sector organisations in Singapore, Hong Kong and Taiwan.

James has more than 20 years corporate experience in such organisations as Wang (UK), Hewlett-Packard, Shell Eastern Petroleum, Cap Gemini Asia and Singapore Telecom, holding executive and management roles in the functional areas of information technology (IT), finance, marketing and professional services delivery. In the mid-1990's, he managed his own Internet services business, and was one of the pioneers of cybercafes in Singapore.

James has an Honours degree in Computer Science and a Masters in Business Systems Analysis & Design, both from the City University, London, UK. He also has postgraduate qualifications in accounting and finance. His professional interests are in e-Government and e-Business strategies, knowledge and learning, as well as organisational innovation. An author of numerous articles and papers, James is also a frequent speaker at conferences. His views have appeared in various regional publications.

Authors *(in alphabetical order)*

Edwin LC Ang is a Security Consultant in the Infrastructure Management and Security Centre of NCS Communications Engineering Pte Ltd, and manages a team of security delivery specialists. With 12 years of Infocomm working experience, he has been focusing on IT security since 1997. He comes from a software product development and management background, with emphasis on data communications and application data security. He specialises in solutions relating to cryptographic implementations, including PKI systems, content security, and access control security.

Edwin graduated from Ngee Ann Polytechnic with a Merit Award in Computer Studies and subsequently from the Queensland University of Technology in Australia. He is currently a member in the Security Standards and Privacy Technical Committee of SPRING Singapore/Infocomm Development Authority (IDA), which recommends security standards suitable for Singapore. He also serves in the Accreditation Evaluation Committee of the National InfoComm Competency Centre (NICC) as a technical evaluator for IT-related courses.

Bok Hai Suan is the Director of Information Systems with NCS. He is responsible for the group's information systems and IT infrastructure in the region.

He has more than 10 years experience in managing information systems departments of government and commercial organisations. The key areas he has worked on include strategic IT planning and architecture, IT policy and performance management, project and facility management, knowledge management, and competency development.

A certified IT project manager, Bok has served on the executive committee of the Certified IT Project Manager chapter of the Singapore Computer Society. He is also a member of the Association for Information Systems and an editorial member of various newsletters.

Dr Chong Yoke Sin is the Assistant Chief Executive of NCS, and a key person involved in charting NCS' overall directions. As the government solutions leader, Yoke Sin successfully grew the business by three times since NCS' corporatisation, including garnering new major projects in Hong Kong and Australia.

Yoke Sin also manages the Business Solutions Group in NCS. This group of 1,700 experienced professionals comprises the client service and business delivery functions of NCS. There are many government domain-specialised groups such as Healthcare, Government Finance, Government Administration, Transportation and Logistics, National Communications and Infrastructure, National Defense, Justice and Security and Education.

Yoke Sin oversees many project implementations in the various agencies of the Singapore and Hong Kong governments. These engagements include visioning, branding, management consulting in finance and human capital development, systems integration, bespoke software development and outsourcing.

Yoke Sin sits on many committees in the government think tanks including: SPRING, and Ministry of Health. She has written many articles on e-Government and IT in government, and is a regular contributor to the *Straits Times* and *Business Times* (Singapore). She has also speaks frequently at regional conferences on e-Governance and e-Government.

Yoke Sin has a PhD in Chemistry from the National University of Singapore. She joined IBM in 1983 as systems engineer and became the Asia product head for CICS in 1987. During her stint at IBM, she managed many commercial sector and government sector clients. She left IBM in 1991 and was with Hitachi Data Systems as consulting manager until joining NCS in 1996. In 1998, Yoke Sin completed the Advanced Management Programme at the Harvard Business School.

Lee Kwok Cheong is the Chief Executive Officer of the NCS Group. Previously, KC (as he is known to all) headed both the Government Systems Division and the National Information Infrastructure Division at the former National Computer Board (NCB), now known as the Infocomm Development Authority of Singapore (IDA). In those capacities he managed Singapore's Civil Service Computerisation Programme and IT 2000 programme.

KC serves on the boards and advisory committees of various education and research institutions. He was an Adjunct Associate Professor at Singapore's Nanyang Business School (1999–2002) and co-authored a book, *Hi-Tech Hi-Touch Branding,* with branding guru Dr Paul Temporal in 2001.

His public service contribution includes sitting on the 4th University Committee, the Academy of Law Technology Law Study Group and the National Crime Prevention Council Board. On the sports front, he was a racing steward and management committee member with the Singapore Turf Club, and a member of the Singapore Island Country Club's Finance Committee. Internationally, he sits on China's Suzhou Industrial Park International Advisory Council and the Singapore-India Infocomm Technology Task Force.

KC was born in Hong Kong. After studying at MIT and the University of California at Berkeley, he worked for Andersen Consulting. He came to Singapore in 1983 to join NCB (now IDA). He attended the Stanford Executive Programme in 1995 and the INSEAD AVIRA programme in 2001.

For his contribution to the IT industry, KC was conferred the "IT Person of the Year" Award by the Singapore Computer Society in March 2000.

Janice Leong Lau Kheng is a Group General Manager under the Global Business division of NCS, and manages NCSI (HK) Ltd. She holds directorships of NCS' overseas subsidiaries and is an international manager.

Janice is a Certified IT Project Manager (Senior) conferred by the Singapore Computer Society and the Infocomm Development Authority (IDA). Her experience covers software engineering, application development, database administration, procurement, project management of turnkey solutions, strategic IT planning, business process reengineering and outsourcing management.

She has held positions as Head, IT department, Deputy Director, CIO in government positions advising government clients in exploitation of IT. Janice holds an Honours degree in Computer Science from the UK and an MBA in Management of IT from Singapore. She has been a frequent speaker in IT and trade conferences.

Lim Hiap Koon is a Consultant with the Business Solutions Group of NCS. He joined NCS in 2002 and is currently focused on designing and implementing e-learning solutions.

Hiap Koon was the founder of tertiary community portal, Funkygrad.com. Created in 1999, Funkygrad is a leading integrated content solutions provider, taking the perspectives of tertiary students and catering to all aspects of tertiary lifestyle. Funkygrad reaches 100,000 tertiary students across Singapore, Malaysia and Australia by providing Internet content, strategic applications, data management services and marketing expertise to student communities. Hiap Koon was involved in kick-starting operations in the aspects of management, strategic planning, collaboration, and business innovation.

Hiap Koon has an Honours degree in Computing (Information Systems) from the National University of Singapore (NUS). His professional and research interests are in e-Government, e-Business strategies, computer-mediated communication, inter-organisational innovation, e-community development and knowledge management.

Praba Nair is a Director with the Institute for Insights & Innovation in NCS. Prior to joining NCS, he has held various management and consulting positions in Singapore and the region over the past 14 years.

Praba specialises in the areas of knowledge management, learning and change management. He focuses on planning and aligning knowledge with the business objectives of the organisation and formulating change management programmes to enable collective learning and sharing within the organisation. As a keen proponent of these disciplines, he is a frequent participant in local and regional forums, seminars and conferences on these themes. Praba regularly conducts KM seminars at the Institute of Systems Science, NUS as an adjunct teaching staff. He has been a faculty member of the Regional Advanced Management Consulting programme jointly organised by the Productivity and Standards Board (PSB) and Japan International Co-operation Agency. He is also an editorial board member of the *Journal of Information and Knowledge Management*. His views have been published in the *Computer Times* and *Business Times* in Singapore.

Praba holds Bachelor of Commerce and MBA degrees from the University of Newcastle, Australia. He also has a Certificate in Management Consulting from JICA (Japan International Cooperation Agency).

Poranee Phureesitr is a Thai national. She holds a Bachelors degree in Computer Engineering from Chulalongkorn University in Bangkok. She was a Bank of Thailand scholarship recipient and completed her MBA from the Fuqua School of Business, Duke University in the US. Poranee joined the Bank of Thailand in 1996 and was involved in the development of the national electronic fund transfer systems. During that time, she also lectured at the Southeast Asia University in Bangkok.

In 2000, Poranee joined NCS in Singapore as a consultant in the e-Business Consulting practice. She then moved to the US for more than two years, where she worked as a management consultant, focusing on financial solutions. One of her projects involved the implementation of a financial system for a US federal government agency. Upon her return to Singapore, Poranee was an independent consultant when she was invited to contribute to the development of this book, focusing particularly on Thailand's initiatives.

Sameer Sachdeva is currently working as a Project Manager for the World Bank project on "Capacity Building for Good Governance" and is employed with Department of Administrative Reforms, Government of India. He had previously worked with Cupid Software and Tata Consultancy Services. Sameer holds a graduate degree in Electrical Engineering and postgraduate qualifications in Management from University of Roorkee (IIT-Roorkee).

He was the founder Editor-in-Chief of *Parivartan*, a newsletter on e-Governance. As a consultant, he has helped the Department of Information Technology, GOI to evolve a strategy for carrying out an e-readiness assessment of India. Sameer has also been awarded by the National IT Council, Malaysia for his contributions to e-Governance.

Sameer has published articles on government process reengineering, e-Governance initiatives and issues, routes of e-Governance, legal frameworks for e-Governance, information management and security issues for e-Governance. He has also developed concept papers on "National Information Infrastructure", "e-Readiness Assessment", "Single Window for E-BIZ", "e-Governance Strategy for India", "e-Governance Action Plan for India" and "School for e-Governance". He has contributed to various publications such as *E-Commerce* and *ICT4D*. He is also an advisory member of the planned Commonwealth Centre for Electronics Governance and is associated with the National Productivity Council, Ministry of Commerce and Industry in their e-Governance endeavours. Sameer moderates India's first e-group on e-Governance called India-egov@yahoogroups.com.

Jeffery BH Tan is a Director with the Institute for Insights & Innovation (I^3) in NCS. He returned to NCS in 2000 after a stint running a SingTel-supported start-up focused on promoting Digital Rights Management services in the region. Prior to joining I^3, Jeffery took charge of the e-Business Consulting unit of NCS where he led various strategic consulting engagements for government and commercial organisations in the region.

Jeffery has more than 13 years of experience spanning various technical and management positions. His career started in the then Institute of Information Technology (then the research and development arm of NCB), where he participated and led projects in application of innovative IT solutions. He has since been involved in many other areas of technology management including product development, strategic IT and e-Business consulting. During the late 1990s, he pioneered an e-Commerce bureau service targeted at SMEs while serving as Technology Manager for SingTel's e-Commerce Division.

Jeffery received his Bachelor of Science (Information Systems & Computing Science) from the National University of Singapore. He has completed an advanced executive management programme jointly organised by the Singapore Institute of Management and the international Institute for Management Development (IMD) in Switzerland.

Contents

Perspectives

Scope

e-Government: Enabling Public Sector Reform

James SL Yong and Lim Hiap Koon

▲ ▼ ▲ ▼ ▲ ▼ ▲ ▼

The art of government simply consists in making things right,
or putting things in their right places.
When the ruler himself is "right", then the people
naturally follow him in his right course.

Confucius (551–479 BC)

▲ ▼ ▲ ▼ ▲ ▼ ▲ ▼

ON GOVERNMENT

Today, with the possible exception of organised religion, the institution of government probably touches the lives of more people worldwide than any other institution in the history of mankind. Government policies and programmes impact numerous facets of individual and organisational development and growth. The public sector is the single largest source of employment in most countries. Government-led economic strategies and spending play a pivotal role in determining the growth or decline of entire industry sectors within the nation. Indeed, government has become a pervasive influence on everyday life.

In this study, *e-Government in Asia*, it is apt to begin our journey by reflecting on the word "government" and considering some fundamental questions. Questions such as: What really is government? Why do we need government? What is the primary purpose of government?

What is government and why do we need it?

The first two questions are intractably linked. The definition of government is often phrased in terms of key requirements that society places on its government.

The New Oxford English dictionary defines government as "the system by which a state or community is governed" or "the action or manner of controlling or regulating a state, organisation, or people".

Other common definitions include "the exercise of political authority over the actions or affairs of a political unit, people, etc, as well as the performance of certain functions for this unit or body" and "the executive policymaking body of a political unit, community, etc". While all these definitions are individually informative, they often do not lend a deep enough appreciation of how government has been perceived by different peoples over different eras.

An etymological view may shed some light. The word "govern" originates from Middle English, from Old French *governer*, from Latin *gubernare* meaning "to steer or rule", and from the Greek *kubernan* or "to steer". It is interesting to note that after many decades of governments steeped in controlling, or at least having a large (and possibly invasive) role in multiple facets of citizens' lives, current thinking on the government's role seems to gravitate towards "steering and not rowing". In other words, governments are now advised to undertake more the role of a catalyst and facilitator rather than trying to provide all the services themselves.

We can also find a wealth of meanings when we look at some Asian words, characters or scripts for "government". Let's consider a few examples.

The Chinese characters for "government" (shown on the right) are read as "zhèng fǔ".

The first character "zheng" is made up of two radicals. The leftmost radical "zheng" means "proper", "right" or "correct", while the radical on the right denotes a hand holding a stick. Thus "zhèng" has connotations of someone using punitive means to enforce the right behaviour.

Figure 1-1: Chinese

The second character "fǔ" is made up of an upper radical "yan" which looks like a roof, and depicts a shelter or building. Beneath this is the radical "fu" which means "handing over, usually of papers or money". So the complete character "fǔ" connotes a building where documents are consigned or money handed over.

Hence the combined characters "zhèng fǔ" embodies very rich meaning — associations with a punitive authority which tries to enforce proper behaviour, and which is normally housed in some official building where documents and money change hands. Such are the origins of government in ancient China.

In the Malay or Indonesian language, the word government is *kerajaan* which comes from the root word *raja* or ruler. In the ancient Malay world, the authority of the ruler was final, and the ruler was effectively the government.

सरकार

Figure 1-2: Tamil

In the Indian sub-continent, there are multiple variations of words meaning "government". In Tamil, government is *aracankam* from the root word *arac — atchi —* which means rule or reign of a king or of an elected member of a political party. There are more than 30 different variations of the word government in Sanskrit. These include administration, guidance, government business, system of government, good government, exercise of government, principles of government and instruments of government. Most of the descriptions tend to emphasise what it means to have a good government.

Government consultants and authors Osborne and Gaebler[1] wrote simply that:

> Government is the mechanism we use to make communal decisions: where to build a highway, what to do about homeless people, what kind of education to provide for our children. It is the way we provide services that benefit all our people: national defense, environmental protection, police protection, highways, dams, water systems. It is the way we solve collective problems: drug use; crime; poverty; homelessness; illiteracy; toxic waste; the spectre of global warming; the exploding cost of medical care. How will we solve these problems? By acting collectively. How do we act collectively? Through government.

The difference between government and governance is often raised. Governance, according to the New Oxford English dictionary, is defined as "the action or manner of governing". Rather than engage in a debate on semantics, for the purposes of this study we found Osborne and Gaebler's distinction a convenient and practical one to adopt: "Governance is the process by which we collectively solve our problems and meet our society's needs. Government is the instrument we use."

It has been noted that there are two broad forms of government: totalitarianism and constitutionalism, both of which exist in varying degrees in different countries. Totalitarianism is a system in which the government attempts to control all aspects of the individual's life. The totalitarian system usually has one leader at the top of the government pyramid who rules for life. He is typically surrounded by a group of advisors who carry out his dictates. Examples from history are Nazi Germany and the former USSR. Constitutionalism is a government form that attempts to limit the scope of government in the average citizen's life and attempts to guarantee individual liberties. Examples would be the USA, UK and France.

What is the primary purpose of government?

This question is more profound than one might expect. There are several possible levels of approach. A seemingly obvious way is to just accept observations of current practice as the basis for our definition of the proper role of government. We start listing such areas as: defence, economic management, healthcare services, law enforcement, transportation, trade and industry regulation, immigration, foreign affairs, education, and so on. At the end of the exercise, we realise we are merely mouthing the names of the existing government ministries and agencies that we are familiar with.

A second way is to revert to some arbitrarily chosen historical period and list what some governments of that era did. We then try to weed out those actions which have no modern equivalent or relevance, to leave behind the roles that may be construed as fundamental. This usually produces a shorter list, but suffers from a strange assumption that a past age had especially enlightened government, which is often not a valid premise.

A third approach is to try to think what the roles *should be* rather than what they are or were. This can be much tougher as it can be very difficult to clear one's mind of current practice and historical precedent. Some examples of such roles may be "obtaining the greatest good for the greatest number" or "resolving conflict between people living in societal groups". It would be nice to base a theory of government on one simple, generally agreed description from which all other aims of government could be developed, rather than starting with an arbitrary collection of unrelated aims, but this writer is not convinced whether such an ideal is achievable.

Modern governmental bodies carry out and engage in a range of activities, some directly derived from statutory powers as defined by legislation, some not. Some of these functions include:

- foreign diplomacy;
- military defense (protection of national sovereignty);
- maintenance of domestic order;
- administration of justice;

- provision for public goods and services;
- promotion of economic growth and development (leading to more jobs and higher incomes); and
- operation of social programmes to alleviate poverty.

At the local government level, these functions may translate into more "tangible" facilities or amenities. These include housing and building, roads and road safety, public utilities (ie electricity, water supply and sewerage), development incentives and controls, environmental protection, recreational amenities, agricultural support, education, health and welfare to name but a few.

In constitutional democracies, the functions of government also include protection of civil liberties and making provision for and regulating the conduct of elections.

PUBLIC SECTOR REFORM

The traditional portrait of many governments worldwide — that of a massive bureaucratic machinery operating at high cost, agencies delivering inefficiently, unresponsive officials shirking accountability — is gradually fading. Over the past two decades, a series of initiatives to transform government processes, "reinvent the government", create the "new public management (NPM)" or set up "Government 2.0" has been widely discussed and selectively adopted in an attempt to address perceived short-comings and generally make government "work better". As pointed out by B. Guy Peters,[2]

> ... the definition of "working better" may differ across governments, and even across components of the same government. The basic point, however, is that if government is to be able to overcome the discontent and distrust of its citizens, it must find ways to become more efficient and effective in the processes of making and implementing policy. At the same time, however, there are also pressures for government to become more responsive to the public and to be more transparent in the way in which it makes decisions.

Some reforms have been radical while others are more incremental. However, it is difficult to find a political system that has not seriously examined its public administration and imposed some form of change. The degree of the change may vary, but almost invariably there has been change.

The global nature of this public sector reform movement is also striking. The concept of the "new public management" has caught the attention and gained momentum across governments, nations, continents and cultures.

An impressive number of public administrations have picked up the gauntlet — from Western nations such as New Zealand, Sweden, USA and UK to Asian governments in Hong Kong, South Korea, Malaysia and Singapore.

Various studies[2, 3] have revealed that the ideas and principles underlying the government reform movement are remarkably consistent:

- **Market Alignment**

  The key idea has been based on the assumption that the public sector organisation would be more efficient and effective if it were more like the private sector entity. The reforms suggested hinge on trying to use private sector methods, and market-style strategies and incentives to drive public policy, strategies and behaviour. Some examples of reforms driven by market alignment are introduction of rewards and incentives based on measurable civil servant performance, and privatisation of selected state-owned enterprises.

- **Productivity Enhancement**

  The relentless search of greater efficiency — often driven by public demand for more services to be provided without commensurate increase in taxes — leads public administrations to review their key processes, eliminating or streamlining them where possible.

- **Service Orientation**

  In an attempt to make the government more "customer-friendly" and "service conscious", public administrations have tried to reinvent their service delivery programmes. Instead of designing programmes from the perspective of the service providers (especially government officials) and managing them through existing bureaucracies, reformers have literally turned the system on its head and tried to put the service recipients (mainly citizens and businesses) first. In some cases, this strategy has meant giving citizens choice among alternative service systems or providers.

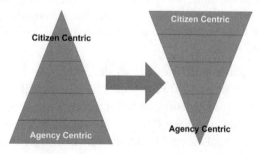

Figure 1-3: Reinventing Service Delivery

- **Decentralisation**
  A key structural reform that has been implemented has been to breakup tightly integrated ministerial departments and replace them with an "agency model", which allows programme implementation activities to be moved to relatively autonomous agencies while policymaking remained in a central unit. Such empowering of agencies is geared towards developing programmes that are more responsive and effective.

- **Separation of Policymaking and Service Delivery**
  By splitting the roles of purchaser of services (the policy function) from that of providing the service (the service delivery function), government administrations can remove a potential conflict of intentions and improve their policymaking and monitoring. After doing this, these governments have sought to improve the efficiency of service-delivery, which might or might not remain in the hands of government, while improving their purchasing capacity.

- **Accountability**
  To improve their ability to deliver what they promise, governments try to get officials to focus on outputs and outcomes, rather than processes and structures. In addition, the citizen-centric approach makes them accountable for their performance not only up the chain of command, but also to their customers.

At the broadest level, these reforms seek to replace traditional rule-based, authority-driven processes with market-based, competition-driven tactics.

At one period, the NPM or public sector reform trend was seen to be geared towards downplaying or downsizing government. Subsequently, the focus shifted more towards government transformation, and on re-affirming and revitalising the role of the state and public sector, with a new *modus operandi* (that of a steering state), rather than focusing primarily on size of government per se.[4]

Different nations have chosen different paths for implementing public sector reform. In the 1990s, work by consultants Osborne and Gaebler has influenced some of the governmental policies and strategies with their proposals of broad principles for reinventing government (refer to Endnote 1):

- steering rather than rowing;
- empowering rather than serving;
- injecting competition into service delivery;
- transforming rule-driven organisations;

- funding outcomes, not outputs;
- meeting the needs of the customer, not the bureaucracy;
- earning rather than spending;
- prevention rather than cure;
- from hierarchy to participation and teamwork; and
- leveraging change through the market.

There is the perennial question of whether NPM as a new administrative paradigm has achieved its claims and intentions to bring about a better and more efficient government. Answering this question involves debates on how to define and measure performance and productivity in the public sector. Empirical studies of reform implementation are still needed to provide analytical tools and perspectives to facilitate such debates.

EMERGENCE OF E-GOVERNMENT

It was observed after some years of effort on public sector reforms that progress had been much more limited than originally envisaged. Specifically, practitioners and academics cited the lack of an enabler to achieve significant leaps needed to effect reforms.

One such enabler came in the form of Information and Communications Technology (ICT). The advent of the Information Age has resulted in important transformations to many facets of life. Rapid advances in computing technology and connectivity have forever changed how people live and work, how companies carry out business and how governments serve their constituents. Witnessing the speed at which the private sector had exploited emerging technologies to create new business models, services and delivery channels, the public sector too began to experiment in the early 1990s and were soon exploring in depth how technology could be leveraged on to enhance efficiency and public services.

At the same time, increased exposure to the possibilities of the Internet and other ICTs had begun to redefine citizens expectations of their government and its services. As emerging ICTs diffused into the society, citizens demanded services of similar quality to those found in commercial organisations. Consequently, public sector leaders grappled with how to deliver these.

The use of technology by government to enhance access to and delivery of public services to benefit citizens, business partners and employees has been labeled "Electronic Government", or e-Government for short. It can be said that e-Government creates a new paradigm of public service. The traditional administrative focus of governments has gradually shifted to become customer-focused, serving citizens and business partners directly by providing integrated and seamless services, information and transactions. Indeed, e-Government has the potential to profoundly transform citizens' perceptions of civil and political interactions with their governments.

Although much of the attention and excitement have centred on public service delivery through the Internet, e-Government affects every aspect of a public organisation. It is not just about technology, infrastructure, business processes or human resources. It is all these areas (and more) combined and integrated. Delivering such integrated services require inter-agency cooperation, coordinating and collaborating between different departments and levels of government. In essence, it provides a new way forward, fundamentally reshaping workflows and innovating new processes.

E-GOVERNMENT DEFINED

When the e-Government movement began in earnest just a few years ago, the Internet presented governments around the world with a set of theoretical possibilities for new service delivery. Many governments were looking toward the future and wanted to capitalise on the tempting potential of revolutionizing the government-customer relationship through emerging web-based technologies.

A large number of public administrators, academics and technologists were enticed to invest significant efforts in the research and development of e-Government. As a result, different initiatives refer to their own programmes by different names. During the course of our study, interactions with various stakeholders revealed terms such as "digital government", "internetworked government"[5] and "government online". For the purpose of this paper, we have deemed all these terms to be synonymous.

In order to make progress in understanding the trends and issues involved in digitizing the government, it is important to develop a clear understanding of what the term e-Government means to both academics and practitioners.

A number of definitions for e-Government have been offered in existing literature. Very often, these definitions have come to imply e-Government as the government's use of technology, in particular, web-based Internet applications to enhance access and delivery of government services to citizens, business partners, employees and other government entities.

To a large extent, the phenomenon of e-Government can be explained unambiguously by adopting a definition of e-Government that includes all electronically executed transactions between government agencies and citizens.

In particular, the adoption of Internet technologies has enabled governments to embrace a citizen-centric approach to service delivery and be the public service that operates "one-stop" and "non-stop".[6] Customer-centric governments are embracing Internet technologies to share information, track customer behaviour, link up legacy systems, and integrate technology across horizontal functions. For example, instead of having to visit multiple agencies to effect the change of a residential address, a citizen can change his address details with all the government agencies through a single interface at the click of a mouse.

These predominantly Internet-driven activities increase the value of customer self-service and encourage citizen participation in the governmental process. The relationship is no longer just a one-way, us-versus-them proposition; rather it is about building a partnership between government representatives and citizens.[7, 8]

Despite the citizen-centric focus, the definition of e-Government is not limited to a service-based view of offering electronic public services to citizens. It has been observed that e-Government in this information age has also become an inter-organisational phenomenon, and that technological improvements have implied more cooperative initiatives between government departments and organisations in complex, diverse and often divided political systems.

Therefore, to envisage e-Government comprehensively, it is necessary to include the concept of "e-Administration",[9] which implies the application of electronic media for the management of the internal public organisation.

Within the administrative perspective, e-Government acts as a catalyst or a "guiding vision" to transform governments. Efforts to use new technologies to transform public organisations can cover changes at multiple levels through reengineering and renewing organisational structure, business processes, network and scope.[10, 11, 12, 13]

Although there are different views on the concept of e-Government, the adoption of ICTs by the public sector will almost consistently affect (i) public service delivery, (ii) organisational settings and (iii) the social/political system. First, service enhancement initiatives will improve reliability and accessibility. Second, ICTs can be used with organisational transformation to generate phenomenal gains in organisational efficiency and effectiveness. Third, increased interactions between government and citizens encourage citizens to be more participative. This in turn allows governments to be more responsive and effective.

The ultimate goal of e-Government is to continuously improve the interactions of the government, business and citizens, so as to stimulate political, economic and social progress of the society.

In this chapter, we have adopted a perspective on e-Government that is grounded on the broad concept of emerging ICTs transforming the role and function of various stakeholders in public administration. With regard to this view, e-Government implies the adoption of such technologies by the government to reform and reinvent public organisations. This initiative enables the government to steer and serve the society in a citizen-centric nature, resulting in more efficient and effective governance.

PERSPECTIVES OF E-GOVERNMENT

The struggle to define a common perspective of e-Government is partially rooted in the phenomenal expansion of the Internet and its penetration into markets, communities and public organisations. Yet, it also reflects our continuous search for better ways to adapt in order to meet new spatial, digital and demographic realities. It has long been realised that e-Government cannot be simply derived by imposing new technology on existing governance models.

As the public sector adapts itself to a new environment, it must also serve as a catalyst for guiding all stakeholders toward a common path. E-Government invariably becomes intertwined with the broader governance transformations, reshaping our economy, society and polity.

In order to facilitate understanding and implementation of e-Government, academics and practitioners develop frameworks to provide a schematic description of the e-Government system, theory, and phenomenon. Many of these proposed frameworks or models also serve to present a simplified view of the relationships between different stakeholders.

A generally accepted e-Government strategic framework (Figure 1-4) is centred on critical dynamics between different bodies within the society. These bodies include the "government", "citizens" and "businesses". To move these three critical sectors towards the e-Government vision, the "government" sector functions both as an "initiator" and a "reactor", which continuously engages in two-way interactions with other critical sectors.

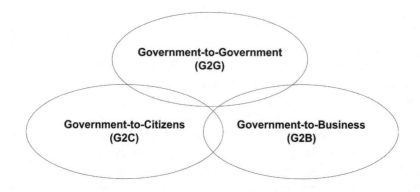

Figure 1-4: Interactions with Critical Sectors

The Government-to-Government (G2G) sector represents internal systems and procedures which form the backbone of public organisations. G2G involves sharing data and conducting electronic transactions between governmental actors. This includes both intra and inter-agency interactions between employees, departments, agencies, ministries and even other governments.

Government-to-Business (G2B) initiatives have been receiving a significant amount of attention, partly because of the dynamic nature of commercial activities in general and the potential for reducing transaction costs through improved procurement practices. Shifting government transactions online provide the opportunities for companies to simplify regulatory processes, cut through red tape, keep legal compliance and start operations quicker and easier through electronic filing, and statistical reporting. Rather than travelling to a government office to fill up paper forms, a contractor, for example, will find it more convenient to apply for building permits over the Internet.

The delivery of integrated, single source public services also creates opportunities for businesses and government to partner together to offer a hybrid of public and commercial services under the same umbrella. For instance, an online portal to renew a vehicle license also provides drivers with the option to purchase car insurance or schedule for maintenance.

Government-to-Citizens (G2C) initiatives have been designed to facilitate citizen interaction with the government. The focus of G2C is customer-centric and integrated electronic services where public services can be provided based on a "one-stop shop" concept. This implies that citizens can carry out a variety of tasks, especially those that involve multiple agencies, without needing to initiate contacts with each individual agency. A single access point also reinforces citizen participation in democratic processes since they can access administrative proceedings readily and articulate their needs more conveniently to public officials.

As researchers seek to deepen their understanding of relationships between stakeholders, new frameworks which evolved from a redefinition and refinement of fundamental relationships were developed. For example, Heeks (refer to Endnote 9) presented the domains of e-Governance, consisting of "e-Administration", "e-Citizens and e-Services" and "e-Society" (Figure 1-5).

While e-Administration initiatives improve internal government processes, e-Citizens and e-Services deal with improving communication and quality of service between government and citizens. Finally, e-Society initiatives concern interactions of government with businesses and civil communities. As each domain develops and progresses, e-Government initiatives may increasingly fall into overlaps. A successful e-Government project therefore constantly strengthens connections within government, between government and citizens, and between government and other civil society institutions.

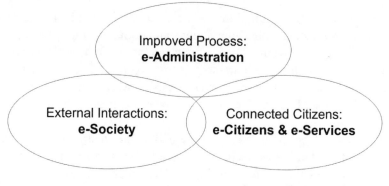

Source : Heeks (2001)

Figure 1-5: Overlapping Domains of e-Governance

The concept of a "relationship" between government and each of its stakeholders has been unique and dynamic. While many frameworks are rhetoric in nature and developed based on segments of transactions between stakeholders, a robust framework for e-Government also seeks to analyse issues from the perspectives of "knowledge", "process" and "tele-cooperation" (refer to Endnote 10).

Knowledge management represents an effective way of looking at and improving how a public organisation uses its intellectual resources. The "knowledge" perspective recognizes that the role of public administrators and their work are sources of knowledge in public organisations. While redesigning transactions in e-Government, it is important that both explicit and tacit knowledge of the organisation be adequately captured to prevent any knowledge loss.

From the "process" perspective, the utilisation of ICT to enhance service delivery efficiency in public organisations can fundamentally reorganise and redesign business processes within the public administration. This exercise can lead to a rethinking of the workings of government, where organisational boundaries fade and give way to innovative organisational design.

The "tele-cooperation" perspective deals with the interactions involving various agencies and trading partners in a work process. A partnership-driven e-Government, which delivers more integrated and collaborative services, will imply a major organisational challenge for the government to simultaneously manage partnerships both internally across governments and externally across sectors.

Today's conventional thinking about e-Government has to go beyond seeking theoretical explanations to the e-Government phenomenon in terms of rhetoric stakeholder interactions and domain perspectives. Since the e-Government movement began, much attention has also been devoted to plotting its evolution, including the genre and order of new services and capabilities that would evolve. What emerged were generally accepted models that described and predicted e-Government growth in stages or strategic phases.

The question, on the minds of every public administrator, technology analyst and academic has been, "Is there a better way to understand the e-Government evolution and develop e-Government successfully?"

E-GOVERNMENT DEVELOPMENT MODELS

As much as it seems that a successful e-Government integrates strategy, people, process and technology, governments have been working very hard to formulate comprehensive development models and effective action plans to chart successful implementation.

Many have turned to a stage-based approach, describing discrete phases of e-Government development and analysing structural transformations.

The table below depicts a variety of development models that have been proposed:

Proposed by/ Source	Stage 1	Stage 2	Stage 3	Stage 4	Stage 5	Stage 6
Deloitte Research[14]	Information publishing/ dissemination	"Official" two-way transactions	Multi-purpose portals	Portal personalization	Clustering of common services	Full integration and enterprise transformation
Elmagarmid & McIver[15]	One-way communication	Two-way communication	Complex transactions	Integration across government administration	—	—
Layne & Lee[16] (Figure 1-7)	Catalogue	Transaction	Vertical integration	Horizontal integration	—	—
Watson & Mundy (refer Endnote 7) (Figure 1-8)	Initiation	Infusion	Customization	—	—	—

Figure 1-6: e-Government Development Models

Generally, the initial stages of e-Government evolution involve publishing or cataloguing information on the Web. Subsequently, the internal systems are connected to online interfaces and citizens are able to transact electronically with the government.

The focus on developing citizen-centric portals presented citizens with a single point of entry where citizens are able to customise the portals with desired features of their own. In doing so, governments build "one-to-one relationships between themselves and their citizens", thus establishing two-way communication channels.

At the final stage of evolution, the perception of different government departments will disappear and the public will view the government as one entity. Full integration and enterprise transformation eliminate "silos" at different levels (vertical) and functions (horizontal) of government services. Through a "one-stop shopping" concept, citizens can contact one point of government and complete any level of government transaction, eliminating redundancies and inconsistencies in the information bases.[14, 15, 16]

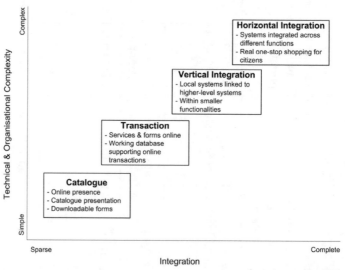

Source: Layne and Lee (2001)

Figure 1-7: Dimensions and Stages of e-Government Development

While traditional models of evolution were adequate for the times when governments and analysts alike were exploring new territory, it does not seem to be so now. Development models, which depict growth in discrete stages, have since been deemed to be flawed and unrealistic.

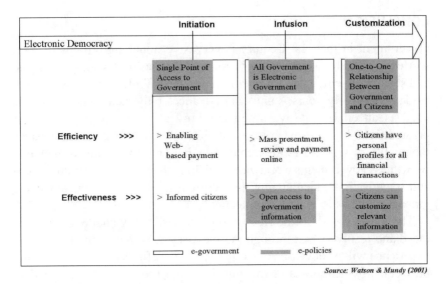

Source: Watson & Mundy (2001)

Figure 1-8: Strategic Phases of e-Government Development

Critics have commented that these traditional models are purely functional charts which just show different complexities of portal development.

In particular, while most traditional models place "enterprise-wide transformation" as the final stage in e-Government evolution following four or five technological stages, organisational change at the enterprise level is not necessarily an end result. In fact, recent e-Government developments have incorporated enterprise-wide transformation as the driving force behind the design, development and implementation of each new service that would appear on each development stage.[17] This allows governments to continuously look for opportunities to improve service and realise economic benefit for each service at each stage.

While new paradigms of understanding the e-Government phenomenon have been discovered, the challenge remains for governments traversing on the e-Government journey to chart, formulate and develop evolution models that fit tightly to their unique context and operating environment.

Almost certainly, there can never be a single development model that fits all e-Government implementation and guarantees success. In particular, the issues that have been raised or will be put forward in subsequent sections are by no means comprehensive or representative of all e-Government projects. Nevertheless, we hope to provide a foundation for further analysis and offer practical guidelines for governments to implement successful e-Governments.

CONCLUSION

Government in the 21st Century is pervasive, touching billions of lives worldwide. Public sector reform is not new, and has been widely discussed and selectively embraced for over two decades. While some progress was made in the early years, significant advances only came when ICT was used as an enabler. Governments, taking a cue from private sector organisations, began to experiment with ICT to boost efficiency and enhance the quality of services to the public. Moving onto the e-Government era, we witness governments worldwide rethinking their interaction with citizens and organisations, challenging their current models and conceptualising innovative ways to leverage on technologies and talents.

The journey will not be free from obstacles. Many challenges will be faced and resolved, and through these experiences, much knowledge and experience will be developed. In transforming the fundamental relationship between government and the public, government agencies need to continually ask of themselves:

- With the advent of Internet technologies as a catalyst, how have the roles and functions of governments changed — then and now?
- How can we responsibly transform our current business models, while incorporating new and emerging technologies?
- Are these new business models reflective of the collective concerns and priorities of the public; or do they threaten the public trust?
- What real (and measurable) results are being achieved?

In this chapter, we have attempted to forge a deeper understanding of the e-Government phenomenon through a study of definitions, frameworks and development trends. However, as we learn more, we also realise the knowledge accumulated is never sufficient or exhaustive. The journey is one without end. Indeed, as traditional mindsets of governance are surpassed by new concepts, principles and best practices of new governance — no doubt enabled by new technologies — we move closer to the day when all "e-Government" will simply become "Government".

Endnotes

1   Osborne, D and Gaebler, T, *"Reinventing Government: How the Entrepreneurial Spirit is transforming the Public Sector"*, Addison-Wesley (1992).

2   Peters, BG, *"The Politics of Bureaucracy"*, Routledge (2001).

3   Kettl, DF, *"The Global Public Management Revolution — A Report on the Transformation of Governance"*, The Brookings Institution (2000).

4   Cheung, ABL and Lee, JCY, *"Public Sector Reform in Hong Kong: Into the 21st Century"*, The Chinese University Press (2001).

5   Tapscott, D, *"The Digital Economy: Promise and Peril in the Age of Networked Intelligence"*, McGraw-Hill (1995).

6   Lawson, G, *"Netstate"*, Demos, London (1998).

7   Watson, RT and Mundy, B, *"A Strategic Perspective of Electronic Democracy"*, Communications of the ACM, Vol. 44, No.1, January 2001.

8   UNPAN (United Nations Online Network in Public Administration and Finance), www.unpan.org.

9   Heeks, R, *"Understanding e-Governance for Development"*, iGovernment Paper No. 11, IDPM, University of Manchester (2001) (http://www.man.ac.uk/idpm/idpm_dp.htm).

10   Lenk, K and Traunmuller, R, *"A Framework for Electronic Government"*, in Proceedings of the 11th International Conference on Database and Expert Systems Applications, London (2000).

11   Aichhlozer, G and Schmutzer, R, *"Organisational Challenges to the Development of Electronic Government"*, in Proceedings of the 11th International Workshop on Database and Expert Systems Applications, London (2000).

12   GBDe (Global Business Dialogue on electronic commerce).

13   Gartner Group, *"Key Issues in e-Government Strategy and Management"*, Research Notes, *Key Issues*, 23 May 2000.

14   Deloitte Research, *"At the Dawn of e-Government: The Citizen as Customer"*, Public Sector Institute (2000).

15   Elmagarmid, AK and McIver, WJJ, *"The Ongoing March Toward Digital Government"*, IEEE Computer, February 2001.

16   Layne, K and Lee, J, *"Developing Fully Functional e-Government: A Four Stage Model"*, Government Information Quarterly, Vol. 18, No. 2, 2001.

17   Deloitte Research, *"The Transformation Is Now: Michigan's Innovative Formula For e-Government Success"*, Public Sector Institute (2002).

CHAPTER 2

In Search of e-Government Excellence

Dr Chong Yoke Sin

▲ ▼ ▲ ▼ ▲ ▼ ▲ ▼

Nothing in the world is so powerful as an idea
whose time has come.

Victor Hugo

▲ ▼ ▲ ▼ ▲ ▼ ▲ ▼

WHAT IS EXCELLENCE IN GOVERNMENT?

Governments have an inherent accountability to their people in terms of fiduciary responsibilities, making available services such as education, healthcare, housing and public utilities, and creating an economic climate conducive for commerce in the country. By definition, governments should also govern the country and its people and ensure that national resources are utilised for the continued growth of the nation. In return, the people expect social equity and basic human freedoms to be respected.

The standard test of good government therefore lies in its ability to improve the quality of life of the people. Towards this end, many governments measure and pride themselves in their ability to achieve high scores in traditional Human Development Indicators such as per-capita GDP, education level of the population, life expectancy, mortality rates, etc. To a certain extent, these indicators measure excellence in government. The result of the excellence in government is then reflected in the polls when the ruling parties seek re-election.

In order to enhance productivity and service levels, many governments now extend governance into the digital realm. Moving government online is an extension of the mode of governing and provision of public service. Excellence in digital or online government therefore requires the implementation of processes and technology to improve efficiencies, communication and services to satisfy all the stakeholders.

While the indicators mentioned above are important at the macro level, a separate set of more detailed measures are also required to measure excellence in government in the digital realm. A number of parallels can be drawn between commercial enterprises and governments. This suggests that the same measures of commercial excellence also apply to government excellence (albeit with some adaptation). Figure 2-1 shows the analogy between a commercial enterprise (private sector) and government (public sector).

Public Sector	Private Sector
Prime Minister	Chief Executive Officer
Prime Minister's Office	Chief Financial Officer
Finance Ministry	Finance Department
Trade and Industry	Sales and Marketing
Healthcare	Health Line of Business
Education	Education Line of Business
National Development and Urban Planning	Property and Real Estate Line of Business
Tourism	Hotel, Retail and Beverage
Law and Justice	Legal Line of Business
Police and Defence	Securitgy Services Line of Business
Foreign Affairs	Alliance/Partnership Management
Front-line Public Enquiry Services	Call Centre/CRM

Figure 2-1: Comparison between Public Sector and Private Sector Governance

Similarities can be drawn between governments and enterprise service providers that collect monies from their customers and in return provide goods and services, thus maintaining equity of the system. Whilst companies are measured by their revenue, profitability and company culture, governments can be measured by their GNP,[1] reserves and the quality of life of their citizens. Similarities can also be drawn between the way goods and services are provided by governments and commercial enterprises. One difference here is that governments in ensuring social equity must also take care of the disadvantaged and provide support mechanisms for them to keep up with the rest of society. Government's role, therefore, is to ensure that this group does not become a burden for the rest of the population, who are paying a reasonable tax regime to benefit from public goods and services. Hence, social welfare programmes must be provided for in a national budget.

Given these parallels, some argue that governments should be run more like businesses — maintaining the same fiscal prudence, keeping an eye on the operating costs and bottom line, being more responsive to customers needs, etc. There is, however, a crucial difference between the two entities — governments are elected by the people and have the sole power to tax the people and in return ensure the delivery of public goods and services and provide for security. In contrast, businesses need to compete in the marketplace and exist primarily for the pursuit of profits. Pursuit of excellence in government, therefore, has to take into consideration that governments are obliged to carry out their duties under this social contract, but to do so as efficiently and effectively as possible.

HOW DOES E-GOVERNMENT ENABLE GOVERNMENT EXCELLENCE?

What is the difference between government and e-Government? Imagine a future in which citizens can log onto a single Internet site, easily find the government services they need and use that site to perform a transaction or simply search for information; a future in which a business can fill out one single Internet form for all its regulatory compliance requirements; a future in which government officials procure goods and services, collect taxes, hold elections, approve permits and deliver other services electronically. Fathom the conveniences, the savings in waiting time, the increase in responsiveness and the improvement in efficiency. This is the promise of e-Government.

Four categories of government interaction are said to exist, and within these categories are opportunities for governments to transform service delivery:

- **Government-to-Citizens (G2C)**: Enabling existing over-the-counter services and in some cases providing a "first-stop, one-stop" access to all online government services for the convenience of citizens;

- **Government-to-Business (G2B)**: Reducing bureaucracy and cost in licensing, regulating and approvals for businesses;

- **Government-to-Government (G2G)**: Promoting government-to-government and international relationships; G2G initiatives could be from country-to-country, international or regional groupings; and

- **Government-to-Employee (G2E)**: Improving effectiveness and efficiency of government departments in serving their internal customers eg government employees.

e-Government enables government excellence by improving interactions with the citizens, businesses and government (intra-governmental and inter-governmental). The type of improvements achievable can be seen at two levels — internal to the government and external to the government.

Firstly, governments focus on internal initiatives that strengthen the pre-conditions of growth and performance. The areas of focus include: information sharing, internal communications and organisational alignment, wellness programmes supporting employee physical and mental well-being, office functionality/redesign, team building, mentoring and coaching, leadership, and internal training.

Secondly, governments focus on improving service delivery and innovation by transforming existing government processes so as to function more productively. Areas of focus include: initiatives that improve internal operational efficiency and/or services provided to the public; one-stop business services; access to educational resources; processes to enhance direct service delivery; community outreach; and web-based service delivery.

Over and above providing new ways of working with constituents, e-Government is also about creating an integrated environment for the development, deployment and maintenance of online solutions and services. Governments need to explore collaborative efforts, working with the private sector to share their experiences in e-Government planning and implementation, and to identify areas to strengthen economic integration and enhance competitiveness. With this infrastructure, governments can enable a powerful network of information, knowledge and commerce.

Among the potential benefits of digital government are savings in time and finances for government, constituents and businesses. If banks are able to cut their transaction costs by 90 percent through online banking, similar savings for government are possible. Moreover, users of government services will benefit by greater $24 \times 7 \times 365$ access to higher quality services. Most important, e-Government promises to foster closer relationship between citizens and government. By fostering an open digital economy with greater transparency and accountability through the free flow of information, citizens would feel they have more say in the governance of their lives. This would create more trust in and respect for the government. Success in e-Government is, therefore, only a means for government to achieve a larger end, that is, serving the constituents — citizens, businesses and employees — better.

THE E-GOVERNMENT JOURNEY

Advancements in technology have fundamentally changed and influenced the way businesses operate and how people go about their daily lives. Governments have also seized the opportunities presented by new technology to reshape traditional public service structures and improve cost-effectiveness and service delivery standards. However, e-Government is not simply about moving government transactions online. A holistic approach is needed to guide the e-Government journey from traditional service counters to online provisioning. It is necessary to develop a framework consisting of four main focus areas to guide the development of e-Government systems, namely: vision, target, theme and strategic objective.

Vision	Delivery of world-class public services in the digital economy			
Target	CITIZEN	BUSINESS	EMPLOYEE	Government
Theme	Citizen Care	Business Made Easy	People Matter Most	Connect Together
Objectives	Offer citizens faster, more responsive, more convenient and less complicated means to public services	Enable businesses to interact, transact and communicate with the government online, with greater speed and convenience	Develop and cultivate IT capabilities among public service officers to deliver efficient and cost-effective services	Promote greater productivity, efficiency, flexibility and convenience through integrated platforms for delivery of public services

Figure 2-2: Strategies for e-Government Journey

In Thailand, for example, e-Government aims to reform public services by reducing paperwork and streamlining public service processes, and by allowing citizens to access public services anytime and anyplace. To help achieve this vision, the government launched the "4Rs campaign", which denotes Red-tape reduction toward one-stop service, Rapid Response, Rural Coverage, and Round-the-clock service.

STAGES OF E-GOVERNMENT

In their quest to achieve their e-Government vision, governments typically move through distinct stages of development. The report entitled "Benchmarking e-Government: A Global Perspective. 2001. Assessing the Progress of the UN Member States" defines five stages of e-Government as follows:

Emerging Presence: A country commits to becoming an e-gov player. A formal but limited web presence is established through a few independent government websites which provide users with static organizational or political information. Sites may include contact information (i.e. telephone numbers and addresses of public officials). In rare cases, special features like FAQs may be found.

Enhanced Presence: A country's online presence begins to expand as its number of official websites increase. Content will consist more of dynamic and specialized information that is frequently updated; sites will link to other official pages. Government publications, legislation, newsletters are available. Search features, and e-mail addresses are available. A site for the national or ruling government may also be present that links the user to ministries or departments.

Interactive Presence: A country's presence on the internet expands dramatically with access to a wide range of government institutions and services. More sophisticated level of formal interactions between citizens and service providers is present like e-mail and post comments area. The capacity to search specialized databases and download forms and applications or submit them is also available. The content and information is regularly updated.

Transactional Presence: Complete and secure transactions like obtaining visas, passports, birth and death records, licenses, permits where a user can actually pay online for a services pay parking fines, automobile registration fees, utility bills and taxes. Digital signatures may be recognized in an effort to facilitate procurement and doing business with the government. Secure sites and user passwords are also present.

Seamless or fully integrated: Capacity to instantly access any service in a "unified package". Ministerial/ departmental/agency lines of demarcation are removed in cyberspace. Services will be clustered along common needs.

Figure 2-3: Stages of e-Government

CASE STUDY: TRANSACTIONAL PRESENCE

Inland Revenue Authority of Singapore e-filing System

The Inland Revenue Authority of Singapore (IRAS) has developed an e-filing system, which is an example of a key e-Government application in the Transactional stage. The system was implemented to address efficiency and cost concerns in processing income tax returns.

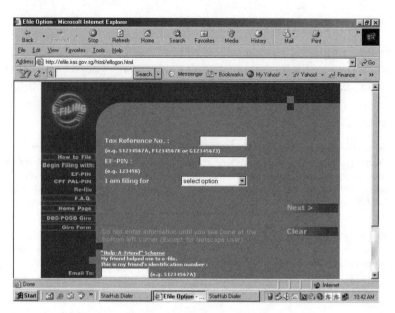

Figure 2-4: IRAS e-filing

The transition to an online e-Government flagship application for IRAS involved exploring different modes of submitting income tax returns and taking progressive steps to leverage technology to improve existing ways of doing things. When the application was introduced in 1995 and individuals were allowed to file income tax by telephone, most taxpayers chose to continue submitting paper returns as they were not comfortable with the new mode of filing. A web presence was established in 1998 with direct electronic filing for individual taxpayers with employment income. In 2000, e-filing was extended to individual taxpayers with business income.

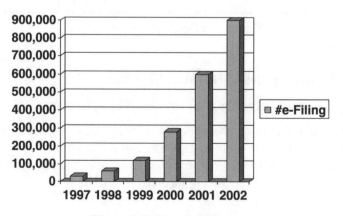

Figure 2-5: No. of e-Filers

The process of completing the form has been made extremely simple. The response time on the Internet is fast. In the "e-filing" example, the success was the result of a sustained change management campaign that ensured popular appeal to the citizens. The IRAS, not only brought the individual citizens online, but also got all the government departments and the major commercial entities in Singapore to directly transmit the income details of the employees thereby gaining the acceptance of businesses.

To prepare the population for e-filing, IRAS launched a campaign to promote the benefits of e-filing by holding road shows in public places and offering incentives and lucky draws for using e-filing. With higher PC and Internet penetration, coupled with greater familiarity with using online services, the number of e-filers took off from the year 2000 onwards.

In building e-Government systems, it is also important to have a set of guiding principles. These guiding principles seek to establish high-level critical e-Government aims and objectives for various government agencies and departments to take note of, when they moved their services online. The principles may include the following:

- **Accessibility:** It should primarily be one-stop, easily accessible, intuitive and cater to the needs of different stakeholders.

- **Availability**: It should be available 24 × 7 × 365, at home, at work, in schools, in libraries and other convenient public locations.

- **Security and Accountability:** Standards should be set for resolving security, privacy, non-repudiation and authentication issues to engender trust in the e-Government.

- **Integrate-bility:** It should be able to link seamlessly to existing back-end systems and across different agencies and platforms.

- **Sustainability:** It should eventually be transaction-based, revenue generating and self-financing.

MEASURES OF EXCELLENCE IN E-GOVERNMENT

e-Government Vision and Leadership

To achieve excellence in e-Government requires an integrated vision that is politically inspiring and administratively pragmatic. This is the initial step. The resolve and the sustained ability to pull the necessary resources together in order to convert this vision to reality pose the bigger challenge. To reflect the commitment to e-Government and ensure e-Government leadership, governments have setup specific agencies to oversee e-Government initiatives. These initiatives are also positioned as part of the larger effort to achieve government excellence.

In Malaysia, the Malaysian Administrative Modernisation and Management Planning Unit (MAMPU), a unit within the Prime Minister's Department, is the central agency for developing information and communications technology (ICT) and automation programmes within government agencies. MAMPU also oversees administrative reforms and facilitates change within government.[2] This is imperative in helping all government agencies focus on the fundamental elements of sound governance such as culture, management integrity and collaboration between the private and public sectors.

A Singapore e-Government tagline reads: "Many agencies, one government". A key strategy to achieve this vision, as outlined in the Singapore e-Government Action Plan, is to deliver integrated electronic services that are customer-centric and accessible online, anytime, anywhere. The vision and strategy require fundamental shifts in public service practices that transcend the agency-centric outlook to one that is citizen-centric. The e-Government office was established within the Ministry of Finance to help realise the e-Government vision. The approach is one that provides a holistic perspective and focuses on other areas such enhancing total organisational excellence, promoting innovation among public sector organisations and minimising bureaucracy.

In India, an Electronic Governance Division and Centre for e-Governance within the Department of Information Technology (DIT) was established to better coordinate and drive its e-Government movement. They found it necessary not only to address the operational aspects of IT but also deal with the more strategic mission of reinventing government and orchestrating the fundamental changes needed to better enable government operations, service delivery and legislature.

Infrastructure

Governments all over the world are endeavouring to capitalise on the Internet to boost their countries' efficiency and enhance their competitive edge. However, in order to reap the benefits brought about by globalisation and the IT revolution, countries must first ensure that the basic ICT infrastructure is in place. The ICT infrastructure serves as the backbone for countries' e-Government agenda and is crucial to e-Government sustainability. ICT infrastructure encompasses not only telecommunications capability — in terms of wireless or broadband networks — but also policies and programmes to educate and speed up the adoption of computers and the Internet in the country.

The lack of a robust and high bandwidth capacity network impedes the delivery of e-Government services through the Internet and Government-to-Business e-commerce. The current infrastructure capability in many countries was designed primarily for telephone use and hence not able to cope with the heavy broadband traffic required for certain e-Government services.

Huge amounts of resources and technical know-how are required to build up ICT infrastructure. Governments would be better-off leaving the private sector and foreign investors to take the lead in infrastructure modernisation through a co-funding model. Linkages to the global information superhighway through the opening of the telecommunications market and economy in general must also be made to attract the necessary foreign expertise and investment.

Connectivity

The "digital divide" describes the chasm between the web-savvy and fully enabled user, desiring to do business electronically, and the web-disconnected majority. In many developing countries there exists a group of citizens without access or any real knowledge of the tools required to use the web as a medium for communicating and transacting. Many governments are beginning to address this problem through various initiatives such as providing free PCs and access to Internet for the rural community and individuals from poor socio-economic backgrounds.

Some commonly used measures to gauge the size of a country's digital divide are listed below.

PCs per 100 individuals: For now, PCs are the primary device for accessing the internet until access becomes universally available through other mediums like television; this statistic is fundamental in quantifying a country's capacity to deliver online service.

Internet hosts per 10,000 individuals: Measures internet penetration. Obviously, the greater the number of internet hosts and service providers, the greater the opportunity for citizen access.

Percentage of a nation's population online: Estimates how many are citizens are using the web.

Telephone lines per 100 individuals *(also called density)*: This is the basic measure for infrastructure. The greater the number of telephone lines the likelihood increases for access.

Mobile phones per 100 individuals: Indicates a country's potential for wireless capacity. Wireless connectivity is extremely important in many developing countries. This could play an important role in the near future, as mobile access becomes more comprehensive.

Televisions per 1000 individuals: This indicator was included to assess the prospects of web TV Cable and satellite TV potentially offer the highest rate of access of any hardware device.

Source: 2001 International Telecommunications Union Report and the 2001 UNDP Human Development Report. 2002.

Figure 2-6: Common Measures of Digital Divide

The increasing number of Internet cafes emerging in major urban centres and in other parts of a country may also be used as a proxy measure of connectivity. The proliferation of such cafes is a sign of the growing e-literacy among the population.

Reliability

What is the quality of the infrastructure? Can the telecommunications and government infrastructure be relied upon to provide dependable services round the clock? In countries where the telecommunications infrastructure has limited capacity and bandwidth, Internet and e-commerce transactions would be hampered and prone to congestion, cut-off and snail's pace downloading speed. This would seriously hamper government efforts to go online and discourage businesses and citizens from transacting over the Internet. Investing in a reliable and robust telecommunications network is therefore crucial. As the telecommunications network sits on top of the energy infrastructure, frequent power outages would negate the effectiveness of the telecommunications network. Thus, governments need to ensure that the basic infrastructures such as power and utilities are reliable and able to support the e-Government systems.

e-Literacy

How proficient are citizens in using the Internet? How receptive are employees, businesses and citizens to e-Government? What are the technical skills required? e-Government initiatives alter the way services are delivered and therefore require staff to be equipped with electronic capabilities. Armed with this knowledge, staff will be able to think innovatively about process and service delivery redesign. In addition, change management would also be required to help traditional users transition to the new service delivery methods.

Improving national education levels, especially in science and technology, is a top priority. In many Asian societies, a high social value has historically been attached to education. It is also a developmental imperative. The overarching goal, however, is to prepare the workforce of tomorrow and to support continued economic development. The approach, however, varies greatly from country to country. For example, Malaysia is building up both basic and advanced literacy levels and also has a unique programme within its "Vision 2020" plan to instil in workers a work ethic that supports greater productivity as well as to train personnel in specific high-tech skills required by industry. For the short-term, the focus is on improving the country's e-literacy level by offering affordable IT manpower conversion programmes and IT courses.

Change management is also another important aspect. Unless people are comfortable with the new tools available, they will revert to their old working patterns and habits. Embracing e-Government requires a willingness to experiment and innovate both by the government and the people. Governments will need to engage in national-wide campaigns to educate people in embracing a change in the way public goods and services are delivered.

Relevance

How relevant public e-services are will depend on the value they are able to offer citizens and businesses. Does e-Government improve the lives of citizens? Do e-services help businesses operate more efficiently or foster better relationships with government? What critical role does e-Government play in solving problems for its citizens and businesses?

There are many approaches to achieve e-readiness, ie big-bang, quick-win, least-cost, or big-impact. In determining the most effective approach, governments typically use measures such as cost effectiveness and productivity gains to justify a particular e-service programme. However, the impact that the e-service has on the customer, ie citizens or businesses, is a key factor to be considered. Citizens and businesses will be willing to transact online with government agencies if it is convenient, efficient and cheaper as compared to transacting over-the-counter. In order to understand better what information, goods and services government can and should provide online, it is therefore to focus on the needs and expectations of users. When an e-service is relevant to businesses and citizens, it provides a catalyst for the introduction of new services or service improvements.

TradeNet in Singapore and DagangNet in Malaysia are examples of e-Government services that are extremely relevant and crucial to businesses. By integrating the import, export and transshipment documentation processing procedures, the system reduces the costs and turnaround time for the preparation, submission and processing of trade and shipping documents, and this expedites cargo clearance.

Trust

With heightened awareness of online privacy and security issues and media coverage of high-profile Internet security breaches, public trust has becomes one of the most critical aspects for online success. For e-Government to be successful, issues relating to public trust must be addressed. There are three components of public trust when using e-Government services:

(1)   Privacy policy for personal or proprietary information provided online

(2)   Confidence that personal information will not be misused

(3)   Security of online transactions, particularly financial transactions and online payment

As in the case of e-Commerce, where commercial ventures specify their security and privacy policies, government should similarly state clearly its policy and provide an assurance of privacy and confidentiality, as the average citizen tends to be wary of government initiatives given that governments have certain powers vested in them. Moreover, any legal action taken against the government is cause for embarrassment and would reflect an unstable government.

The security policy has to be supported by a comprehensive and robust technology infrastructure, to ensure acceptance by the public. A 2002 survey by Taylor Nelson Sofres, shows the level of trust that the public has in online interactions with government. Is there something that we can learn from Singapore, Malaysia and Hong Kong where almost 40 percent the population trust the online mode of transacting with its government?

In 2002, Which Countries Consider Government Online To Be Most ...?

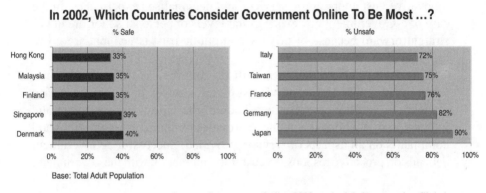

Base: Total Adult Population

Source: Government Online 2002 — A global perspective Global
Annual Report Taylor Nelson Sofres. November 2002.

Figure 2-7: Survey on Trust in e-Government

Clearly, to encourage wider acceptance and participation in e-Government, more needs to be done to make people trust e-Government. Issues such as security, privacy and authentication need to be adequately addressed.

Satisfaction

User satisfaction is a measure of expectation versus experience, and satisfaction with e-Government services will depend on the perceived value to the citizens and businesses. In order to meet the needs of its users while carrying out its administrative duties, governments provide many channels of service delivery. Consistency of services provided across these various delivery channels is a minimum requirement for customer satisfaction.

Some attributes of expectation and experience are access, ease of use, graphical user interface, information quality, features and speed of transaction. Good performance on each attribute would contribute positively towards user satisfaction levels while a small blemish in one of these attributes tends to have a large negative impact on satisfaction levels.

e-Business is another typical benchmark used by citizens and business to evaluate e-Government services. Users have become accustomed to the level of service and quality provided by commercial providers in their e-business offerings and expect similar levels of service quality from the government.

In the e-Business environment, service providers are able to capture insights into customer behaviour and use the information to deliver innovative customer-centric services and personalised experiences. In the case of e-Government however, similar levels of personalisation are not as straightforward because of privacy and public trust issues that are given top priority.

In order to achieve success with the Internet as delivery channel, governments must aim to provide superior services in a quick and easy manner. In addition, government should also allow for greater public interaction by enabling the public to provide compliments, suggestions and complaints on all aspects of services provided. Successful e-Government depends on proactive response to customer interaction with the government.

Integrated services

Integrated e-Government service delivery requires a seamless organisational function that is transparent to users. As physical barriers are erased, service delivery is made possible over the Internet, mobile phone, PDA or any other such devices that may be introduced in the future.

The integration of services requires government to institute bold measures such as reengineering current departmental boundaries around the needs of citizens and businesses. To achieve this, government must have a citizen relationship management philosophy. Moreover, to achieve true integration of services, the private sector must be included either in an outsourcing capacity or as a direct service provider. An example is payment services to government agencies that include banks and financial institutions in the value chain.

The Singapore e-Government journey began with the conceptualisation of the eCitizen Centre which is positioned as the first-stop for government services on the web. The Centre provides useful information and online services that are intuitively grouped along the important events in the lives of Singaporeans, and more importantly according to their needs and perspective. This model transcends the boundaries of individual government agencies and epitomises the resolve to shift from agency-centric to customer-centric service delivery.

Singapore's approach of centralising the coordination and management of integrated services has contributed greatly to the achievements it has made so far. The eCitizen Centre is owned by the Ministry of Finance (MOF) and project-managed by the Infocomm Development Authority of Singapore (IDA) — the information and communications technology arm of the government.

Singapore has also put in place a common platform to empower and enable various government agencies to provide their online services in a more cost-effective and efficient manner. In January 2001, the Public Service Infrastructure (PSi) was commissioned as a central infrastructure for the rapid development of e-forms equipped with gateways for electronic payments and authentication. Some of the services that were implemented included Renewal of Road Tax, Search for Vehicle Insurance Particulars and Renewal of Driver's License.

In the G2B space, the concept of "Business town" serves as a single convenient point for businesses and companies to access e-services in an enterprise-centric manner according to business segments and different stages of the "business cycle". A good example of the integrated services between both the public and private sector would be the One.motoring portal launched by the Land Transport Authority in October 2000. The portal provides comprehensive information about vehicle related products and services, as well as a one-stop service for purchasing of vehicle related products

The South Korean government procurement system is another excellent case of integrated services for the business community. The system is a single nationwide procurement web portal that ensures the timely delivery of quality products at reasonable prices in a competitive procurement market. The system serves government at all levels including 55 central agencies, 248 local governments, and approximately 700 non-governmental public bodies.

FUTURE SUCCESS OF E-GOVERNMENT

The future success of e-Government is dependent on a few key areas. Firstly, the ability to achieve personalisation to the user needs and preferences would be likely to attract more citizens and businesses to come onboard. It would likely be a citizen or business-centric model where government activities are organised around the lives of citizens and businesses. Citizens can create their own MyCareer, MyFinance, MyBusiness, MyEducation, MyHealth, etc. Similarly business can create their BizApplications,

BizLoans, BizReports, BizLicenses, etc. Governments can then organise and integrate their services and activities around the needs of the citizens and businesses. The ability for different government agencies to cross deliver their services would enhance the experience of citizens and businesses with government agencies. The dreaded experience of being "bounced from one agency to another" would be replaced by a few seamless clicks within the e-Government system.

At the end of the day, the future success of e-Government is dependent on continuous value-adding to the provision of public goods and services, and in reducing the distance between government and the people through the innovative use of technology.

Endnotes

1   GNP refers to Gross National Product.

2   Message from the Director General of MAMPU.

3   Benchmarking e-Government: A Global Perspective. 2001. Assessing the Progress of the UN member states, 2002.

4   Government Online 2002 — A global perspective Global Annual Report Taylor Nelson Sofres, November 2002.

5   2001 International Telecommunications Union Report and the 2001 UNDP Human Development Report, 2002.

Vision

CHAPTER 3

The Journey to e-Brunei

James SL Yong

▲ ▼ ▲ ▼ ▲ ▼ ▲ ▼

It is good to have an end to journey towards,
but it is the journey that matters in the end.

Ursula Le Guin

▲ ▼ ▲ ▼ ▲ ▼ ▲ ▼

"Selamat datang" a cheerful lady behind the counter called out as Halim entered the cybercafe in the heart of the capital city, Bandar Seri Begawan.

"A PC — for about half an hour. And an iced tea please."

The lady gestured to Halim to take the first PC by the window. He smiled, as that was his favourite seat, with a serene view of the famous water village, Kampung Ayer.

Visiting the cybercafe was Halim's usual routine. Several days a week while on his way home from work, he would pop by one of the cybercafes along his route, to check his e mail account, and visit a few favourite fishing websites. He still marveled at how connected his life had become ever since he started using the Internet three years ago, usually at one of the more than 50 cybercafes around the city.

Today he remembered he had to check out the procedures for renewing his passport, as he was planning a holiday soon. He deftly surfed to the website for the Immigration and National Registration Department, and quickly found out what he needed to bring along — identity card, birth certificate and photos — and where he had to go to submit the application.

"That was easy", Halim said to himself, as he hopped over to another site to explore the latest in fishing gear ...

BACKGROUND

History[1]

Brunei Darussalam has been called "a new nation but an ancient country". It gained full sovereign independence relatively recently in 1984, but has had a long and colourful history. Records as early as the 6th Century show that it was then known as "Puni" or "Poli". Annals of both the Sung

Dynasty and Marco Polo reflect thriving trade between China and "Puni" up to the 12th Century.

By the 10th Century, Brunei had emerged as a kingdom of the Buddhist Srivijaya empire of Sumatra, and subsequently it came under the Hindu Majapahit empire of Java. The Majapahit empire was itself overthrown by Muslim invaders in the 15th Century, resulting in independent rule by the Sultans of Brunei.

Between the 15th and 17th Centuries, the Sultanate of Brunei's control extended over much of the island of Borneo and even southern parts of Philippines. Borneo was notorious as a pirate haven until the middle of the 19th Century when the British navy destroyed many of the pirate fleets. Brunei subsequently entered a period of decline brought on by internal struggles, piracy and encroachment by European powers. Many territories were ceded to Sarawak during the time of the White Rajah, James Brooke. In 1888, Brunei opted to become a British protectorate with a British Resident appointed to advise the Sultan on all matters except those pertaining to Islam and Malay customs.

The fortunes of the nation changed radically starting from 1929 when oil was discovered at Seria. Oil and natural gas continue to be the key basis for Brunei's immense wealth.

The previous ruler, Sultan Omar Ali Saifuddien III, resisted British proposals to merge Brunei with Sarawak or British North Borneo (Sabah), or to join Malaysia. In 1959, Brunei was given constitutional self-rule under British protection. The present ruler, Sultan Haji Hassanal Bolkiah, ascended the throne in 1967 and paved the way for full independence in 1984.

Geography[2]

The Islamic sultanate of Brunei Darussalam lies on the north-west coast of the island of Borneo. It is bounded on the north by the South China Sea and on all other sides by the Malaysian state of Sarawak. Brunei has a total area of 5,770 sq km. The name "Brunei Darussalam" means "Abode of Peace", and indeed there is a certain old world tranquility of the land. The country is divided into four districts: Brunei/Muara, Tutong, Belait and Temburong. The capital city Bandar Seri Begawan has many modern business areas, hotels and shopping centres. Seventy percent of the land is untouched, primary rainforest — a higher proportion than any other Asian country — making Brunei Darussalam an eco-tourist paradise.

Brunei has a population of just 350,000, with Malays making up more than seventy percent of the population. The other racial communities include mainly Chinese, Indians and Ibans, among others. The official language is *Bahasa Melayu* (or Malay) but English is also widely used.

The people of Brunei live a peaceful and relatively austere Islamic lifestyle. Public sale of liquor is forbidden and the nightlife is relatively quiet. The political culture has been described as one of harmonious acquiescence to the edicts of the Sultan. Most Bruneians' basic needs are taken care of with free healthcare and education, cheap loans and tax-free wages. Serious crimes are almost unheard of, making Brunei one of the safest places in the world.

Economy

With some of the region's richest petroleum and natural gas deposits, it is hardly surprising that oil and gas form the key industry in Brunei. GDP is US$ 4.5 billion and Brunei has one of the highest per capita incomes in the world. Brunei's major trading partners are ASEAN, Japan, Taiwan, South Korea and USA.

Economic policy has been formulated in a series of development plans. The latest is the Eighth National Development Plan (2001–2005). Over the years, the government has been endeavouring to diversify the economy and move away from over-reliance on oil and gas. Some industry sectors being emphasised include financial services, ICT, tourism, fishing and agriculture. Greater private sector participation to spearhead the diversification is also being urged.

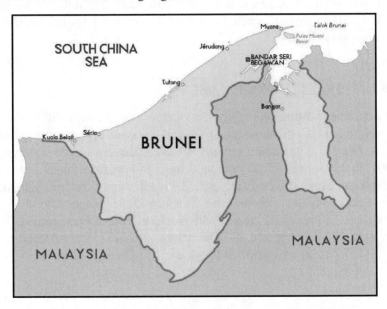

Government

Brunei Darussalam's government is a form of constitutional monarchy, referred to as Malay Islamic Monarchy in official documents.[3] The country is ruled according to established Islamic values and traditions. The same family has now ruled Brunei for over six centuries. The present head of state, Sultan Haji Hassanal Bolkiah, is the supreme executive authority and serves as Prime Minister, Minister of Defence and Minister of Finance. The overall government structure is as follows:

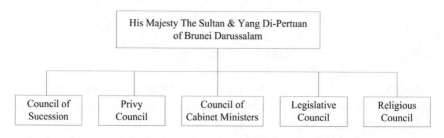

Figure 3-1: Overall Government Structure

Other than the Prime Minister's Office, there are 11 other Ministries: Defence, Finance, Foreign Affairs, Home Affairs, Education, Industry and Primary Resources, Religious Affairs, Development, Health, Culture, Youth and Sports, and Communications.

In addition to the Council of Cabinet Ministers, the Sultan is advised and assisted by a Privy Council, Council of Succession, Legislative Council and Religious Council.

THE NATIONAL ICT PROGRAMME

ICT adoption in Brunei generally was, and to a large extent still is, led by the government. Computerisation of the civil service began as early as the 1970s. The computerisation initiatives were relatively ad hoc up to early 1990s. In 1993, the various computer units in key government agencies (notably the Brunei Investment Agency, Treasury and Economic Planning Unit) were combined to become the Computer Division under the Ministry of Finance. This was later merged with the State Stores Department leading to the formation of an Information Technology and State Stores Department (ITSSD) in 1996. A national IT strategic planning framework was formulated in 1997 and the first National IT Strategic Plan took off starting in 2000.

From late 2000, Sultan Haji Hassanal Bolkiah indicated his clear commitment to bring Brunei and its people into the global IT mainstream. At the APEC 2000 conference, the Sultan sent the clear message to the world that "Brunei is open for business". The ruler highlighted efforts to establish e-Government and e-Business in particular and "e-Brunei" (which was, in short, a core strategy aimed at driving toward a paperless society) in general. There was also the need to further develop Brunei's services sector to create new jobs and sources of economic growth, diversifying beyond oil and gas reserves, and financial assets. In addition, there was an emphasis on encouraging the private sector to play a greater role in the national programme. Since then, various initiatives have begun or been given renewed impetus.

The national IT vision is:

Brunei Darussalam to exploit IT to its fullest potential for national prosperity.

The national IT mission is:

Brunei Darussalam through its National IT Council aims to lead and facilitate the strategic development and diffusion of state-of-the-art IT for the entire nation.

The national strategic IT plan, called "IT 2000 and Beyond", includes goals such as raising the level of IT literacy, promoting effective application of IT in the public and private sectors, and ensuring sufficient supply of IT-skilled manpower to fuel growth in the sector. To achieve these goals, the plan highlighted strategies to create a paperless society, to push towards introduction of electronic government through better training programs and IT coordination, as well as to create better incentives for IT adoption and e-Business deployment in the private sector.

Under the Eighth National Development Plan (2001–2005), the Brunei government had allocated almost B\$ 1 billion (US\$ 570 million) for the development of the ICT sector.[4] A substantial part of this budget is devoted to the development of infrastructure for the e-Government initiative to apply ICT to the operations of government. The year 2005 has been set as a deadline for the full implementation of the e-Government system. This initiative will expand the breadth and depth of the fledgling ICT industry in Brunei from piecemeal projects addressing vertical needs, to multi-million dollar projects which address the breadth of government needs.

KEY ORGANISATIONAL STRUCTURES

The following councils, committees, and other governmental agencies have played key roles in the development of the national ICT programme in Brunei Darussalam.

Brunei Information Technology (BIT) Council

The BIT Council is a high-powered agency established in 2000 to lead and facilitate the strategic development and diffusion of ICT to the people, as well as guide Brunei in harnessing ICT to its fullest potential for the nation. It is chaired by the Minister of Communications and is made up of representatives from government, the private sector, the IT sector, academia and community representatives.

To achieve its overall mission, the BIT Council established ten goals that covered such areas as: leadership, needs, IT literacy, manpower, applications, R&D, links, economy, business and relevance.

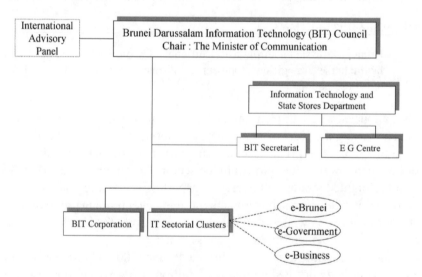

Figure 3-2: BIT Council and Supporting Agencies

Information Technology and State Stores Department

The ITSSD, under the Ministry of Finance, is involved in the national IT development programme, and managing the state supplies and stores through good governance, sustainable development and electronic services delivery.

ITSSD is the Secretariat for the BIT Council. In this role, it supports the activities of the BIT Council, monitors the implementation of the National Strategic IT Plan, spearheads the formulation and implementation of the national IT policy and plans, nurtures alliances with ICT clusters and appropriate organisations, and manages corporate communications and publicity.

e-Government Programme Executive Committee (EGPEC)

EGPEC is an affiliate of the BIT Council. The members of the EGPEC comprise the Permanent Secretaries from all government ministries. EGPEC functions as the advisory and consultative body to the BIT Council for the development and implementation of the e-Government programme listed in the e-Government Strategic Framework for Action 2001–2005. EGPEC is tasked to appraise, study and further propose steps to implement the e-Government program including preparing a specific Plan of Action towards fully attaining the mission of the program fully within five years. This will serve as an engine to advance IT diffusion in the public service, and advance the development of "e" related services or activities currently being undertaken by various ministries and government agencies in Brunei Darussalam.

e-Business Programme Executive Committee (EBPEC)

EBPEC is an affiliate of the BIT Council. It is the equivalent of EGPEC, but focused on commerce rather than government. The members of the EBPEC consist of recognised IT leaders and representatives from the private sector, academia and the civil service. It is tasked to coordinate the IT application drives of the private and the public sector; identifying linkage-building strategic opportunities for local IT businesses with others and directing the necessary assistance to the IT sector.

Ministry of Communications

The Ministry of Communications (MinCom) plays a key role in planning, creating and developing the transportation industry (ie maritime, land and air) and the communications industry (ie global post and telecommunications). It prepares and updates the country's laws and regulations as well as strives to establish a competitive and conducive climate for growth of industries. MinCom also develops and promote services offered by its various departments.

Today, Jabatan Telekom Brunei (JTB or Brunei Telecoms) is one of the departments under the Ministry of Communication and offers a wide range of domestic and international telecommunication services in voice, message and data communications. Being a national telecommunication services provider, JTB has been committed to play a leading role in facilitating the development of infocommunications in the country. In 2003, JTB is likely to be corporatized, forming Telekom Brunei Berhad (TelBru), with its previous regulatory functions transferred to a new "Regulatory Unit" in the Ministry of Communications.

Authority of Infocommunication Technology Industry (AiTi)

A new statutory body, the Authority for Info-Communications Technology Industry (AiTi), was created in early 2003, under the Authority for Information and Communications Technology Industry Order 2001. This represents a significant development in the ICT industry in Brunei, as AiTi will function as an independent body for regulating and developing the ICT industry in the country.

ICT INFRASTRUCTURE

The earliest telecommunication services were introduced in Brunei Darussalam in the 1920s when the first international wireless telegraph circuits were installed to link Brunei Darussalam and Labuan (a nearby Malaysian island). The introduction of telephone services in the 1930s marked the beginning of a radical change in the way people communicated in business, government and society.

Jabatan Telekom Brunei (JTB) was established as a government department in 1952 to administer the telecommunications services, taking over from the Post and Telegraph Office. Drastic transformation and modernisation became more obvious especially after Brunei's independence in 1984.

Between 1996 and 2000, the Brunei government invested more than B$ 124 million in high-speed IT infrastructure under RKN7. These included the construction of RaGAM21,[5] a high capacity and high speed nationwide backbone optical fibre cable system, the CBD-NET optical fibre access network linking the government and business areas within the Brunei-Muara district, and the SEA-ME-WE3 submarine cable system connecting Brunei Darussalam to the global community.

Teledensity in Brunei is relatively high. By the end of 2002, some 95 percent of households had fixed line telephones, and mobile phone penetration was 40 percent.

The first Internet Service Provider (ISP) in Brunei was BruNet, started in October 1995 by JTB. Internet development in Brunei took a step forward with the November 2000 launch of E-Speed, a broadband alternative to JTB's dial-up service that employs the faster ADSL (Asymmetric Digital Subscriber Line) technology. ADSL enables access speed of up to 512 kbps. The government's support of ICT development led to the liberalisation of ISP licencing. The second ISP, Simpur made its debut in 2000 under the flagship of DST Multimedia Sdn Bhd. However, the Internet penetration was still below 20 percent (although accurate figures are hard to come by because of the widespread usage of pre-paid cards, eg Netkad). It is estimated that on average, one in three Bruneian households in urban areas and one in nine rural households are connected. This gap between basic access and Internet usage raised some concerns.

There are two operators providing telecommunications services in Brunei — the government department JTB and a private company DSTcom. Up until early 2003, JTB played the role of both an operator and a regulator. As an operator, it provided a wide range of telecommunications services. JTB's regulatory role was in support of a Regulatory Unit under the Ministry of Communications which tried to ensure healthy development in the telecommunications industry in Brunei. At the time of writing, the government is working on the corporatisation of JTB in 2003, forming the new Telekom Brunei Berhad (TelBru).

As part of its liberalisation and corporatisation policy, Brunei has opened up its telecommunications services for competition. In 3G mobile licensing, the government has already allocated the appropriate 3G spectrum for service providers in the economy, and will be awarding two 3G licenses, including one to the incumbent mobile operator.

E-GOVERNMENT — VISION AND DIRECTIONS

The key message of the e-Government programme is:

EG21 — Governance and Services Online.

The vision of the Brunei administration with respect to e-Government is:

> To be an E-Smart Government in line with the 21st Century Civil Service Vision.
>
> The vision of the civil service is one that continually strives to be more innovative, productive, effective, efficient, competitive and dynamic. A key facet of the vision is the creation of a "paperless bureaucracy".

The e-Government programme mission reads:

> His Majesty's Government aims to establish electronic governance and services to best serve the nation.

There are many flagships under the overall e-Government programme. Specific ministries or agencies have been clearly identified to spearhead each of them:

• PMONet, HRM flagship	Prime Minister's Office
• Defence ICT infrastructure	Ministry of Defence
• TAFIS, EG Centre, IT manpower devt	Ministry of Finance
• <flagships being finalised>	Ministry of Foreign Affairs
• MSC flagship, Mukim.Net	Ministry of Home Affairs
• e-Education	Ministry of Education
• <flagships being finalised>	Ministry of Industry & Primary Resources
• Zakat Information System, e-Kiosk, Islamic Information System	Ministry of Religious Affairs
• e-Heritage	Ministry of Culture, Youth & Sports
• eMincom, eLATIS	Ministry of Communications
• e-Health	Ministry of Health
• MOD *e*	Ministry of Development

In addition, an EG Value Chain Implementation Blueprint has been developed to provide effective alternatives for supporting the government ministries and agencies in their e-Government projects. The services framework outlined in this blueprint comprises three areas: the EG Centre, EG Bandwidth and EG Agency.

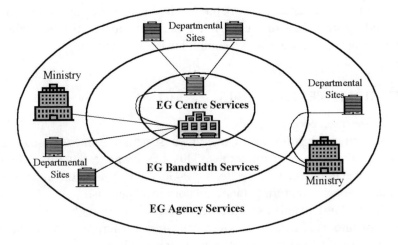

Figure 3-3: e-Government Value Chain Implementation

EG Agency Services

The ministry or department users are offered two models to choose from. They can either have their own ministry IT center at their own departmental site, or they can have ITSSD host it at the EG Center for them. There will thus be 12 ministry IT centers to deal with specific ministerial IT visions and missions. Each center thus handles transactions on the Internet, Intranet and Extranet.

The EG Agency services offered include outsourcing applications, multi-channel access devices, agency infrastructure, common office environment tools, manpower, training, architecture framework, marketing and quality assurance.

EG Bandwidth Services

This is managed by the Ministry of Communications. Building on the excellent telecommunications infrastructure — RaGAM 21, DST, etc — this helps provide the last-mile connection to government premises. In other words, the EG Bandwidth Services provide outsourcing of broadband network connectivity up to the routers/switches.

EG Centre Services

This will be managed by ITSSD. It is designed for the common services such as hosting co-location facilities, facility management, data center, disaster recovery center, network operation center, service operation center (including certification authority, e-mail services, portals, website customisation, gateways and common business services).

KEY STRATEGIES AND GOALS

There are three core strategies.

The first is to institute an e-Government structural framework to realise and sustain bona fide outcomes. This requires the development of institutional infrastructure, architecting e-Government solutions and putting in place proper monitoring and regulatory mechanisms.

The second involves injecting smart capital to build reliable infrastructure. This includes e-Government infrastructure, and both common and specific e-Government applications and services.

The third core strategy requires the development of societal resources to leverage capacity, capability and innovation at the forefront of the ICT-led economy.

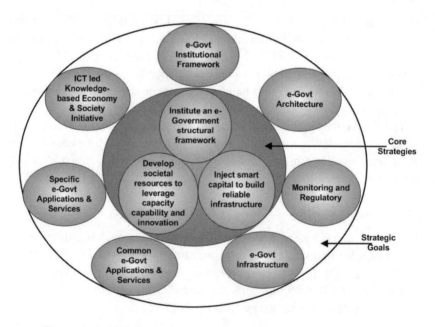

Figure 3-4: BIT Council's Core Strategies and Strategic Goals

In line with these core strategies, seven strategic goals were outlined.

(1)   To establish the e-Government framework.

(2)   To establish the e-Government architecture.

(3)   To establish monitoring and regulatory.

(4)   To establish e-Government infrastructure.

(5)   To deploy common e-Government applications and services.

(6)   To deploy specific e-Government applications and services.

(7)   To establish ICT led knowledge-based economy and society initiatives.

STATUS OF INITIATIVES

The following are some of the more visible e-Government initiatives in Brunei. Some have been rolled out, while others are in various stages of development.

TEMA: the IT Program for the Civil Service

This initiative for the civil service, called TEMA (short for "TEknologi MAklumat", Malay for "Information Technology"), was launched by the Prime Minister's Office in 1995. The objectives of TEMA were threefold. Firstly, it was to raise the general IT awareness among civil servants. Secondly, it promoted planned IT programmes under the leadership of the user ministries or departments. This was done via the IT Committee at the ministry level and project steering committees at department levels. Thirdly, TEMA pushed for updates to the processes and service levels in project implementation and IT systems maintenance at the various ministries and departments.

Through Program TEMA, ITSSD has developed very good rapport with the other ministries and departments. All these ministerial IT Committees, normally chaired by the Permanent Secretary of the ministry, and comprising members from departments under the ministry, are responsible for evaluating each request from the ministry and its departments before further action from ITSSD.

Program TEMA has increased awareness and commitment of the ministries and departments to handle the information technology request issues and making it conducive for ITSSD to carry out the planning, management and implementation of an effective information technology and IT diffusion.

With Program TEMA, the ministries and departments can send their requests for IT hardware and services. ITSSD has handled different types of projects — development, technical and supply of systems — for a wide spectrum of departments and ministries in Brunei.

TAFIS

By the end of 2002, the Ministry of Finance was continuing to implement the government-wide Treasury Accounting and Financial Information Systems (TAFIS). The main objective of TAFIS is to improve the efficiency of government's financial transaction processes.

The baseline version of TAFIS has already gone live since March 2002 and business process reengineering (BPR) has been done after the completion of the first milestone. Preparation for the second milestone on rolling out the implementation to four ministries has already commenced. TAFIS will enhance the efficiency of managing the Government financial services, promote accountability in the use and tracking of government finance, besides providing transfer of knowledge and skill based on technology and moving towards paperless government. In other words, the end result will be an enhancement of efficiency and effectiveness in completing the task in terms of process and shorter delivery time.

With TAFIS, the Ministry of Finance has focused on the core services to achieve desired outcomes and starting small from baselines, follow up with business process reengineering and scale up fast to rollouts. We believe that with this sort of approach, utilisation will be maximised, unnecessary wastage minimised, and duplication avoided. Rather than duplicate, it will leverage on existing opportunities that can "test" the integration of technology and infrastructure.

E-Education

The Ministry of Education is currently focusing on an e-Education initiative under the e-Government programme. The increased emphasis on ICT in

Brunei's education system should bring about significant improvement in the quality of teaching and learning in classrooms, and lead to greater IT literacy. The strategies formulated under the e-Education Roadmap will drive programmes on EDUNET, e-Learning, Education Information System (EIS), Digital Library, and Human and Capacity Building. All this is made possible by significant government funding, in particular a part of the ICT-led and related funds allocated in the Eighth National Development Plan.

E-Health

The vision of the Ministry of Health is to enhance medical services through e-Health. E-health refers to healthcare services being available through the Internet. E-Health is about the use of informatics and telemedics in the way we use information, telecommunication and technology in medical care, prevention, education and training.

E-health, which is included in the health plan 2000–2010 highlighted in October, also has the mission to provide excellent medical service and care to the people in Brunei Darussalam. The action plans laid down by the ministry among others aimed for the quality of health care, to promote excellence in health services and enhance cost effectiveness in service delivery, and to achieve excellence in reference clinical laboratory services.

The broadband network of RaGAM21 links hospitals in various locations in Brunei, eg Kuala Belait, Tutong and Temburong with the RIPAS Hospital. According to the ministry, these services and expertise can be integrated through e-Health. In this way, medical care can be brought to the patient rather than patient to the medical care.

Multipurpose Smartcard

The smartcard was first introduced in Brunei in 2000.[6] Since then, some 280,000 have been issued in the form of official identity cards. The card can be used as a driving license, school registration document or for other purposes. It has also been identified for use in other multipurpose functions such as a travel document or passport. It may be used for immigration clearance at immigration control posts or for future e-Government areas.

Eco-Cyber Park

In line with the call to diversify Brunei's economy from being overly oil-based, there has been a series of proposals geared towards creating an economy focused on ICT as an engine of growth. One such proposal is the creation of the Brunei Eco-Cyber Park. This is an important information infrastructure project aimed at creating a strategic cluster of leading ICT (and other technology) companies and building up a critical mass of professional talent in Brunei.

It is envisaged that the Eco-Cyber Park will serve as an incubator for the dynamic development of ICT services (including data communications and multimedia content development), as well as help attract foreign companies and investments into the country. It will also provide opportunities to promising local companies and develop human capital to help Brunei compete in the new economy.

The proposed site of the Eco-Cyber Park is a 100 acre (0.4 sq km) area in Lambak Kanan Timor, about 10 km from Bandar Seri Begawan. The development will comprise intelligent offices equipped with shared ICT infrastructure and facilities, a centre suitable for exhibition, retail, educational and entertainment purposes and quality public housing.

The "Eco" in the name refers to the environmental protection aspect of the project. While achieving the goals mentioned above, the proposed Eco-Cyber Park will also aim to provide a healthy working environment and strive for efficiency in work practices, and use of resources and energy.

Tenders for the development were called in September 2002, and work on the project is expected to begin in 2003. Indeed, planning has already gone beyond the ICT part of the Eco-Cyber Park to conceptualising other initiatives for the Park such as a Nova Hub, Nano Hub and Life Sciences Hub.

Mukim.Net

The Mukim.Net project is an attempt to reach the *mukims*[7] and *kampungs* throughout Brunei. The activities and online access will be centred around community centres as well as rural post offices. The goals are twofold: to make Internet services available to people who do not have access to this technology in their own homes, including school children, retirees, the elderly and housewives, and to bring business capabilities into the villages and fostering greater levels of entrepreneurship.

Quick Quotes

Mr Mohammed Reeda Malik, General Manager of SapuraBrunei, is an active member of the Brunei ICT scene. He shared three key challenges[8] that he sees facing the realisation of e-Government in his country.

The first challenge is in the area of human resources. How does Brunei develop sufficient numbers of professionals to service the ICT industry both within and outside Brunei? Brunei's ICT industry requires a new breed of "knowledge workers". The industry emphasizes the need for creativity and innovation. Brunei's education system may need to adjust itself according to the requirements of the new economy.

The second challenge is the government itself. How quickly can government turn itself into a leading edge user? How do we address the problem of "over-cautiousness" and inertia in government? With the current drive towards e-Government, the Brunei government has the opportunity to move up the IT maturity scale fairly quickly. The problem of "over-cautiousness" can be addressed when there is an increase in empowerment within the ranks of the civil service to make certain decisions that will benefit the nation at the end of the day.

And thirdly, how do we foster a private sector able and willing to anticipate and seize opportunities rather than simply reacting to developments? Brunei Darussalam's E-Initiatives present a unique opportunity for the private/business sector to develop itself through implementation of large scale IT projects like the e-government flagships. This is an opportunity not to be missed and the private/business sector needs to adopt a pro-active approach in educating and creating awareness among their government counterparts on what is available out there.

Sources: Asia-Inc, interview with Mr Malik

KEY CHALLENGES AND THE WAY AHEAD

While it may have started later, Brunei Darussalam is well on its journey towards e-Government. The key drivers have been thought through, the goals and strategies clearly set out, the coordinating bodies established, various policies and frameworks are in place, and the financial budgets allocated. The Sultan and senior officials have reiterated their support for this initiative since 2000.

Progress has been made in many areas, with early 2003 reviews indicating that current e-Government benchmarks have been clearly surpassed. It is evident to the leadership that the potential benefits to the nation in terms of economic growth, development and overall competitiveness make ICT development (including e-Government and e-Business) an imperative that cannot be allowed to stagnate. The Bruneian administration needs to continue to move swiftly to achieve the goals stated in its national IT strategic plan "IT 2000 and Beyond", keeping pace with neighbouring nations which are also achieving milestones of their own.

The journey is, however, not without challenges.[9] Some of the challenges faced relate to the actual implementation of e-Government programmes. These include getting adequate commitment from different entities involved, effecting necessary process changes, enacting legislative instruments, and managing change for those impacted.

It is recognised that the key challenges go beyond technology. Many are clearly people and process related. One official commented:

> Integration is not just getting two or more computer applications to share data. Integration covers integrating processes across department, linking job specifications with system capabilities, replacing manual processes with computerized processes, mapping workflows with physical layouts, performance management at multiple levels and many other factors. The key to successful integration process is taking a total and holistic approach to implementation. Total consideration should not just be on the technology element but should also involve the human processes, organisational, security, laws and regulations and environments.

It is generally agreed that many of the challenges relate to people rather than technology. The ability to change mindsets, and consequently behaviours, is a key success factor.

Getting executive sponsorship and managing change are the key challenges to be faced, according to Haji Mahmud, Director of the ITSSD. (Refer to interview later in chapter.)

Quick Quotes

Mr Lim Boon Guan, General Manager (Brunei) for NCS, commenting on e-Government in Brunei Darussalam, said, "It is an ambitious and laudable goal that the Brunei government has set for itself. E-Government is a very important strategic move for the nation. One can clearly see many projects already underway, championed by various ministries and agencies. Going forward, it is important that the government adopt an active public-private partnership model in order to benefit from a larger pool of talents and technologies in this transformation journey."

Mr Lim, who has many years experience in public sector IT and telecommunications, also added, "It is by adopting and adapting the knowledge and experience of various governments worldwide, for example Canada and US in the west or closer to home, Singapore and Hong Kong, that Brunei will be able to achieve its objective of leapfrogging into a leadership position in ICT within the region. Welcoming global participation will guarantee that Brunei benefits from the best the world can offer, and also ensure technology and expertise transfer to home-grown SMEs."

Source: Interview

From an observer's viewpoint, it appears that all the favourable conditions are in place for e-Government to take off in Brunei Darussalam. The bold national plans stipulate 2005 as the target year for e-Government systems to be in place. What is key is the national will to persevere, and adequate senior leadership to spearhead the initiatives. It is necessary to keep the momentum for the national programme going. One factor that is needed is a strong sense of urgency among the leadership and the people. Brunei's oil wealth certainly puts the nation at a distinct economic advantage. However at times it is easy for the blessed populace to be lulled into a sense of complacency and not realise the importance and urgency of economic diversification and the need to move more rapidly into the ICT age.

The Permanent Secretary at the Prime Minister's Office, Dato Paduka Haji Hazair, speaking at an e-Government seminar in late 2002 said it best, "Year 2005 is just three years away. We must act now and move forward ... We need to show good example and good leadership ...".[10]

PERSPECTIVES OF AN E-GOVERNMENT LEADER

Haji Mahmud bin Haji Mohd Daud,
Director of the Information Technology and State Stores Department
and Secretary for the BIT Council,
Brunei Darussalam

Awang Haji Mahmud bin Haji Mohd Daud is the Director of the Information Technology and State Stores Department, which is under the Ministry of Finance. He is also the Secretary for the Brunei Information Technology (BIT) Council, the body which facilitates ICT development and deployment in the nation. In addition, he is the Joint-Secretary for the E-Government Program Executive Committee (EGPEC).

Haji Mahmud has played a key role in the e-Government programme for Brunei Darussalam.

In June 2003, the author (JY) had the privilege of an interview with Haji Mahmud (HMD) at his offices in Bandar Seri Begawan.

JY   : **What does e-Government really mean to you and to Brunei Darussalam?**

HMD : Beyond the obvious — that e-Government is about transforming public service through process redesign and ICT enablement, we have learnt that e-Government is really about aligning multiple stakeholder views. Although there may be a common e-Government framework, the participants in that framework may be at different levels of induction, some high, others at the bottom — so each will have their own perspectives and requirements. It is very important to get "buy-in" from the different parties — for instance, at the national level, ministry level, department level and individual level. We know we have achieved some alignment when people can see the total picture but also can identify their own role in the overall scope. In this way, we can achieve greater ownership.

By aligning the e-Government directions to our national development and civil service vision, we have tried to achieve tight linkage with our economic and business drivers. Brunei's National IT Agenda and Strategy — called "IT 2000 and Beyond" — has three areas of focus: a public sector drive towards e-Government, private sector drive towards e-Business and national drive towards a paperless society or "e-Brunei". In the longer term, we hope these initiatives will help us diversify Brunei Darussalam's economy beyond oil and gas.

IT 2000 and Beyond
(National IT Strategic Plan)

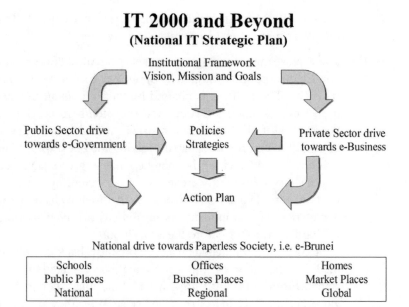

Institutional Framework
Vision, Mission and Goals

| Public Sector drive towards e-Government | Policies Strategies | Private Sector drive towards e-Business |

Action Plan

National drive towards Paperless Society, i.e. e-Brunei

Schools	Offices	Homes
Public Places	Business Places	Market Places
National	Regional	Global

JY : **In your e-Government programme, there must be many competing priorities. How did you decide on the key priorities to focus your resources on?**

HMD : Generally we briefed the various ministries in Brunei that each of them needed to champion at least one e-Government flagship project. In the early days, we had tried suggesting the projects they should be doing, but we found this method did not lead to real ownership of the projects. There tended to be abdication of responsibilities along the way, and accountability was either not there or not sustainable.

Now each of the ministries come up with their flagship projects and business plans, but they need to justify their proposals to the EGPEC and BIT Council. For example PMONet is spearheaded by the Prime Minister's office, TAFIS by the Ministry of Finance, e-Health by the Ministry of Health, e-Education by the Ministry of Education, e-Heritage by the Ministry of Culture, Youth and Sports and so on.

JY   : **How is the management and progress tracking of Brunei's e-Government flagship projects carried out?**

HMD : The way we make the flagship projects get realised faster is through our Electronic Government Programme Executive Committee (EGPEC).The EGPEC is chaired by the Permanent Secretary of the Prime Minister's Office, and the members are Permanent Secretaries of all the other ministries. At each meeting, we have the EGPEC chairman repeatedly asking the question "Where are you now?", and each of the members has to give a status update.

In short, it implicitly creates an aura of cajoling and shaming, but that helps. I have begun to observe that we now have Permanent Secretaries of every ministry getting directly involved — something we hardly ever had before the year 2000.

EGPEC was launched on an interim basis back in 1999, before the BIT Council was set up. After that it was elevated to its current status. From 2000 until now, it has done much better. We have gained greater buy-in from everyone else. What they are now doing is drawing up all the concept plans and going ahead with the implementation.

JY   : **What are some of the key challenges to Brunei's e-Government implementation?**

HMD : Two key areas are crucial. Firstly, there has to be executive sponsorship. Secondly we have found that it isn't so much about technology issues, but more about change management and process adaptation issues which need to be managed in conjunction with changes in the technology infrastructure.

JY   : **What are some of the critical success factors (CSFs) for an e-Government programme?**

HMD : We have recognised several CSF's. Firstly we need leadership and sponsorship from senior members of the government. Secondly, we need to focus on achieving business results. To do this, we have to begin with core services and to drive them with proven IT strategies. Thirdly, we should start with small, manageable projects but scale quickly. Fourthly, managing of the change is crucial. Finally, the solutions we deploy must be easy to operate and support.

JY   : **In the planning and deployment of Brunei's e-Government programmes, what is the government's overall relationship with the private sector?**

HMD : With its small population and limited resources, Brunei would certainly face resource constraints if it did not outsource its e-Government implementation. Our view is that so long as we address the critical success factors, due diligences and economic drivers in the e-Government initiatives, we are quite glad to see government and private sector working hand in hand. In addition, as government leads certain initiatives, we are confident we have the full support of the private sector.

Endnotes

1   Mason, C, "*A Short History of Asia*", Macmillan Press (2000).

2   "*Country Profile 2001: Brunei*", Economist Intelligence Unit, 2001.

3   "*Brunei Yearbook 2002*", Borneo Bulletin.

4   "*Brunei allocates $1 Billion for ICT projects*", Brudirect.com, 10 September 2002.

5   RaGAM21 is short for "Rangkaian Global Aliran Multimedia 21" (or Global Multimedia Network System 21).

6   "*Smart Card System promises Smarter Passport Processing*", Brudirect.com, 12 November 2002.

7   *Mukim* is a Malay word. The aggregation of *kampungs* (villages) is a mukim, and the aggregation of mukims becomes a *daerah* (region or district).

8   Malik, MR, "*Driving the ICT Industry through e-Government*", Asia Inc, July 2002.

9   "*2005 deadline for E-Government*", *Borneo Bulletin*, 28 August 2002.

10   "*ICT projects to boost employment*", *Borneo Bulletin*, 22 October 2002.

Useful Websites

www.bit.gov.bn	Official website of Brunei Darussalam IT Council
www.e-government.gov.bn	Official e-Government website for Brunei
www.brunei.gov.bn	Official website of the Government of Brunei Darussalam
www.brudirect.com	A popular informational website on Brunei
www.brunet.bn	Website of Internet service provider under Jabatan Telekom Brunei (or Brunei Telecom)
www.simpur.net.bn	Website of Internet service provider under DST Group
www.netkad.com.bn	Website for pre-paid Internet access card.

CHAPTER 4

Enter the Dragon — Informatization in China

James SL Yong

▲ ▼ ▲ ▼ ▲ ▼ ▲ ▼

There are many paths to the top of the mountain,
But the view is always the same

Chinese proverb

▲ ▼ ▲ ▼ ▲ ▼ ▲ ▼

BACKGROUND

History

In Mandarin, China is "Zhong Guo", which literally means "Middle Kingdom". The ancient Chinese believed that China was the geographical centre of the world, and represented the only true civilisation. Indeed, Chinese civilisation has existed continuously for about 3,500 years.

A succession of dynasties shaped the nation we now know as China. The earliest known dynasty was the Shang (1600–1026 BC). Next came the Zhou dynasty (1027–256 BC) which produced great philosophers like Confucius and Mencius. The Qin empire (221–207 BC) is remembered for the unification of China by Emperor Shi Huangdi. It was also during his rule that the 2,000 mile Great Wall was built to keep out invaders. The Han dynasty (206 BC–220 AD) imbued the united state with characteristics that we today recognise as Chinese. After Han, came a period of disunity before the Tang dynasty (618–906 AD) rose to power, bringing great advances in learning and culture. Astronomy, mapmaking and Chinese arts flourished. Mongol invaders from the North ended Tang rule, and it took a half-century before the Chinese regained control under the Song dynasty (960–1279 AD). The Mongols eventually overcame the Chinese forces, and the Yuan dynasty (1279–1368 AD) came about. The best known ruler was Kublai Khan who brought progress to the nation in trade, scholarship and the arts.

For centuries China outpaced the rest of the world in the arts and sciences. During the Ming dynasty (1368–1644 AD), China reached the zenith of its power. Chinese armies reconquered Annam, as northern Vietnam was then known, and kept the Mongols back in the North. All the while Chinese fleets under the command of the famed Admiral Chenghe sailed far and wide.[1] China's power and influence led many maritime Asian nations to send envoys bearing tribute to the Chinese emperor.

The Ming maritime expeditions stopped suddenly after 1433 for reasons which are still unclear. Historians speculate that it could have been the huge expense of large-scale expeditions at a time of preoccupation with northern defenses against the Mongols. This may have been coupled with opposition by factions of conservative imperial court officials. Pressure from the powerful Neo-Confucian bureaucracy led to a revival of a strict agrarian-centred society. The stability of the Ming dynasty, coupled with advancements in economy, arts, culture and politics, promoted a belief among the Chinese that they had achieved the greatest civilisation on earth, and that nothing foreign was needed or welcome. The Middle Kingdom then went into a period where a strict "closed door" policy was enforced.

This period of isolation was broken only in the mid 19th Century, with the arrival of foreign powers. The Chinese defeat by the British in the Opium War of 1839–1842 led to a series of treaties where China was forced to open five ports to foreign trade. Similar concessions were later made to France and the US.

In the first half of the 20th Century, China was beset by major famines, civil unrest, military defeats, and foreign occupation. After World War II, the Communists under Mao Zedong established a regime that, while ensuring China's sovereignty, imposed strict controls over everyday life and cost the lives of tens of millions of people. After 1978, his successor Deng Xiaoping gradually introduced market-oriented reforms and decentralised economic decision-making. Output quadrupled in the next two decades and China now has the world's second largest GDP. Political controls remain tight even while economic controls continue to weaken.

Geography

With a total area of around 9.6 million sq km, China's vastness essentially encloses many different worlds within a single country. From bustling cities to the vast grasslands of Inner Mongolia — with deserts, mountains, and imperial ruins — China is a land of cultural and geographic diversity of epic proportions.

China's population stands at a staggering 1.3 billion people — which implies that almost one out of every four persons on earth is Chinese. The main languages used are *Putonghua* (Beijing Mandarin dialect) and Cantonese. Although the official religion is atheism, there are large followings of Confucianism, Buddhism, Taoism, Islam and Christianity. Almost 900 million (70 percent) live in rural areas, while the remaining 400 million are urban dwellers. The major cities include Beijing (the capital), Shanghai, Guangzhou, Shenzhen and Shenyang.

The country is divided into 22 provinces, 5 autonomous regions, 4 municipalities and 2 special administrative regions (SARs). The autonomous regions are Guangxi, Inner Mongolia, Xinjiang, Ningxia, and Ziziang. The four municipalities that are governed directly from the central government are Beijing, Shanghai, Tianjin and Chongqing. Hong Kong, a British Crown colony until 1997, and Macao, a Portuguese colony until 1999, are the two SARs.

Economy

After the Cultural Revolution was over, and Deng Xiaoping had been brought back to the helm, he began to pursue his vision of the "Four Modernisations" — targeting the four areas of agriculture, industry, defense and science for rapid development. With this, mass importation of modern technology and equipment, mainly from the West began in earnest.

Deng focused on transforming China into a modern economy. His often quoted words, "It does not matter if it is a yellow cat or a black cat, as long as it catches mice", captures the essence of the rapid changes in the Chinese economy since the mid-1980s. Deng acknowledged the failure of the previous economic system, and argued that there was no use in everyone having the same amount if all were poor. He offered a new kind of socialism that he termed "socialism with Chinese characteristics". Today, while China's official doctrine remains Marxist, the reality is unbridled capitalism in most areas, practiced under the label of "socialist market economy", one which reduces central control in favour of market forces.

Deng's "open door" policy also led to the creation of four Special Economic Zones (SEZs) in Fujian and Guangdong provinces in 1979.[2] These areas were set up in China's coastal regions as export zones, with tax incentives to attract foreign investors. Effectively, they were China's earliest experiments in capitalism.

China's economy experienced a growth rate averaging 9–10 percent during the 1990s, and GDP was around US$ 1,100 billion by the turn of the millennium. In December 2001, China gained entry into the World Trade Organisation.

Government

The governmental system is communist republic. It is also a one-party Marxist state, with political power resting firmly with the Chinese Communist Party (CCP), with a central committee and politburo elected every five years.

There are 28 ministries in the government. The list of ministries and commissions reads as follows: Foreign Affairs, State Development and Reform Commission, Commerce, Education, Science and Technology, Commission of Science, Technology and Industry for National Defense, State Ethnic Affairs Commission, Public Security, State Security, Supervision, Civil Affairs, Justice, Finance, Personnel, Labour and Social Security, Land and Natural Resources, Construction, Railways, Communications, Information Industry, Water Resources, Agriculture, Culture, Health, State Population and Family Planning Commission, China Banking Administrative Commission, People's Bank of China and the Auditing Administration.

The Ministry of Commerce was created only after the National People's Congress (NPC) which concluded in March 2003. This ministry consolidated two bodies — the State Economic and Trade Commission (SETC) and the Ministry of Foreign Trade and Economic Relations

(MOFTEC). Another significant act at the NPC was the downgrading of the State Development Planning Commission, the agency long entrusted with carrying out the traditional five-year plans of the Communist Party's planned economy. It was renamed the State Development and Reform Commission, and became more of a policy think-tank. This move signaled a clear shift away from central planning.

The Chinese leadership transition proceeded in a peaceful and orderly fashion, also concluding in March 2003. Hu Jintao was elected state President and Chairman of the Central Military Commission, Wu Bangguo as Chairman of the NPC and Wen Jiabao as Premier. Among the outgoing "third-generation" leaders,[3] only President Jiang Zemin stayed on as head of the military, while NPC chairman Li Peng and Premier Zhu Rongji both officially retired, ceasing to play any direct role in politics.

Political analysts believe that it is unlikely that the new team's approach will be radically different from their predecessors. Hu has already committed to carry on Jiang's economic liberalisation policies and to uphold the "Theory of the Three Represents", Jiang's doctrinal legacy.[4]

INFORMATIZATION IN CHINA

Over the last decade, there have been phenomenal changes in the modernisation of the People's Republic of China (PRC), fuelled by the commitment of government leaders to transform China into a market economy. Nowhere is such growth more evident than in the ICT sector.

It has been documented that the very first Internet email from China was sent by an academic in September 1987.[5] Today, the Internet (or *hu-lian-wang* in Mandarin) has become an indispensable part of many Chinese people's lives in urban areas. The number of Internet users has doubled every year for the past five years. Latest estimates (for the first quarter of 2003) are that there are between 45 and 65 million Internet users in China, depending on which research body, official agency or publication one references.[6] It should, however, be noted that even these huge numbers represent only a mere 5 percent of the total population. Internet diffusion has only now started to move into the vast rural areas, with information and communication centres being set up. Computer literacy among the younger generation is enhanced by special education programmes in schools.

The information industry (including hardware, software and content) has become an important pillar of China's commercial sector. Chinese IT firms, such as Legend and Founder, have been successful competing against powerful foreign brands in the domestic market. Chinese portals — Sina.com, Sohu.com and Netease.com — have become well-known even outside China. China's telecommunications equipment market has several rising Chinese firms, including Julong, Datang, Zhongxin, Huawei and Jinpeng, which have developed and marketed their own brand-name products such as digital switches and mobile systems. With China's entry into the WTO in 2001, major restructuring of all ICT businesses in China is expected over the next decade.

A popular phrase in Chinese leadership circles over the past few years is "xin xi hua", which connotes the meaning of "ICT promotion". This term has been translated into English as "informatization".[7] The highest echelons of China's central leadership have shown that they clearly recognise the criticality of ICT for national growth and development. As early as 1984, Deng Xiaoping pointed out the importance of developing information resources in order to promote the realisation of the Four Modernisations.[8] Deng also emphasised repeatedly that "telecommunication is the starting point of economic development".[9] Past President Jiang Zemin reiterated these points. Once he even revealed in an interview that he had a PC in his Zhongnanhai home and often logged onto foreign websites.

Thus, similar to many national initiatives, Internet development in China is very much a top-down effort by the Chinese government. The authorities played a crucial role in building a national information infrastructure and developing an information economy. All of the telecommunication infrastructure in China, including the Internet backbone, would have been impossible without government support and funding. Government-supported academic and research networks such as CSTnet and CERnet were the forerunners of the modern Internet in China. The "Golden Projects" (to be highlighted later) built upon this information infrastructure.

Government Internet Policy

The position of the Chinese government tends to be paradoxical. While publicly supportive of Internet development, the Government also struggles to control its every aspect. The leadership certainly intends to quickly develop sound ICT infrastructure and nurture a people familiar with cyberspace, as they perceive the adoption of the Internet as a necessity for economic growth. Yet, some in government are very wary that the Internet may be a potential challenge, if not an outright threat, to their authority. There is an ongoing cautiousness of what an open Internet may introduce, as well as a fear that the Internet may be difficult for the government to control.

The Internet sector in China is specifically governed by two regulations: *Interim Regulations on International Interconnection of Computer Networks in PRC,* and *Measures for the administration of Internet information services.* The Interim Regulations specify that all ISPs provide access to the Internet through Interconnecting Networks, and these Interconnecting Networks connect into global Internet via a gateway administered by China Telecom.

Key themes covered by the government Internet policies include the definition of directions (with informatization of the whole country being a key goal), and the setting up of high-tech zones. In these designated zones, high-tech startups can enjoy five years of significant tax breaks, seed money, lower tariffs, favourable foreign investment and foreign sales regulations, and standard setting (mainly technical standards managed by the MII). The Chinese government has also planned for national information infrastructure development.

In line with their commitment to utilising the Internet to promote economic development in China, the government has decided to focus on "Government Online" and "Enterprise Online".

Informatization Blueprint

In China's 10th Five-Year Plan (2001–2005), the use of ICT or informatization as a tool to help drive China's industrialisation was highlighted as one of the key measures of "national economic strategic adjustment and restructuring".

In 2000, the government also introduced a measure which was called "National Informatization Quotient" (or NIQ), which is meant to evaluate the informatization levels of different regions of China.

In July 2002, China's first informatization blueprint called "The Layout of National Economy and Society Informatization", was mapped out.[10] While conceptually not entirely new, this blueprint builds on work already being done over the past half-decade, and puts the overall effort in perspective. In particular, it urges the further development of four key programmes:

(1)   information resource development;

(2)   information infrastructure development;

(3)   application of informatization; and

(4)   information products.

The blueprint proposes that China set up a national information network with sound structure and security considerations in order to achieve the rapid development of information industry. To fulfill the blueprint, China needs to work out the national informatization technology standards and refine the relevant laws and regulations.

At the same time, the aims of China's e-Government development were determined:

- to set up a fully functioning and safe e-Government information network platform under a uniform standard;
- to achieve impact on key business systems and the basic and strategic e-Government information warehouses;
- to enhance sharing rates of information resources; and
- to set up a basic e-Government security system.

THE KEY AGENCIES

A handful of government agencies have wide-ranging influence on the ICT landscape in China: the Ministry of Information Industry, the State Informatization Leading Group, China Internet Network Information Centre, and the newly formed Ministry of Commerce (from the merger of SETC and MOFTEC in 2003).

Ministry of Information Industry (MII)

Formed in 1998, the MII regulates telecommunications and IT-related products and services, including data and wireless communications, satellites, multimedia, broadcasting, electronics, computers, software and the Internet. The MII reports to the State Council, and comes under the purview of the State Informatization Leading Group.

As the telecom market continued to grow under the market opening policy and the encouragement of fair competition, the MII officially relinquished its control of manufacturing and services. In reality, however, MII still has much influence on market directions through its regulations, inspections and recommendations, as well as through informal networks.

The MII has played a key role in shaping telecom development in China, in areas such as developing the national telecom policy framework, network planning and regulation, developing technical standards, overseeing Internet operations and security, and management of international services. MII is also acknowledged for its efforts in nurturing the competitive telecom market in China. In 1999, the MII spearheaded the breakup of China

Telecom into multiple operating entities, each focusing on different types of services (refer next section). The intent behind the breakup was to accelerate the development of a larger number of telecom services sectors.

With China's admission into the WTO, the MII faces some new challenges. These include protecting domestic companies while opening the market to foreign participation, developing China's first telecom law, managing the convergence of telecom, cable TV and the Internet, managing feedback on high service charges, and enforcing Internet regulations to curb "negative" effects from the cyber world while making it conducive to growth.

State Informatization Leading Group (SILG)

The SILG was formed to provide top-level coordination on intra-agency issues related to IT and telecom issues. In the wake of emerging Internet service and computer crimes (such as security breaches, fraud and "harmful" content), the SILG acts as a "super government agency" that oversees links between the Central government, the MII, or other information policy development bodies.

The SILG is a virtual organisation with half a dozen senior members who are heads of various government agencies, including MII and the Communist Party Propaganda Department. Ex-Premier Zhu Rongji was a key proponent of the SILG. The Office is more of a contingency agency, to be called on when needs arise — such as when there are major changes of China's information policy and enforcement measures. Despite its unassuming appearance, the SILG, with its high-profile members, wields tremendous influence over other government agencies, and through them, has control of the industry. The group approves and modifies frameworks for industry regulations and future directions for the telecom, industry as well as enforcement and execution issues. On rare occasions, the SILG has been known to reverse MII proposals or key decisions.

Ministry of Commerce

At the NPC meeting of March 2003, it was announced that the new Ministry of Commerce would take over the functions of two former bodies: SETC and MOFTEC.

The SETC's role was to monitor and regulate the national economy, to implement the objectives, policies and measures for near-term economic operations; to resolve major problems arising from economic operations, and to provide feedback and recommendations to the State Council.

The policies of MOFTEC impacted the telecommunications industry in many ways, especially in its regulation of foreign trade and investment, joint ventures, use of foreign exchange and exports. All foreign investment in China's telecom industry needed MOFTEC approval. Its jurisdiction included all forms of foreign investment, scope of restrictions, approval of foreign-funded limited liability companies, representative offices, and products under China's quota system. MOFTEC played the role of chief negotiator for China's WTO membership.

China Internet Network Information Centre (CNNIC)

Founded in 1997, CNNIC is a nonprofit organisation, reporting to the MII, but functioning under the leadership of the Chinese Academy of Science. The main responsibilities of CNNIC include domain name registration, IP address distribution, managing a national catalogues database, publishing statistics on Internet development in China, and providing services relating to attestation of net station visitor flow.[11] CNNIC also provides various Internet technology and applications training for different levels of society. CNNIC liaises with other Internet network information centres such as InterNIC and APNIC. It also undertakes scientific research projects related to the Internet and offers technology consultation services.

THE TELECOM SCENE IN CHINA

China began the deregulation of its telecommunications industry in 1993. Prior to this, China's telecommunication services (both basic and value-added) were all operated and administered by the Ministry of Post and Telecommunication (MPT), now part of MII. Overlapping governmental sectors and the mixture of governmental functions and enterprise functions in China's telecommunication field, seriously slowed its development. China Telecom was eventually separated from MPT to focus on operating the telecommunication services, while MPT only handled policy and strategy aspects.

In 1994, China decided to allow certain companies (ie those not under MPT's jurisdiction) and private investors, to participate in a limited area of value-added telecommunication operations. Two telecommunication companies, China Unicom and Jitong, were established to compete with China Telecom's monopoly. Unicom was permitted to engage in basic telecommunication services, such as long-distance phone, local phone services and value-added telecommunication services. Jitong (owned by the Ministry of Electronics Industry) focused instead, on the domestic information services market. In spite of this move, the new entrants were found to be too small to compete with the giant incumbent.

Between 1999–2001, the MII spearheaded the breakup of China Telecom's four main service divisions into separate operating entities. Four state-owned companies were thus formed: a *new* China Telecom (the fixed-line business of the old China Telecom), China Mobile, China Satellite Com and China Unicom (which absorbed the paging business).[12] Other smaller players included Jitong, Railcom and Netcom.

In early 2002, the authorities further split the fixed-line services of China Telecom into two. The services for ten northern provinces were merged with Netcom, with China Telecom maintaining the rest of the fixed-line services. By mid-2002, China's telecom market was dominated by four large players, China Telecom, China Mobile, China Netcom and Unicom; and two smaller players: Railcom and China Satellite.

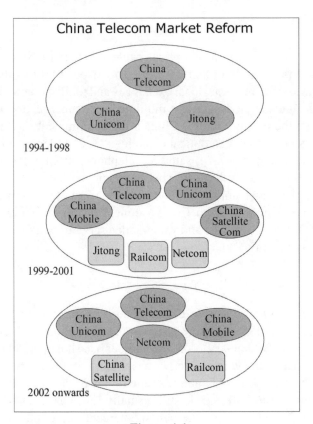

Figure 4-1

ICT MATURITY INDICATORS

Teledensity

China has rapidly emerged as the world's largest telecommunications market, ranking first in the size of its mobile market and second in fixed-line phones (after the US).[13] By 2002, there were 145 million mobile phone users and 179 million fixed-line subscribers. China's overall telephone penetration (fixed and mobile combined) rose from less than 1 percent in 1991 to 30 percent by mid-June 2002.

Growth in Short Message Service (SMS) has also been phenomenal. In 2000, about one billion SMS messages were sent within China. This sprang to nearly 16 billion in 2001 and 90 billion in 2002. It was reported that during the eight-day Chinese New Year holiday in February 2003, almost 8 billion SMS messages were routed.[14] Some analysts say the figure could balloon to 200 billion for the year 2003.

Networks

The estimated total length of optical cable laid within China exceeds 1.5 million km — as long as two round trips from Earth to the Moon! Long distance transmissions, local exchanges and mobile communications have been digitised, and data and multimedia communication networks span almost the entire country. China's telecommunications networks, centred on some two dozen optical cable lines, is complemented by other networks such as microwave, satellite, telephone, mobile phone, digital communications, and multimedia communications.

In 2002, the major domestic players in the China telecommunication market include: China Telecom, China Mobile, Unicom, and China Netcom. Under WTO rules, both basic and value-added services market have begun to open to international players.

Internet

The Internet was introduced to China much later than to other industrial nations. As late as 1999, there were fewer than 9 million Internet users in mainland China. By January 2003, the number had shot up to 59 million.[15] This works out to an average Internet penetration of 450 users per 10,000 persons. The reality is that Internet penetration in cities is significantly higher, while in rural areas, it is still dismally low. One is also reminded that 59 million users represent a mere 4.5 percent of the total population. Nonetheless, overall Internet growth in China continues to be astounding.

About two-thirds of the Internet users use dial-up access, a third on leased line connections while a small percentage are on ISDN or broadband. In 2002, China's Web-surfer population reportedly exceeded that of Japan.[16, 17]

The major Internet Service Providers are ChinaNet, ChinaGBN, CERnet and CSTnet. In addition to these, there are more than 500 other ISPs in China, most of them providing some kind of Internet access and other services for particular geographic markets. Internet access in China is under the regulatory category of "value-added services", which has been open since the mid-1990s. That is any company can apply for a license from the MII to provide the service to the public.

THE GOLDEN PROJECTS

It could be said that China first launched its national ICT programme in December 1993, when the State Council formed the high-level Joint Committee of National Economic Informatization to oversee the progress of a series of national initiatives, called the "Golden Projects". These were far-reaching initiatives with ambitious goals, including:

(1) building a national information highway leading to modernisation and economic development;
(2) driving development of IT in China; and
(3) unifying the country by connecting the centre to the provinces, and by allowing the government to act across ministerial and industrial boundaries.

These three goals overlap somewhat, but are also different. The first is most tangible — creating an information infrastructure over which data can flow. The second is emotional — a rallying cry for China to become a modern nation. The third is a combination of the first two goals — it is clearly the most important, and the driver for the other two. Attaining this will allow the central government to regain administrative control by becoming an "information gatekeeper" for the country.

Since then, a series of Golden Projects has been inaugurated at the Joint Conference. The projects can be categorised into four tiers or phases.

Tier One comprised the "Golden Gate", "Golden Bridge", "Golden Card" and "Golden Sea" projects. The first three of these have remained the most high-profile, even among the many other Golden projects subsequently launched.

The **Golden Gate**, also called "Golden Customs" project, first proposed by then Vice Premier Li Lanqing in 1993, was aimed at creating an integrated trade information link between MOFTEC, the Customs Bureau and a host of foreign trade companies and banks. Prior to 1978, only the foreign trade ministry and its 12 trade corporations were permitted to engage in international trading activities. By the early 1990s, the "open door" policy had resulted in more than 9,000 organisations providing international trade services. The Golden Gate Project was thus designed to develop an information network to recentralise administration and control of China's foreign trade activities. The system was intended to speed up customs clearance and enhance the authorities' ability to detect and prevent illegal activities (eg smuggling), and collect taxes and duties. It also allowed companies to submit import and export declarations to the customs bodies, compute duty payments and check trade statistics.

This second project, the **Golden Bridge**, focused on infrastructure. The goal was to create an infrastructure backbone for the first national economic information network. It was intended to support Internet access, email, EDI, information and application services. Since it was proposed in 1993 by then Vice Premier Zhu Rongji, it has been formed out of a hybrid of satellite and landline networks, which tie together regional nodes into a network hub in Beijing. The Golden Bridge project spurred the creation of ChinaGBN, which is today a major ISP. Up until 2002, the Golden Bridge Network has been constructed as a medium-speed "information highway", but the ultimate goal is to upgrade it into a high bandwidth multimedia network over which other Golden projects can transmit and receive data.

The **Golden Card** project was initiated to create a unified payment settlement system to enable the wide use of credit and debit cards. Unlike the case in many other developing countries, such cards have yet to gain widespread adoption. Apart from the neglect of the local commercial banks to promote the consumer credit market in the past, strict government control over the banking system has also contributed to the slow development of an effective payment system.[18] This project was initiated by former President Jiang Zemin in June 1993 when he called for the creation of a nationwide credit card system. China's fragmented banking system has also made it extremely difficult to clear transactions, thus forming a major barrier to commerce, especially e-Business. The "Golden Card" project was launched in 1995 and 1996 in a dozen trial areas, including most key cities and provinces. Implementation will progress in three stages: the pilot stage (1994–1996), the dissemination stage (1997–1999) and the popularisation stage (2000–2003). A number of regional "Golden Card Offices" have started their own Internet payment gateway companies in Beijing, Shanghai and Guangzhou. These are companies which are "licensed" to offer Internet payment gateway solutions to e-Commerce providers that are linked to the "Golden Card Project" inter-bank settlement systems.

The **Golden Sea** project was conceived as an information system linking China's top government leaders, providing them instant access to data from institutions, organisations, and offices under the direct control of the Communist Party Central Committee.

The projects in **Tier Two** were designed to apply information networks to economic reform. These comprised "Golden Macro", "Golden Tax", "Golden Intelligence" and "Golden Shield".

The **Golden Macro** project was developed to serve the government's Central Economic and Financial Leading Group in macro-control over China's national economic activities.

The **Golden Tax** project involved building a data network to link the State Tax Administration's auditing centre in Beijing with 50 regional offices and 800 bureaus. It also allows customs departments to verify through the network, a range of data in order to facilitate customs management and prevent illegal activities.

The **Golden Intelligence** project concerns the setting up China's Internet service.

The **Golden Shield** was initiated in 2000, and the project goals are to promote "the adoption of advanced information and communication technologies to strengthen central police control, responsiveness, and crime combating capacity so as to improve the efficiency and effectiveness of police work". This was in effect, an ambitious plan to create a nationwide digital monitoring network, linking national, regional and local security agencies in a panoptic web of surveillance. At its core is supposedly a database system which offers immediate access to records on every citizen in China.

Projects in **Tier Three** had to do with sector-specific applications of the new IT programme. They included "Golden Enterprise", "Golden Agriculture", "Golden Health", "Golden Information" and "Golden Housing".

The **Golden Enterprise** project pushed for the construction of intranets, extranets and various inter-connections between China's 12,000 large and medium-sized enterprises, based on the different business sectors.

Under the **Golden Agriculture** project, a databank and services network was set up to provide agricultural information, weather reports and market information.

The Ministry of Public Health spearheaded the **Golden Health** project to develop a high-speed information exchange system for hospitals.

The **Golden Information** project is a network linking the various statistical collection departments across the country.

The **Golden Housing** project is aimed at the nationwide sharing of information on real estate.

The Fourth Tier of projects have so far comprised the "**Golden Cellular**", a consortium of eight of China's largest domestic mobile communications manufacturers; and "**Golden Switch**", a programme to develop China's domestic digital switch manufacturing industry.

	Name of Project		Stakeholders
(1)	Golden Customs (or Golden Gate)	*JinGuan*	Ministry of Foreign Trade, Customs, Jitong Co.
(2)	Golden Bridge	*JinQiao*	Ministry of Electronics, State Information Centre
(3)	Golden Card	*JinKa*	PBoC, Ministry of Electronic, Ministry of Internal Trade, Great Wall Computer Co.
(4)	Golden Sea	*JinHai*	State Statistical Bureau, PBoC, State Information Centre
(5)	Golden Tax	*JinShui*	Ministry of Finance, Ministry of Electronics, National Tax Bureau, Great Wall Co.
(6)	Golden Macro	*JinHong*	China Ex-Im Bank, Ministry of Finance, State Information Centre
(7)	Golden Intelligence	*JinZhi*	State Education Commission
(8)	Golden Shield		
(9)	Golden Enterprise	*JinQi*	State Economic and Trade Commission
(10)	Golden Agriculture	*JinNong*	Ministry of Agriculture
(11)	Golden Health	*JinWei*	Ministry of Health
(12)	Golden Information	*JinXin*	State Statistical Bureau
(13)	Golden Housing		
(14)	Golden Cellular	*JinFeng*	Ministry of Electronics and Information
(15)	Golden Switch	*JinKai*	Ministry of Electronics and Information, Ministry of Posts and Telecoms (now MII)

Sources: www.mii.gov.cn, www.virtualchina.com

Figure 4-2: China's Golden Projects

China plans to spend more than US$ 120 billion over the next 5 years to spur the development of its information industry, according to MII. Half of this investment will be earmarked for telecom. MII said that priority will be given to the application of IT to boost social and economic development. Financing will be raised from domestic and international capital markets, and both Chinese and foreign investment in the sector will be encouraged.

THE GOVERNMENT ONLINE PROJECT

The various Golden Projects were meant to establish the operational backbone for propelling China into the information economy. Once these infrastructural foundation initiatives had been launched, the Central Government announced, between 1999 and 2001, a new series of plans based on three specific areas: Government Online, Enterprise Online and Family Online.

Government Online is a broad effort to drive government agencies to utilise ICT, to interconnect and to disseminate information to the people.

Enterprise Online is targeted at encouraging industries to aggressively adopt Internet technologies and to strive for greater transparency.

Family Online focuses on increased use of network resources by families across China, bringing the population at large onto the new e-platform.

Government Online (or e-Government) is recognised as an important area of focus for China and here are a number of policies and plans in place to facilitate its development. The project is part of a wide-ranging informatization programme.

Year 2002 was designated the "Year of e-Governance" (*dianzi zhengwu*) by the Central Government. At a high-level conference in December 2002, Mr Lou Qinjian, Vice Minister of the Ministry of Information Industry, pointed out that promotion of e-Government will be treated as one of the crucial goals of informatization. He said that in particular, e-Government promotion will serve to expedite the development of IT manufacturing, telecommunications, and the software industry. It will also serve to strengthen the standard implementation of e-Government and set up an overarching secure network.[19]

In conjunction with the Government Online Project, the Chinese administration carried out a major initiative to reduce bureaucratic red tape. In 2001, China announced that in the previous year it had abolished almost 20 percent of the more than 4,000 administrative approvals required by more than 60 government departments. Lovelock and Ure described the Government Online Project as a three-stage initiative:[20]

- Stage One focuses on introducing the enabling technologies, in particular, connecting some 1,000 government offices and agencies to the Internet.
- Stage Two focuses on information sharing, by having offices and agencies move their information systems into compatible electronic form.
- Stage Three is only expected to happen sometime late in the decade. It will see government offices and agencies going paperless.

The key goals of China's e-Government Online project are:

- to set up two integrated Internet platforms: an internal network to handle government affairs at all levels, and an external web to handle interactions with enterprises, public services and between governments;
- to establish several key databanks (eg on demographics, natural resources, law and enforcement, and the macro economy);
- to transform government by promoting 12 priority application projects (including customs, taxation, finance, public security, social security, and agriculture and water resources); and
- to ensure information security, and protection (data integrity/security)
- to build an information standardisation system and policy system.

The "Government Online Project" was conceived to cover eight areas:[21] online electronic information exchange, online government procurement bidding, online welfare payment, electronic delivery, information centre, electronic document management and publishing, electronic taxation, and digital identity.

Building Blocks of e-Government in China

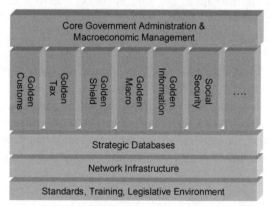

Figure 4-3

The ambitious Government Online Project attempts to inter-connect government agencies in every province, autonomous region and municipality. Establishment of official government agency websites to provide information and services will be strongly encouraged. It will also facilitate collaboration between the government and the nation's growing number of IT enterprises (such as ISP's, software and hardware manufacturers). By putting in place the basic infrastructure and encouraging government agencies to embrace Internet technologies, the government hopes to set the tone for online development and eventually e-Commerce.

Some cities have put in place particularly strong e-Government programmes (eg Beijing and Shanghai). It was reported that by the end of 2000, four out of five government agencies, both local and national, had established websites.

The Chinese government is promoting the construction of network infrastructure in preparation for this. Significant progress appears to have been made. Reports as of mid-2002 indicate that China has established 52 governmental websites, and that government domain names have increased from 145 at the start of the initiative to nearly 5,000.

China has set as its Electronic Services Delivery (ESD) target as "enabling 80 percent of the services of municipal government agencies to be delivered on the web by 2005". In this regard, the Chinese government intends to conduct all government purchasing online to enhance the transparency of business transactions. Departments involving trade, finance, public health, medicine supervision, logistics and large state-owned enterprise have all promoted online purchasing since 2001, as well.

Government agencies at all levels are estimated to have set aside a total of 1 trillion yuan (US$121 billion) for e-Government projects, ranging from office automation and government websites to sponsoring e-Commerce for local businesses.[22] E-Government spending in China is expected to grow at a CAGR of nearly 40 percent.[23]

The State Council will review two regulations on e-Government, which will lay a stable foundation for the promotion of building an online government in the country. These two regulations relate to digital signatures and information publicity.

The digital signature regulation will establish the basis for online approval between government departments, while the government information publicity regulation will push government departments to publicize their contact information and regulations on the Web, and give free access to the public.

E-GOVERNMENT: DEVELOPMENTS FROM BEIJING

Originally built in the late 13th Century by Kublai Khan as the capital of his Yuan dynasty, the city was first called *Dadu,* meaning "great capital", before the Ming rulers renamed it *Beijing* (or "northern capital") in the 15th Century. Today Beijing is China's political and cultural centre, and home to 14 million residents. Beijing district spans some 17,000 sq km in the Northeast part of China.

Casual visitors to Beijing would probably remember the Forbidden City, Summer Palace, and Temple of Heaven more than the fact that this city is the heart of China's central government machinery. But if one wanders westwards of the Forbidden City towards an area called *Zhongnanhai*, one can peer into a compound which holds the residences and offices of the highest ranking members of the Communist Party. Beijing, an independently administered municipal district, accommodates both the central and municipal government. Not surprisingly, government administration is a prime source of employment. As the de facto national showcase to the outside world, Beijing boasts many grand infrastructure projects, such as ring roads, a subway system and rail and air hubs. Many sports facilities are also being added in readiness for the 2008 Olympics.

Beijing's e-Government Journey

An ancient Chinese saying goes, "The journey of a thousand li begins with the first step".[24] So it is with Beijing's journey to enable its public administration through the use of ICT. As early as 1998, the Beijing municipal government had taken its first steps to bring government onto the Internet, making it one of the earliest cities in mainland China to initiate online office work. By the end of 2000, various information networks and databases had been established, covering such areas as population, taxation and human resources management. Not surprisingly, Beijing's municipality e-Government projects tend to be intertwined with China's national initiatives, such as the Golden Projects.

Zhongguancun and the Haidian "Digital Park"

Launched in 2000, in the Zhongguancun Science Park (ZSP)[25] (www.zhongguancun.com.cn), the Digital Park at Haidian[26] is a key part of Beijing's e-Government initiative. Running on the Digital Park Internet-based platform are many traditional government functions, such as business registration and regulation, tax declaration and data collection, etc.

The parallel structure of the Digital Park is very different from the hierarchical bureaucracy of government. Such a transition entails changing not only existing laws and regulations, but also calls for a significant change of work style for both the government staff members and visitors.

The Digital Park is in fact a software platform on which the administrative authorities can process their internal and external affairs. This enables the government to provide its services and conduct its administrative duties, using latest communications technologies and gaining the inherent benefits of fast information flow. Four major features of the Digital Park system are: openness, interactivity, "all-in-one" site (single point of access), and "all-on-one-sheet" (simplified documents). The first phase of the Digital Park went into operation in August 2000. The system includes five key functions:

- *e-application*: A Web-based program that provides applicants with all forms and documents to be prepared as well as related laws, regulations, requirements and procedures ie words, all that people need to know about setting up a company in the Park. The applicants can complete the forms online if they wish.
- *e-registration*: After a company is initially approved, it must provide additional information to register with other ZSP departments, eg statistics bureau, finance bureau, quality control bureau, etc. This can be done online as well.
- *e-administration*: Several other documents that companies must file on a regular basis can now also be filed online.
- *e-reporting*: Each high-tech company must report about 100 pieces of operational data, such as revenue, tax, costs, cash flow and so on, to the appropriate government offices each month. This is done entirely online. Companies must however, pay a fee to have a digital identity established by the Certification Authority.
- *e-consulting*: Government officials can provide interactive online consulting services about any of these procedures, and can provide answers to FAQ's by email or fax.

Ever since the Park went online in 2000, more than 6,000 businesses in the ZSP have been able to apply for a license, file monthly financial reports, submit tax statements and conduct dozens of other "G2B" and "G2C" functions online. The system has helped to increase government transparency, and reduced the opportunities for corruption. The government's stated intent is that if the Digital Park is a success, within 5 years most government administrative functions in Beijing will also be performed online in a similar manner.

Beijing Government Intranet

The creation of Beijing's government Intranet is not a simple exercise of hyperlinking together the websites of individual government departments, but rather, the integration of their backend information systems and databases. This is no mean feat, as there are more than 130 government units; the data resources of which need to be reviewed and integrated. For instance, on the same Intranet there should be available information from the Taxation Bureau, the Forestry Bureau and so on. There should not be any necessity for citizens to log onto the individual departmental websites to hunt for the information required.

However, difficulties such as uniform standards and the redefinition of responsibilities of individual government departments stand in the way of full integration. "We still lack a clear uniform standard in constructing e-Government, since different departments have different standards. Also, it's very difficult to redefine the work responsibilities of those departments" lamented a government official. The next step will combine the information of another 600 government departments. The main purpose is to maximize the availability of government information to the general public. However, it is hard to say when and what proportion of government functions can be realised through the Internet.

e-Government Website

After some experimentation, the Beijing municipal government launched their e-Government website (http://eservice.beijing.gov.cn) in late 2002. Through this website, Beijing residents are able to access all 15 departments of the municipal government included in the e-Government plan. These will include bureaus involved in the granting of about 70 types of approvals related to the setting up of new institutions, qualification appraisals, HR management, license applications and construction plans. Some of the municipal bureaus include the Public Security Bureau, Commission of Economy and Trade, Bureau of Land Resources and Housing, Industry and Commerce Administration, and Civil Affairs. For example, online services offered by the Public Security Bureau would include the processing of ID cards, international travel and entry documents, and applications for immigration to Hong Kong and Macao, while the Bureau of Land Resources and Housing would offer issuance of licenses for new real estate projects and relocation plans.

Figure 4-4: **Website of Beijing Municipal Government**
http://eservice.beijing.gov.cn

E-GOVERNMENT: DEVELOPMENTS FROM SHANGHAI

Shanghai is sometimes referred to as the "dragon's head" of China due to its location at the mouth of the Yangtze River. Shanghai is an excellent sea and river port, with easy access to the vast hinterland. Shanghai's population is about 17 million.

During the 1930s, Shanghai was considered the most cosmopolitan and vibrant city in Asia. This changed during World War II. However, in the 1990s Shanghai began to regain its former glory and is now very much in the headlines. Shanghai in 2003 is the showcase of China's fast growth and a bonanza of tourist attractions, business opportunities and cultural activities. It has firmly re-established itself as a premier financial and commercial centre.

Shanghai's telecommunication infrastructure is among the best in China. There are now more than 6 million fixed-lines, 7 million mobile subscribers and 3 million Internet users.

Shanghai's mid to long-term strategic programme for social and economic development is to build the city into a leading economic, financial, trade and shipping centre in the world, and to establish the city's status as an international metropolis featuring socialist modernisation.

Informatizing Shanghai

With aspirations to join the ranks as one of the world's most connected cities, Shanghai has taken major steps towards informatization. Wiring up the city and providing enhanced Internet services have long been a key objectives. The city of Shanghai is committed to develop its IT infrastructure. All government departments now use IT to improve their performance. Tax forms, retirement benefit applications, and other documents can now be requested and accessed online. The city has also introduced electronic social security, transport and banking cards for its citizens. All schools are now connected to the Internet, with one computer for 15 students at the elementary school level and one for 10 beyond the junior-high level. Libraries have been e-enabled, with cross-lending possibilities.

In January 2002, senior city officials highlighted eight clear priorities for Shanghai's information development in the years ahead. These were: e-Government, a computerised credit rating system, companies' internal information systems, city-level geographic information system (GIS) platform, next generation information infrastructure, information security, public service information system, and the information industry (especially software and digital TV).

Shanghai's Targets under the Tenth Five-Year Plan

Under China's Tenth Five-Year Plan (2001–2005), Shanghai government leaders have set themselves some detailed targets in order to sharpen the city's competitive edge.

The targets include:

- sharpening Shanghai's overall competitive edge and transforming it into a city with large-scale, high-grade industries and strong resource distribution capacity both in China and worldwide;
- improving the city's overall services to provide both Chinese and overseas investors more business opportunities and a promise of lower costs;

- optimising the city's comprehensive development environment to turn it into an ideal location, for starting a new business and for living;
- enhancing the city's creative capacity and developing new systems and mechanisms to nurture sustainable innovation;
- upgrading the city's administration, and introducing a new system of modern urban administration, featuring the concerted participation of the government, society, market and citizen; and
- improving the overall quality of citizens' lives and to create a spiritual outlook of a modern international metropolis.

Shanghai's e-Government Programme

The city had started on its e-Government project early. From 1996, some government departments had already begun to develop their own websites. At that time however, the concept of e-Government was relatively unclear. Most of the information and resources tended to be isolated in individual government institutions.

After investing heavily for several years in an IT infrastructure, the city government of Shanghai is now ready to start building applications and information systems to tap that hardware's potential and make Shanghai more "digitised". Accelerating the pace of IT development will lead the local government to become more open, fair and efficient.

In order to benefit from global experience and best practices, Shanghai organised and hosted a series of annual international conferences "High-Level Forum on City Informatization in the Asia and Pacific Region" (CIAPR) starting in 2000. These were attended by representatives from all around the world. The first conference had the theme "Promoting City Informatization for a Better Future", the second in 2001 was on "Bridging the Digital Divide: Solutions and Best Practices in City Informatization", while the 2002 conference focused on "e-Government and City Informatization".

Several high-profile projects such as the e-Government portal, social security card and community informatization, have boosted Shanghai's overall e-Government programme.

China-Shanghai: e-Government Portal

In September 2001, the Shanghai city administration launched "China-Shanghai" (www.shanghai.gov.cn) as the official website of the Shanghai Municipality — effectively the city's e-Government portal.

The website offers information on government matters, news events, policies and regulations, lifestyle matters, investments, as well as online services and advisories. The site also offers a new channel for people to participate in the deliberation and administration of state affairs, thus helping to increase the transparency of government work and keeping citizens well informed. All of Shanghai's government bodies are eventually to be connected to the site.

In the area of hardware deployment, Shanghai has taken a slightly different approach from Beijing, which had set up specialised information offices to take care of this. As the cost of building and maintaining an e-Government system is high, the Shanghai government has gone into partnership with China Telecom and other IT companies. These operators and vendors, with highly developed networks of resources, and large pools of IT professionals, are in a good position to develop, run and maintain the e-Government system. This approach not only ensures service quality, but also greatly reduces costs.

Figure 4-5: Official Website for Shanghai Municipality
http://www.shanghai.gov.cn

Shanghai Info-Port

As early as 1994, Shanghai started making plans to develop what became known as the "Info-Port". The Info-Port project was to be a massive

Shanghai municipal government initiative to connect the entire province through a high-speed network. The project exemplified the local government's commitment to facilitate the growth of high-technology information businesses both in and around the city. The project comprised an integrated network infrastructure that delivered all the necessary elements for the development of information businesses.

In 1996, Shanghai started work on deploying the Shanghai Info-Port, with the intention of using it as the foundation of a 10–15 year programme of urban informatization. Estimates put the whole project cost at US$ 10 billion. This included investments in communications and other key infrastructure areas, promoting value-added information services and the development of IT applications. Different ways were developed to allow people to connect to the network. One such connection method, for example, is through public online computer kiosks. These terminals allow Shanghai residents to carry out such tasks as scheduling doctor appointments, donating money to charities, and filing for marriage licenses.

Social Security Card Project

Since 1999 the Shanghai municipal government has put much effort into developing the Social Security and Citizen Service Information System (SSCSIS). The structure of the SSCSIS includes five sub-systems: labour, social security, public security, civil administration and medical insurance. The SSCSIS is also linked to the Shanghai Information Service Centre.

The public can use their social security cards as electronic keys to various systems, thus benefiting from a variety of social security and related services provided by the government. Some examples of such services include job searches, applications for unemployment subsidy, registration for medical insurance, and application for public housing funding. More electronic functions will gradually be added to the cards. The city has now issued more than 7 million cards covering more than 90 percent of its urban residents above 16 years of age.

e-Government at the Community Level

Another approach that is being tried in Shanghai is what has been called "community informatization". In this approach, citizen communities in various sub-districts of Shanghai will progressively be exposed to aspects of informatization and e-Government services. The communities will then facilitate penetration for informatization of the city.

In 2002, a community informatization experiment was conducted in the Wuliqiao sub-district of Luwan District, and the Shimener Road sub-district of Jing'an District. Local residents are now offered the convenience of online processing of employment and social insurance; acquiring knowledge of procedures, policies and statutes; and accessing information on catering, recreation and transportation within the community. The community cadres help to pass documents online or acquire information of administration affairs.

CONCLUDING REMARKS

Challenges and Obstacles

Deployment of e-Government programmes in any country rarely happens without challenges and obstacles. More so in a country as vast, diverse and complex as the People's Republic of China. The reality is that e-Government in China is only available in a practical sense in selected urban locations, in particular, the major cities such as Beijing or Shanghai, and in some of the more developed provinces, eg Guangdong, Liaoning and Fujian. These are generally the locations where the ICT infrastructure is more ready to support e-Government applications, where the citizens or businesses have adequate access to PCs and the Internet, and where the computer literacy of the people is sufficiently high.

Research suggests that the seven key obstacles were faced in the implementation of e-Government projects in China:[27, 28]

(1) **Bureaucracy**
     Zhang describes the situation as one of "digital or non-digital "warlords" at various levels of the government". A common issue in e-Government in both Beijing and Shanghai is how to break the protectionism of the "warlords" in government units. This is essential if the government units are to be successfully integrated into a common e-Government system.

(2) **Lack of financial resources**
     With the many competing national priorities, this is a perennial problem. Budgets need to be spread over many projects and initiatives and often, e-Government projects are delayed due to lack of adequate funding.

(3) **Lack of technical standards**

The lack of technical standards gives rise to problems of systems integration. Different programme modules cannot talk to each other. Different systems cannot be seamlessly integrated. Without appropriately integrated systems, "islands of automation" will result in different government agencies, and the overall e-Government interface will remain disjointed.

(4) **Gaps in legal framework**

The legal system in China still lags its technological advances, and many areas of ambiguity arise in areas of e-Government and e-Business interactions.

(5) **Security problems**

The Chinese government continues to try to control many aspects of the Internet, taking a harsh view of "subversive" online activities and "spiritual pollution" of content.

(6) **Relatively low numbers of e-Government users**

There is still a lack of a critical mass of users for the various e-Government applications that have been introduced. Various measures are in place to boost the numbers, but these will take time to achieve results.

(7) **Digital divide**

This is probably the most challenging problem. With China's population of 1.3 billion, spread over a vast expanse of land, the effort to impart an adequate level of computer literacy is a mammoth task that will take many years. Today, computer literacy for the masses may be conceivable in the major cities and the more developed coastal provinces, but for the majority of the population living in the inner reaches of the country, the priorities are more of basic amenities (like drinking water and electricity) rather than on Internet access.

E-Government in China may be regarded as being at an early stage. The path to the top of the mountain still appears to be a long one, fraught with hurdles and pitfalls. However, China seems to have fully opened up to learning from other nations that are further along their journeys, borrowing and adapting their best practices and experiences. With the commitment and tenacity that the national leadership and people have shown so far, it can only be a matter of time before the summit of the e-Government mountain is reached.

Endnotes

1   Compelling new evidence uncovered by Gavin Menzies seems to indicate that Chinese fleets may have traveled much further than historians have given them credit for Menzies' book "*1421: The Year the China discovered the World*", Bantam Press, London (2002) reveals that the Chinese reached the great continents years before the Europeans set foot there, including arriving at America in 1421, some seventy years before Columbus, and circumnavigating the globe almost a century before Magellan.

2   The SEZs were in Xiamen (in Fujian province) and Shantou, Shenzhen and Zhuhai (in Guangdong).

3   The first generation leadership was led by Mao Zedong, the second by Deng Xiaoping, and the third by Jiang Zemin.

4   The Three Represents theory, first raised by Jiang Zemin in 2000, states that the Communist Party must (1) represent the most advanced productive forces, including private business, (2) represent the most advanced culture, and (3) represent fundamental interests of the broad masses — ie not merely a "revolutionary party" but one that stands for all Chinese.

5   On 20 September 1987, Professor Qian Tianbai sent China's first email titled "Crossing the Great Wall to Join the World", marking the beginning of the use of the Internet by the Chinese. Professor Qian was in charge of CANET (Chinese Academic Network), an Internet-related scientific research project launched by the Beijing Municipal Computer Application Research Institute in 1986 in cooperation with Karlsruhe University, Germany. The mail sent by Professor Qian at a speed of 300bps officially realised the store-and-forward function (CNNIC website).

6   ChinaWN.com, link to "Internet" section, "*Statistical Mistakes — the Number of Net Users in China*", www.websitesaboutchina.com/internet/internet_3.htm.

7   Some groups have used slightly different renditions of this word. So far, the authors have come across three other variations: informationisation, informationalisation and informisation. For the purposes of this article, we will stay with informatization, but we regard the different terms to be synonymous.

8   Zhao, Xiaofan, "*Promoting Informatization in China*" presentation, Department of Informatization Promotion, Ministry of Information Industry, PRC, 1999.

9   Quoted in "*A Critical Review of the Development of Chinese Government*", paper by Junhua Zhang, Perspectives, Vol 3, No 7, December 2002 (www.ovcf.org).

10 "*China maps out first Informatization Blueprint*", *AsiaInfo Daily China News*, 5 July 2002.

11 Attestation Service of Net Station Visitors Flow: In order to promote the healthy development of Internet information services in China, and have a standard of attestation of net station visitors flow, CNNIC provides visitors flow services to all net stations.

12 Wu, Yanrui, "*Growing through Deregulation: A Study of China's Telecommunications Industry*", Dept of Economics, University of Western Australia, 2000.

13 ITU "Asia-Pacific Telecommunications Indicators 2002" report.

14 www.BDAConnect.com

15 CNNIC statistics, January 2003 (www.cnnic.net.cn).

16 Auchard, E and Greenberg, J, "*China Becoming World's No. 2 Market for Web and PCs*", 31 July 2002, CIBT.

17 Greenspan, Robyn, "*China pulls ahead of Japan*", internet.com, 22 April 2002.

18 Hoong, YL, "*New China Rising*", 2001.

19 China Information World, 16 December 2002.

20 Lovelock, P and Ure, J, "*e-Government in China*", 2001.

21 Xiong, Chengyu, "*e-Government in China — Present and Future*", International Seminar for "*e-Administration for the benefit of citizens*", Paris, January 2002.

22 "*Easier Access*", *China Daily* (HK Edition), 21 October 2002.

23 "*e-Government initiatives expected to grow in Asia*", asia.internet.com, 26 February 2002.

24 A *li* is a Chinese mile.

25 Zhongguancun Science Park, established in 1988, is the first and biggest national science park in China. Located in Northwest Beijing, it covers about 100 sq km. Inside the Park, more than 6,000 high-tech enterprises in the fields of IT, biology, medicine, etc. have their offices. Large multinational IT corporations such as IBM, Motorola, Microsoft, Lucent, HP, and Epson have R&D institutes here. Many prominent universities, such as Tsinghua University and Beijing University are also located within the Park. Many companies have moved into the Park, attracted by its high-tech environment and preferential tax treatment.

26   The Haidian Science Park (HSP) is widely known as China's Silicon Valley. With generous tax incentives and other preferential treatment, it has been the country's leading incubator of high-tech businesses, and has gained global attention as a major cradle of the knowledge-based economy in China. Advanced communications infrastructure make HSP an attractive place for businesses.

27   Zhang, Junhua, *"Assessing China's e-Government"* presentation, Free University Berlin.

28   Simon, LD, *"NetPolicy.Com — Public Agenda for a Digital World"*, Woodrow Wilson Centre Press, 2000.

CHAPTER 5

Digital 21 and Hong Kong's Advancement in e-Government

James SL Yong and Janice LK Leong

▲ ▼ ▲ ▼ ▲ ▼ ▲ ▼

There is always gold on the streets,
it depends on whether one has the ability to pick it up

Chinese saying

▲ ▼ ▲ ▼ ▲ ▼ ▲ ▼

BACKGROUND

History[1,2]

China's national flag and the Hong Kong SAR *bauhinia* flower flag now fly where the Union Jack had previously, reflecting the momentous transition in 1997 when the island and its surrounding territories reverted to Chinese rule.

In 1842, the British pressured the Chinese to cede the island of Hong Kong to them in perpetuity, following the Opium Wars. In 1898, the British also gained a 99-year lease on the New Territories, which they felt was essential to protect their interests on Hong Kong island. In December 1984, the British agreed to hand over the entire colony when the lease on the New Territories ran out in 1997, rather than hang on to a truncated colony consisting of Kowloon and Hong Kong island. Hong Kong thus became the Hong Kong Special Administrative Region (SAR) of China on 1st July 1997. In this agreement, China promised that, under its "one country, two systems" formula, China's socialist economic system would not be imposed on Hong Kong, and that the territory would enjoy a high degree of autonomy in all matters except foreign and defense affairs for the next 50 years.

Despite its British colonial past, Hong Kong never lost its Asian roots and traditional Chinese culture. Being a globally reputed trading port and a key entry point to southern China, Hong Kong had always been inextricably linked to mainland China in both economic and social terms.

Family ties across the border are very strong, and Hong Kong investment in China has always been large. There was, understandably, some apprehension in the years leading up to July 1997, but the smooth transition and relatively little interference in Hong Kong affairs by China's central government have largely restored confidence.

Geography

Hong Kong, which means "fragrant harbour", lies on the Southeast coast of China, at the mouth of the Pearl River Delta. It comprises four main areas — Kowloon, Hong Kong Island (also called Victoria), the New Territories and the Outlying Islands — with a total area of about 1,100 sq km.

Looking down from Victoria Peak, the summit of Hong Kong island, one has a panoramic view of the world's busiest, deepwater port, and a vibrant, global city. The population is about 7 million, with the vast majority being of ethnic Chinese descent. Hong Kong also has substantial British and American communities. Cantonese and English are widely spoken, and ever since 1997 Mandarin is also slowly becoming popular.

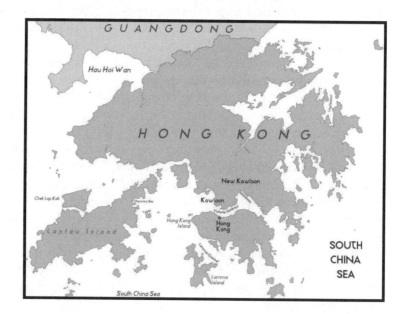

Economy

Hong Kong has come a long way since the 1840s, when a British minister at the time infamously labeled it a "barren rock". Its position as one of the world's key economic centres is based on several factors. It is located midway between Japan and Singapore, and lies astride the main shipping and air routes of the western Pacific. Hong Kong has also long served as a major port of entry and trade for China, which had used Hong Kong as a primary link to the world economy. Trading had been the bedrock of Hong Kong's business. Furthermore, Hong Kong has a very pro-business culture and working environment.

Hong Kong has a dynamic free market economy highly dependent on international trade. Natural resources are limited, and food and raw materials must be imported. Hong Kong's per capita GDP compares with levels in the advanced countries of Western Europe. GDP growth averaged a strong 5 percent in 1989–1997.

Soon after its return to China, Hong Kong was hard hit by the Asian crisis in 1998. Although there was rapid recovery in 2000 (with about 10 percent growth), fortunes dipped again in 2001/2002 following a global economic slowdown. The early years of the new millennium were difficult and Hong Kong's administrators showed resilience as they faced challenges of financial deficit, economic revival, terrorist threats, global uncertainties, and viral outbreaks.

In Chief Executive (CE) Tung Chee Hwa's policy address of January 2003, he shared a roadmap for Hong Kong's future economic development. In addition to capitalising on Hong Kong's natural advantages and enhancing its four pillar industries of financial services, logistics, tourism and producer services, Hong Kong would also foster the development of creative industries, promote innovation and technology, and support SME development in new business areas. Economic integration with the Pearl River Delta would be accelerated to facilitate economic restructuring.

Hong Kong and the Pearl River Delta

Social and economic ties between Guangdong province and Hong Kong expanded in almost all dimensions in the 1990s. The development of these links is influenced by the economic complementary nature and social contacts between the two areas, as well as the political and administrative compromises between the governments on both sides.

The complementary strengths of Hong Kong and the rest of the Pearl River Delta (PRD), if combined, can potentially give rise to phenomenal growth. Hong Kong is the hub for business, logistics, finance and services for the region. The PRD has interlocking clusters of internationally successful industries and services, a continuous stream of start-ups, as well as many SMEs. The PRD also displays great flexibility in meeting changing market needs as one of the world's leading bases for manufacturing.

Professor Michael Enright, an authority on international competitiveness, has said, "the delta has been the fastest-growing part of the fastest-growing province in the fastest growing large economy in the whole world".

Hong Kong and the PRD together are often positioned as a "total solution" for overseas companies wanting to enter the vast China market. The proposed mainland/Hong Kong Closer Economic Partnership Arrangement (CEPA) will help promote trade and investment flow, and provide Hong Kong service providers and manufacturers with greater access to the mainland market.

Currently, Hong Kong handles 40 percent of the mainland's foreign trade, and is the major source of inward investment to the mainland, accounting for nearly half of all external investment in the Chinese mainland, and 70 percent of that in Guangdong Province. At the end of 2001, there was US$ 79 billion realised direct investment. Of the more than 3,000 regional offices and headquarters established in Hong Kong, about 80 percent are responsible for mainland businesses. A study by the University of Hong Kong showed that about 11 million workers were employed by Hong Kong companies in manufacturing facilities in the PRD.

After two decades of high growth, the PRD is now ready to take on new challenges. The combined GDP of Hong Kong, Macao and the rest of the PRD reached US$260 billion in 2001, placing the region amongst the top 20 economies in the world. The combined GDP of Hong Kong, Macao and the PRD will reach well over US$500 billion in 10 years time.

Hong Kong and the PRD have developed a very productive synergy since China's reform and open policies began in the 1980s. The highly successful "front shops, back factories" model of economic cooperation is now classic.

The vision is to develop the PRD into a major competitive economic region. It will not only be a manufacturing base with new technology inputs, but also a principal provider of modern services to China and the Asia Pacific. It will host clusters of internationally competitive enterprises, engaging in logistics, professional and financial services, tourism and entertainment, communication, consumer and personal services, in addition to other high value-added activities.

Source: Various speeches by senior HK officials, 2002 and 2003

Government

Hong Kong is governed under the Basic Law approved in 1990 by the National People's Congress of China. The chief of state is the President of China, and the head of the government of Hong Kong Special Administrative Region (HKSARG) is Chief Executive Tung Chee-hwa, who assumed the position at the handover in 1997.

The Chief Executive (CE) is advised in key policymaking matters by an Executive Council, and a 60-member Legislative Council. The Executive Council comprises fourteen Principal Officials appointed under the Accountability Scheme[3] and five non-official members. The Principal Officials hold the following positions: Chief Secretary for Administration, Financial Secretary, Secretary for Justice, Secretary for Commerce, Industry and Technology, Secretary for Housing, Planning and Lands, Secretary for Education and Manpower, Secretary for Health, Welfare and Food, Secretary for the Civil Service, Secretary for Home Affairs, Secretary for Security, Secretary for Economic Development and Labour, Secretary for the Environment, Transport and Works, Secretary for Financial Services and the Treasury, and Secretary for Constitutional Affairs.

The Legislative branch is formed by the unicameral Legislative Council (often called Legco), which has 60 seats, with members serving four-year terms.

The main political parties are the Democratic party, the Liberal Party, and the Democratic Alliance for the Betterment of Hong Kong.

THE DIGITAL 21 IT STRATEGY

In 1998, the Chief Executive of HKSAR launched a "comprehensive and visionary programme of initiatives" and a road map to Hong Kong's digital future. This was embodied in the "Digital 21 IT Strategy" policy document (www.digital21.gov.hk). The strategy set out the initiatives and programmes that aimed to enhance and promote Hong Kong's information infrastructure and services in order "to position Hong Kong as a leading e-Business community and digital city in the globally connected world".

Between 1998 and 2001, the initiatives arising from the Digital 21 Strategy were largely completed. Hong Kong's information infrastructure had been substantially enhanced. A business environment conducive to IT adoption in business, government and daily life was also forming. Thus a new version of the strategy, called the "2001 Digital 21 Strategy", was published in May 2001. This allowed the strategy to be fine-tuned to cope with the technological changes and global e-Commerce developments.

Five Key Result Areas (KRAs) were identified in order to strengthen Hong Kong's position as a leader, and not a follower, in the digitally connected world. These five KRA's were:

(1)   to enhance the world-class e-Business environment in Hong Kong;
(2)   to ensure that the Hong Kong government leads by example;
(3)   to develop Hong Kong's workforce for the information economy;
(4)   to strengthen the Hong Kong community for digital exploitation; and
(5)   to leverage Hong Kong's strengths in exploitation of enabling technologies.

ICT MATURITY INDICATORS

The ICT-related indicators for Hong Kong reflect an environment that is very technology-ready.

Teledensity

The number of mobile phone subscribers in Hong Kong overtook the number of fixed-line phones in 1999. Analysts[4] estimate that by mid 2002 more than 80 percent of the population, or 5.8 million people in Hong Kong, own a mobile phone, as compared to some 3.9 million business and residential (fixed) lines in Hong Kong.

Internet

Hong Kongers are one of the most intense Internet users in the world. ITU reported that in mid-2002, they averaged 12:12 hours per month of Internet use. About 60 percent of households have personal computers, and more than 50 percent of all households are connected to the Internet. There are some 2.6 million Internet accounts. All schools are linked to the Internet.

Broadband

Broadband services have grown rapidly. Hong Kong is one of the world leaders in broadband deployment — an achievement driven by low prices and wide availability of services. However, broadband services are probably not yet profitable.[5] Overall broadband penetration is about 12 percent. The broadband infrastructure reaches more than 95 percent of households, and practically all commercial buildings. About a third of households now use broadband.

Others

3G services are expected to kickoff by the end of 2002. There are four network licensees, all of whom plan to run on W-CDMA, and four MVNOs (Mobile Virtual Network Operators) who will purchase capacity from the licensees. In the lead-up to 3G, most operators have adopted GPRS networks, but this has not seen enough growth to be profitable as yet.

With China's admission to the WTO, some of the larger Hong Kong players have positioned themselves to move into the mainland market.

THE E-GOVERNMENT PROGRAMME

As noted previously, one of the five KRA's of the "Digital 21 Strategy" seeks to ensure that the Hong Kong government leads by example. This is to be done by driving e-Government, providing e-options for more services, and actively pursuing e-procurement and outsourcing. The vision is "to transform traditional government into a citizen-centric e-Government". The Government Information Centre website further spells out the purpose of e-Government as being "to provide seamless electronic services to the public and business in an efficient and customer-centric way."

Specific policy objectives of the e-Government programme include: improving service delivery, achieving efficiency gains, and driving the adoption of e-Commerce in the private sector. Two specific e-Government targets set out in the 2001 Digital 21 Strategy were:

(1) to provide an e-option for 90 percent of the public services which are amenable to the electronic mode of service delivery by end-2003; and

(2) to conduct 80 percent of government procurement tenders through electronic means by end-2003.[6]

The overall approach to carrying out the development of e-Government in Hong Kong is based on mutually beneficial cooperation between government and the private sector.

In an interview, Ms Joyce Tam, Principal Assistant Secretary in the e-Government Division of the Commerce, Industry and Technology Bureau (CITB), said that "The Hong Kong government has had a very long and established policy with regard to working with the private sector. We try to outsource and use private sector resources as far as possible. The target we set for ourselves was two-thirds but in fact it often exceeds 80 percent. We are extending this into applications management duties as well. Eventually we hope to take one more step beyond simply involving the private sector — we want them to become real partners to government."

The HKSARG administration plays two essential roles in relation to computerisation. Firstly, it acts as a facilitator in building up the necessary infrastructure so that the IT industry can operate and support the various business communities effectively. Secondly, it acts as a user of IT to support its own operational and managerial needs.

The key building blocks,[7] or foundations for success, of the e-Government programme in Hong Kong have been identified as:

- leadership from the highest levels of the government;
- e-Government Coordinator;
- strong governance and management framework;
- legal framework;
- robust Information Infrastructure;
- interoperability framework;
- information security policy and practices;
- outsourcing; and
- commitment to innovation.

MAJOR E-GOVERNMENT INITIATIVES

The deployment strategy for e-Government in Hong Kong calls for a number of different projects to be pursued. For clarity, these can be categorised into G2C (government-to-citizen), G2B (government-to-business), G2E (government-to-employee) and G2G (government-to-government, or intra-government).

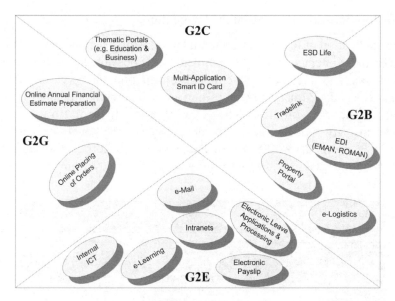

Figure 5-1

Enhancing Government Efficiency

The HKSARG aims to achieve universal accessibility to IT facilities for all its government officers. To promote a paperless and electronic government, more government officers are equipped with IT tools and email facilities to assist them in their work. The government internal IT infrastructure was also enhanced to support the wider adoption of electronic transactions. These, together with the adoption of proper Software Asset Management practices and the implementation of the Confidential Mail System across the government, have helped build a solid and comprehensive information infrastructure within the government for the adoption of various types of IT applications and electronic transactions.

All bureaus and departments are linked by a government-wide Intranet. By mid-2003, there will be 47,000 users of the system, with 8,000 having confidential email connections.

A parallel programme was also implemented to provide officers with access to Government-to-Employee (G2E) applications such as electronic leave application and processing, electronic payslip, checking of various employment benefits, e-learning and electronic training administration. Similarly, Government-to-Government (G2G) applications are also being rolled out, such as online annual financial estimate preparation, and online placing of orders for common store items and the printing government publications.

Transforming Government-Public Interaction

The application of ICT has the potential to transform the manner in which government interacts with its constituents. It is possible to provide single point access to interactive government information and services. All the bureaus and departments in Hong Kong are online with bilingual (English and Chinese) websites. The Government Information Centre (www.info.gov.hk), the most popular website of the government which attracted more than 500 million page views in 2001, is a one-stop information portal providing easy access to all other government websites.

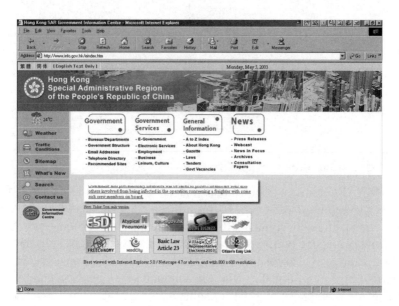

Figure 5-2

Major policy proposals or issues of community interest are often the subject of consultation. The public can give their feedback and views on public policies and regulations through the websites of the bureaus and departments. Over 1,400 official forms are available for downloading from the government websites, with some 200 e-forms that the public can complete and submit electronically. A consistent brand image and "look and feel" to government websites has been adopted to heighten the sense of familiarity and trust between the government and citizens.

Other innovations include an online news bulletin to provide a new channel, for multimedia dissemination of government news and information, online forums and features for the constituents to personalise their user interfaces, so as to receive only information aligned to their personal preferences.

Electronic Services Delivery (ESD)

The ESD Scheme, one of the key e-Government initiatives, aims to transform the way public services are delivered in Hong Kong. It seamlessly integrates public and private sector services in a customer-centric approach.

By the end of 2002, there were more than 140 types of public services provided on the "ESDLife" portal, from more than 40 government departments and agencies. Citizens can carry out a wide variety of activities — ranging from payment of government bills, filing tax returns, renewing driving and vehicle licences, booking government leisure and sports facilities, booking appointments at various government agencies, and registering for public examinations. Businesses can apply for licences and permits, register job vacancies and order government publications.

Launched in 2000, the ESD Scheme allows the public to transact business with the government round-the-clock through a diversity of access channels. These include personal computers with Internet connections, public computer facilities, ESD kiosks (installed at train stations, shopping malls and supermarkets), and even mobile devices. Through ESD, public service efficiency can be enhanced and delivery costs reduced. At the same time, ESD helps to nurture the development of electronic commerce in Hong Kong.

Kiosks in public places are a significant part of the whole initiative, bridging the digital divide for those unable to afford their own access device. The kiosk includes a scanner to read paper documents, slots for ID or credit/debit cards, and even a printer. Some commercial services such as purchasing tickets for events are also provided at the kiosks, as are printable location maps.

The ESDLife portal has been well received by Hong Kong residents and businesses. As at July 2002, the average daily hit rate of the ESD web site was around 2 million, and the accumulated total number of visitors exceeded 32 million since the launch of the programme.

Figure 5-3

The ESD Scheme was developed based on an innovative public-private partnership approach. Under this approach, both the government and the private contractor have to invest. The government will pay for the system on a per-transaction basis only after the contract period, or after the cumulative number of chargeable transactions exceeds an agreed volume.

The private sector can put in their advertisements, which can generate income for them. They can also include in the portal, various additional services. For example, one section of the ESDLife site deals with booking for wedding registration dates. In that same section, there are links to wedding planners and advertisements for gold items and top-quality brandy — both traditional features of Hong Kong weddings.

There are some rules for the portal that service providers must heed. On pages built around government services, one rule says there should be a minimum of 60 percent government content. But relevant graphics are encouraged, even some animation. A manager shared that high quality graphics often help to "create stickiness", encouraging people to use and return to the online service.

The ESD effort has received international recognition. In 2001, it was named as a winner of the Stockholm Challenge Award 2001 under the Public Service and Democracy category. The judges were impressed by ESD's innovative creation of a one-stop public and commercial service portal for the community under a public-private sector partnership.

Multi-Application Smart ID Card

Another significant e-Government initiative is the replacement of some seven million identity cards with Smart ID cards, beginning in mid 2003. The whole cycle is expected to take 4 years to complete.

Besides using for immigration purposes, cardholders will be able to use the card for other value-added applications, such as using it for the library, as well as for driving license-related functions. Cardholders can also opt for a free digital certificate to be embedded in the Smart ID Card, which will allow for the conduct of secure e-Business over the open network. Capacity has also been reserved for the future implementation of an electronic purse if deemed appropriate. In short, the Smart ID card will become a vehicle for the provision of more efficient and better quality services to the community.

With the deployment exercise covering some 7 million people, this Smart ID card project will probably make Hong Kong one of the largest populations in the world using Smart ID cards and the e-Cert facility.

Electronic Procurement

Electronic procurement is a key initiative driving the adoption of e-Business in the private sector as well as increasing the efficiency of the government procurement process. The government has set itself a target of conducting 80 percent of procurement tenders through electronic means by the end of 2003 in order to provide an incentive for private sector companies to also go online and adopt e-Business.

For non-works tenders, an Electronic Tendering System (ETS) has been in use by the Government Supplies Department (GSD) — the central procurement authority — since April 2000. The ETS provides an online infrastructure for supplier registration, notification of tenders, downloading of tender documents, receiving and responding to enquiries, submission of tender offers and contract award notices. All these functions are carried out on the Internet, which means that government tenders will be accessible on a 24 × 7 basis, making it far easier for suppliers across the world to take part in the procurement process.

The system is now capable of handling all non-works tenders originated by GSD and will soon cover the non-GSD originated non-works tenders, currently issued by individual departments.

With the ETS, the procurement process has been made swifter and more responsive. GSD can reach a much wider range of potential suppliers so that more competitive bids may be obtained. For suppliers, this is a cost-effective method of submitting tender offers. Subscribers will gain real time access to information and, because of instant transmission, they have more time to prepare their tender bids. Subscribers will save time — receiving and submitting tender documents — and costs for postage and packing. The whole process cuts down on paperwork and increases efficiency.

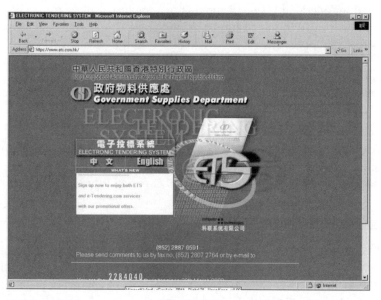

Figure 5-4

For works tenders, which normally entail voluminous requirements and bulky submissions, and therefore involve more complex considerations, the process is currently not handled by the ETS. However, the use of electronic means would greatly improve the efficiency of the engineering and works professions in preparing and submitting tender proposals as well as the government in subsequent processing. The government already issues works tenders and receives tender proposals through CD-ROM. The Environment, Transport and Works Bureau has completed a study on the feasibility of submission of works tenders through the Internet. It has concluded that such an approach is feasible and is now formulating an implementation plan.

For low value purchases,[8] the Hong Kong authorities are considering the development of an Electronic Marketplace System (EMS) to automate the currently manual procurement processes and increase operational efficiency. A trial for the EMS was conducted in 2002.

Electronic Trading Systems

Global trade is a cornerstone of the Hong Kong economy. As a free port, Hong Kong has relatively few import and export licensing requirements. Most products do not need licenses to enter or leave Hong Kong. However for the required documentation, the HKSARG has mandated that electronic data interchange (EDI) be used for submission and processing of these trade documents. This began in 1999 with the restrained textiles export licence. It was extended to production notification, trade declaration and certificate of origin in 2000. Development of EDI services for cargo manifests and dutiable commodities permit are now underway.

With EDI, companies can have speedy interchange of business documents, such as purchase orders, shipping orders and other government documents in electronic form.

Tradelink

In 1997, Tradelink Electronic Commerce Ltd (www.tradelink.com.hk) was created as a joint-venture between the HKSARG and private sector shareholders, mainly key players in the international trade cycle. The agreement with the government (signed in 1992) called for Tradelink to provide a "single electronic gateway" between the trading community and the HKSARG for a range of specified trade transactions.

Currently the government holds about 42 percent share in Tradelink, a figure which many in the industry expect, will be reduced as competition is to be introduced when Tradelink's franchise ends in December 2003. Tenders for two more service providers were called in mid-2002, heralding the end of Tradelink's monopoly.

Tradelink's stated mission is "to enhance the productivity and competitiveness of Hong Kong's trading community by making available a range of value-added electronic commerce services, with equal emphasis on automating commonly-used trade transactions of the Hong Kong SAR government and the commercial sector."

Since all import and export shipments involve government documentation at some stage, Tradelink is jump-starting the adoption of e-Commerce in Hong Kong by providing electronic services for the most commonly-used government transactions, linked to a programme of migration from paper to full electronic submission. The goal was to speed up the processing of the documents required, thereby helping to reduce time-to-market.

As of mid-2002, Tradelink had an impressive customer base of over 53,000 companies. All trade declarations are now submitted electronically and the Tradelink system handles more than 70,000 transactions per day.

Tradelink currently offers five trade documents: trade declarations, certificates of origin, dutiable commodities permits, production notifications and restrained textile export licences. The latest development will include e-manifests.

In addition to providing an electronic link to the government, Tradelink's services offer a number of value-added transaction management facilities including message checking, matching and validation, message authentication and security, electronic billing and payments, and message archiving and audit trail services.

Cargo Manifests

Hong Kong is also moving towards e-Government for industrial applications with the mid 2003 commissioning of a system for the electronic submission and processing of cargo manifests (EMAN). With this service, the air, sea, river and rail carriers are now able to submit cargo manifests through the Tradelink system to three key departments — Customs and Excise, Census and Statistics, Trade and Industry. This system was implemented from April 2003.

In addition, carriers can make use of other ancillary functions of the service to receive detention notices and release vouchers issued by the Customs and Excise Department, submit import and export statements for dutiable commodities, and reply to queries raised by the government. Carriers will also no longer be required to prepare manifests manually on paper and submit different copies to separate government departments.

ROMAN is another EDI system involving road manifests which is planned for implementation.

E-logistics

In 2003, the government invited bids for the creation and management of a billion-dollar Digital Trade Transport Network (DTTN). This initiative effectively attempts to develop an electronic network for the whole logistics industry. With the goal of achieving operational efficiencies, the DTTN will transfer online, the management of the US$ 400 billion in merchandise which moves through Hong Kong's maritime terminals, borders and airport each year, including the regulatory documentation governing it.

Joined-up Government Projects

The E-government Coordination Office is working on a number of "joined-up projects", including a property portal and a business portal. By putting together property-related information kept by various departments in a single property portal, public and trade access to such information is made more transparent and convenient. Another project is that of providing an entry point for businesses to different business-related websites in Hong Kong. Such an integrated business portal would help companies, especially the SME's to access the necessary business-related information. "We have been coordinating among the various parties involved to facilitate cross-departmental collaboration to make these portals possible. We will also explore opportunities to partner with the private sector in the development of such projects. A further initiative the E-Government Coordination Office is helping with is one to provide an integrated Criminal Justice System, which will link the paper flows of those agencies involved in the Justice system," said Alex Ma, Assistant Director, ITSD.

INNOVATIVE BUSINESS MODELS

The Hong Kong e-Government programme has showcased several innovative business models. The following are three prominent ones:

Government portals

In this model, the government bears the entire initial investment and the operating cost. An example of this is the development of the Government Information Centre, and the websites of most of the bureaus and departments.

The "Service" Approach

In this model, the government buys services from a business partner. There is an agreement on the deliverables and the services levels expected. An example of a project using this approach is the Electronic Tendering System.

Public-Private Partnership[9]

To speed up the implementation of e-Government initiatives, the Hong Kong SAR administration has been pursuing a vigorous outsourcing strategy. The primary objectives are to enlarge the delivery capacity for IT services and to accelerate the delivery of IT solutions. As at end-2002, more than 80 percent of all new IT projects were already outsourced. Outsourcing of IT services on a departmental basis was also achieved. This created and fueled the cost competition in the IT provider market, providing cost advantages and savings to the HKSAR government.

The HKSARG has also entered into standing offer agreements with a large number of companies under the Information Technology Professional Services Arrangement (ITPSA) for the provision of professional services to undertake IT services for the government. Such arrangements will further accelerate the delivery of IT solutions and increase industry participation in government IT services.

Another free market competitive bid is the reissue of the Server Bulk Tender to 3 categories of IT providers proving the e-options and procurement choices to HKSARG users. The approach is expected to streamline and save time in having individual departments bid for the hardware, software and services for those tenders that do not require complex systems integration. It is an attempt at freeing market monopoly by a single contractor even for the period of two to three years.

MILESTONES AND CHALLENGES

Key Milestones

Since the official launch of the Digital 21 Strategy and the national roadmap to Hong Kong's digital future, steady progress has been made in Hong Kong's e-Government programme. The Hong Kong administration has developed a strong foundation in terms of infrastructure and the legal framework to support electronic transactions. There have also been concerted efforts by the E-Government Coordinator and the EG Division of the CITB collaborating with staff in various bureaus and departments.

By the end of 2002, about 80 percent of public services had been made available via the electronic mode of delivery with an e-option. The flagship ESD programme had achieved a 40 percent increase in monthly transaction volume, with the ESDLife website reaching some 2 million hits a day. There has also been good progress in the Multi-Application Smart ID Card programme, which is to be progressively rolled out from the middle of 2003, paving the way for further e-Government service adoption.

A number of joined-up e-Government initiatives are being explored. These include a study on an Integrated Criminal Justice System, an e-option for citizen address change notification and the creation of thematic portals for business, property, and licensing operations.

Key Challenges

Probably the greatest challenge in the tough economic climate is managing the e-Government programme under tight budgetary pressures. Bureaus and departments find themselves squeezed with budget cuts on the one side, and the need to deliver value-adding e-services on the other. Targets for containment or reduction of recurrent IT expenditure add to the pressure. In true Hong Kong fashion, this has led government officers to review their needs, crystallise the value of their ICT investments, and embark on innovative working models with their suppliers. The challenge is to manage demands for changes in the recurrent phase by reflecting on the development phase and managing within the affordable budget.

There are also various operational challenges in getting e-Government deployed. Ms Joyce Tam, Principal Assistant Secretary, EG Division of the CITB, recounts three:

(1) getting departmental management on-board. This means getting their full commitment and agreement to carry out a BPR exercise before the actual deployment. This is in fact, one of the reasons why the e-Government Coordinator/EG Office is needed, ie to drive the initiatives and to continue to make it visible to senior bureau and department officials;

(2) continuing to fight against inertia at the operational level; and

(3) educating and convincing the public to use the online services, once they are available. The EG office conducts IT awareness courses (especially for women, elderly, physically handicapped, etc) in partnership with the Home Affairs Department and the Social Welfare Department. It helps to tackle the digital divide problem.

CLOSING REMARKS

The momentum of e-Government in Hong Kong has clearly been created, and despite external and internal challenges, it is likely to continue growing from strength to strength. Beyond just productivity and service, there has been an evident shift towards aligning e-Government activities with overall national programmes for generating economic growth.

In his keynote address at a recent seminar on e-Government,[10] Mr Francis Ho, Permanent Secretary for the Information Technology and Broadcasting Branch, CITB, shared his thoughts on four high-level priorities for Hong Kong's e-Government initiative. The first was that e-Government projects had to be directly linked to Hong Kong's economic competitiveness. The second was that e-Government was a key driver of higher productivity — not only internal to the government, but also making the whole interaction of government with the society-at-large more convenient and efficient. The third priority was to translate the output of e-Government services into financial savings for the public service. Finally, e-Government is a key impetus to Hong Kong's progress into an innovation-driven economy.

These sentiments aptly capture the motivations behind Hong Kong's e-Government programme today, and into the future.

Endnotes

1   CIA The World Factbook 2002, on Hong Kong.

2   Patten, C, "Hong Kong History" (article written on 30 June 1997).

3   The Accountability Scheme of government was introduced in Hong Kong in July 2002. The new system has been described as a hybrid of the British Westminster and the American Presidential systems. It is intended to make the top layer of officials accountable for their decisions and answerable to the Chief Executive It also ends the dual identity of key public servants, who would no longer have to make political decisions while trying to remain neutral. Political observers see this change may encourage outsiders to join the government, and to make it easier to interchange talent between the public and private sectors.

4   Figure is consistent from Gartner, Research and Markets and ITU.

5   Milburn, R, *"A Glimpse at Hong Kong's Telco trends"*, 25 June 2002 (http://asia.internet.com).

6   Stone, M, *"Hong Kong's e-Government Developments"*, presentation of Technology Task Force, ABAC Third Meeting, 8 August 2002.

7   Mak, S, *"Developments in Hong Kong's IT Infrastructure"*, Information Technology Services Department, 17 August 2002.

8   Purchases below HK$ 1.3 million each, which are now conducted through invitation for quotation or direct purchase.

9   Yau, C, *"e-Government in Hong Kong: Public-Private Sector Partnership"*, CIAPR III — Shanghai 2002, 14 June 2002.

10   NCS Public Sector Seminar, *"Managing Change for a Digital Government"*, Hong Kong SAR, 16 January 2003.

CHAPTER 6

India: e-Progress in the States

James SL Yong and Sameer Sachdeva

▲ ▼ ▲ ▼ ▲ ▼ ▲ ▼

Eighteen languages, 500 dialects, some 30 religions, a million Gods and Goddesses, 300 million individuals, an infinity of castes and sub castes, and a population (that is) practically illiterate and half of which (are) beggars or thieves ... Good luck, sir! Such a nation is ungovernable! It'd take you centuries to get anywhere!

Lord Bevin to Gandhi, 1947

▲ ▼ ▲ ▼ ▲ ▼ ▲ ▼

Fifty-five years on, India with its one billion population, is the largest democracy in the world. The country is an emerging industrial giant, with technological capabilities spanning from satellite launching to offshore oil drilling. It is positioned at a strategic location in Asia, looking across the seas to Arabia and Africa on the west, and to Myanmar and Malaysia on the east. The Himalayas on the north set it apart from the rest of Asia.

A promising software superpower, India is one of the world's leading software exporters, the second largest business process outsourcing centre in Asia, as well as the largest supplier of software professionals in the global IT industry.[1]

BACKGROUND

History[2]

India derives its name from the Indus river valley, home of one of the oldest civilisations in the world. The great ancient cities Mohenjodaro and Harappa are the places believed to be where Hinduism originated. The Indian Heritage has its influences from the Aryan and Dravidian tribes, the Vedic culture, Buddhism, and a succession of empires such as Mauryan, Gupta, Mughal, Maratha, Arabs, Turks, and the British during the late 18th Century.

The British East India Company was established around 1600 as a trading entity. Later, the company was involved in Indian politics and by 1803 had control of most of the country. Eventually, India became part of the British Empire in 1857. In 1947, the country gained its freedom under the leadership of Mahatma Gandhi, but it was divided into India and Pakistan. When the dividing line was announced, the greatest exodus in the history of mankind took place as Muslims moved to Pakistan while Hindus and Sikhs relocated to India. More than ten million people changed sides and hundreds of thousands were killed. Mahatma Gandhi's support for secularism and his principles of non-violence led to his assassination in 1948.

India's first Prime Minister Jawaharlal Nehru championed a secular constitution, socialist central planning, and a strict policy of non-alignment. Nehru's daughter Indira Gandhi was elected Prime Minister in 1966. While she continued Nehru's pro-poor and socialist policies, her regime was marred by her declaration of a State of Emergency in 1975 when she perceived her power to be threatened. After her assassination in 1984, her son Rajiv Gandhi became Prime Minister. Rajiv brought new and pragmatic policies to India. Foreign investment and the use of modern technology were encouraged, import restrictions were eased, and many new industries were set up.

True liberalisation of the Indian economy started in the early 1990s with then Finance Minister Manmohan Singh. But with the rise of Hindu nationalism (*hindutva*), the Bharatiya Janata Party (BJP or Indian People's Party) gained more control of the Central Government. The BJP came to power and led several coalitions to victory under the dynamic leadership of AB Vajpayee. To appease its coalition partners, the BJP government later slowed down its nationalistic agenda and bound itself with the National Democratic Alliance (NDA) manifesto.

Geography

The Indian subcontinent lies north of the equator, bound by the Indian Ocean, the Arabian Sea and the Bay of Bengal. India shares borders with Pakistan and Afghanistan to the west, and Bangladesh and Myanmar to the east. Below its southern tip lies the island nation of Sri Lanka. The northern borders are defined by China, Tibet, Nepal and Bhutan.

The Indian mainland comprises the northern mountains, the Indo-Gangetic plains, the western desert, the Deccan plateau, and the eastern and western Ghats.

India is a union of 28 states: Andhra Pradesh, Arunachal Pradesh, Assam, Bihar, Chhattisgarh, Goa, Gujarat, Haryana, Himachal Pradesh, Jammu and Kashmir, Jharkhand, Karnataka, Kerala, Madhya Pradesh, Maharashtra, Manipur, Meghalaya, Mizoram, Nagaland, Orissa, Punjab, Rajasthan, Sikkim, Tamil Nadu, Tripura, Uttaranchal, Uttar Pradesh and West Bengal.

The biggest state is Madhya Pradesh; the smallest is Goa. These states are governed by the state governments.

The capital city of Delhi is also known as the National Capital Region (NCR). The central government administer the NCR and six other union territories, which are the Andaman and Nicobar Islands, Chandigarh, Dadra and Nagar Haveli, Daman and Diu, Lakshadweep, and Pondicherry.

The area of the country is about 3.3 million square kilometers. With over a billion people, India is the second most populous country in the world. The population comprises 72 percent Indo-Aryan, 25 percent Dravidian and 3 percent others. Over 80 percent of the population is Hindu. The remaining are Muslim, Christian, Sikh, Buddhist, and Jain.

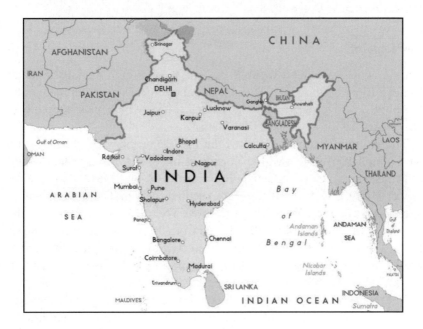

Economy

India adopts a mixed economic policy and plans its national policy every five years. At present, the tenth plan is in progress.

The Indian economy encompasses traditional village farming, modern agriculture, handicrafts, a wide spectrum of modern industries, and a multitude of support services. More than a third of the population is below the poverty line. The international payments position remained strong in 2002 with adequate foreign exchange reserves, moderately depreciating nominal exchange rates, and booming exports of software services, though growth in manufacturing output slowed, and electricity shortages continued in many regions.

GDP stands at around US$ 460 billion in 2001. Almost half of this is contributed by services, with industry accounting for 28 percent, while agriculture accounts for 24 percent. The average annual growth rate during the ninth plan (1997-2002) was around 5.4 percent, which was supported by a growth rate of 5.7 percent in agriculture, 3.3 percent in industry and 6.5 percent in services.[3]

The major industries in India are textiles, chemicals, food processing, steel, transportation equipment, cement, mining, petroleum, machinery, and agricultural products. Key trading partners include USA, Hong Kong, UK, Japan, Germany, Belgium, Saudi Arabia and Russia.

Government

India practices a federal republic system, a Sovereign Socialist Secular Democratic Republic, with a parliamentary form of government. The Republic is governed under the Constitution, which was adopted on 26 January 1950.

The union executive comprises the President, the Vice-President and the Council of Ministers with the Prime Minister as the head. The Council of Ministers, which is collectively responsible to the House of People (or Lower House), is vested with real executive power. The government is federal in structure but unitary in features. There are 245 members of the Upper House who are indirectly elected from the states, and 545 members of the Lower House who are directly elected by the people. The current President is Dr APJ Abdul Kalam, and the Prime Minister is Shri Atal Bihari Vajpayee.

Each state has its own elected assembly. The governor is the head of state while the Council of Ministers, headed by the Chief Minister, has the real executive power. The Council of Ministers is collectively responsible to the State Legislative Assembly.

THE NATIONAL ICT PROGRAMME

Information and Communication Technology (ICT) has been viewed as an enabling tool for the delivery of products and services to both the public and private sectors in India. The country, however, has extensively been burdened with archaic bureaucracy and the government has struggled with economic reform since the early 1990s.

With the increasing pervasiveness of the Internet, public governance has inevitably been affected. There has been a fundamental shift in the manner by which the states deliver public services. Most state governments have carried out computerisation projects at the departmental level. A large number of public agencies have set up at least informational websites. According to the National Association of Software and Services Companies (NASSCOM), Indian federal and state governments spent some US$ 890 million in 2001–2002 on e-Government.

The Information Technology Action Plan

1998 was a significant year for the IT industry development in India. Intent on accelerating IT growth, Prime Minister AB Vajpayee set up a National Technology and Software Development Task Force led by several high-profile individuals and many eminent representatives from government, industry, and academia. The mission of the task force was to formulate a National Policy on Informatics to enable India to emerge as an IT superpower within ten years. A related goal was to recommend action steps the government needed to take to remove bottlenecks and give a sharp boost to the development of the industry.

Based on the Information Technology Action Plan recommended by the task force, a number of regulatory and promotional measures have been implemented to remove impediments and enable IT growth in the country. The plan focused on three basic objectives:

(1) **Info-Infrastructure Drive:** This was to accelerate the creation of world-class Info Infrastructure including fibre optics, satellite communications, and wireless networks in order to seamlessly interconnect Local, National and Global Informatics Infrastructures. (LII, NII and GII).

(2) **IT Exports:** The second area of focus was to increase IT exports. Aiming to tap the potential US$ 2 trillion global IT industry, India needed to create a conducive policy ambiance for its IT industry to reach the target of US$50 billion in annual exports of IT software and services by 2008.

(3) **" IT for all by 2008":** The third objective was to make computer literacy nationwide. This would be achieved through spearheading the use of computers and IT in education, culminating in what was called the "Operation Knowledge" national campaign.

Specific initiatives following the IT Action Plan are shown in the following diagram:

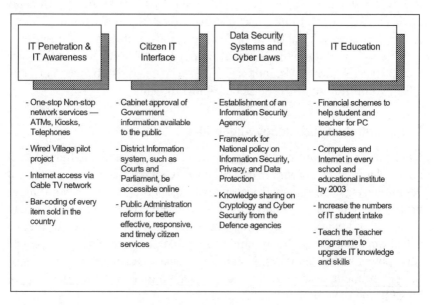

IT Penetration & IT Awareness	Citizen IT Interface	Data Security Systems and Cyber Laws	IT Education
- One-stop Non-stop network services — ATMs, Kiosks, Telephones	- Cabinet approval of Government information available to the public	- Establishment of an Information Security Agency	- Financial schemes to help student and teacher for PC purchases
- Wired Village pilot project	- District Information system, such as Courts and Parliament, be accessible online	- Framework for National policy on Information Security, Privacy, and Data Protection	- Computers and Internet in every school and educational institute by 2003
- Internet access via Cable TV network			
- Bar-coding of every item sold in the country	- Public Administration reform for better effective, responsive, and timely citizen services	- Knowledge sharing on Cryptology and Cyber Security from the Defence agencies	- Increase the numbers of IT student intake
			- Teach the Teacher programme to upgrade IT knowledge and skills

Figure 6-1: Initiatives under the National IT Action Plan

Information Technology Policy

India is one of the few early nations in the world that have given recognition to digital documents and signatures. It is one of the first nations to enact such legislation. The following are key legal and policy frameworks for IT development in India:

Information Technology Act 2000

This Act, endorsed in October 2000, is the fundamental law for e-Governance. It serves to provide legal recognition for transactions carried out by means of electronic data interchange (EDI) and other means of electronic communication, which involves use of alternatives to paper based methods of information communications and storage. The Act also provides for other related issues to e-Governance, such as security, penalties, offences, and adjudication.

Communication Convergence Bill

In 2001, the Government of India released a draft Communication Convergence Bill that aims to provide a clear regulatory framework for the convergence of telecom, Internet, and broadcasting services. Passage of the draft made India the second country in the world (after Malaysia) to adopt legislation covering the convergence of high-tech media. The objective of the bill is to create a regulatory environment, which is flexible enough to accommodate and propagate any permutation or combination of technologies and services. In order to achieve a technology-neutral and service sector-neutral environment, the bill outlines the creation of four categories of licenses that include network infrastructure facilities, network services, application services and content application services.

Agenda for e-Governance Policy

Drafted by the Department of Information Technology (DIT), this Agenda charts a roadmap for e-Governance policies and projects. It ensures that the basic infrastructure is planned for, including technology standards, funding mechanisms, and human resource development strategies.

Freedom of Information Bill 2002

The Parliament of India took another step towards transparency in governance by passing the historic Freedom of Information Bill 2002. The Bill aims to provide access to government information and files to every citizen in an effort to promote openness, transparency and accountability in administration.

Telecommunications Policy

New Telecom Policy (NTP) '99

The NTP '99 focused on provision of telecommunication services to rural areas. The policy set a target to achieve a teledensity of 7 by 2005 and 15 by 2010. It also envisaged transformation of the telecom sector into one of greater competitiveness, by providing equal opportunities for all the players.

Corporatisation

With effect from 1 October 2000, the service providing functions of the Department of Telecommunications had been divested to a newly created corporate entity – Bharat Sanchar Nigam Limited (BSNL) in order to provide functional autonomy and decision making powers to the incumbent operator in the emerging competitive environment.

Strengthening the Regulator

The Telecom Regulatory Authority of India (TRAI) Act was amended to restructure and strengthen the Regulator by giving additional functions and making it mandatory to seek its recommendations in several fields. A separate high-powered body, the Telecom Disputes Settlement and Appellate Tribunal (TDSAT) was also set up for expeditious disposal of telecom disputes.

Private Sector Participation

The telecommunication sector, including telephone, cellular phone, and Internet services has been opened for private participation and competition is encouraged. The Department of Telecommunications has opened up national long distance as well as international long distance services for private participation. 100 percent foreign direct investment (FDI) is now permitted in the manufacturing of telecom equipment, Internet services (excluding provision of international gateways), and certain infrastructure providing email and voicemail services. Up to 74 percent FDI is permitted for the provision of international gateways, and radio paging service. Up to 49 percent FDI is permitted for national long distance service, basic telephone service, cellular mobile service and other value added services.

ICT MATURITY INDICATORS

Better connectivity normally implies greater readiness to e-Governance. The following are some key indicators of the National Information Infrastructure that reflect India's situation:

Teledensity

Teledensity (number of telephone lines per 100 persons) is still very low in India, although there has been considerable improvement over the past few years. As of mid-2002, the overall teledensity was 4.4 and rural teledensity was only 1. Public telephones are a lifeline for connectivity in rural areas. In fact, for a developing country like India, the prevalence of public telephones is a better gauge of connectivity than the possession of home telephones. There are approximately one million public call offices and half a milllion village public telephones. Apart from this, there are some 30,000 STD[4] stations operating in the country.

As at March 2002, there were 38 million Direct Exchange Lines (DEL's) provided by the government-owned telephone service providers and about a half million DEL's of private companies. Apart from the basic DEL's, the country is also connected by coaxial cable, optical fibre, microwave, and UHF.[5] There are more than 400 VSATs[6] working in the country.

Cellular phones

With the corporatisation of government-owned telephone service providers and their entrance into the cellular business, the number of licensed cellular operators rose to 89. The cellular mobile industry had 42 networks, serving over 1,400 towns and cities and thousands of villages. This industry has been growing at a rate of 85 percent per year, and with improved affordability and better coverage, the number of cellular subscribers has already exceeded 6.5 million.

Internet Access

Internet access in India was initially dominated by a state-owned Internet Service Provider (ISP), Videsh Sanchar Nigam Limited (VSNL). VSNL has now been diversified, though the government still holds some stake. With the new National Telecom Policy, the ISP market was privatised and some 500 Internet licenses have been issued. About 140 ISPs are providing services to over 300 major cities and towns. The number of Internet subscribers reached 4.1 million in March 2002. The number of cybercafes and public access kiosks has exceeded 12,000. More than 45 ISPs have been approved to establish international gateways.

The number of Internet hosts per 10,000 inhabitants is exceedingly low at 0.35 as is the number of personal computers per 100 inhabitants at 0.45. Less than one percent of PCs are connected to the Internet.

National Connectivity

In order to provide a national backbone, BSNL initiated the Sanchar Sagar Project, a National Information Infrastructure and Internet Backbone, to make domestic bandwidth on demand available for almost all the district headquarters in India. The first phase of this project has been completed. This project covers a route length of over 17,000 kilometers and provides very high-speed connectivity linking 33 cities all over the country. The second phase of the project is under execution, covering a route length of 36,000 kilometers that will provide connectivity to 150 more cities.

E-GOVERNANCE IN INDIA

India's vision for e-Governance is "to apply Information Technology in the processes of government functioning to attain a S.M.A.R.T. government". The acronym represents:

- **S**imple;
- **M**oral;
- **A**ccountable ;
- **R**esponsive; and
- **T**ransparent.

The strategic imperatives laid out to achieve this vision are:

- Developing the institution of nodal officers[7] both within the Department of Information Technology and in other corresponding departments in the government for quick initiation and transfer of suitable technologies and packages enabling e-Governance.
- Leveraging resources of various Indian ministries, departments, and other public sector institutions to enable the adoption of electronic service delivery.
- Encouraging development of similar mechanisms and dedicated institutions at the state level.
- Encouraging various Constitutional agencies to adopt e-Governance for effective delivery of services and administration.
- Addressing privacy concerns through a clear statement of continuous commitment to the data protection and Internet security system, both in the public and private domain.

Agenda for e-Governance

The government of India, in association with the Department of Information Technology, laid out the following agenda on e-Governance in 2000:

- Each Ministry and Department must set up LANs and provide PCs with necessary software for all officials up to the Section Officer level.
- There must be training for every staff member who needs to use computers for office work.

- Each Ministry and Department must start using the Office Procedure Automation software developed by the National Informatics Centre for the documents filing system in the department.
- Payroll, accounting, and other housekeeping software should be put in place for day-to-day operations.
- Notices for internal meetings should be sent by email to the officers and put up on online notice boards of the Ministry and Department.
- Ministries and Departments should provide the web-enabled complaints filing system.
- Each Ministry and Department should have its own website.
- All Acts, Rules, and Circulars, along with other published material of interest or relevance to the public, should be converted into electronic forms, made available on the Internet, and be accessible from the Information and Facilitation Counters.
- The websites of Ministries, Departments, and Organisations should specifically contain a section in which various forms to be used by citizens are available. The forms should be available to print, or to complete and then print out for submission. Attempts should also be made to enable completion and submission of the forms online.
- The Hindi version of the contents of the websites should be developed simultaneously.
- Each Ministry and Department should also make efforts to begin electronic delivery of services to the public.
- Each Ministry and Department should have an overall IT strategy for a five-year period, which should encompass specific action plans and targets (including the minimum agenda) to be implemented within one year.

KEY GOVERNMENT AGENCIES

Department of Information Technology

In 1999, the Ministry of Information Technology was established in India to facilitate all initiatives in the IT sector. The Ministry was then merged with the Communication Ministry to form the Ministry of Communication and Information Technology (MCIT). Currently the Department of Information Technology (DIT), under the MCIT, works as a nodal agency for Information Technology. The Department of Telecom and Department of Posts are the two other key departments under the MCIT.

The following are some key offices related to the DIT, which are responsible for e-Governance:

- **The National Informatics Centre (NIC).** This provides the major backbone networks in the country. It renders computer support to all departments in the Central and State governments, and more than 500 district administrations. It has a satellite-based computer communications network for providing services such as email, Internet, file transfer, access to databases, electronic data interchange (EDI), and video-conferencing facilities. NIC has also computerised the functions of various legislative courts (including supreme, high, and lower courts) to streamline functions and enhance transparency.
- **Electronics Research and Development Centre of India (ER & DCI).** The ER & DCI was established to undertake application-oriented, region-specific research, design and development in the state of the art electronics technology including rural applications to generate, deliver know-how, and commercialise the R&D for the manufacturing sector in the country.
- **NISG — National Institute for SMART Governance.** This is a non-profit entity being promoted by the Department of Information Technology, Department of Administrative Reform, Government of Andhra Pradesh and the National Association of Software & Services Companies (NASSCOM). The company provides technology consultancy to various Central, State and local government agencies for the implementation of e-Governance.

e-Governance Initiatives

Several of the e-Governance initiatives in India are carried out by the Central government, with the driving force being the DIT. Many more high-profile projects are championed by the State governments of India.

NATIONAL LEVEL INITIATIVES

India Country Gateway

The Country Gateway project was implemented by DIT on behalf of the Development Gateway Foundation.[8] It aims to develop and facilitate the participation of local and professional communities in virtual discussions. DIT has developed a prototype for the project, which covers key areas such as health, education, rural energy, and agriculture. The prototype portal was launched in late 2002.

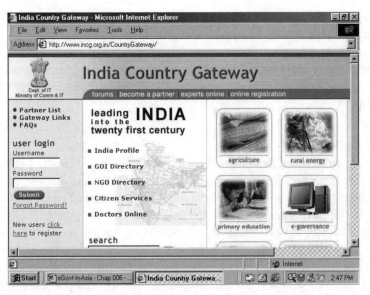

Figure 6-2: The India Country Gateway website

The India country gateway contains links to the websites of key government agencies and constituents, such as the Indian Parliament. The Parliament website provides lists of daily synopses, Parliamentary questions, debates and proceedings, details of members, parliamentary committees, Bills, and Acts and so on. Moreover, this website also allows citizens to submit feedback to their elected representatives.

The Central Vigilance Commission (CVC)

In an effort to further the idea of zero tolerance for corruption, the Central Vigilance Commission (CVC) in India has been sharing with citizens a large amount of information related to corruption. The CVC website (www.cvc.nic.in) provides practical information on how to complain about the corrupt acts. The website has published the names of officers against whom investigations have been ordered or penalties imposed for bribery. Newsweek magazine carried an article about this effort, calling it "e-Shame".

In August 2001, the CVC published a document entitled "A Citizen's Guide to Fighting Corruption". Two months later, the CVC declared a "vigilance week", urging the public to monitor and report corrupt actions by public authorities. The CVC has also proposed the development of a corruption perceptions index that ranks all government departments according to the bribes required. All departments in the state were recently ranked in a "corruption league table".[9]

By January 2003, some 240,000 visits had been registered on the site and the media has actively promoted the CVC website throughout the country.

ePost

The Department of Posts launched its first web-based product ePost in 2002. The pilot project was launched in five states: Andhra Pradesh, Kerala, Goa, Maharashtra, and Gujarat. This product links Internet users with those who do not have direct access to the Internet. Each post office is given an email ID based on its Postal Index Number (PIN), a unique identifier. Internet users can send email to those who do not have a PC or Internet access of their own. The email would go to the identified post office, then get printed out, and delivered in hardcopy at the doorstep of the intended recipient. This is a part of the programme for bridging India's digital divide. There are plans to give an ePost ID to every citizen in India.

Computerisation of the Elections Commission

The Elections Commission has set up a network for 750,000 polling stations across the country involving more than 600 million voters. The system, including ballot forms and directories, accommodates 14 languages and nine scripts that are in use in India. The electoral lists and voting cards are being computerised. Electronic voting machines were first used in November 1998 and have been used in all subsequent elections. It has reduced considerably the time needed for vote counting in this highly populous country.

CRISP

The Computerised Rural Information Systems Project (CRISP) was launched in 1986 by the Ministry of Rural Development to assist staff of the District Rural Development Agencies (DRDAs) in the monitoring exercise of poverty alleviation schemes using a computer system. Since 1986, several versions of the CRISP application software package have been designed and developed for DRDAs. The latest in the series is RuralSoft, which is a scalable web-based solution that helps in monitoring the poverty alleviation schemes. The system, which is inter-connected by a satellite network, has been implemented in 15 districts.

TRADENIC — A Trade Portal

TradeNIC is a one-stop online trade information resource being developed by NIC catering to the information needs of exporters and importers, investors, and buying organisations abroad. The site provides the links to several websites containing important trade related information including commercial and economic information from different countries, tenders, calendars of trade fairs and trade statistics.

Multipurpose National Identity Cards

The Government of India has for many years been planning to carry out compulsory registration of all Indian nationals above the age of 14 and issuing them with multipurpose national identity cards (MNICs). Past proposals had fallen through after some States expressed reservations on the grounds that it was too gigantic a task to issue such a card to each citizen. The union government under the Home Ministry is planning to enact a legislation to make such cards mandatory. The government plans to use the MNICs for the purpose of passports, driving licenses, and employment cards. A pilot project was launched in 13 states from April 2003.

Nationwide replication of e-Governance

The government plans to replicate successful projects which have originated in certain states, such as the Bhoomi project from Karnataka. The replications are to be implemented in one district for each state. Each state would select a model district on the basis of parameters such as IT infrastructure, affordable connectivity, presence of technical and professional educational institutions, and relevant growth indicators to implement the project. DIT would provide funding for each selected district in all states and union territories.

To facilitate knowledge sharing, the e-Governance National Resource also launched the website www.egovdatabase.gov.in to archive and disseminate information on e-Governance applications in the country. The project enables any organisation planning an IT project to instantly ascertain whether any similar project has already been implemented anywhere in the country. The intending implementers would then know who the key people in similar projects are and how to contact them. For implementing agencies, be they government-owned organisations or private IT companies, the database offers a unique opportunity to share the knowledge resource from the existing projects both domestically and internationally.

In order to showcase technologies in area of e-Governance, a Centre of Excellence was established at DIT in August 2000. The Centre, the first of its kind in the country, showcases various e-Governance applications and solutions that have been implemented, and also offers other services such as technical consultation, proof of concept, and technical presentations. It conducts programmes for creating awareness among decision-makers in the Central and State governments and helps them in defining and implementing policy and process changes. The centre draws upon expertise from leading companies, technical institutes and business partners in India and abroad to help initiate certain projects to address specific needs.

KEY INITIATIVES BY INDIAN STATES

e-Governance in Andhra Pradesh

Andhra Pradesh is one of the most prominent states in India for IT progress and development. The chief minister of the state, Chandrababu Naidu, is quite a celebrity within India, recognised for his vision of Andhra Pradesh's IT future.

The vision of the state for the IT sector is embodied in the following statement:

> Andhra Pradesh will leverage Information Technology to attain a position of leadership and excellence in the information age and to transform itself into a knowledge society.

The strategic directions of the state are reflected in a blueprint called "Vision 2020", which sets out the goals, milestones, strategies and plans needed to realise the vision. The main goals are "transparency, accountability and speediness".

Some of the major projects undertaken by the Andhra Pradesh government are outlined below.

Andhra Pradesh State Wide Area Network (APSWAN)

APSWAN is the backbone network for the state of Andhra Pradesh, which was first operational in November 1999. It connects the state capital Hyderabad to some 25 centres (including all the District Headquarter towns). APSWAN was the first state-wide network in India. The government Intranet, which is used for voice, data and video communications, started with a capacity of 2 mbps (which is scalable to 600 mbps), and has provided some real communication benefits. For example, video conferencing is used for administrative reviews and conferences, online distance training for government officials, demonstration of best practices from the departments and fast data transmission. In subsequent phases, it is planned to connect Mandal headquarters and other towns/villages with dedicated lines, dial-up and wireless facilities.

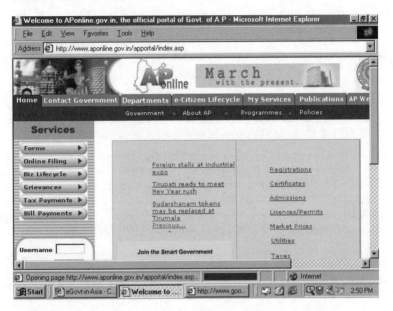

Figure 6-3: The website of Andhra Pradesh state

CARD: Computer-aided Administration of Registration Department

Land registration offices throughout Andhra Pradesh now operate computerised counters to help citizens to complete registration requirements within several hours instead of days or even weeks, as was necessary under the earlier system. This is made possible by the CARD project at the Registration and Stamps Department of the state. Under this project, the manual system of registering the sales deed for a property was made easier, faster and more transparent through computerisation. The project was completed in 1998 and has since been expanded to more than 200 centres.

APDMS: Andhra Pradesh Development Monitoring System

APDMS is a pioneering project of the Planning Department, which was started in 2000. The purpose is to create base maps with habitation patterns. This includes the road network, the community infrastructure, demographic data, soil and geo-morphological data. It combines the GIS (Geographical Information System) with data from remote sensing devices. This information is used along with inputs from the Land Information System, socio-economic indicators, household survey database, and human development indicators.

---

e-Seva

If one happens to reside in Hyderabad, capital of Andhra Pradesh, all one needs to do is to click on *www.esevaonline.com* to access a wide selection of online services relating to public utilities like water, electricity and telephones.

The e-Seva centre is a 24 × 7, one-stop shop for 32 government-to-consumer (G2C) and business-to-consumer (B2C) services. From payment of utility bills to the issue of birth and death certificates, permits and licenses, reservation of bus tickets and receipt of passport applications, the e-Seva centres offer a wide range of services under one roof. Internet services like electronic payments, downloading of forms and government orders, and filing of applications on the Web are also offered.

e-Seva is the improved version of a project started in 1999 called TWINS (Twin Cities Network Services) providing similar services for the twin cities of Hyderabad and Secundrabad. According to the e-Seva director, these services will be set up in 229 centres in 117 municipalities within Andhra Pradesh by March 2003.

All services are delivered online to the citizens by connecting to the respective government departments and providing online information at the point of service delivery. The software is deployed in an n-Tier environment, each tier being physically located in a different departmental office.

- "Tier 1" is the point of service delivery, ie Integrated Citizen Service Centre (ICSC), which has counters offering more than 20 services, with an electronic queuing system.
- "Tier 2" is the Central Hub for routing all transactions to the respective departments
- "Tier n" is the Database related to consumer information available at respective Government departments

This Project is also part of the Andhra Pradesh State Government's "public-private" partnership initiative.

Figure 6-4: The e-Seva website

e-Governance in Gujarat

The State of Gujarat has articulated its mission to help improve processes in government agencies by using computing devices, communication systems and software to provide better delivery systems to the citizens.

In 1999, the Gujarat state government set up Gujarat Informatics Ltd (GIL) as a nodal agency in the public sector for the development of IT in the state, promotion of Gujarat as an IT destination, and evolution of e-Governance for the state.

Figure 6-5: The website of Gujarat state

Some of the notable achievements of the state are:

City Civic Centre of Ahmedabad

The Citizen Convenience Centre, also called "City Civic Centre", recently launched at the Ahmedabad Municipal Corporation (AMC), is the latest e-Governance product from the GIL basket. GIL played a key role by investing in the development of software and retains the Intellectual Property Rights, even as AMC and a local private company designed and implemented the project.

The civic centre provides citizens with public services such as property tax payment, birth/death certificates issuance, filing for a water tap/drainage connection request, application for building plan approval, lodging a complaint, or making miscellaneous payments. The citizens can track the status of their applications through the corporation website. The system helps management to internally monitor the disposal and redressal of such applications, including any possibility of delay or harassment which may lead to nepotism or corruption. The operations of the city civic centre have also been connected to the web thereby bringing in transparency in the number of applications received and the department to which they relate.

The "Mahiti-Shakti Project"

This project from the Panchmahal tribal district won an award in 2002 from the Computer Society of India. Called the *Mahiti Shakti* (meaning "power of information") project, it has made life easier for thousands of villagers in the region. Launched in late 2001, this G2C project leverages on already available infrastructure in the towns and villages, eg network of dairies, STD/PCO booths, etc. which have computers with Internet connectivity and are regularly frequented by the people. The so-called Mahiti Shakti *kendras* (or kiosks) have trained operators to help villagers access the information they require. They supply printouts of almost all types of forms required by Government departments. A small, affordable fee per form is levied. The project has been so successful that the Gujarati administrators are planning to replicate it in other districts. The Mahiti Shakti kendra becomes a single window clearance for some 200 forms and other information that people in small towns and villages may require.

IT at Milk Collection Centres

Milk production is important to India. Milk is one of the main sources of protein and calcium for a largely vegetarian population, and dairying provides a livelihood for millions of Indian farmers and additional income for a large number of rural families. It is also a means for women to participate in economic activity in rural areas.

The use of IT in cooperative diaries in Gujarat brings benefit to more than 60,000 farmers. The project, which started at Amul dairy, is replicated in 70,000 villages in some 200 Indian districts. By using computers in thousands of rural locations for processing transactions related to milk buying and selling, a half million people are exposed to the benefits of IT each day.

The project has been developed through extensive collaboration with the co-operative dairy unions of Gujarat. The farmers benefit from this project as payment to them is now based on a quick and accurate measurement of fat content and weight, and is not subject to the malpractice and underpayment common with other traditional systems used. Traditional methods require hours to calculate fat content, as the measurement process is much more cumbersome, and payment to farmers was made every ten days due to the inability of the collection centres to calculate the payment immediately. The IT system enables prompt, accurate, and immediate payment. The queues at the centres are short despite the number of people selling their milk being quite large. As 2,500 centres receive milk from 400,000 farmers daily, a ten-minute savings per farmer each day amounts to a total savings of 180,000 man-days per month.

The software can incorporate the revenue from daily milk sales to the local villagers and expenditure incurred. Since the accounts are kept accurate and up-to-date there is less likelihood of fraud and corrupt practices (e.g. temporary use of the funds by individuals). The simple technology uses a weighing machine with a PC interface and online milk tester.

The system reduces the number of employees and increases the availability of daily accounts at the milk collection centre. The profit is calculated on the basis of data received from the dairy regarding the payment made by the dairy for the previous day's collection. These records can be kept over months to maintain an up-to-date accounts.

e-Governance in Karnataka

Karnataka State has a decentralised setup such that most people do not have to come to Bangalore, the capital, for routine day-to-day business. Most decisions are taken at the village or district levels. It was, however, felt that an exhaustive database was needed at a single point and to be made available to all the decision-makers in Karnataka. A comprehensive database was then developed and portions of the database made available to respective decision-makers. The system provides data analysis and a sophisticated decision support system for the use of the Chief Minister.

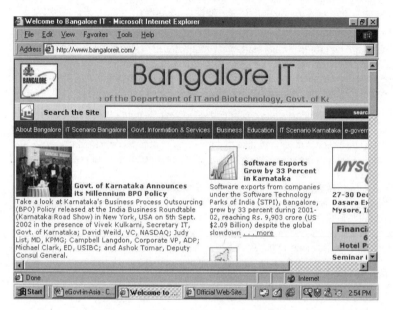

Figure 6-6: The website of Bangalore

Nondani

This project is aimed at making land registration simpler for the citizens in the state of Karnataka. People normally go to the sub-registrar offices for registering a sale deed or mortgage deed, as well as for an encumbrance certificate. This process is manual and is extremely cumbersome. To simplify the procedures for citizens, the government has initiated computerisation of the department. The sub-registrar offices in Shivaji Nagar, Kengeri and Bangalore South have facilities to scan the registration deeds and return the registered documents. Over 100,000 documents have been registered in a computerised environment.

BHOOMI

The record of Rights Tenancy and Crops (RTC), plays a vital role in the life of Indian farmers. The records are required for establishing ownership of land, for recording the succession of ownership, for recording the crop details and for obtaining loans from banks.

The Bhoomi project is the computerisation of land records carried out by the Department of Revenue in Karnataka. Over 20 million records of land ownership of 6.7 million farmers in the state have already been stored in the database.

The project has changed the lives of the farmers who need a copy of an RTC. Before the project was established, there were normally delays, harassment, and bribery. Today, for a fee of Rs.15 (US$ 0.32), a printed copy of the RTC can be obtained online at computerised land record kiosks (Bhoomi centres) in more than 140 offices. Now, the Government of Karnataka is trying to make the system as a web-enabled central database where RTCs would be available online at any Internet kiosk.

The cost of processing an RTC has been roughly estimated at Rs.13, assuming a life of 5 years for the hardware and an activity level of 2 million RTCs issued from all the kiosks (10 percent of all holdings). This cost includes an assumed operational expenditure of Rs.2 for stationery, cartridges and electricity. The current user fee of Rs.15 seems adequate to cover these costs.

By the end of November 2001, Rs. 5.0 million (US$ 107,000) had been collected in user fees for the distribution of 330,000 RTCs through the 140 kiosks. Farmers can now get an RTC for any parcel of land within 5–30 minutes from an RTC information kiosk instead of waiting for days.

Khajane

This project involves intensive computerisation of the treasuries all over Karnataka. The treasury payment system handles over Rs. 0.2 billion (US$ 4.3 million) annually through 225 treasuries. This welfare payment system serves a half million pensioners. In addition, the system serves 1.3 million old-age pensioners, the physically handicapped, and destitute widows. The treasuries act as bankers to 4,500 local agencies at district, block and village, as well as municipal corporations and other funds.

e-Governance in Kerala

The major IT initiatives carried out in the state of Kerala are:

Figure 6-7: The website of Kerala state

Aksharya

Akshaya addresses the issues of the digital divide in the state in a holistic way. It provides ICT access to all sections of society by setting up multi-purpose community technology centres to develop minimum skill sets for people through functional IT literacy training, and the creation of relevant local content. Two progammes on the introduction of computer training in government schools have been launched by the Kerala state government. The State Education Department has implemented this under an initiative called "IT @ School".

Sevana

The Department of IT in association with the state library council has launched the first computerised rural information centre at Kallara Gram Panchayat library in Trivandrum district. Fourteen rural information centres, one in each district of the state, have also been established. These centres enable the rural citizen to have free access to the Internet. An application package named "Sevana" provides information on various government schemes, programmes, roles and services of local bodies, links to important sites, and other facts relevant to the rural populace.

FRIENDS

The Department of IT, in association with the local bodies and government departments, has set up integrated services centres called FRIENDS (Fast Reliable Instant Efficient Network for Disbursement of Services) with a view to enable a smooth and transparent C2G interface. These centres accept all utility bills, taxes and fees payment pertaining to the participating departments and offer quality services to citizens. FRIENDS has been launched in all 14 district headquarters in the State of Kerala.

The computer server of a FRIENDS centre will be linked to the server of the concerned departments for update of data in real-time, once the computerisation of the departments is completed. Until then, the FRIENDS centre would work on the principle of "collect and remit" and "receive and forward" methods to offer various services including bill payments, tax payments, and license registration. Other services, which work on a "Check and Confirm" mode, such as KSRTC Express Reservation service, booking/reconfirmation of airline tickets, and hotel reservations will be added in future.

OTHER SIGNIFICANT PROJECTS

Some other successful e-Governance projects and initiatives implemented in India include:

- **WARANA Cooperative Complex**
  This is an example of successful integrated rural development resulting from people's participation in the cooperative movement. It comprises 25 cooperative societies in the field of sugar, milk, poultry and construction. The primary objective of the project is to demonstrate the effective contribution of an IT infrastructure in a cluster of 70 contiguous villages around Warana in the Kolhapur and Sangli Districts.

- **SETHU**
  This is an initiative of the government of Maharashtra, which strives for citizen satisfaction through its services. The facilitation centre offers one-stop counter services for all certificates and permits, public grievance redress, availability of information on all administrative processes, and the progress of applications, among other services.

- **GYANDOOT**
  This project of the Government of Madhya Pradesh in the Dhar district
  is a computer network connecting rural cybercafes. It caters to the
  everyday needs of the masses in providing information and transaction
  services relating to commodity/Mandi marketing information system,
  income certificates, domicile certificates, caste certificates, landholder's
  passbook of land rights and loans, rural Hindi email, public grievance
  redress, forms for various government schemes, below poverty line
  family list, employment news, rural matrimonial procedures, rural
  market, news, advisory module, e-learning, driving licenses, and so on.

- **CHOiCE Centres**
  This is a project by the government of Chattisgarh for connecting all
  villages and towns through wireless solutions. "CHOiCE" is the acronym
  for CHhattisgarh Online information system for Citizen Empowerment.
  CHOiCE also stands for the choice available to citizens to avail services
  from public offices with care, courtesy and utmost ease. CHOiCE centres
  provide a wide range of services including connectivity, information,
  IT education, e-Governance and e-Commerce.

- **RajSwift** is an initiative of the government of Rajasthan, which aims
  to facilitate information exchange on a real time basis among a closed
  user group consisting of the Chief Minister of the state, senior level
  functionaries at the Chief Minister Secretariat and District Collectors.
  Collectors/District Magistrates will be able to update the related data
  on a daily basis, for the Chief Minister's review.

OBSERVATIONS OF E-INDIA

Despite various success stories, the road to an integrated e-Government
system in India is still a long one. The projects are emerging disparately
without much replication and interoperability. Even the successes of states
like Andhra Pradesh and Karnataka are not much replicated in other states.
The lack of central government initiatives is another hindrance for these
progressive states. The government of Andhra Pradesh, which has facilitated
a one-stop solution for establishing companies in the state, could not achieve
much because there are various permissions that have to be received from

central government agencies and hence, could not transfer real benefits to businesses. Even in the case of various services to the citizens there are certain subjects which are beyond the authority of state government and a state cannot carry out re-engineering in areas where they are bound by the constitution.

By the same token, the central government has to take the initiative. There is a great need to establish various institutions for e-Governance. If DIT is to be the nodal agency for implementing e-Governance in the country, it needs to be given power to cut across states and departments of the Government of India. There is a great need for a comprehensive national e-Governance Plan. A concept of a National Information Infrastructure connected to the State Information Infrastructure and to the Local Information Infrastructure has to be developed. The interoperability of various networks has also to be taken into account.

The central government and the state governments need to establish state sponsored data centres, which can carry records of land, citizens and property. Though the IT Act provides for the setup of the office of the CCA, the purpose for which the office was created is yet to be clear. There is a need for a DIT interoperability commission to look into affairs of interoperability of e-Governance projects. A School of e-Governance and a R&D organisation are other necessities in the country. A separate institution for awareness of e-Governance may also need to be established.

The Indian e-Governance agenda also needs to address the Accountability Law that holds the civil servants, including elected representatives, accountable for the non-functioning or malfunctioning of their departments. In addition to the IT Act and Freedom of Information Act, a law to protect the privacy of citizens is needed. Such a law will ensure that the personal information of the citizens is not misused. In order to promote the use of electronic records, a law like the US Government Paper Elimination Act (GPEA) should be considered. Amendments to the Consumer Protection Law, Tariffs and Taxation Laws, Intellectual Property Regulations, etc, are also required. Further guidelines for content, technological standards, and electronic payments are also desirable.

Government also needs to introduce the subject of IT in the civil service examinations to promote the admission of IT literate professionals in the civil services. A separate cadre of Indian Information Technology Services is being debated. The first requirement in this area is the establishment of a national e-Governance agency which becomes the centre for all development. The National Association for SMART Governance is proposed as one such body.

In short, for successful implementation of e-Governance in India, standards, infrastructure, legislation, and strategy need to be in place. It also requires the establishment of various institutions under the Department of Information Technology. What is required is global vision but local implementation. And above all, India requires e-readiness in the minds of its citizens and government employees. This chapter will be incomplete without giving a direction to our strategy and this direction comes in the words of Mahatma Gandhi:

> ... Whether what we are doing benefits the common man in any way ...

Endnotes

1   Data on Indian software exports: from the National Association of Software and Services Companies (NASSCOM), 2003.

2   Keay, John, *"A History of India"*, Harper-Collins (2000).

3   GDP: World Bank, Country Data, India: www.worldbank.org/data/ countrydata/aag/ind_aag.pdf.

4   STD: Standard Trunk Dialing.

5   UHF: Ultra High Frequency is a range of the radio spectrum extensively used for satellite communication and broadcasting, in cellular telephone and paging systems, and by wireless services.

6   VSAT: Very Small Aperture Terminal is a satellite communications system that serves home and business users.

7   In India, a nodal agency is usually a State Government Department, which is concerned with the welfare of any vocation/occupation group, a welfare fund or society, village, NGO, and self-help group. Nodal officers are those working in nodal agencies.

8   The Development Gateway Foundation is an independent, non-profit organisation built on public-private partnerships. Its mission is to promote the use of ICT for poverty reduction and sustainable development, and help overcome the digital divide through practical and dynamic programmes. The Foundation's "Founding Members" include Australia, China, Germany, India, Italy, Japan, the Republic of Korea, Mali, Pakistan, Rwanda, and the World Bank.

9   *Times of India*, 1 February 2002.

References

1   UNESCO Report on "e-Government: India".

2   Satyanarayana, J, *"Challenges of e-Government – two success stories from India"* (presentation), www.ap-it.com/egovchallenges.pdf.

3   Himmelsbach, Vawn, *"India develops five-year e-Government plan"*, Technology in Government, Jul/Aug 2002, Vol. 9, No 8.

4   Sachdeva, Sameer, White Paper on *"E-Governance Strategy in India"*, December 2002.

5   *"E- government throws up opportunities in India"*, *Economic Times* (India), 17 October 2002.

6   *"Govt's IT Project Bhoomi eyes Stockholm Award"*, *Economic Times* (India), 3 July 2002.

7   "Andhra Pradesh (India) to collect data from villages daily, via e-mail", *The Financial Express*, 3 October 2002.

8   *"Delhi to become a Cyber-state"*, www.ciol.com.

9   *"E-Governance in India: Too many goals, very little reality"*, Mumbai, 29 June 2001.

10 *"Empowering Dairy Farmers: A Portal and Dairy Information and Services Kiosk Case Study"*, www.digitalpartners.org/disk.html.

Useful websites

home.nic.in	Official website of the National Informatics Centre, an IT organisation providing IT solutions for Government of India
indiaimage.nic.in	Information website on the Government of India
www.mit.gov.in	Official website of the Department of Information Technology, Ministry of Communications & Information Technology, India
www.bangaloreit.com	Official website of the Department of IT Biotechnology, Government of Karnataka, India
www.ap-it.com	Official website of the Department of IT Communications, Government of Andhra Pradesh, India

www.andhrapradesh.com / www.aponline.gov.in	Official website of the Government of Andhra Pradesh, India
darpg.nic.in	Official website of the Department of Administrative Reforms & Public Grievance, Government of India
www.developmentgateway.org	An interactive portal of the Development Gateway Foundation (www.dgfoundation.org) for information and knowledge sharing on sustainable development and poverty reduction website
www.assam.org	The homepage of the State of Assam, India
www.cdacindia.com	Official website of the Centre for Development of Advanced Computing, Ministry of Communications & Information Technology, India
www.esevaonline.com	Main gateway to citizen services (eSeva), Government of Andhra Pradesh, India
www.friendscentre.net	Integrated Services Centre, IT Department, Government of Kerala, India
www.gujaratinformatics.com	Website of Gujarat Informatics Limited, an agency for IT development, Government of Gujarat, India
www.gyandoot.nic.in	An extension of the Gyandoot intranet in Dhar district that connects rural cybercafes and provides network access to the masses
www.keralaitmission.org	Official website of the Kerala State IT Mission, an IT implementation agency for the Department of IT, Government of Kerala India
www.rajgovt.org	Official website of Rajdarpan, Government of Rajasthan, India
www.westbengalgovt.org	Official website of the Government of West Bengal, India

CHAPTER 7

e-Korea: High Bandwidth, High Growth

James SL Yong and Jeffery BH Tan

▲ ▼ ▲ ▼ ▲ ▼ ▲ ▼

Power lasts ten years,
Influence not more than a hundred

Korean proverb

▲ ▼ ▲ ▼ ▲ ▼ ▲ ▼

Having read the newspaper after dinner, Kim Yong-Jun was looking to spend some quality time with his son Soon-Man. "What are you doing?" he enquired as he approached Soon-Man who was seated in front of the family computer. "Just getting clobbered by the Orcs," replied Soon-Man with scenes of battle images fading in and out on the monitor.

"That should be enough online gaming for today," Yong-Jun said as he sat himself beside his son. "Let's check up on how you are doing in school." He deftly navigated to the National Education Information System to retrieve the responses on various questions he posted the day before. Yong-Jun beamed with satisfaction while reading the glowing report from the teachers and Soon-Man gave out a sigh of relief.

"How's about finishing up the article we were working on yesterday?" suggested Yong-Jun. As an avid citizen reporter for OhmyNews, Yong-Jun has contributed numerous reports, some of which has been published on the news agency online edition. He pulled up the working file as father and son deliberated on the article for the next hour.

Having put in the finishing touches, Yong-Jun logged-on to the OhmyNews website and submitted the article to the editors. "I think we have a good chance of seeing it published in a few days," said Yong-Jun while glancing at the wall clock. "It's time for you to retire as there's school tomorrow."

Soon-Man was about to protest, but decided otherwise as he trooped out of the study to his bedroom. Yong-Jun proceeded to review the status of the health insurance he recently acquired for the family. The Social Insurance Service Portal reported that the policy has been approved and he should receive the official documents soon.

With a few more keystrokes, he found himself in the virtual world of Aden. With a twinkle in his eyes, he extended a virtual greeting to his "blood brethrens" as they embarked on their online fantasy adventure ...

BACKGROUND

History

The Korean peninsula is a land with a long and often turbulent history. Over the centuries, the Koreans have survived the rule of Mongols, Chinese, Russians, Japanese and Americans.

Japanese colonialism of Korea ceased in 1945 with Japan's defeat at the end of World War II. The Republic of Korea was then set up in the southern half of the Korean Peninsula while a communist-style government was installed in the north. The Korean War (1950–1953) had the United States and United Nations (UN) forces intervene to defend South Korea (Republic of Korea) from North Korean attacks supported by the Chinese. An armistice was signed in 1953 splitting the peninsula along a demilitarised zone at the 38th parallel.

Over the next three decades, under a succession of Presidents,[1] the Republic of Korea swung between democracy and martial law. By the late 1980s, the country seemed to be in a critical state — plagued by student-led protests, work stoppages around the country, and constant demands for greater political and press freedom. Civil war was narrowly averted only when the authorities found ways to accede to some of the demands.

In 1988, General Roh Tae-Woo was elected President. Roh's regime was considered more democratic. Over his term, Roh was given credit for political reforms and an improved relationship with North Korea. His "North Policy" established formal diplomatic relations with Moscow and Beijing, as well as many other countries. However, critics pointed out flaws in his economic policies and initiatives.

In 1992, Roh was replaced by Kim Young-Sam and his Democratic Liberal Party. Kim took a hard line on corruption, and during his term of office several politicians were prosecuted for abusing the system. Notably, ex-presidents Chun Doo-Hwan and Roh Tae-Woo were put on trial for corruption and imprisoned, though they received presidential pardons later.

In spite of the political issues, South Korea achieved impressive economic growth up until the Asian financial crisis of 1997–98, which exposed various longstanding weaknesses in South Korea's development model. The leadership pushed through painful economic measures, and South Korea emerged to make a solid recovery.

In 1998, former dissident Kim Dae-Jung became President, the first time a non-conservative had led the country since independence. Kim promised to introduce economic and democratic reforms and improve relations with North Korea. By mid-1998, the South Korean economy was going through fundamental restructuring and actually shrinking. Rising bankruptcies and soaring unemployment led to large-scale labour unrest, but the economy then began to move again. By 1999, GDP growth had recovered, reversing the substantial decline of 1998. Seoul has pressed the country's largest business groups to restructure and to strengthen their financial base.

In June 2000, under South Korea's so-called "Sunshine Policy", a historic first summit took place between the south's Kim Dae-Jung and the north's leader Kim Jong-Il. In December 2000, Kim Dae-Jung became the first Korean to win the Noble Peace Prize for his lifelong commitment to democracy and human rights in Asia.

In February 2003, Roh Moo-Hyun took office as the new President of the Republic of Korea.

Geography

Strategically located in the waters of the Sea of Japan, Korea Strait and Yellow Sea, and surrounded by the giants of Japan, China and Russia, the Korean peninsula has been referred to as a "shrimp between whales" in an old Korean proverb. Today, South Korea's remarkable economic achievements make it a rather significant shrimp.

This is a land rich in cultural heritage and esoteric beauty. Much of the entire Korean peninsula comprises forested, rocky mountain ridges, accompanied by numerous offshore islands. In fact, only 20 percent of the total land area is flatland. The Republic of Korea has a total area of about 99,500 sq km and a population of some 48 million. Seoul, which has been the capital for six centuries, has a population of 11 million, making it one of the most densely populated cities in the world.

Economy

Today, the Republic of Korea has a vibrant and prosperous industrial economy with a GDP of US$ 450 billion. This is doubly impressive when one considers that fifty years ago, after the Korean War, the country emerged nearly vanquished, and with hardly any industry. Through incredible growth fuelled by dynamic entrepreneurship and a system of close government-business ties, South Korea achieved in less than four decades what has been called the "economic miracle on the Hangang River", after the river that runs through Seoul. Korea took its place among the world's top economies by the end of the 20th century.

South Korea is often referred to as one of the Four Tigers[2] of East Asia. Its major industries are electronics products, machinery, shipbuilding, metal goods, cars, electronics, machinery and chemicals. Its major trading partners are USA, Japan and China.

From 1997–1999, when the South Korean economy was threatened by the Asian financial crisis, the resolve and resilience of the Koreans were evident. Through faithful implementation of an IMF agreement, the government's drive for reform, and successful negotiation of foreign debt restructuring with creditor banks, the nation emerged on track to resume economic growth.

One element often linked with the South Korean economic system is the *chaebol*.[3] Chaebols are conglomerates of many companies clustered around one holding company. The companies usually hold shares in each other. Chaebols have a significant impact on the South Korean economy – the top four super-chaebols have sales which account for up to 40 percent of South Korea's GDP.

Government

The system of South Korean government is one of parliamentary democracy with legislative power exercised by a 299-member National Assembly elected for 4 years.

The basic principles of the South Korean Constitution include the sovereignty of the people, separation of powers, and the pursuit of peaceful and democratic unification of South and North Korea, the pursuit of international peace and cooperation, the rule of law and the responsibility of the state to promote welfare.

The current Constitution of the Republic of Korea is said to be a major step in the direction of full democratisation. Recent amendments include the curtailment of presidential powers, the strengthening of the power of the legislature, and further devices for the protection of human rights.

There are three branches of government: Executive, Legislature and Judiciary.

Executive

Executive power is exercised by an elected President, who sits at the apex of the Executive Branch, and serves a single five-year term. The President presides over a State Council of Ministers which is responsible for all important government policies.

The Prime Minister is appointed by the President and approved by the National Assembly. As the principal executive assistant to the President, the Prime Minister supervises the administrative ministries and deliberates major national policies.

Members of the State Council are appointed by the President upon recommendation by the Prime Minister. They lead and supervise their administrative ministries, deliberate major state affairs, act on behalf of the President and appear at the National Assembly and express their opinion.

In addition to the State Council, the President has several agencies under his direct control to formulate and carry out national policies: the Board of Audit and Inspection, the National Intelligence Service, and the Civil Service Commission.

Legislature

Legislative power is vested in the National Assembly, a unicameral legislature. The Assembly members are elected by popular vote for a four-year term.

The National Assembly is vested with a number of functions under the Constitution, the foremost of which is making laws. Other functions of the Assembly include approval of the national budget; matters related to foreign policy, declaration of war, the dispatch of armed forces abroad, or the stationing of foreign forces within the country; inspecting or investigating specific matters of state affairs; and impeachment.

The Assembly maintains 16 standing committees with the following functional designations: House Steering; Legislation and Judiciary; National Policy; Finance and Economy; Unification, Foreign Affairs and Trade; National Defense; Government Administration and Local Autonomy; Education; Science, Technology, Information and Telecommunication; Culture and Tourism; Agriculture, Forestry, Maritime Affairs and Fisheries; Commerce, Industry and Energy; Health and Welfare; Environment and Labour; Construction and Transportation; and Intelligence.

Judiciary

The judiciary of South Korea comprises 3 levels of courts: the Supreme Court, High Courts, and District Courts that include the specialised Family Court and Administrative Court. At their various levels, the courts exercise jurisdiction over civil, criminal, administrative, election, and other judicial matters, while also overseeing affairs related to the registration of real estate, census registers, deposits, and judicial clerks.

SOUTH KOREAN GOVERNMENT REFORM

During President Kim Dae-Jung's presidency, the South Korean government focused its efforts on sweeping reforms in the public sector. The administration set three goals for its public sector restructuring programme: "a smaller but efficient government", "a highly competitive government", and "a customer-oriented government".

In light of these goals, reform activities have been pushed forward. Since 1998, ministerial posts have been reduced from 43 to 31, and the government employee base has been shaved by 10 percent. More open hiring was introduced to attract qualified personnel into the public sector, and to boost professionalism and competitiveness. Various initiatives are underway to implement a more customer-oriented "one-stop service" in the civil service.

Kim Dae-Jung's government also worked hard to build the framework for a knowledge-based society. Advanced technologies were introduced and efforts were made in promoting areas of IT and other new industries.

In particular, the government has been very successful in establishing a strong infrastructure for e-Korea systems. By December 2000, the government had completed massive high-speed fibre-optic networks deployment across the nation, interconnecting all major communication zones. The result was a remarkable surge in the overall Internet population, with the number of users reaching 25.6 million people (June 2002) and 10 million households (October 2002).

This had a marked positive impact on the national economy. High-tech industries also helped create more than 150,000 new jobs and increase its exports to US$ 45.8 billion in 2002, or 28.2 percent of the nation's total exports.

The government also undertook numerous initiatives to start-up new sectors — such as movies and games, as the nation's next-generation strategic industries. Modernising the nation's traditional industries, as well as expanding e-Business systems among businesses and consumers were also among the initiatives in the government's IT thrust. In percentage terms,

South Korea now has one of the highest level of online stock transactions in the world.

Under its national project, completed in April 2001, the government built IT facilities to provide the nation's primary and secondary schools with Internet broadband services. As early as 2000, the government fully implementing ahead of schedule, the computer facilities at these schools, giving them high-speed computers and providing all teachers with personal computers. By the same year, the government completed teaching equipment modernisation programmes, providing advanced equipment to all of the nation's primary and secondary schools.

Narrowing the digital divide has been a high priority for the government. The nation now enjoys a high-speed Internet network which spans almost the entire nation and covering 98 percent of local districts.

ICT MATURITY INDICATORS

Teledensity

As recently as the early 1980s, South Korea's fixed-line penetration rate stood at a mere 7 percent. Today, South Korea's fixed-line telephone penetration rate stands at over 50 percent with 23 million subscribers. Mobile telephony has also become a basic telecommunications device for the general public. As of March 2002, the number of mobile subscribers reached 30.3 million (or 60 percent of its 46 million people), surpassing the fixed-line subscriber population.

South Korea has moved beyond the CDMA mobile communications technology by starting a third-generation mobile communication service (3G) in 2002. By mid-2002, there were over 7 million mobile Internet subscribers using 3G.

Internet penetration

A January 2001 Nielsen survey found South Koreans to be the most avid Internet surfers in the Asia-Pacific region. This assessment is based on the number of web sessions per month, time spent online, number of sites visited, and total page views. In fact, it was reported that South Koreans spend more time in front of computers than watching television.

By June 2002, the number of Internet users totalled 25.6 million (68 percent of the population) with 10 million households connected. The country was placed 7th in the ITU ranking of mobile Internet penetration, second only to Hong Kong in the region.[4]

Broadband usage

In early 2002, the South Korean government declared plans to make broadband Internet a universal service for all in the country. A new programme to ensure that all homes can receive broadband was announced in November 2002. This 13.3 trillion won (US$ 11 billion) initiative was funded by KT Corp, one of the country's largest telcos and Internet service providers, with assistance from government loans. The growth in South Korea's broadband subscribers has been impressive — from 4.1 million in 2000, to 10 million by 2002. The most popular broadband access method is ADSL, followed by cable modem. One likely reason that resulted in the quick and widespread adoption of broadband was attributed to the pricing strategy of broadband access. The country's broadband service providers offer either a flat subscription fee or a marginally higher price than narrow-band Internet access plans. The goal is to bring the number of broadband subscribers to 13.5 million by 2005.

THE ROAD TO INFORMATIZATION

The South Korean leadership has continually strived to steer the nation into the information age by investing in leading-edge ICT over the years. The advanced state of the South Korean ICT scene today is a result of the fast and relentless initiatives taken by the government and businesses to infuse a mindset of technology adoption into the society. This achievement is even more impressive when one realises that the country was engulfed by social unrest and anarchy till the late 1980s, when efforts towards industrialisation started to take hold. However, the South Koreans were determined not only to catch up in industrialisation, but in informatization as well. Over the past fifteen years, with strong government and industry commitment to nurture ICT and transform the nation into the digital age, South Korea is now regarded as one of the leading nations in telecommunications services. It has one of the world's highest penetration of mobile and Internet users.

Early Efforts

The Republic of Korea's efforts to enter the digital age can be traced back to 1987, when the National Basic Information System Plan (NBIS) was launched to promote the computer industry. The focus on the computerisation of the public sector provided the initial markets that helped to lay the foundations for the development of an IT industry. The government-led efforts were also expected to raise the awareness of the private sector in the application of IT in their business operations.

Covering the period up to 1996, the NBIS resulted in the establishment of a wide range of independent data networks via the 1st and 2nd Public Business Networking Projects. These networks supported services in the areas of People Identification, Land Registry, Vehicle Registry, Customs-Clearance Management, Fishing Boat Management, Post Office, Industry Property Rights Management, Meteorological Information, Office Supplies Catalogue Management, Economy and Trade, Agriculture Technique Management, Environment Protection, and Inland Revenue.

The telecommunications industry was deregulated in 1990 to further accelerate the development of the information industry. In 1994, the government set up a Korean Information Infrastructure (KII) Policy Committee to consolidate the various disparate networks and create a nationwide high-speed information infrastructure. Chaired by the Prime Minister and run by the Minister for Economic Planning with officials from twenty ministries, the committee focused on four key functions:

(1)   deliberate on and coordinate KII policies and assist in implementing the KII vision;
(2)   develop the KII master plan and manage the implementation funds;
(3)   evaluate technology to be deployed on the KII; and
(4)   review legislations and related regulations for relevance in the information society.

The approach was to use both government and private funding to build an advanced information network, and to develop core applications such as electronic governance services, remote medical care, and distance learning. To forge better collaboration between the public and private sector, a KII Task Force was also established with representation from both sectors as well as academia.

Informatization Promotion (1996–1998)

The enactment of the Framework on Informatization Promotion Act in 1995 led to the formulation of the Informatization Promotion master plan, the first government-led plan for the development on an information society. Released by the Ministry of Information and Communications in June 1996, the plan detailed the framework "to promote informatization in the country and bring information superhighway business to full scale". To support the plan, the Informatization Planning Office, Informatization Planning Committe and Informatization Promotion Fund were also established.

The master-plan outlined the projects that would result in the early establishment of the KII, lay the infrastructure for the information and communications industry to flourish and called for spending almost 70 billion won on networks and applications. Guidelines for these projects were encapsulated in the following ten priority tasks:

(1)   establish a small but efficient e-Government;
(2)   implement an educational information infrastructure to develop qualified human resources for the information society;
(3)   advance the nation's knowledge base by creating an environment for access to academic and research data;
(4)   reinforce corporate competitiveness through informatization promotion throughout industry;
(5)   increase the utilisation rate of social infrastructure through informatization;
(6)   support informatization in rural areas for balanced regional development;
(7)   advance medical services through the use of information technology;
(8)   incorporate informatization in environmental management to ensure pleasant living conditions;
(9)   build a national safety management data system to cope with disasters; and
(10)   secure advanced diplomatic and defense information systems.

In response to the Asian financial crisis in 1997, the plan became a pillar to support and facilitate structural readjustments of the public and private sectors for an early economic recovery and relief from the IMF programme.

Cyber Korea 21 (1999–2002)

Realising the economic significance of a vibrant ICT industry to help lift the country out of the crippling foreign exchange crisis, the government revised the existing Basic Plan for Expediting Information Age and established "Cyber Korea 21" in March 1999 as the second master-plan for Informatization Promotion.

Building on the momentum of the first master-plan, the new plan focused on creating the framework for a knowledge-based society, and to improve national competitiveness and the quality of life to the level of the advanced nations. It envisioned the knowledge-based industries expanding their share of the GDP to levels that would equal or exceeded the OECD levels. Relevant statutes and systems were also considered for streamlining to accommodate the speed at which the information industry was evolving.

The government also supported these industries by introducing knowledge-based management techniques to facilitate the adoption of new technology trends and to boost national productivity. The key undertakings of Cyber Korea 21 included:

- upgrading telecommunications networks, using fibre optics, cable modems, wireless local loop and satellite communications to make high-speed communication services available to all in the nation. This was estimated to cost US$ 8.67 billion with a significant portion coming from the private sector;
- enhancing the IT literacy of the entire population with a computer education program, ranging from basic literacy to advanced classes. The plan calls for connecting every South Korean school to the Internet;
- making revisions to intellectual property, taxation, encryption and legal frameworks to better support e-Commerce. This included the enactment of an electronic signature law to facilitate electronic transaction and document circulation;
- creating an electronic civil service and installing civil service kiosks in public places to permit citizen transactions in areas involving real estate, motor vehicles, and education. By 1999, South Korea had already placed on the Internet more than 4,500 civil service procedures;
- encouraging more extensive use of ICT in businesses to improve productivity and create high value-add industries in software and multimedia content;
- promoting international collaboration in the research and development of advanced information technology.

Representing the government's vision for the digital age, Cyber Korea 21 is expected to require an investment of US$ 23 billion over 4 years in the hope of creating one million new jobs and US$ 100 billion worth of new production.

By 2002, the knowledge-based industry was contributing a similar proportion to the GDP as that of other OECD member nations and South Korea was on its way to becoming one of the top ten information societies in the world.

e-Korea Vision 2006 (2002 onwards)

Based on the accomplishments of informatization projects so far, the government set out the third master-plan in April 2002 to meet the new challenges of the evolving information landscape, as well as to carry out continual reforms in the nation as a whole.

The e-Korea Vision 2006 master-plan has a strong focus on qualitative accomplishments such as increasing productivity through legal and institutional reforms. Moreover, beyond the quantitative expansion of the Internet, the plan also calls for innovations in business processes throughout society.

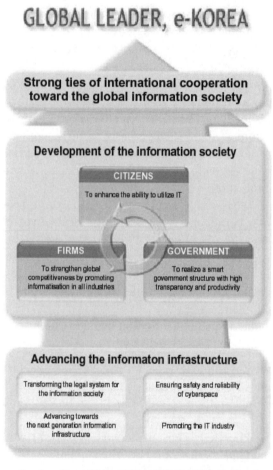

Source: e-Korea Vision 2006 — The Third Master Plan for
Informatization Promotion (2002–2006)

Figure 7-1: e-Korea 2006 Vision

To encourage the development of new industries, the government will focus on upgrading the information infrastructure, supporting venture start-ups, sponsoring research and development and human resource development. With the appropriate legal and institutional reforms, it hopes to provide a foundation on which the private sector could lead in the development of independent and creative industries, and produce goods and services of global standards. To further strengthen the nation's competitiveness in IT, the government will increase investments in core technologies and strategic services, which have the potential to produce significant added value in the future.

The plan also aims to achieve informatization of all industries and to raise the level of productivity to the level of G7 countries. The target is to have approximately 30 percent of total transactions in major industries and 25 percent for other industries to be online by 2006.

Relevant training programmes will be put in place to ensure the continuing development of a highly-skilled knowledge-based workforce that would lead the next generation of information industries. The government also intends to make available, one-stop electronic services for employment searches, employment insurance and job training to provide direct employment opportunities for all citizens.

The advanced broadband communications network is planned to reach every household by 2005. With minimum transmission speeds of 1 Mbps, high quality digital content delivered by digital television and the Internet will serve to enrich the life of every citizen. The infrastructure will also be used to promote lifelong learning among the population.

Other targeted areas for ICT application include enabling environmental improvements to conserve a clean and natural environment, deploying an Intelligent Transportation System to relieve traffic congestion and applying Geographic Information Systems to aid in optimising logistics planning.

The public administration will continue to enhance its online services to encompass the entire civil service by 2006. The government intends to establish a mobile government information infrastructure to make e-Services available from any location within the country. Citizens will also be encouraged to participate in the policymaking process via e-civic forums organised by the government.

E-GOVERNMENT — VISION & DIRECTION

The government of the Republic of Korea has had a long history of IT-based administration. The e-Government initiative had in fact, originated from an executive information computerisation project in 1978. Various Office Automation projects were carried out between 1978 and 1986, which computerised diverse areas such as statistics collection and analysis, civil service personnel records, payments, and pensions.

As part of the NBIS (1987–1996), five major networks were planned; the National Administrations Information System, the Financial Information System, the Education & Research Information System, the National Defense Information System, and the National Security Information System. Among these, the last two were managed by the military and intelligence agencies respectively for security reasons.

The National Administrations Information System involved the computerisation of internal operations of government agencies in support of service delivery to the public. It included subsystems for residents, vehicles, houses and land, employment, customs and clearance, and economic statistics. The government invested about US$ 200 million on these six subsystems, mainly to install computers in local as well as central government offices, and to develop networks and relevant software.

The first stage of the project (1987–1991) mainly involved developing the separate systems. The second stage (1992–1996) emphasised integrating systems so as to allow the sharing of information among government agencies, and to support new management systems for health care, postal services, marine transportation, intellectual property rights, weather information, government procurement, and fishing boats.

The Financial Information System began as a data communications network to link organisations in the banking sector, which included integrating existing networks that were already established by the larger institutions. The Confederation of Financial Institutions and representatives from the Financial Clearing House coordinated the planning and implementation for the system. The network was eventually extended to include other financial companies such as securities and insurance.

The Education and Research Information System involved the networking of universities, libraries, and research institutes. It also calls for equipping schools with computers and applying them to teaching and administration.

Between 1995 and 1998, various concept plans were developed and dialogue on e-Government vision and strategic directions carried out. In 1998, the Ministry of Government Administration and Home Affairs published the document "Toward 21st century electronic government" articulating the national vision and strategy for e-Government. The intent was to promote a knowledge-based government that delivers high quality service and achieves service excellence through IT-based innovation. The strategy was aimed at delivering a one-stop service platform for information distribution and government e-services available anytime-anywhere. The performance of these e-services is to match those of the private sector, and promote an open administration with greater transparency and customer-orientation. To achieve these objectives, six initiatives were set up to focus on:

(1)   electronic delivery of information and services;
(2)   reengineering business processes to support electronic document exchange;
(3)   information-sharing among agencies with adequate privacy protection;
(4)   establishing information technology standards and extensive networking;
(5)   promoting IT literacy in the civil service; and
(6)   modifying laws and statutes to accommodate electronic transactions.

The development of the e-Government programme was supervised by the National Computerisation Agency. With its role as a project champion, the agency functioned as an advisory organisation providing the government with appropriate recommendations on e-Government policies and technologies.

The Action Plan for e-Government

In 1999, the Ministry of Government Administration and Home Affairs and the Ministry of Information and Communication jointly published the "Comprehensive Plan for e-Government". As the blueprint for a more systematic framework for e-Government implementation, the plan incorporated a number of key actions:

* The development of a Comprehensive Information System that connects 21 data networks, the Electronic Ombudsman System, the Family Record On-line System and the Web-based Service Delivery Systems to provide "one-stop and non-stop" access to government services.
* The government will set up various information services to forge a more transparent and customer-focused public administration. These include the Government Information Locator Service, the Open Government Service, the Local Administration Information Bank Web and the Bulletin Board Service of Local Governments.
* An Integrated Call Centre and Integrated Kiosk System are planned so as to ensure consistency in e-services delivery across multiple and diverse delivery channels, and to provide access to all.

To further enhance public sector efficiency, the government will embark on continuous productivity improvements via:

- business process reengineering to streamline procedures;
- electronic document practices to ensure timely and accurate information exchange between public entities;
- government knowledge management to leverage information sources within the whole public administration to better service the population;
- integration of civil service management systems (personnel, payments etc) to allow for optimised operations;
- set up of a government intranet with appropriate data code, IT and resource standards, and a public key infrastructure (PKI) for secure government transactions; and
- providing all civil servants with IT literacy training and email access. A Cyber Training Centre will be created to facilitate the programme.

KEY E-GOVERNMENT INITIATIVES

The e-Government initiatives in South Korea can be broadly classified into three groups:

- innovation of government services to citizens and businesses;
- enhancement of administrative productivity; and
- establishing foundation for e-Government.

A Special Committee for e-Government was established in January 2001 to further accelerated the implementation of e-Government. The committee comprises of experts and professionals from the private sector, members of vice ministry level and academia. A report was submitted to the President in May 2001 putting forward 11 strategic initiatives to be completed by end 2002. The key e-Government initiatives were:

(1)   Innovation of government services to the public
- Government for Citizen (G4C) e-Service Centre
- Integrated Social Insurance Service
- Home Tax Service (HTS)
- Government-wide e-Procurement System (G2B)

(2)   Enhancement of administrative productivity
- National Finance Information System
- Integrated Administrative Information System of local governments

- National Education Information System
- Personnel Policy Support System
- Government e-Document Exchange

(3) Establishing foundation for e-Government
  - Government e-Signature and e-Seal System
  - Government Information System

True to the commitment, the proposed 11 strategic initiatives were completed by 14 November 2002.

Some of these strategic initiatives are now detailed.

G4C — The Single Window e-Government (www.egov.go.kr)

In November 2002, the South Korean administration launched the government e-services website (www.egov.go.kr), which offered access to almost 400 public services. These services included vehicle registrations, checking the status of income tax refunds, application for permits to sell property, etc.

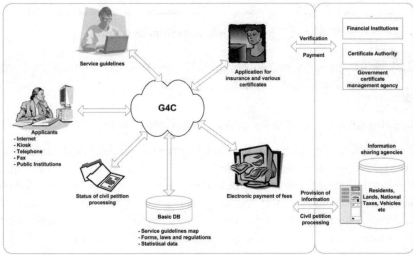

Adapted from Ministry of Information and Communication

Figure 7-2: Government for Citizen — A single window of e-Government

To minimise the need for repeated document submission, a system for information sharing among government agencies was put in place. The portal will gradually encompass the entire civil service with enhancements to allow citizen participation in government affairs.

Figure 7-3: Korean e-Government website

Besides the 400 services, information on up to 4,000 different types of civil matters are available through the portal.

Social Insurance Service Portal (www.4insure.or.kr)

Connecting four major social insurances (unemployment, health, industrial disaster and pension), the Social Insurance Service centralised the common administration of these insurances. The integration has provided citizens with a convenient one-stop service platform to register, revise, withdraw or declare information from the Internet or by visiting any one of the relevant insurance companies. Checking and payment of premium can also be conducted online.

Government-wide e-Procurement System (G2B) (www.g2b.go.kr)

The G2B system is an online e-Procurement system that covers the entire government procurement process (from tendering to payment). Businesses can access the system via a one-time registration to review and submit bids from all public sector tenders. It is expected that some 26,000 government organisations and about 96,000 businesses will use this system and save the public administration about 3.2 trillion won (US$ 2.65 billion) a year.

Figure 7-4: National e-Procurement Portal

Since going live in September 2002, some 13,000 government procurement tenders have been submitted, and a combined 1.85 trillion won (US$ 1.5 billion) worth of contracts signed.

Home Tax Service (HTS) (www.hometax.go.kr)

Managed by the National Tax Administration, HTS is an electronic filing system for tax returns. The service does away with the need to meet with tax officers and all required documents for personal and business filing are available on the HTS website. A myriad of tax-related civil services like business registration certification and tax return registration can also be conducted online.

Figure 7-5: Home Tax Service website

Besides filing, taxpayers can opt for notices to be sent via email or SMS. They can also pay their taxes and related payment like VAT and withholding taxes online.

National Finance Information System

The Ministry of Finance and Economy established an information system to automate the country's national finance administration. The National Finance Information System connects and integrates the financial systems of all agencies to facilitate the processing of government financial transactions — from budget compilation to settlement of accounts. This allows for a more timely and consistent analysis, and forecasting of financial performance, thus aiding the government in its economic decision-making.

The system also saves cost and enhances productivity through streamlining of the finance administration processes, and promotes financial transparency through the consolidation of multiple financial statements.

National Education Information System

All schools nationwide were enabled with Internet access by 2000. The next step was to integrate the administrative functions of schools with the education offices of the local government. This was accomplished via the National Education Information System which connected 16 offices of education with the elementary and secondary schools, and facilitated a standard administrative process to enhance the management of national education.

All educational administrative services like curriculum development, students' academic records and student counselling are handled by the system. This helps to relieve the administrative burden on the teachers who would then be able to focus on the quality of the teaching. Parents can also utilise the system for services such as requests for certificate of student registration and official transcripts (about 5 million certificates are issued annually) via the Internet, and consult with teachers regarding school-life and academic achievement from their home.

Personnel Policy Support System

The Personnel Policy Support System was developed to propagate a standardised process regarding the management (eg employment, promotion, benefits, education and welfare) of civil servants for all agencies. The government has since integrated seven areas of personnel administration into the system.

To establish such a centralised administration, a database of all civil servants was created to facilitate personnel and policy decisions and ensure a more transparent and equitable administration. It is estimated that over 90 percent of personnel-related paper documents will be converted to electronic form thus helping the administration to save millions annually.

Government Electronic Document Exchange

Although government departments and administrations have been exchanging electronic documents for some years, such exchanges tended to be limited to within the department or administration. The main constraint has been the different systems deployed by the agencies. At one point, there were some 20 different electronic document systems within the government.

By establishing standards for electronic document exchange, cross-departmental exchanges is enabled. With all government divisions participating in the pan-governmental document exchange, duplication is vastly reduced and the efficiency of the government is highly improved.

Government e-Signature and e-Seal System

To create a safer environment for electronic information exchange and e-Commerce, the government established the e-Signature and e-Seal services. These services involve the government issuing accredited digital certificates to enable e-Signature for transactions requiring high levels of security and validation.

The e-Seal functions as the electronic version of the present government seal or official seal. Government offices can utilise the e-Seal to make official, electronic documents that are secured with confirmation of the sender and receiver's identity. This helps to establish a more trustworthy document exchange between the various government agencies.

OTHER ENABLING INITIATIVES

The Government Superhighway Network

The Government Superhighway Network (GSN) connects three government complexes within a 160 km radius and almost all departments and administrations are fully connected with the GSN. All the provincial and municipal government networks have also been connected. Some small and remote governmental branches would soon be included by incorporating a satellite solution.

PCs for Public Servants

There are about 800,000 personnel in the civil service (excluding military personnel) of which 73,000 are office workers. Personal computers (PCs) are used by about 86 percent of the office workers. All of the PCs are connected and email is used by about 91 percent of the office workers.

Online Patent Filing

Since 1999, the Korean Intellectual Property Office has been providing online submission, registration, evaluation and notification of patent application via the KIPOnet service. By 2001, approximately 240,000 patent applications were processed online (representing 81 percent of total applications). There are about 3.3 million users and the evaluation timeframe has been reduced by 6 months (from an average of 22 to 28 months).

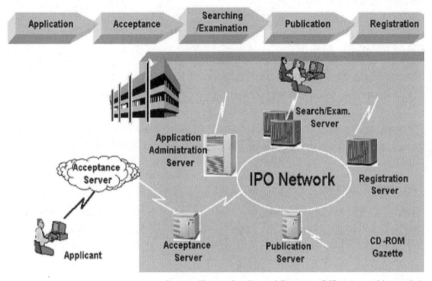

Source: Korean Intellectual Property Office (www.kipo.go.kr)

Figure 7-6: KIPOnet

National Knowledge Information Service

The resources of six major national libraries have been digitised and integrated into one online digital library. This has greatly improved the access to knowledge and narrowed the information divide between regions.

Legislative Changes

Since 1995, annual surveys have been conducted to assess the rules and regulations that should be revised to create a conducive environment for the information society. This resulted in the enactment and revision of 63 legal statutes on the basis of the annual reports from 1995 to 1997. In 1999, the Electronic Commerce Act and the Digital Signature Act were introduced to encourage the widespread use of IT by the private sector. The government will continue to review the relevant legal statutes required to support electronic procurement, the management of information resources, telemedicine and geographical information systems, amongst others.

The Ministry of Legislation and the Korean Supreme Court have also jointly developed the Comprehensive Legal Information Service System to facilitate access to legal resources and improve the citizens' legislative knowledge and awareness.

CHALLENGES AHEAD

The rapid pace with which the Republic of Korea has established its world-class status for telecommunications and information services has created a strong foundation for the nurturing of a leading e-society. Looking forward, the journey still has its share of social and technical challenges, which the South Korean administration is actively addressing.

The Digital Divide

This is a prevalent issue among nations faced with a highly diverse and dispersed population, and the need to ensure equitable development across the country. With a priority on managing the digital divide, the South Korean government has launched various initiatives to bridge the gaps between the "haves" and "have-nots'.

Computer education is now mandatory in all primary schools and the government will expand IT training opportunities to all levels of society, including young children and soldiers. The Ministry of Education (MOE) is promoting a programme aimed at boosting English language proficiency. English proficiency is seen as a basic requirement towards achieving IT literacy. Soldiers are required by the Ministry of Defense (MOD) to sit for web search specialist certification, before being discharged from the service.

To address those outside of the main cities and who are more likely to be left out of the information age, the Ministry of Information and Communication is expanding the high-speed Internet network to about 200 towns. Free public access to personal computers will also be more readily available via public libraries, social welfare centres and most post offices. A programme that gives free PCs and five years of free Internet access service to about 50,000 children in the lower income group is also being studied.

Government Control vs Industry Self-Regulation

Though many have acknowledged the government's role in developing South Korea into one of the most wired nations in the world, some have expressed concern over government tendency to control the Internet in the traditional Korean way. These advocates see the need for more private-sector control in order to create a more sustainable information industry. Reports that the deregulation of the telecommunications sector has made slow progress have also surfaced. These reports claimed that policies and rules in many areas such as interconnection, access, and pricing remain largely unresolved. Some have also criticised that the South Korean Communication Commission (the national equivalent of the US FCC) is not an independent body but exists as part of the government. On a more positive note, South Korea is a signatory to the WTO Agreement on Basic Telecommunications and is thus moving toward more liberalisation and openness in telecommunications.

Public Acceptance

The government's ambitious plans to provide a fully electronic administrative service, has yet to garner overwhelming response from the public. In late September 2002, a hearing at the Science, Technology, Information and Telecommunications committee reported that more than 60 percent of the 143 e-services available then, have never been used. Very low utilisation was also recorded for various other e-services. The advent of the G4C initiative and the continuing streamlining and improvement of processes is anticipated to deliver more customer-oriented e-services which would help to drive more widespread adoption.

Identity Crisis

Since November 2002, the G4C portal has made it relatively convenient for citizens to access e-Government services with the use of a single ID. However, these services are limited in scope due to the disparate identity verification process required for more sensitive tasks. It is estimated that up to 15 different IDs and security numbers are needed to fully exploit the various online services. The government has been exploring the deployment of a "single sign-on" solution to permit single ID access to all e-Services. This issue is not unique to South Korea and in fact, poses one of the greater challenges for aspiring e-Government implementers.

IN CONCLUSION

South Korea's advanced e-Government services have earned many positive reviews from the United Nations in June 2002, whose "Benchmark Report on e-Government" categorised South Korea as one the most advanced in the quality of e-Government services. In September of the same year, Brown University in the United States gave similarly high marks, pronouncing South Korea as second best among nations in its level of e-Government services.

Amidst all the accolades and acknowledgements, the government is not resting on its laurels and is continuing to strengthen the nations' transition to a fully knowledge-based economy. "The e-Government revolution has just begun," said the head of the Special Commission for Electronic Government, Ahn Moon-Seok. "The real agenda lies in individuals and businesses interacting with the government over the Internet, to raise the transparency and competitiveness of society as a whole."

Informatization and the Inter-Korean Relationship

While the Republic of Korea has surged ahead of the global pack to be recognised as a leader in the exploitation of ICT and e-Governance, its northern brethren has not been quite as progressive. The North is not completely immune to the global technological trends. Limited and controlled Internet access has become more readily available with communication reforms starting to take place. As the 2 countries pursue their sometimes conflicting national agendas, it will be interesting to observe what role technology will play in unifying the Korean peninsular.

Some studies have called for a more proactive approach by the South to utilise communications technology to facilitate more open and transparent dealings between the two nations. These speculate that the opening of non-government sectors would provide the catalyst for cooperation and exchanges between private enterprises, leading to more flexible and moderate policies. South Korea lawmakers recently submitted a bill seeking to make non-political interaction with the North through the Internet more open. Currently, a permit from the Unification Ministry is required before any contact can be made. Information technology could very well have a profound impact in establishing the momentum towards unification.

In the short span of 20 years, the Republic of Korea has elevated itself from a war-torn county to become a major global economic force. The growth of the nation has been widely attributed to the government resolve to develop technology as a key pillar of the economy. The impressive achievements in telecommunications and technology exploitation have resulted in a nation that is highly regarded as role model for creating the knowledge-based economy of the 21st Century. As technology progresses unabated and bandwidth increases, South Korea is fast becoming "a shrimp with whale-like proportions".

Endnotes

1   Rhee Syng-Man (1948–60), Yun Bo-Seon (1960–62), Park Chung-Hee (1963–79), Choi Kyu-Hah (1979–80) and Chun Doo-Hwan (1980–1988).

2   The other Asian Tigers being Singapore, Taiwan and Hong Kong.

3   Chaebols first arose in South Korea in the 1920s and 1930s when the country was under Japanese rule. Japan planned Korea's economic development to feed its own markets and set up a series of companies which were privately-owned and run, but strictly controlled by the cuntral government — through credit, the control of trading licenses, and other measures. But paradoxically, the Koreans developed a similar system for themselves once they won independence.

4   "Internet for a Mobile Generation", International Telecommunications Union, September 2002.

References

1   *"Government for Citizen (G4C) Project"*, National Computerisation Agency.

2   *"South Korea claims net 'super' status"* BBC News (World Edition), 6 November 2002.

3   *"Broadband A Hit In North Asia"*, reported on Internetnews.com, 28 March 2002.

4   Suh Sam-Young, President of National Computerisation Agency, *"Korea's e-Government Finally at Hand"*, *The Korea Times*, 12 November 2002.

5   *"Korean Electronic Government: The Action Plan for Electronic Government"*, International Council for Information Technology in Government Administration, 34th Conference on Electronic Government in the Information Society, September 2000.

6   Yang Seung-Taik, Minister of Information & Communicsation, Republic of Korea, paper on *"Digital Divide & Cyber Korea 21 Initiative"*, June 2002.

7   Hwang Eui-Hwan, Director, Technology Standards Division, *"Information Technology and Economic Development"*, Ministry of Information and Communication, 27 April 1999.

8   *"Changing Korea with e-Government"*, Ministry of Information and

Communication and National Computerisation Agency, 2003.

9   *"Launch of the Integrated Government e-Procurement (G2B) Services"*, NCA IT e-Newletter, National Computerisation Agency, November 2002.

10   *"Completion of e-Government Frame by 2002 through Promoting Key e-Government Projects"*, UNESCO, Observatory on the Information Society, 2002.

11   *"Public acceptance and user of national e-Services"*, 17 September 2002.

12   Woo Byeong-Hyeon, *"Seoul Launches into 'e-Gov'"*, Digital Chosun, November 2002.

13   Kang Weon-Sik, *"Informatization and Inter-Korean Relationship"*, The Institute of East Asian Studies, East Asian Review, Spring 2001.

14   *"Lawmakers Submit Bill for Opening of Inter-Korean Internet Contact"*, *The Korea Times*, May 2003.

Useful Websites

www.nca.go.kr	Official website of the National Computerisation Agency, Republic of Korea
www.cwd.go.kr/english/	Website of Office of the President (Cheong Wa Dae), Republic of Korea
english.metro.seoul.kr	Seoul Metropolitan government webpages
www.korea.net	Official website of the Korean Government.
www.mic.go.kr	Official website of the Ministry of Information and Communications, Republic of Korea
www.mogaha.go.kr	Official website of the Ministry of Government Administration and Home Affairs, Republic of Korea
www.csc.go.kr	Official website of the Civil Service Commission, Republic of Korea

CHAPTER 8

Malaysia: Advancing Public Administration into the Information Age

James SL Yong

▲ ▼ ▲ ▼ ▲ ▼ ▲ ▼

In the information age we are living in, the Malaysian society must be information rich. It can be no accident that there is today no wealthy, developed country that is information-poor, and no information-rich country that is poor and underdeveloped.

Dr Mahathir Mohamad, Malaysian Prime Minister

▲ ▼ ▲ ▼ ▲ ▼ ▲ ▼

Ahmad Samedi looked up as his mobile phone buzzed. Another SMS message had been received. He took a look at it and realised that a tender announcement alert had just been issued — this time by the Ministry of Energy, Communications and Multimedia.

"This must be the one we've been waiting for" Ahmad remarked to his business partner Roslan. Both men had been actively servicing office equipment contracts for various government departments for almost ten years, and business had grown.

Ahmad went to the e-Perolehan system using his web browser, keyed in an identity code and inserted his smart card into the attached card reader. Soon he was busy reading through a tender document and discussing various points with Roslan. Both partners were pleased as they felt they were be able to supply the equipment to meet the needs detailed in the tender specification. Their company had provided equipment to the Ministry several times before and they were confident they knew what it took to secure this deal.

Ahmad began preparing a response to the tender, while Roslan started making some calls to his suppliers.

e-Perolehan is Malaysia's new electronic procurement system for Government-to-Business (G-to-B) exchanges on which suppliers maintain product and pricing information for access by government buyers. Around 500 government procurement centres around the capital Kuala Lumpur were e-Perolehan enabled by the end of 2002. Suppliers who register with e-Perolehan can gain access to a variety of benefits including putting up their product catalogues online, processing purchase orders and receiving payment from government agencies via the Internet and submitting quotations.

BACKGROUND

History[1, 2]

The Malays, the largest ethnic group in Malaysia today, have inhabited the area for at least 2,500 years. They are the result of migration and intermingling with people from outside the region, as well as from groups within the Southeast Asian archipelago.

Around the first century BC, strong trading links were established with China and India, which had a major impact on the culture, language and social customs of the country. Large-scale immigration of Chinese and the Indians, the two other key racial groups, came mainly in the 19th and 20th Centuries.

Between the 6th and 13th Centuries, the Malay Peninsula came under the loose control of various empires, including the Sumatran-based (Buddhist) Srivijaya and the Java-based (Hindu) Majapahit. The spread of Islam, introduced by Arab and Indian traders, brought the Hindu-Buddhist era to an end by the 13th Century. The Melaka Sultanate was founded in the early 15th Century and the increase in the Spice Trade turned Melaka into one of Southeast Asia's leading ports.

Melaka's wealth soon attracted European powers. In 1511, the Portuguese captured Melaka and established a number of fortified bases in the region. The ruler of the Melaka Sultanate and his successors fled southwards to Johor. They later forged alliances with the Dutch, who arrived in the region at the end of the century and together, they expelled the Portuguese in 1641. The Dutch then colonised Melaka and over the next century and a half, steadily expanded throughout the region until the Dutch East Indies became the heart of a prosperous colonial trading operation.

After the defeat of the Netherlands by France in 1795, the Dutch chose to pass control of some of their Asian bases and resources to the British in a series of exchanges rather than hand them over to the French. The British already had a thriving port in Penang in 1786 and took over Melaka in 1795. Over the course of the 19th Century, the British gradually took control of the peninsula using economic pressure rather than outright military force. Local rulers were permitted substantial autonomy so long as they posed no threat to British interests. After World War II, the states of Sarawak and Sabah, on the island of Borneo, formally came under British control.

The Federated Malay States were created as an entity in 1895, and remained under British colonial control until the Japanese invasion during World War II. After the defeat of Japan in 1945, the 11 states were once again incorporated as British Protectorates and in 1948 became the Federation of Malaya. Communist guerrillas, who fought the Japanese throughout the occupation, began an armed struggle against British rule in 1948 and Malaya achieved independence in 1957. Sabah, Sarawak and Singapore combined with Malaya to establish Malaysia in 1963, but two years later Singapore left the confederation.

The United Malays National Organisation (UMNO) has been the key political force, with Prime Minister Dr Mahathir Mohamad at the helm since 1981.

Geography and Economy

The Federation of Malaysia, located in Southeast Asia, is geographically divided into two parts — West and East Malaysia — separated by 400 miles (650 km) of the South China Sea. The country has a total area of about 333,000 sq km, and is home to a multi-racial population of 23 million (58 percent Malays and native peoples, 27 percent Chinese, 8 percent Indian). The capital city is Kuala Lumpur.

GDP is approximately US$ 90 billion, and grew by an average of 7 percent per annum over the 1990s. Although more than 50 percent of the GDP is now contributed by the services industry, there is still a large dependence on manufacturing (especially in electrical and electronic products, textiles and rubber-based products). Agricultural and mining activities are still widespread, with Malaysia being one of the world's largest exporters of rubber, palm oil, tropical timber, pepper and tin.

The combination of political stability, foreign investment and steady growth, had earned Malaysia global acclaim as an "economic miracle", until the Asian financial crisis of 1997 which severely affected many Southeast Asian economies. During the crisis, the Kuala Lumpur stock exchange plunged, Malaysia rejected IMF-recommended remedies and imposed strict financial and currency controls. The Ringgit was pegged at a fixed exchange rate to the US dollar. By 2000, however, Malaysia had shown signs of recovery.

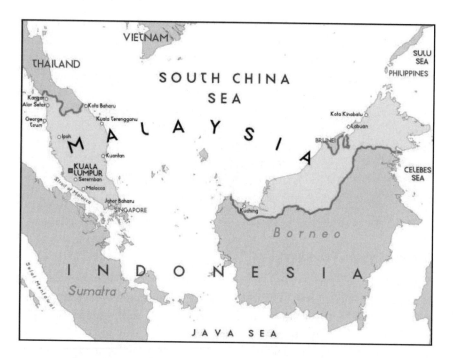

Government

Malaysia's government is based on the concept of a parliamentary constitutional monarchy with a Federal Government structure. The constitution, with its parliamentary and cabinet system, is modeled on the British Westminster structure. Malaysia has a unique system of constitutional monarchy which gives each of nine Sultans a chance to be King (or *Yang di-Pertuan Agong*)[3] for five years in rotation. The King is head of state and acts on the advice of the Cabinet and the Prime Minister.

The government, headed by the Prime Minister and his cabinet, is an alliance of parties representing different racial groups. The Prime Minister's Department oversees and coordinates the policies of the Government and their implementation.

There are three main components of Government — Executive, Legislative and Judiciary. The Executive is the cabinet of ministers, headed by the Prime Minister. The Legislative council is made up of the Dewan Negara (Senate or upper house) and the Dewan Rakyat (House of

Representatives). The Judiciary comprises the Superior Courts and the Subordinate Courts, with the Federal Court of Malaysia being the highest court.

There are 25 government ministries: Agriculture, Culture Arts & Tourism, Defense, Domestic Trade & Consumer Affairs, Education, Energy Communications & Multimedia, Entrepreneur Development, Finance, Foreign Affairs, Health, Home Affairs, Housing & Local Government, Human Resource, Information, International Trade & Industry, Land & Cooperative Development, National Unity & Social Development, Primary Industries, Prime Minister's Department, Rural Development, Science Technology & Environment, Transport, Works, Women & Family Development and Youth & Sports.

There are state governments in each of the 13 states. Each state has its own constitution, a council of state or cabinet with executive authority, and a legislature that deals with state matters. Three federal territories exist: Kuala Lumpur, Labuan and Putrajaya.

The Barisan Nasional (National Front) coalition has been the dominant political entity in power. A rocky political situation ensued in 1998 when the deputy Prime Minister was sacked and arrested, drawing some national and international outcry. Nevertheless, Barisan Nasional won the elections of 1999. By the beginning of the 21st Century, the social upheavals had faded to a distant rumble and the Malaysian economy was edging upwards again.

Dr Mahathir's political control remains firm, but at the end of 2002, he announced that he would step down in October 2003, after having led the country for 22 years. Dato' Seri Abdullah bin Ahmad Badawi is expected to take over.

ICT MATURITY INDICATORS

In terms of teledensity,[4] fixed line telephones reach 22/100 of the population, while the corresponding figure for mobile phones is around 30/100. For a large and geographically diverse country like Malaysia, an average teledensity index belies the significant differences in the situation between urban and rural population. For instance, taking the fixed line figure of 22/100, it is actually 32/100 in urban locations and a mere 11/100 in rural areas. What is also significant is that the growth (CAGR, 1999–2001) of fixed lines is 15 percent whereas mobile is increasing at 40 percent.

By 2001, there was on average 13 computers per 100 persons.[5] According to official sources, the number of Internet subscribers stood around 2 million by mid 2001. However, much of the Internet usage in Malaysia is through corporate organisations and public access points (eg cybercafes). PIKOM, the Association of Computer and Multimedia Industry of Malaysia, estimated that there were 4.8 million users at mid 2001, which translates to about 20 percent of the population. This was triple the number of Internet users recorded in 1998. Market watchers expect the Internet user population to exceed 10 million by end 2003.

Despite strong governmental emphasis on multimedia and the MSC, broadband usage levels had been relatively low up to 2002. Apart from the business sector, few homes had broadband access by end 2000. This was probably because of the limited cable TV market in Malaysia and also slow ADSL rollout. Wireless broadband access approaches, such as, Direct-to-Home satellite and Fixed Wireless Access are being explored. However, by the end of 2002, there were indications that broadband usage in Malaysia was beginning to rise more sharply from the low base of the previous years. Projections by market watchers indicate that about 96,000 subscribers will access the Internet via broadband in 2003, up nearly four-fold from 2002.[6]

THE NATIONAL ICT PROGRAMME

In Malaysia, the shift towards a knowledge-based economy (frequently referred to as KBE in Malaysian literature) started to gain momentum from the mid 1990s. Rising wages coupled with plateauing productivity had somewhat eroded Malaysia's position as a low-cost production base. This concern spurred on the nation's leadership in their search for new drivers of growth, one being the move away from labour-intensive towards knowledge-intensive industries. Furthermore, Malaysia recognised that low wages did not necessarily translate to competitiveness. To achieve sustainable economic growth, it was imperative for Malaysians to embrace the knowledge-based economy. The nation needed to harness the innovative potential of its people by leveraging on an educated and skilled workforce, and investing in the right infrastructure, particularly in the area of ICT.

The Multimedia Super Corridor

It was against this backdrop that the Multimedia Super Corridor (MSC) was launched in 1996, conceived as a key engine of growth and Malaysia's principal vehicle to leapfrog from the industrial to the information age. While computerisation programmes in both the public and private sectors had been ongoing for several decades, it was with the MSC that Malaysia caught the attention of the world with this unique initiative to create an entire "cyber-region" and a base for a world-class technology, multimedia and content industry.

The idea of the MSC has been directly attributed to Prime Minister Dr Mahathir Mohamad and is rooted in the "**Vision 2020**"[7] master-plan. This paper expressed the vision for Malaysia to be a "fully developed, industrialised and knowledge rich country by 2020" but argued that Malaysia must go its own way in leveraging on the technology, while preserving its cultural identity and managing its ethnic and racial challenges.[8]

The MSC is located along a greenfield "corridor" south of the nation's capital Kuala Lumpur. It is some 50 km long by 15 km wide, and stretches from the Kuala Lumpur City Centre (KLCC, better known as the world's tallest building, the Petronas Twin Towers) down south to the Kuala Lumpur International Airport (KLIA). Located within this Corridor are two new smart cities: **PutraJaya**, the new seat of the Malaysian Government and administrative capital of Malaysia and **CyberJaya**, the favoured site for ICT companies investing in the country. A new multimedia university was set up at CyberJaya to help provide a sustainable supply of skilled workers.

The MSC has the latest facilities and infrastructure such as fibre-optic networks, world-class infrastructure including a 2.5–10 Gbps multimedia network. In addition, the MSC creates a holistic environment for professional and personal lifestyles, with new highways, high quality homes, schools, shopping malls and business and recreational areas.

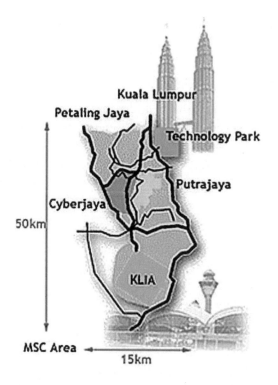

Figure 8-1: The Multimedia Super Corridor (MSC)

The creation of the MSC was accompanied by special Cyberlaws, policies and practices tailored to enable smart partners to achieve maximum benefits from technology and multimedia.

To attract investors, the Malaysian Government offers high-technology companies, both local and foreign, incentives to locate in the Corridor. Approved companies, which are granted "**MSC Status**", will enjoy tax-free status for up to ten years, tax exemptions, relaxed immigration rules for expatriates, and other economic perks. By mid-2002, it was reported that more than 700 companies had been granted MSC status.

To allay concerns of some investors, the Malaysian government created a **Bill of Guarantees** to apply within the Corridor, providing for strong intellectual property protection, freedom from Internet censorship, freedom of ownership, competitive financial incentives, and competitive telecom tariff. The government also developed a more comprehensive national framework for electronic commerce and among the laws drafted or already passed, are those dealing with digital signatures, electronic contracts, computer crime, data protection, and electronic government.

In conjunction with the creation of the MSC, a group of globally renown ICT experts were invited to be members of an **International Advisory Panel (IAP)**. This panel included luminaries such as Gates of Microsoft, Gerstner of IBM, McNealy of Sun Microsystems, Miyawaki of NTT, Murthy of Infosys, Shih of Acer, Bonfield from BT and management guru Ohmae. The IAP held annual meetings chaired by the Malaysian Prime Minister. The IAP was consulted on a variety of issues ranging from their views on the progress of the MSC, new and emerging Internet technologies, global ICT trends, market potential for multimedia applications, venture capital, intellectual property rights, and future challenges. In short, the IAP was a valuable resource to government leaders and planners in charting and fine-tuning the directions of the MSC.

Quick Quotes

Ms Ng Wan Peng is a Senior Manager at the Multimedia Development Corporation in Cyberjaya. She shared some of the thinking that led to the creation of the MSC project.

"In the mid 1990's when our national leaders sought to address a number of critical issues facing Malaysia, they looked at three broad areas, namely: the economic factor, the social factor and the global factor.

(The Economic Factor)   How do we sustain our economic growth towards 2020? Before the economic downturn in 1997, Malaysia had been showing impressive growth every year, but this slowed after 1997 — as has been the case for most Asian countries. It was recognised that Malaysia was losing its comparative advantage in some of its traditional economic sectors. It is therefore important to drive the economy towards higher productivity through technology and high value-added economic activities. We saw the need for adoption and application of ICT to enhance competitiveness of the manufacturing, banking, finance, tourism and service sectors.

(The Social Factor)   How do we ensure equitable and efficient access to public goods, services and information? We know that as a country develops, some people will get more and some people may get left behind. We wanted to find a way to bridge the gap and ensure no one loses out. Of course it can never be 100 percent achieved — but we should try. We should do our best to bridge any Digital Divide.

(The Global Factor)   How do we deal effectively with the forces of globalisation and the challenges of the knowledge age? Malaysia was severely hit by the effects of globalisation in 1997, and it left a deep impression on us that we needed to find effective ways of countering such forces in the future."

Source: Interview, July 2002

The Flagship Applications[9, 10]

The MSC plan identified seven "Flagship Applications" for priority development. These applications are divided into two categories — "multimedia development" (which offer concrete business opportunities to facilitate the MSC's development) and "multimedia environment" (which provides an optimal environment that supports companies entering into the MSC). This is illustrated in Figure 8-2.

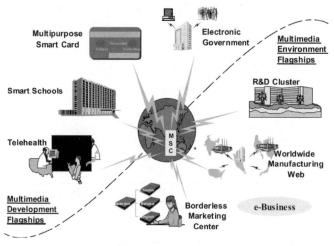

Figure 8-2: MSC Flagship Applications

Electronic Government

The objective is to transform the workings of government by improving the way it operates internally and how it provides services to the public. The lead agency is the Malaysian Administrative Modernisation and Management Planning Unit (MAMPU).

Multi-Purpose Card

Malaysia launched the world's first national smartcard to improve the ease of transacting with government agencies and private sector companies. The Multi-Purpose Card or MPC contains the owner's identity code and electronic signature in a plastic card with an embedded microprocessor chip. It allows a multitude of transactions such as personal identification, driving licence, passport information, health application, as well as cash withdrawal and payment. The government MPC, known as *MyKad*, was launched in early 2002. The Central Bank of Malaysia is the lead agency for the deployment of this flagship.

Smart Schools

In order to nurture a technologically literate and thinking workforce that will be critical to transform Malaysia into a knowledge-based economy, the Smart Schools flagship application was implemented to totally revamp teaching and learning practices and processes, while addressing all aspects of school management. The lead agency is the Ministry of Education.

Telehealth

The goal of this flagship application is to promote Malaysia as a regional centre for telemedicine. This will be achieved by providing greater access to, and increased knowledge on, healthcare. The flagship also encourages individuals to manage their own personal health, and integrates information to allow smooth flow of products and services throughout the healthcare system. Rural clinics will be linked with medical experts in the city and renowned clinics worldwide using new tele-instruments for remote diagnosis. The lead agency is the Ministry of Health.

R&D Cluster

It has long been recognised that R&D is a critical pillar in support of Malaysia's goal to be a developed nation. This flagship was developed to help ensure that the MSC becomes an attractive location for companies seeking to develop next generation multimedia technologies and innovations. It tries to foster collaborative efforts among leading R&D firms, local universities and public research institutions, as well as supporting the growth of Small and Medium-sized Enterprises or SMEs. The lead agency is the Ministry of Science, Technology and the Environment.

The next two flagships were individually introduced but because of their complementary nature, were later combined into what was called the **"e-Business Cluster"**.

Worldwide Manufacturing Web

This flagship strives to position Malaysia as a preferred location for manufacturing firms to locate their hubs to support and control their manufacturing operations in the region more efficiently and cost-effectively. The objective is to develop a conducive environment for high value-added manufacturing and related services, ie R&D, design, engineering, logistics support, manufacturing control, procurement and distribution. The lead agency is the Ministry of International Trade and Industry.

Borderless Marketing Centre

This flagship leverages on technology to enable businesses to transcend traditional barriers of time, space or form to better serve their customers. It is an initiative to spearhead the growth of multimedia based service industries in the MSC, with emphasis on telemarketing, online information services, electronic commerce and digital broadcasting. The lead agency is the Multimedia Development Corporation (MDC).

An eighth flagship of the MSC was added at the end of 2001. The purpose of the **Technopreneur Development** flagship was to drive entrepreneurship in ICT and other high technology arenas. One growth area identified is biotechnology. Bio Valley, a dedicated zone within the MSC for biotech companies, has recently been launched. It is expected that activities in this area will spawn and nurture more SMEs in Malaysia. The lead agency is MDC.

The MSC master-plan envisions a 20-year time-frame for the full implementation and execution of the entire programme. This time frame is broadly divided into three phases, as shown below:

Phase I (1996–2002) Successfully create the MSC	• One super corridor • Core of 50 world-class companies • Launch 7 flagship applications	• Introduce leading framework of cyberlaws • CyberJaya an PutraJaya as intelligent cities
Phase II (2003–2009) Link MSC to other cybercities in Malaysia and wordwide	• Create a web of corridors • 250 world-class companies • Set global standards in flagship applications	• Harmonised global framework of cyberlaws • 4 intelligent cities linked to other global cybercities
Phase III (2010–2020) Transform Malaysia into a knowledge society	• All across Malaysia • All across Malaysia • 500 world-class companies • Global test-bed for new multimedia applications	• International CyberCourt of Justice in the MSC • 12 intelligent cities linked to global information highway

Encouraging signs of progress include the large number of firms that have applied for MSC status. A target of 750 MSC status companies by the end of 2003 had initially been set. Before the end of 2002, there were already 745 MSC status companies already approved, with another 100 companies in the pipeline. Of this total figure, more than 600 of these companies are already operational and located at the MSC, while the remaining are still at the gestational stage. European companies made up the largest number of investors, followed by those from the USA and Japan.[11]

The MSC is a symbol of high-tech entrepreneurial activity, a risk taking culture, knowledge sharing and technology transfer among the high-tech communities. It has made some headway attracting international technology companies such as Sun Microsystems, Microsoft and Ericsson. Other firms like DHL, HSBC and Shell have also established centres in the MSC.

The Government has invested heavily in world-class infrastructure which contains a high-speed link (10Gbps network) connecting the MSC to Japan, ASEAN, the US and Europe. It is capable of supporting extensive public administration, education and business applications. The Government is aiming to continue the establishment of basic telecommunications infrastructure, with plans for 250 Internet access points, 250 mobile phones and 500 fixed lines for every 1,000 people within the next 5 years.

The Cyberlaws

In parallel with the development of the physical ICT infrastructure, the Malaysian government also focused on a set of legislation which was seen to be essential to curb abuses of the new digital environment. These cyberlaws addressed such issues as: information security, integrity and confidentiality, legal recognition of online transactions, and protection of intellectual property.

As of end 2002, five cyberlaws had been enacted, namely:

(1) Communications and Multimedia Act 1998 — which provides the policy and regulatory framework for convergence of the telecommunications, broadcasting and computer industries.

(2) Digital Signature Act 1997 — regulates the legal recognition and authentication of the originator of electronic documents.

(3) Computer Crimes Act 1997 — imposes criminal penalties on activities such as computer related crimes, hacking, cracking, planting of viruses and other offences related to misuse of computers.

(4)   Copyright (Amendment) Act 1997 — provides protection for creators of copyrighted works such as music, books, films, educational content, entertainment products and information, and other creative efforts.

(5)   Telemedicine Act 1997 — enables and regulates the practice of medicine through the multimedia and communications channels in Malaysia.

Proposed legislation being drafted include a Private Data Protection Legislation Bill, which will provide assurance of proper management in the collection, processing and utilisation of all personal data transmitted online, an Electronic Transaction Bill and an Electronic Government Activities Bill.

KEY ORGANISATIONAL STRUCTURES

The following are some of the important organisations involved in spearheading the ICT programmes in Malaysia.

e-Government Steering Committee (EGSC)

This is the highest level of the e-Government implementation structure. The Steering Committee is chaired by the Chief Secretary to the Government. Members of the EGSC include representatives from various government agencies, such as the Economic Planning Unit, Implementation Coordination Unit, INTAN, Treasury, Ministry of Energy, Communications and Multimedia, MAMPU, Office of the Auditor-General, Public Service Division and MDC. MAMPU acts as the Secretariat to the EGSC.

The key roles of the EGSC are to provide the policy direction and approve the e-Government programmes and activities. In addition, the committee also monitors the implementation progress of each pilot project under the responsibility of the lead agencies.

The Multimedia Development Corporation (MDC)

Established in 1996, the MDC leads the development and implementation of the Multimedia Super Corridor. A government-backed organisation, it acts as champion and international promoter of the MSC. Its stated mission is "to shape a world-leading environment, attract and nurture leading-edge and world-class companies, facilitate knowledge transfer and wealth creation, and build a value-based, highly effective institution."

MDC acts as a "one-stop shop" facilitating applications from companies to re-locate to the MSC. It shapes MSC-specific laws, policies and practices by advising the Malaysian government and standardises MSC's information infrastructure and urban development.

In facilitating the establishment of company operations within the MSC, the MDC serves as champion, facilitator and partner. As a performance-oriented, client-focused agency, it endeavors to cut through bureaucratic red tape to provide timely information and good advice, expedite permit and license approvals, and introduce companies to potential local partners and financiers.

One division of the MDC is the MSC Venture Corporation, created to provide venture capital to innovative and emerging ICT enterprises and multimedia companies at the start-up, growth and pre-IPO stages.

Malaysian Administrative Modernisation and Management Planning Unit (MAMPU)

MAMPU was set up in 1977 as an agency within the Prime Minister's Department. It was entrusted with the task of introducing administrative reforms in the public sector to upgrade the quality, efficiency and effectiveness of the Malaysian public service in accordance with national goals.

MAMPU advises the Government in the area of organisational management and acts as consultant to various agencies for organisational development. It also provides technical and management expertise as the central agency for ICT development and office automation in the public sector.

MAMPU has been intimately involved in the implementation of two key programmes, namely, the ISO 9000 quality standard and the Electronic Government flagship of the MSC project.

THE ELECTRONIC GOVERNMENT FLAGSHIP

Electronic Government or e-Government is one of the flagship applications of the MSC project. Broadly the goal is to improve both how the government operates internally and how it delivers services to the people of Malaysia. It seeks to improve the convenience, accessibility and quality of interactions with citizens and businesses; simultaneously, it aims to improve information flows and processes within government to enhance the speed and quality of policy development, coordination and enforcement.

The Malaysian vision of Electronic Government is "for government, businesses and citizens to work together for the benefit of the country and all its citizens". It is envisaged that the vision will be realised when, through the use of ICT and multimedia, government agencies become more efficient and effective in their delivery of public services and consequently more responsive to the needs of the citizens.

The e-Government vision is directly applicable in three broad areas:

(1) **Public/Business to Government**
   • Service Access (ie one-stop, single point of contact, multiple delivery channels, multilingual)
   • Service Quality (ie high quality, reliability, security/privacy, accountability)
   • Service Delivery (ie efficiency/quick turnaround time, cost-effective/productive)

(2) **Intra-Agency**
   • Improved process
   • Enhanced profile
   • People development

(3) **Inter-Agency**
   • Enhance the capability of government machinery in engineering the success of the e-Government initiatives
   • Provide government agencies and the general public access to information on the progress of the e-Government initiatives
   • Provide a model of best practices in interactive multimedia information, collection and dissemination
   • Utilise IT to enhance processes in the public sector.

In a speech by the Minister of Energy, Communications and Multimedia in 1998, the objectives for e-Government in Malaysia were aptly summarised:

• introducing greater customer orientation in the delivery of services;
• effecting changes in the structure of public organisations towards greater efficiency, better responsiveness to clients and more effective decision-making;
• enhancing accountability and discipline;
• nurturing values of excellence in the civil service; and
• encouraging the private sector to make greater use of IT for business transactions.

The e-Government initiative is spearheaded by MAMPU. It has envisioned its e-Government initiative as being to "drive public services towards excellence", and its mission is "To bring changes in the public administration services to achieve high quality, efficient, effective and strong management in line with the national goals.

The vision calls for both reinventing government (using multimedia and information technology to dramatically improve productivity, reviewing processes and standards), and creating a collaborative environment that fosters the ongoing development of Malaysia's technology and multimedia industry.

E-GOVERNMENT PILOT PROJECTS

Five pilot projects were identified as the first wave of e-Government, namely the Generic Office Environment, e-Procurement, Human Resource Management Information System, Project Monitoring System and e-Services. These projects were selected both for their impact as well as to showcase different aspects of e-Government, as shown in the figure below.

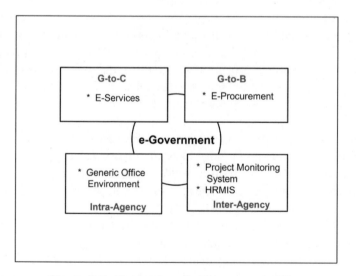

Figure 8-3: Categories of e-Government Pilots

A team comprising of lead implementing agencies and private sector representatives developed the "Concept Requests for Proposals" (CRFPs), which outlined the requirements for each of these pilot applications and then gave consortia of private sector companies the flexibility to innovate and deliver the best solutions.

Generic Office Environment (GOE)

This pilot project is about creating an "electronic office" environment to enhance productivity through better information management, communications and collaboration. The immediate objective of GOE is to provide a fully integrated, distributed, and scaleable paperless office environment for the Prime Minister's Office by deploying multimedia and ICT. Civil servants will be provided with quick and easy methods to access up-to-date, accurate information. Focus is placed on ensuring that the right information gets to the right people at the right time.

The GOE pilot application, which has been successfully completed, comprises various modules — document management, search and retrieval, executive information manager, online information filter, messaging system, electronic meeting, bulletin board, decision tracking, meeting management and a discussion forum.[12]

Electronic Procurement

It has been estimated that Malaysian government agencies spend 35 billion Ringgit (US$9.2 billion) annually on goods and services. When completely rolled out, the Electronic Procurement pilot will have over 4,000 government procurement points and 30,000 registered suppliers will use the system.[13, 14] The system, known as *"ePerolehan"*,[15] is expected to streamline government procurement activities and improve the quality of service provided. Over time, it is expected that ePerolehan will convert traditional manual government procurement processes into electronic procurement on the Internet.

The electronic procurement system will reengineer, automate and transform the current procurement system. ePerolehan supports the entire procurement cycle; from central contract, request for quotations, request for tender and direct purchase. The system even allows alerts or notifications by email, short messaging (SMS) or fax.

The objective of ePerolehan is to ensure best value for money as well as transparency and accountability in line with established procedures. The system will enable the government to become a smarter and more efficient buyer by reducing costs and leveraging economies of scale, achieve faster turnaround time, as well as improve control and accuracy in the ordering and billing process. Government will also reap the benefits of up-to-date supplier information and better management of supplier performance.

With the system, suppliers both large and small will be IT-enabled and will benefit from increased transparency and faster payment turnaround time. Other benefits include increased efficiency due to more accurate orders, fewer product returns, lower cycle time, and reduced operation costs due to electronic retrieval and submission of quotations. Suppliers will also be able to extend their reach to new customers on a global basis through the use of an electronic catalogue with internationally recognised product classifications.

In essence, ePerolehan is the link between government suppliers and government agencies. It is the medium through which the purchaser and the supplier will conduct their supply and demand activities.

Human Resource Management Information System (HRMIS)

HRMIS is a system which provides full Human Resource Management (HRM) functionality for the government to develop and manage its human capital. The objectives of the HRMIS project are:

- to achieve effective staffing and "rightsizing" of the civil service through better availability of HRM information;
- to automate the current manual HRM operational processes;
- to build up-to-date consolidated HRM information for effective planning among agencies;
- to achieve better communication, horizontal integration and streamlined processes through establishment of a richer collaborative systems environment among agencies;
- to improve paperless HRM capabilities; and
- to provide an open and flexible HRM system to meet the information requirements of both operational and managerial processes.

The HRM functions include resourcing, remuneration and benefits, competency assessment, career management, performance management, human resource development as well as other supporting functions.

Project Monitoring System (PMS II)

This pilot project is an online end-to-end project monitoring system to create a collaborative environment for better management of development projects.

The scope of PMS II provides three categories of services, namely application services, data services and communication services to improve project management. Under this pilot project, an online end-to-end mechanism for monitoring project implementation will be created.

As the PMS II pilot is primarily a G2G application, its benefits tend to be more visible within the government's operations than the general public.

For instance, PMS II will enable government officers to monitor about 40,000 ongoing projects nationwide, and make more informed and better decisions based on analysis and forecasting of project information made available through PMS II.

e-Services

This pilot project was selected to showcase various government to citizen services. It provides an alternative means for the public to transact and interact with government ministries and agencies faster and more conveniently. It will be deployed in different ways and through a variety of electronic channels, for instance, through interactive voice response (IVR) systems, the home or office PC, public kiosks in shopping malls, and wireless devices.

To date, e-Services covers services from a variety of ministries and agencies. Some examples include: the Road and Transport Department (for driver and vehicle registration, licensing and summons, test scheduling services), the Ministry of Health (for online health information), Tenaga Nasional Berhad (for utility bills payments) and Telekom Malaysia Berhad (for telephone and Internet bills).

Electronic Labour Exchange

In 1999 a sixth pilot e-Government project was launched — the Electronic Labour Exchange (ELX). This pilot was aimed at improving the mobilisation of the nation's human resources and optimising manpower utilisation through systematic matching of job seekers to job vacancies. The main applications of the ELX were to the Job Clearing System, Labour Market Database and the Office Productivity System. ELX is designed to be a one-stop hub for labour market information that is accessible both within Malaysia as well as internationally.

e-Syariah

In 2002, the government launched a seventh e-Government initiative called *e-Syariah*, a web-enabled integrated electronic application system for *Syariah* Courts nationwide. This project helps to reform and upgrade the service quality of the *Syariah* Courts by enhancing the effectiveness of the Islamic Justice Department in coordinating and monitoring the respective agencies. e-Syariah also enhances the productivity and efficiency of the *Syariah* Courts management.

Some applications being developed as part of e-Syariah are: Court Case Management System, *Syarie* Lawyers Registration System, e-Syariah Portal, and a Library Management System.

EG*Net: The Key Link for e-Government

This Wide Area Network (WAN) is the single service network designed to link all e-Government applications and systems. EG*Net is provided by an entity called the Government Integrated Telecommunications Network or GITN.[16] GITN has the responsibility to provide a single network to link not only the government entities and civil servants but also businesses and citizens via the Internet.

The Electronic Government flagship applications of the Multimedia Super Corridor were implemented in phases, beginning with the pilot phase towards the end of 1999. GITN plays a very important role in providing a reliable and efficient communications network, complete with security features, dedicated to the Government. This infrastructure forms a framework, which encompasses a nationwide high-speed network, based on the frame relay technology, upgradeable to Asynchronous Transfer Mode (ATM).

CHALLENGES AND ASPIRATIONS

Having followed the development of the MSC since early 1997, and seen a huge but empty stretch of real estate south of Kuala Lumpur being transformed from acres of oil palm plantations into the brand new cities of Putrajaya and Cyberjaya, bordered in the north by a huge skyscraper in the Petronas Twin Towers, and a gleaming new KLIA airport in the south, one cannot help but be awed by the vision and the commitment of the nation.

As one speaks with various executives and officials involved in the Multimedia Super Corridor initiatives, it becomes clear that the MSC goes beyond being a mega-ICT project. It is in many ways an embodiment of Malaysia's global aspirations and a reflection of national pride.

Malaysia has taken some very significant strides down the road towards the knowledge economy. It has not been an entirely smooth road. Some external factors have been beyond the control of the project implementers. Other factors stem from within.

There have also been no shortage of critics and nay sayers. An old saying goes "Whether a cup is half full or half empty depends more on the observer than it does the cup". Proponents focus on the milestones and advances made. Critics highlight the project misses and shortfalls. Despite many challenges, both internal and external, faced along the way, the project has slowly but surely edged forward.

Key Challenges

The progress of the MSC flagships and projects are continually being reviewed. At one such review of the e-Government flagship in mid 2002, some obstacles to change and progress were shared. Conversations with officials involved in the e-Government initiatives elicited comments along the lines of:

- "The size and complexity of the projects cannot be under-estimated"
- "Cross-agency integration is paramount"
- "There are issues integrating the new with the legacy systems"
- "It's a talent war out there. We need more skilled knowledge workers."
- "Resistance to change is the key hurdle"
- "We must strive to develop common standards ..."
- "The digital divide is a key issue to be tackled"

The pilot projects under the e-Government flagship are at different stages of testing or launch. As the project continues, new ones are also being considered.

Many lessons have been learnt along the past 5 years on project management, planning, contracting models, infrastructural pieces, talent development, and the management of mindset change. All these will become even more valuable in the next phase of the journey.

Moving Ahead

The external environment continues to be tumultuous. Even before the region had emerged from the Asian crisis of 1997 and 1998, a global recession hit, triggered by the technology bust. In quick succession came the terrorist attacks of 9/11, war on Iraq, and the SARS outbreak in 2003.

It is still too early to assess the success of the MSC as Malaysia like all its neighbours, has been affected by the environmental uncertainties in Asia. To date, the number of companies recruited is still within the targets set. Most projects are still progressing, albeit delayed in some cases. A balanced analysis may only be possible in a few years.

The spirit of "Malaysia Boleh" (loosely translated as "Malaysia Can Do It") is alive even though the nation, together with other regional countries, has gone through the environmental turbulence. The vision of making Malaysia as one of the global leaders in ICT remains unchanged, and redoubled efforts continue to make the vision a reality.

A DIALOGUE WITH
DATUK DR MUHAMMAD RAIS BIN ABDUL KARIM,

Director-General, MAMPU, Malaysia
Prime Minister's Complex, PutraJaya

Datuk Dr Muhammad Rais bin Abdul Karim joined the Malaysian Civil Service in May 1969 after graduating with a BA (Hons) degree from the University of Malaya. He also holds a Masters in Public Administration from the University of Southern California and a PhD in Economic and Social Development from the University of Pittsburgh.

After various postings in different agencies he assumed his current position as the Director-General of MAMPU in 1996. In this capacity, Dr Rais spearheads modernisation and innovation efforts in the civil service. He also leads the implementation of Electronic Government, one of the MSC flagships and sits on numerous Committees charged with overall administrative and IT improvements in government.

At the international level, Datuk Dr Muhammad Rais is a Board member of the Commonwealth Network of Information Technology for Development (COMNET-IT) and is actively involved in the Commonwealth Association of Public Administration and Management (CAPAM) and the Eastern Regional Organisation for Public Administration (EROPA). He recently served on the International Committee of Jurists for the CAPAM International Innovation Awards and sat on the United Nations Panel of Experts on Public Administration and Finance in 1995 and 1997.

Datuk Dr Muhammad Rais edited the book entitled *Reengineering the Public Service: Leadership and Change in an Electronic Age* (Pelanduk Publications, 1999). He also has edited several publications such as *Malaysia Kita, Citrakarya* and *Malaysian Development Experience*, which have become basic texts within the Malaysian Civil Service. He is also co-author of the book *Ibu Tunggal* (Pelanduk Publications, 1999). Most recently, he co-authored the 2003 publication *e-Government in Malaysia*.

The author (JY) had the privilege of speaking to Datuk Dr Rais (DR) in October 2002.

JY : **You first wrote about e-Government in your book *Reengineering the Public Service* in 1999. Since then, many of the Malaysian e-Government initiatives have been launched. Has your view of the definition and scope of e-Government changed in any way?**

DR : Not really. e-Government still means the same thing. For Malaysia, e-Government is one of the flagship projects under the MSC programme. It is about using technology (mainly IT, communications and multimedia) and other means (reengineering, change management) to reinvent government , in order to attain:

- more effective access to service delivery
- higher quality services
- greater impact through better processes and systems
- better and more efficient communication
- more transparent and faster decision making, and
- more empowered people

JY : **On the key challenges faced in implementing e-Government in Malaysia, I recall reading in one of your speeches, you spoke of the two components "e" and "Government" that make up "e-Government" and how the magnitude of the challenges were in the order of 10 percent: 90 percent. Could you elaborate on that?**

DR : e-Government involves both the technology and the people. e-Government is about back end systems interoperability, sharing of data among agencies (often in ways not previously done), redefined data custodians, new reporting mechanisms, report presentation formats, new approval processes, and amended division of responsibilities, etc.

There are often disagreements to some of the changes and invariably there will be turf fights. Some Heads of Departments (HOD's) are used to their approval authorities and processes, and sometimes resist changes. Some departments prefer to use vendors familiar to them. In general, effort is often needed to come to agreement on data sharing and new responsibilities.

New skills are often needed for the reengineered and ICT-enabled processes. It needs to be decided whether the new skills can be found or developed in-house, or whether it is necessary to buy-in the new skills. Change management needs to be incorporated in the transformation process.

e-Government is often accompanied by a steamlining of the public sector organisation. There is often a reduction in the number of ministries needed, through consolidation of existing ministries or closing down some redundant units. In Malaysia, there are currently 25 ministries (including the Prime Minister's Department). India has around 40. Pakistan has 24. Singapore has 15.

JY : **In moving the e-Government programme forward, what role does MAMPU play?**

DR : The role of MAMPU is to support the e-Government vision, especially from the public service side. MAMPU is the lead agency for the e-Government flagship application and its role includes planning and coordinating the implementation of the e-Government projects.

For stand-alone systems, individual government agencies are allowed to select themselves; however when they require systems to be networked with other agencies' systems, they need to consult MAMPU.

MAMPU is also represented in many high-level committees on governance, eg GITIC, NITC, Steering Committee on Electronic Government, etc.

MAMPU is not directly involved in general infrastructure deployment, nor in legal areas (eg enacting Cyber Laws).

JY : **How does the vast geographical size and diversity of Malaysia impact its e-Government deployment?**

DR : Size is relative. Malaysia is small compared to some of the states in the US or countries in Europe. However, there are indeed certain challenges that geographical size brings to an e-Government implementation.

One key area is network connections. As a geographically dispersed country, divided into West and East Malaysia by sea, we are not as well wired up as we would like. In certain areas, eg MSC and urban centres, the connections are more widespread and access to e-Government services is easier. Despite the common adage "death of distance", in the more isolated rural areas, we still need to focus on the "last mile" connection either by wired or wireless technologies. But even with wireless technologies, we need to connect to certain wireless hub points.

In some areas we still have electrical power glitches to sort out. These are teething issues, but will definitely affect e-Government service deployment.

JY : **There has been some debate on whom does e-Government really benefit — is it the constituents eg citizens, businesses or is it government? Also does e-Government lead to better governance?**

DR : The goal of e-Government is that it will benefit the citizens (in being able to receive better services), the government (in becoming more efficient, effective and service-oriented) and the private sector (in easier legal compliance and access to government services).

In practice, it is still too early to answer who Malaysia's e-Government programme is benefiting today, and how. We are still in the pilot stage of many of our initiatives, and the benefits cannot be clearly seen. In the long run, we are confident that all parties will benefit.

JY : **How does the Malaysian government promote e-Government services? How do you motivate the constituents (eg citizens, businesses, etc) to make use of e-Government services?**

DR : e-Government, as part of the MSC flagships, has been widely publicised.

The Project Monitoring System (PMS II) launched in May 2001 is a very successful project under the e-Government flagship. PMS II provides the capability for government agencies to monitor development projects planned and approved by the Malaysian government under the Five-Year Development Plans. PMS II connects government personnel at all levels — from federal to state and district levels — in monitoring the numerous government-related projects.

Electronic Labour Exchange (ELX) launched in May 2002 will improve the mobilisation of the nation's human resources and ensure optimum utilisation of manpower through the systematic matching of job seekers to job vacancies. This project will also act as a one-stop centre for labour market information, accessible to government agencies, the private sector and the general public.

JY : **How does MAMPU help to nurture an environment of public sector innovation?**

DR : We're doing quite a lot of different things. There are ongoing systems studies, ISO initiatives, Public Service Innovation Award, quality inspectorates, papers submitted, PM Quality Award, Public Sector Quality Award (fashioned after the Malcolm Baldridge award), etc.

We are open to suggestions and welcome feedback on how to do things better. We would, however, prefer the providers of feedback to specify which areas are perceived lacking and could be improved, rather than making sweeping remarks on allegedly less than adequate performance of the public service.

At the end of the day, what we are trying to nurture is a mindset and culture of service orientation and quality consciousness.

JY : **Can you share some key metrics that you look at to monitor the progress of your various e-Government initiatives? Also what benchmarks do you employ?**

DR : We definitely do benchmark our efforts with the best in the world. We have been making study trips to countries like Ireland, UK, and India. We have been watching Singapore's progress closely. We will be making a trip to Brunei soon.

While we have many metrics to monitor the status of the e-Government projects, at the end of the day, nothing is more concrete than programmes delivered by the government. Without this, all e-Government initiatives are meaningless. The image that a country projects is not through the systems it has, but in what the country has achieved.

JY : **How does the public sector generally measure the value of ICT deployed?**

DR : This is related to the often-referenced "Information Paradox" which questions the link between ICT investments to improvements in business performance. It's true that ICT benefits don't always clearly and directly commensurate with the investment put in. But that does not mean we will invest less in ICT. There is no substitute for ICT to help create faster, more transparent e-Government.

The important thing is to be able to manage the cost. For that reason, public sector executives need to be not only numerate but also knowledgeable about what the technology can do. They must know how to apply ICT solutions to real-life problems. They must know when is the right time to apply ICT, and when not to keep chasing technology (eg upgrades or versions touted by a host of ICT vendors). Sometimes negative outcomes result from inappropriate application of technologies.

Usually, measurement of value of ICT needs to be by indirect measures. For the overall public sector, one needs to look at national indicators — the country's progress, GDP growth, overall competitiveness, etc.

At the functional level, there may be various appropriate indicators. Take a port for example. The ICT applied must be able to monitor or track the ships entering and leaving, efficiently handle tax computations and compliance issues, communicate with local authorities where relevant, help to be vigilant against diseases, etc.

Endnotes

1   Mason, C, "*A Short History of Asia*", Macmillan Press (2000).

2   Baker, J, "*Crossroads — A Popular History of Malaysia and Singapore*", Times Books International (1999).

3   Supreme leader.

4   The teledensity numbers quoted are for 2001.

5   *The Economist*, 2001.

6   IDC Asia-Pacific projections.

7   The document "*The Way Forward — Vision 2020*" was unveiled in February 1991 by the Prime Minister, Dr Mahathir Mohamad. Broadly speaking, it is a master-plan for transforming Malaysia into an industrial country by the early 21st Century. Vision 2020 outlines nine challenges to be met, in the areas of: Unity, Self-confidence and self-respect, Mature consensual oriented democratic society, Moral and ethical society, Scientific and progressive, Innovative and forward-looking, Mature and liberal society, Caring society, Economically just and Prosperous, resilient economy.

8   Ahmad Sarji Abdul Hamid (ed), "*Malaysia's Vision 2020: Understanding the Concept, Implications & Challenges*", Pelanduk Publications (1993).

9   Multimedia Development Corporation, "*Multimedia Super Corridor Flagship & Applications — Malaysia's Experience*" presentation (2002).

10 Tan SM, "*Strategies in developing Electronic Government: Malaysia's Perspective*" presentation, MAMPU, 2001.

11 Information from the MDC website and MSC.comm publications.

12 "*Online Government*", MSC.comm, September 2002.

13   Muhammad Rais Abdul Karim (ed), *"Reengineering the Public Service: Leadership and Change in an Electronic Age"*, Pelanduk Publications (1999).

14   Muhammad Rais Abdul Karim and Nazariah Mohd Khalid, *"E-Government in Malaysia"*, Pelanduk Publications (2003).

15   In the national language Bahasa Malaysia (or Malay), *perolehan* means "benefit" or "enablement".

16   GITN was originally formed as a joint venture between Permodalan Nasional Berhad and Telekom Malaysia Berhad. Today, it is wholly owned by the latter.

Useful Websites

www.cmc.gov.my	Communications & Multimedia Commission
www.ktkm.gov.my	Ministry of Energy, Communications & Multimedia
www.mimos.my	MIMOS Berhad official website
www.mdc.com.my	Website of the Multimedia Development Corporation
www.eperolehan.com.my	Website of the Electronic Procurement system

CHAPTER 9

Many Agencies, One Government — Singapore's Approach to Public Services Delivery

Jeffery BH Tan and James SL Yong

▲ ▼ ▲ ▼ ▲ ▼ ▲ ▼

Every service that can be delivered electronically shall be electronically available.

Mr Lim Siong Guan,
Head, Singapore Civil Service

▲ ▼ ▲ ▼ ▲ ▼ ▲ ▼

It has been a hectic workweek and Tan Chin Siong and his wife Julie were relieved that the weekend had finally come around. Resting on the couch after a late Saturday morning breakfast, the couple contemplated their leisure activities for the day and their upcoming vacation.

"Boy, these last 5 days have really been exhausting," said Chin Siong. "I'm glad we finally have some time to relax and look forward to our week long vacation."

Julie thought for a moment and then turned to her husband, "Did you remember to renew the road tax for our car? The current one expires next week and our flight is on Monday morning."

"Oh no … I forgot! It's already 11.45 am and the office closes at 12 pm," exclaimed Chin Siong. "No point rushing down now as we probably won't make it in time."

A moment of silence passed as they traded accusing glances at each other.

Suddenly Chin Siong stood up and said, "There was an article in the papers the other day about the new services on the eCitizen portal. I remember that road tax renewal is now available online." With that he scurried into the study room and started up the home computer.

Within minutes, the eCitizen portal was gleaming on the monitor. With Julie standing by his side, he deftly navigated to the relevant site, checked out the procedures and conducted the necessary transactions all before the clock struck noon.

Beaming with relief, Julie sat herself besides her husband and took control of the mouse. "Let's start our vacation now," she said as the screen displayed a scenic picture of their holiday destination …

BACKGROUND

History

Singapore owes its existence to its prime geographical location at the meeting point of sea routes at the southern tip of the Malayan Peninsula. Towards the west is the vast Indian Ocean and on the east is the South China Sea. During the 14th Century, this small but strategically placed island was bestowed with the name "Singa Pura", meaning "Lion City". Legend has it that a visiting Srivijayan prince saw an animal he mistook for a lion and that was how Singapore's modern day name came about.

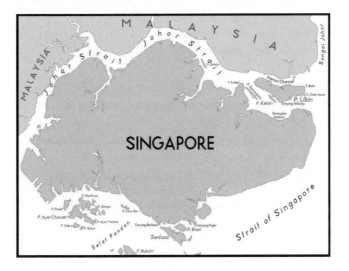

In 1819, a British colonial administrator Sir Stamford Raffles established a trading settlement in Singapore. The policy of free trade made Singapore an attractive port of call for various sea craft from all over Asia and from as far afield as Europe and the Middle East. In 1832, Singapore became the centre of government for the British controlled Straits Settlements (comprising Penang, Malacca and Singapore). The opening of the Suez Canal in 1869 and the advent of the telegraph and the steamship enhanced Singapore's importance as a centre for the expanding trade between East and West.

During World War II, Singapore fell to the Japanese in 1942. After the war, Singapore became a Crown Colony. The growth of nationalism led to self-government in 1959, with Lee Kuan Yew as Singapore's first prime minister. There was a brief period of union with Malaysia, until finally in 1965, Singapore became an independent republic.

Geography and Economy

The island Republic of Singapore, roughly 682 sq km (250 sq miles) in size, is home to a multiracial population of 4 million (about 76 percent Chinese, 14 percent Malay, 8 percent Indian). The major languages in used are English, Mandarin, Malay and Tamil. The key religions include Taoism, Buddhism, Islam and Christianity.

Singapore's compact size belies its economic growth. In merely 150 years, Singapore has grown into a thriving centre of commerce and industry with an annual GDP of US$ 89 billion.[1] It is one of the world's major oil refining and distribution centres, as well as a major supplier of electronic components and a leader in shipbuilding and repair. Singapore is one of the busiest ports in the world and has also grown to become a key financial centre in Asia. Other major industries include tourism, logistics and medical services.

Business dealings are facilitated by Singapore's superb communications network that links the Republic to the rest of the world via satellite and 24-hour telecommunication systems.

Over the past 30 years Singapore experienced rapid economic growth with a large volume of foreign investment that helped to transform the economy, expand trade and creat jobs. The positive trend slowed in 1997 when the Asian financial crisis swept through the region although Singapore emerged relatively unscathed. This was followed by the global meltdown brought about by the dot com crash of 2000, the looming terrorist threat following the 9/11 disaster in New York, the war on Iraq and the deadly SARS[2] virus outbreak of early 2003 that sent tremors of uncertainty across the world. Another major economic factor after the 1997 crisis was that attention was increasingly being concentrated in North Asia with China emerging as a major economic force in the region. Singapore and many of its Southeast Asian neighbours experienced disparate and weaker growth due to lower foreign direct investment and falling demand from their trading partners.

In the midst of this challenging period, the Singapore Government embarked on an ambitious plan aimed at transforming the nation's economy and ensuring Singapore's relevance and success in the new economy. An Economic Review Committee (ERC) carried out a comprehensive review of economic policies and proposed ways to develop a vibrant and competitive private sector. The ERC submitted its recommendations to the government in early 2003.

Government

Singapore has a parliamentary system of government. The President, who is directly elected for a 6-year term, appoints the Prime Minister and Cabinet. Goh Chok Tong has been Prime Minister since 1990. There is a single-chamber parliament with 84 elected MPs, some elected from single-member constituencies but the majority from group represented constituencies (GRCs). In addition to elected MPs, the constitution provides for a number of non-constituency MPs and nominated MPs (usually highly regarded professionals) to sit in parliament. The People's Action Party (PAP) has been in power since independence. Over most of Singapore's modern political history, there has not been much opposition representation in the parliament.

In addition to the Prime Minister's Office, there are fourteen other ministries: Community Development & Sports, Defence, Education, Finance, Foreign Affairs, Health, Home Affairs, Information, Communications & The Arts (MITA), Law, Manpower, National Development, Environment, Trade & Industry, and Transport.

Since independence, Singapore has built up a reputation for political stability with a clean, effective public administration. The government places strong emphasis on economic development, fostering a sense of nationhood and social stability. Years of successful economic policies have led to Singapore having one of the highest standards of living in the world.

THE NATIONAL ICT PROGRAMMES

On an island with practically no natural resources except the people, generations of Singaporeans have learned to combine their skills and diligence with education and technology to sustain the momentum of their economic growth. There was very early recognition that IT would be needed to leverage Singapore's intellectual capital in order to move into the ranks of developed nations. A concerted effort to harness computing power began in the early 1980s with the government taking the lead.

Singapore has a clear and integrated approach to national computerisation. Over the past two decades, there has been a succession of national programmes, each designed to build on the successes of the previous, in a relentless journey to transform Singapore into a vibrant wired nation.

To date, there have been five key phases, each framed by a national plan with clearly articulated goals, policies and projects.

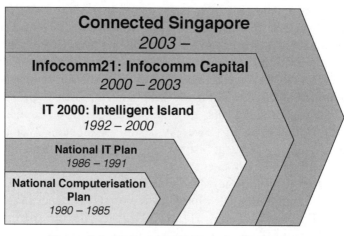

Figure 9-1: National ICT Plans in Singapore

National Computerisation Plan (1980–1985)

This first phase officially began in 1980, with the formation of a Committee for National Computerisation, led by a Cabinet Minister. In 1981, this committee released a 5-year National Computerisation Plan with primary focus on three areas:

(1)   computerisation of the civil service,

(2)   development of the local IT industry to expand software and services, and

(3)   growing a pool of IT professionals to meet the future needs of the industry.[3]

The Civil Service Computerisation Programme (CSCP), launched in 1982, was aimed at turning the whole civil service into a world-class IT user. A new statutory board in charge of IT matters — the National Computer Board (NCB) — was created to plan and implement the CSCP. Early applications were mainly in the areas of transaction processing, data modelling and database management. CSCP applications were designed to enhance productivity within the public sector and to connect the various government ministries and agencies.

National IT Plan (1986–1991)

Building on the momentum of the National Computerisation Plan, another 5-year plan was launched in 1986. Known as the National IT Plan (NITP), it was jointly developed by the NCB, Economic Development Board, the telecommunication authority and the National University of Singapore.

The NITP encapsulated a multi-pronged strategy that included of the following.

- Developing IT professionals and experts. This included applied research efforts into enabling technologies like software engineering, expert systems, and electronic data interchange (EDI).
- Improving the ICT infrastructure through the installation of fibre-optics and integrated services digital networks (ISDN).
- Developing a strong export-oriented ICT industry, involving alliances with global software firms to build engineering skills for the local IT sector and a global plan to export these capabilities.
- Coordinating and collaborating between various ICT-promoting organisations by developing networked communities.
- Establishing a culture that was receptive to ICT by promoting IT awareness through organised events for society at large, eg IT Week.
- Encouraging creativity and entrepreneurship.
- Increasing ICT applications in workplaces by leveraging networking and communication technologies to integrate applications and provide one-stop efficient services to diffuse the use of IT in selected industries.

During this phase, a number of nationwide electronic services were introduced, which successfully enhanced various government functions and improved interaction with the constituents. These EDI-based networks (eg TradeNet and Portnet for the trading, shipping and freight forwarding community; MediNet for the healthcare community and LawNet for the legal community) enabled the electronic exchange of structured documents between the industry and various government agencies. The Integrated Land Use System (ILUS), a GIS-based[4] information system that helps the planning authority in city and road planning, facilitated the management of scarce land resources. The One Stop Change of Address Reporting Service (OSCARS) provided citizens with a single point reporting for change of residential address.

TradeNet in particular was seen as a major national success as the electronic network allowed traders and government departments to exchange trade documents conveniently and efficiently. It has been widely quoted in leading publications and journals as a reference case on the successful application of technology in transforming public administration. On a national basis, it was estimated to be saving Singaporean traders about one billion US dollars a year.

By the early 1990s, Singapore had a thriving IT industry with a growing number of indigenous IT firms exporting to the region, the US, and Europe. Research centres were established, developing advanced technologies and applications for industry and state-owned enterprises.

IT 2000 Masterplan (1992–2000) — Intelligent Island

The key goal of the IT 2000 Masterplan launched in 1992 was to transform Singapore into an "Intelligent Island", based on an advanced National Information Infrastructure (NII) connecting computers in virtually every home, school and office. The Intelligent Island was meant to be a place where IT was pervasive, with services readily accessible by every citizen — at work and play.[5]

The IT 2000 vision was based on five sub-visions: developing a global hub, transforming the economy, enhancing the potential of individuals, linking communities locally and globally, and improving the quality of life. The plan was initiated with a rather ambitious agenda covering eleven sectors including construction and real estate, education and training, manufacturing, media, publishing and information services, and transportation.

The NII was conceived as an advanced information infrastructure to enable access and assimilation of information from diverse sources. The technological elements considered key to the developments of such an infrastructure include broadband networks, multimedia, telecommuting, and technical standards. This resulted in the creation of Singapore ONE (One Network for Everyone), the world's first nationwide broadband network, available to nearly every home, all schools and many public and private organisations. Singapore ONE has become a platform for innovative multimedia services — from online banking to entertainment on demand. By end 2002, there were some 200 applications and more than 1.24 million users (or two out of five Internet users in Singapore).[6]

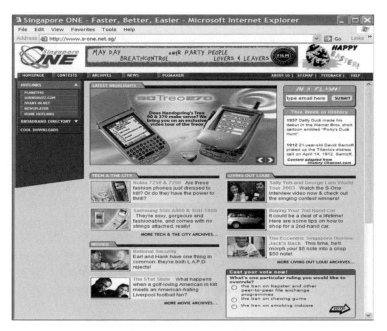

Figure 9-2: Singapore ONE Website

Singapore ONE

Singapore ONE is the national broadband framework to deliver a new level of interactive, multimedia applications and services to homes, businesses and schools throughout Singapore.

It comprises two distinct but integrated levels:

- A broadband infrastructure level of high capacity networks and switches.
- A level of advanced applications and services that take advantage of the infrastructure's high-speed and high-capacity capabilities.

Having established a broadband infrastructure that covers about 99 percent of the island with access via ADSL,[7] cable,[8] wireless,[9] and fibre,[10] the network is capable of carrying voice, data, audio, and video information simultaneously and at high speed to homes, businesses, schools, and other public places throughout the country.

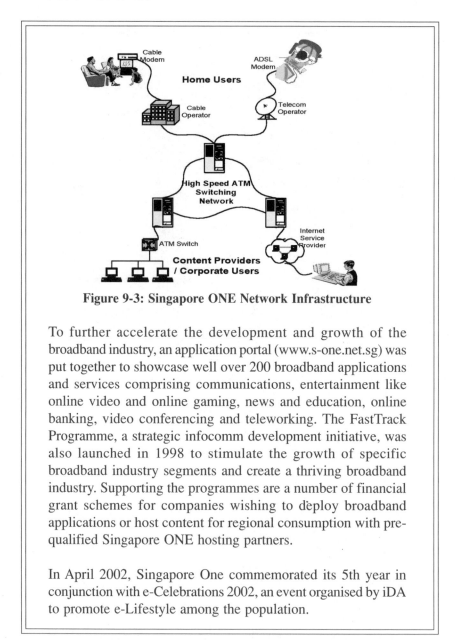

Figure 9-3: Singapore ONE Network Infrastructure

To further accelerate the development and growth of the broadband industry, an application portal (www.s-one.net.sg) was put together to showcase well over 200 broadband applications and services comprising communications, entertainment like online video and online gaming, news and education, online banking, video conferencing and teleworking. The FastTrack Programme, a strategic infocomm development initiative, was also launched in 1998 to stimulate the growth of specific broadband industry segments and create a thriving broadband industry. Supporting the programmes are a number of financial grant schemes for companies wishing to deploy broadband applications or host content for regional consumption with pre-qualified Singapore ONE hosting partners.

In April 2002, Singapore One commemorated its 5th year in conjunction with e-Celebrations 2002, an event organised by iDA to promote e-Lifestyle among the population.

Other notable applications include a nationwide digital library system that links up the catalogues and resource materials of major libraries, automated immigration-clearance at key checkpoints through the use of smart cards and electronic filing of income tax returns via phone and Internet.

Singapore also has one the highest PC and Internet penetrations in the world. With increasing online filing, applications and registration in many areas it is a clear indication of the effectiveness of the government's drive to develop a nation of IT savvy citizens.

In December 1999, a new statutory board, the Infocomm Development Authority (iDA) was established with the merger of the National Computer Board (NCB) and Telecommunications Authority of Singapore (TAS). This was part of the government's strategic response to the convergence of the IT and telecommunications arenas.

The Technopreneurship 21 (T21) initiative was launched in 1999 to prepare and lay the foundation for the successful development of a technology sector in Singapore. A joint effort by the government and private sector, the programme covers four areas which were deemed critical for the technology sector to flourish; education, facilities, regulations and financing. A Science Hub with world-class facilities to attract international talent working in knowledge industries was planned for and a US$ 1 billion Technopreneurship Investment Fund was launched to attract more venture capital activities into Singapore.

The success of IT 2000 is attributed to the joint effort of government agencies, the private sector, academia, research institutes, community groups and civic and voluntary organisations, which have played important roles in the conceptualisation, planning and the implementation of the IT 2000 plan.

Infocomm21 (2000–2003) — Infocomm Capital

As IT 2000 was being implemented progressively, the global technology and economic landscape also experienced massive changes. The globalisation of businesses, liberalisation of markets, emergence of e-Commerce and e-Business, proliferation of the Internet, broadband and wireless technologies, and convergence of IT, telecommunications and broadcasting have caused paradigm shifts that called for a review of strategies. To stay ahead of the changes, the Singapore Government embarked on a new plan in 1999 — Infocomm21 (Information and Communications Technology for the 21st Century).

The overall Infocomm21 vision is: "Singapore as a dynamic and vibrant global Infocomm Capital with a thriving and prosperous e-Economy and a pervasive and thriving e-Society".

Adopting a more industry-focused and industry-led approach, the government will perform the role of the catalyst by functioning as facilitator, promoter, educator and "anchor tenant" for the testing and pilot deployment of new applications.

Five strategic thrusts were defined as the focus of Infocomm21:

(1)   Singapore as the premier Infocomm Hub. Key to this development is the liberalisation of the telecommunications sector and putting in place a conducive business and regulatory framework.

(2)   Increase the competitiveness of Singapore businesses. The aim is to be among the top nations in the Asia Pacific for e-Commerce infrastructure and e-Business readiness.

(3)   Enhance the e-lifestyle of Singaporeans. To develop Singapore into a leading infocomm-savvy society with a pervasive net-centric lifestyle.

(4)   Create one of the world's leading e-Government. Deploying more extensive government services online to better serve the population.

(5)   Develop Singapore as an infocomm talent capital. Establish Singapore as the location of choice for high-calibre infocomm workforce and as a leading e-learning hub.

Through a consultative process with the industry, the iDA charts the vision, trends and developments of the infocomm landscape in Singapore for the next 5 years. Known as the Infocomm Technology Roadmaps (ITR), the aim is to align Singapore's technological developments with global infocomm trends and to give the local industry a competitive edge in business and economic opportunities brought about by technological advancements.

Connected Singapore (March 2003 onwards)

Announced in March 2003, "Connected Singapore"[11] represents the new blueprint for infocomm development in Singapore. With infocomm contributing 7 percent to the GDP and helping to create in excess of 100,000 jobs, the blueprint lays out the vision, strategies and goals that would further develop the infocomm industry over the next three years. It outlines opportunities for individuals, organisations and businesses to lead Singapore to become one of the world's premier infocomm capitals.

Continuing with the emphasis on greater industry participation, Connected Singapore is positioned to encourage and forge a new era of industry-government partnership. The government continues to play more of a supporting role and have the industry drive the development of the programme.

STANDARDS AND LEGISLATION

Singapore IT Standards

The Information Technology Standards Committee (ITSC) was formed in 1990, under the purview of the Standards Council appointed by the Productivity and Standards Board (now known as SPRING Singapore). It is an industry-led effort made up of volunteer members from the industry and supported by SPRING Singapore and the iDA. It is a neutral and open platform for interested industry and government parties to come together to agree on technical standards.

ITSC promotes and facilitates the national infocomm standardisation programmes and serves as Singapore's representative in the international infocomm standardisation efforts. It appoints various technical committees and work groups to undertake standardisation activities with emphasis in the following areas: automatic data capture, construction industry IT standards, information exchange, learning standards, multimedia representations, security and privacy, cards and personal identification, and e-financial services.

Collectively, the standard recommendations are referred to as Singapore Standards which includes the NII standards. The Singapore Standards are reviewed at least once every 5 years.

Electronic Transaction Act

The Electronic Transaction Act (ETA) was enacted in July 1998 in response to the need for a commercial code to define the rights and obligations of transacting parties. The Act aims to address the important issues of providing a legal foundation for electronic transactions and to give predictability and certainty to electronic formation of contracts.

Beyond providing legal status on the use of electronic records and signatures, the ETA also contains an omnibus provision for government departments and statutory boards to be able to accept electronic filing and issue permits and licences electronically without having to amend their respective Acts.

The ETA also includes provision for the appointment of a Controller of Certificate Authorities[12] and the liability of network service providers with regards to third party content.

ICT MATURITY INDICATORS

As of end 2002, Singapore's teledensity was about 1.25, comprising of an estimated 1.93 million fixed lines and 3.25 million mobile users. With a population of just over 4 million, Singapore has one of the world's highest mobile penetration, almost 78 percent of the population.[13]

Of the estimated 2 million Internet subscribers (representing about 48 percent of the population), about 11 percent or 222,000 were broadband users. This represented an increase of 60 percent from 2001 figures; much of it attributed to the falling subscription rates.[14]

The growing interest in wireless communication also resulted in a proliferation of "WLAN hot spots"[15] with up to 5 operators covering hundreds of public places like the airport, cafes and convention centres.

THE JOURNEY TOWARDS E-GOVERNMENT

The various National ICT Programmes resulted in a myriad of government administrations and services that exploited technology to enhance efficiency, service quality and accessibility via electronic channels. These achievements were working examples of government e-services that would be forerunners to e-Government as we know today. To better address the foregoing opportunities and challenges, the government has put forth targeted initiatives to further galvanise the efforts towards a digital economy.

Public Service for the 21st Century

Since its launch in 1981, the CSCP has redefined the way the Singapore Government works, interacts and serves the public. As technology continues to evolve at a breakneck speed, the challenge has been to keep pace and exploit opportunities for innovative approaches to governance.

Launched in May 1995, the "Public Service for the 21st Century" (PS21) became the standard bearer for the government to undertake the change that would prepare the civil service for the 21st century and be a model for efficiency, creativity and excellent service. The programme is expected to impact the mindsets, organisational culture and norms pertaining to the civil service to accomplish the following two basic objectives:

(1)   to nurture an attitude of service excellence in meeting the needs of the public with high standards of quality, courtesy and responsiveness; and

(2)   to foster an environment which induces and welcomes continuous change for greater efficiency and effectiveness by employing modern management tools and techniques, while paying attention to the morale and welfare of public officers.

The Government Information Infrastructure

To realise the PS21 vision of service excellence to deliver integrated and user-friendly electronic government services on the web to all Singaporeans, the Government Information Infrastructure (GovII) was conceived in 1997 to make communications and transactions within the civil service and between the government and the public more accessible and convenient. Developed on various Internet technology and standards, GovII was designed to provide easy access to the government on-line services and bring the "Connected Government" to Singaporeans all around the world.

Some of the services deployed on GovII include:

- the Government Intranet and Messaging Infrastructure for communication and sharing of information within and between government departments
- the Government Website (www.gov.sg) was setup in 1995 to provide the public with updated information on the government
- the eCitizen Portal (www.ecitizen.gov.sg) provides the single gateway to public information and e-services on the web under the e-Government Action Plan

To cater for the projected growth in transactional volume and network traffic, the Government Data Centre was built and began operations in May 2001 to provide a secure, non-stop and robust hosting environment. Designed for applications implementation this central facility also allows government agencies to deploy application systems within short lead times.

The Service-Wide Technical Architecture (SWTA) was developed to meet the government needs to create an environment of information sharing and interoperability within the public service. It is essentially a set of principles, standards and guidelines for public sector agencies in the design, acquisition, implementation and management of infocomm technology. This common set of principles and standards also provide a semantic framework for information sharing and interoperability of systems across all agencies.

The e-Government Action Plan

One of the key thrusts of the Infocomm21 Strategic Plan is to enable the Singapore Civil Service to harness ICT to better serve the public. The challenge is not simply of technology exploitation but rather one of reinventing government in the digital economy. This transformation of government and governance cuts across all aspects of the public sector from leadership, delivery of electronic public services, internal government operations, and ultimately economic competitiveness. The vision of the civil service was to move from operating as separate entities to serving the public as "One Government". This is encapsulated in the "customer-centric" approach to e-Government with the focus on CARE:[16]

- Courtesy — providing e-Government services in the most user-friendly, speedy and convenient way that minimises the effort to obtain the services.
- Accessibility — proving convenient and easy access to e-Government service, "anytime-anywhere" if possible.
- Responsiveness — delivering services promptly with minimal bureaucracy.
- Effectiveness — effectively meeting the public need in a secure and reliable manner without creating complexity in the process.

To drive this initiative, the Singapore government launched the e-Government Action Plan in June 2000, setting aside a budget of S$ 1.5 billion (US$ 870 million) to support the programme for the next 3 years. The e-Government Action Plan was drawn up as the blueprint that charts the strategic thrusts and programmes guiding the public service in realising the e-Government vision.

The stated vision of the Singapore Government is "to be a leading e-Government to better serve the nation in the digital economy".

Key Strategies and Areas of Focus

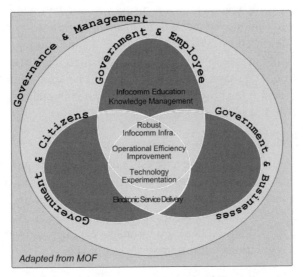

Figure 9-4: e-Government Strategic Framework

The strategic thrusts of the e-Government Action Plan are as follows:

Strategy 1: Delivering Integrated Electronic Services
Adopting the tenet of *"Many Agencies, One Government"*, the emphasis is on delivering services from a customer-centric perspective. Citizens will be able to access greater public services delivered online, anytime, anywhere. The eCitizen portal launched in April 1999 is one such example. As of March 2003, more than 1,600 public services were enabled for online delivery.

Strategy 2: Using Infocomm Technologies to build new capability and capacity
The public sector will leverage infocomm technologies to continually innovate and adapt its business and operational processes. To create new value and make quantum leap in service delivery, radical re-engineering and transformation are to be considered and applied, if necessary. Examples include the use of infocomm technologies to enable collaborative knowledge management to provide instant knowledge and processing capability.

Strategy 3: Innovating with Infocomm Technologies

Going beyond tried and tested ways of deploying technology, the public sector will experiment with new technologies to learn and develop capabilities, at times taking a leadership role in promoting new technological trends. Procurement and project management practices will be kept flexible to avoid deploying obsolete technology while maintaining practicality and pragmatism.

Strategy 4: Being Proactive and Responsive

Adopting a "sense and respond" approach to anticipating new trends, services are to be delivered at "Internet speed" with continuous fine-tuning in response to customer needs and feedback. The public sector will harness the power of infocomm technology to enhance policy delivery, simplify regulations and improve service levels.

Strategy 5: Reinventing Government in the Digital Economy

The public sector will systematically cultivate a better understanding of the impact of infocomm technologies to make meaningful decisions in all aspects of governance and to continually innovate to harness the benefits of infocomm technologies in its public services.

Six programmes were identified to drive these strategic thrusts:

(1)   Knowledge-Based Workforce — Public officers will be empowered to be knowledge workers who engage in active and collaborative learning and knowledge-sharing as part of a culture of continuous learning. Learning itself will increasingly be performed online, ie e-learning. Public officers will tap the power of infocomm technologies to improve service delivery, processes and teamwork.

(2)   Electronic Services Delivery — Public services which are suitable for electronic delivery should be re-engineered accordingly and delivered electronically.

(3)   Technology Experimentation — Public sector agencies will be encouraged to experiment with new technologies that could potentially revamp the way they work. Agencies can pioneer initiatives, which are "first-of-its-kind" or "first-in-its-series" in the public sector, on a trial or pilot basis, to better understand what new capabilities these technologies can offer and how they can benefit their organisations and customers.

(4)   Operational Efficiency Improvement — The public sector will continue to identify and invest in new systems that improve operational efficiency. In doing so, public officers should however, actively ask radical and fundamental questions to review the relevance and usefulness of functions and processes, and whether these could be streamlined to take advantage of the new capabilities offered by the Internet age.

(5)   Adaptive and Robust Infocomm Infrastructure — The rapid convergence of telecommunications, broadcasting and information technology has opened up possibilities for networked government at lower cost. A well-designed and reliable infrastructure is critical to support the e-Government vision.

(6)   Infocomm Education — ICT education programmes must go beyond learning about systems and applications to harnessing ICT to improve work processes and service delivery, and to developing policies more relevant in the new economy.

This section looks at some of the more visible projects within the overall e-Government programme, and gives a brief update on the progress to date (as of early 2003).

GENERAL INFRASTRUCTURE

PSi: A Central Infrastructure for Government e-Services

The CSCP programme and its subsequent follow-ups created pockets of closed networks in the early 1990s resulting in time consuming and frustrating experiences for citizens and businesses when dealing with multiple agencies. The need to rapidly develop Internet-enabled applications provided the catalyst for a complete end-to-end platform for government agencies to develop and deploy their applications on the Internet efficiently and rapidly.

Launched in January 2001 by the Ministry of Finance and iDA, the Public Service Infrastructure (PSi) is possibly the first integrated government-wide infrastructure in Southeast Asia for the development, deployment and operations of e-services. Designed as a central platform for different agencies to share common components (like payment gateways, electronic data exchange, authentication services and other security services), PSi enables large-scale deployment of public services rapidly through online portals with a secured, scalable and central government-wide infrastructure.

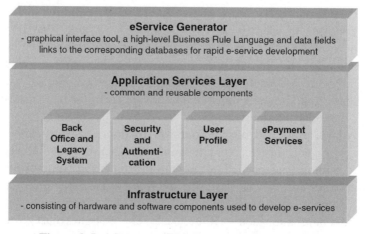

Figure 9-5: 3 Layers of Public Service Infrastructure

Integrating Layers of Government

The goal of PSi was to tie the disparate processes and data resources of the government into a single working infrastructure, supporting existing government services over the Internet and development of new electronic services. It comprises of 3 component layers; infrastructure, application services and e-service generator.

Designed to be secure, robust, scalable and highly available, PSi allows new upgrades to be added without affecting the current e-services that are already deployed or in production. A browser-based System Management Console allows assigned users from agencies to administer accounts, log reports, application services and e-services.

The renewal of Road Tax and Bizfile (online filing of incorporation of companies and businesses) showcase how the advantages and versatility of the PSi have been deployed. New e-services are also launched in relatively short periods of time like the encashment of New Singapore Shares (NSS) and its website, which was conceived and deployed in 3 weeks.

Wireless Programme

With the growing proliferation and adoption of wireless technology, the Wired with Wireless programme was initiated by the iDA in October 2002 to position Singapore as a living hub for wireless development in Asia. In collaboration with the industry, the programme serves to identify, develop and launch key wireless projects through pilots and trials across various industries in the areas of wireless multimedia, mobile commence and location-based services. The overall objectives of the programme include:

- creating a vibrant wireless industry for Singapore and enable companies to build and export wireless products and services globally;
- building a world-class wireless infrastructure that the industry can leverage for greater competitive advantage in the wireless arena; and
- promoting and enabling a wireless lifestyle for Singaporeans.

The widespread adoption of mobile devices has created opportunities for the government to leverage the wireless infrastructure as a viable delivery channel. e-Services are being enhanced with mobile facilities wherever possible (eg use of SMS[17] for notification and transactional services). The evolution of what some termed as "m-Government" would further enhance the accessibility and convenience of government e-services.

Web Services

The iDA unveiled the Web Services development framework in October 2002. Working with key industry players (including major technology vendors, market research firms, educational institutions and end-user organisations), the programme is intended to foster Singapore's leadership in significant emerging technologies. It currently consists of 3 initiatives to encourage growth of Web services:

(1) Intellectual Capital — to develop the necessary manpower and intellectual property management services;

(2) Living Lab — to jumpstart Web services adoption by positioning Singapore as an attractive facility for Web services development; and

(3) Enabling Infrastructure — focuses on interoperability, network identity, Web services management and other industry-wide issues.

A Web Services Innovation Zone is being planned to address and support the challenges of these initiatives.

Inline with government efforts to keep Singapore abreast of global technological developments, it is hoped that these initiatives would help to lay the foundation for Singapore to be a leading hub for Web services development and deployment.

SingPass

SingPass (Singapore Personal Access) was announced in March 2003 as a common authentication system for accessing government e-services. With SingPass, the public would only require one password to interact with different government agencies. All Singapore citizens above the age of 15 years are eligible. Employment pass holders and their dependants can also apply on a need basis. The government expects all e-services requiring authentication to offer SingPass access by end 2004.

CITIZEN SERVICES AND PROGRAMMES

Online Tax Filing

In 1995, the Inland Revenue Authority of Singapore (IRAS) introduced filing of personal income tax by telephone. This evolved into the e-Filing service where individual taxpayers with employment income supply IRAS with filing information directly on the Internet (efile.iras.gov.sg). Though the system was simple, and many incentives were offered, only 10 percent of the taxpayers opted for the system when it was first introduced in 1998. By 2000, some 30 percent of all taxpayers (364,000) filed electronically (a further 119,000 filed through the telephone) and the service was extended to individual taxpayers with business income.

The system presents an electronic version of the tax form and filers key in the appropriate details to be submitted. Further enhancements were made to allow employers to participate in an auto-inclusion scheme where employee income data are submitted electronically to IRAS (as of 2002, there are more than 1,900 companies participating in the scheme). This was subsequently extended to include data on dividends paid by Singapore-listed companies (obtained from the Central Depository) and other tax relief information reported from such sources as the Ministry of Defence.

Actively reacting to feedback from the public, IRAS continues to make improvement to the service. In 2003, a re-efile option was introduced to allow amendment of errors after submission. Through a partnership with the People's Association (PA) and 22 eClubs island wide, taxpayers without Internet facilities can approach volunteers at the clubs to help e-File their returns.

In 2002, about 808,000 taxpayers filed their tax assessment via the online system representing about 52 percent of total submissions.

eCitizen Portal

Launched in 1999, the eCitizen portal is the first stop on the web to a wide range of government information and services. Owned by the Ministry of Finance and managed by the Infocomm Development Authority of Singapore, in close collaboration with all government agencies, the key goal is to build a leading e-Government, which delivers more convenience and benefits to all Singapore residents.

An initiative to transform the way the public interact with the government, the eCitizen portal cuts across all agencies, integrating the e-services to provide a customer-centric single point access to all government e-services. Designed with the constituents' needs in mind, services and information are organised into 16 categories which cater to various essential touch points in life — Arts & Heritage, Business, Defence, Education, Elections, Employment, Family, Health, Housing, Law, Library, Recreation, Safety and Security, Sports, Transport and Travel. Users can search for and access a diversity of information and conduct a wide range of online government transactions. This customer-centric approach allows for a more intuitive experience in accessing the e-services.

To facilitate members of the public with no Internet at home or workplace, a nationwide network of community clubs and facilities under the eCitizen Helper People-Private-Public (3P) Partnership Programme, provides the public with Internet access as well as helpers to guide users to transact with the government. The partnership is a joint collaboration between the government and other public and private sector organisations and forms part of the government's commitment to ensure that no user is deprived of the benefits and convenience of government e-services.

A recipient of the 2002 Stockholm Challenge[18] award in the category e-Government, the eCitizen portal has been recognised for excellence in harnessing ICT to benefit Singapore's people and society. The eCitizen portal has an average monthly hit of over 8.7 million as of February 2003.

More details on the structure and development of the eCitizen portal can be found in Chapter 12.

Enabling the e-Lifestyle

To promote the development and trial of innovative infocomm products and services to homes and communities, the Connected Homes Programme was officially announced by the iDA in April 2002. The aim of the programme is to provide a test-bed environment for the industry to develop, pilot and deploy innovative and integrated end-to-end solutions for homes and the community. Leveraging on the existing Singapore ONE infrastructure and services, the programme is to enable consumers and communities to realise the benefits of an e-lifestyle.

The Connected Homes Programme has 2 strategic thrusts comprising:

(1)   Connecting the Home — development of home-based networking solutions to connect a multitude of communication devices for the intelligent home.

(2)   Connecting the Community — development of a suite of services that aims to connect aspects of the community ranging from health providers, educational institutions, community groups and businesses.

Industry partners are encouraged to collaborate and develop such integrated solutions for the homes and conduct trials of the solutions with real-life home users.

BUSINESS SERVICES

TradeNet

TradeNet — implemented in January 1989 — is one of the first nationwide Electronic Data Interchange (EDI) systems that facilitates the electronic exchange of structured trade messages and information between various parties from the public service (encompassing 35 government controlling units) and the private sector. This includes the electronic submission and processing of import, export and transhipment documents, resulting in reduced cost, and shorter turnaround time.

Before TradeNet, every declaration amounted to a tremendous amount of paperwork involving a minimum of four documents escalating to over 20 documents for more complex shipments. In 1987, the Trade Development Board (TDB, now known as IE Singapore) was handling almost 10,000 declarations per day. Servicing more than 15,000 traders and 700 shipping companies, the need to streamline the procedures and remain competitive motivated the TDB to explore automation and reduce the myriad forms into a single user interface.

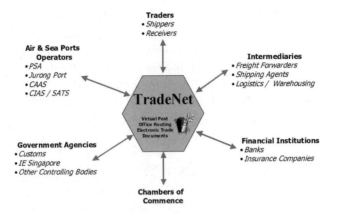

Figure 9-6: Linking the Trading Community

With TradeNet, trade documents are processed in less than 10 minutes and prior to the arrival of a ship. This significantly cuts the stay time, saving trading firms and agents up to 30 percent in administrative costs. Other benefits include reduction in inventory cost and lower submission error rates.

TradeNet was migrated from a private network solution to a web-based system as part of a major update in 1998.

Online Government Procurement

The Government Electronic Business (GeBIZ) portal (www.gebiz.gov.sg) facilitates procurement and revenue tenders activities between businesses and the government.

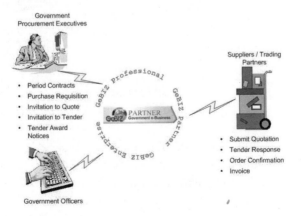

Figure 9-7: Government Electronic Business

Launched in June 2000, GeBIZ comprises of three components: GeBIZ Enterprise for decentralised procurement by government officers, GeBIZ Professional designed for procurement executives in administering complex tenders, and GeBIZ Partner for the supplier community to source and response to government-wide business opportunities.

Today, more than S$ 500 million worth of government procurement activities have been conducted through the portal.

GOVERNMENT EMPLOYEE SERVICES

PaC@GOV

The government "Pay n Claim" portal (PaC@GOV) provides the civil service with a one-stop access to all payroll related services. This includes the ability to request for electronic payslips that can be viewed via the portal or delivered to the recipient's email account. Claims such as transport and other allowances can be uploaded into the system for subsequent processing.

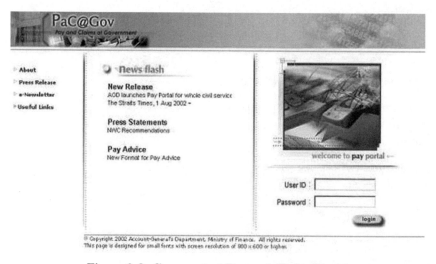

Figure 9-8: Government Pay and Claim Portal

Upgraded in late 2002, the system also offers self-service functions like varying the amount of regular donations to approved charity bodies (eg Community Chest) and updating of bank accounts for salary crediting.

This helps to minimise the amount of manual paperwork and remove the need for the tedious process of liaising with the finance staff.

PRAISE

PRAISE (Promotion, Ranking, and Appraisal System) is a Web-based solution on the Government Intranet that integrates the appraisal, ranking and promotion processes of more than 65,000 civil servants working throughout the government's Ministries. Designed as an effective talent management system, PRAISE provides a graphical and intuitive user interface to capture appraisal information via standardised and password protected forms.

With its high accuracy, security, and flexibility, civil service personnel have more confidence in their appraisal, ranking, and promotion outcomes. Users now achieve faster response times with increased efficiency and reduced work effort in talent management.

TRAISI

Introduced by the Ministry of Education (MOE) in September 1999, the Training Administration System On Intranet (TRAISI) allows MOE staff to plan their individual training roadmaps and keep track of their training records online. TRAISI provides a user-friendly, web-based interface for all MOE staff to manage and administer training and assume ownership for his or her own development. Training courses can be sourced via the system which also tracks individual training history and provides statistics to help plan for training.

PM2S

The Singapore Civil Service People Matters Management System (PM2S) is the second-generation government-wide human resource management solution. The system will facilitate the integration of the generic human resource needs of the Singapore Civil Service and the specific requirements of the various government agencies. Designed to manage human resource functions it consists of modules such as selection and appointment, deployment and posting, manpower planning, service conditions and exit.

One of the key features of the PM2S is the implementation of a self-service portal for staff benefits and services. Employees would be able to perform leave application, file declarations on investment and indebtedness, update personal information and provide feedback through surveys.

PM2S will be implemented over a two-year period starting from March 2002, and is expected to be commissioned in the first quarter of 2004.

DRIVING GOVERNMENT EFFICIENCY

e-Courts of Justice

The Singapore Courts have been actively applying ICT to improve the court administration and judicial adjudication processes. It is harnessing the Internet, telephony, kiosk and video-conferencing technologies so as to enable more efficient delivery of court-related services. With a view to create the court of the 21st Century, the Courts have embarked on the use of document imaging and workflow technology to improve case management; applied multimedia technology to facilitate trials; implemented an integrated criminal justice system with partner agencies; and automated court administration and corporate support systems to enhance service quality and efficiency.

The Electronic Filing System (EFS) was launched in 2000 to facilitate the electronic submission of documents by law firms. Originally designed to run on a dedicated private network, the system was migrated in 2001 to a web-based application accessible via the Internet. With EFS, civil litigation court hearings are facilitated with electronic document management solutions that would free lawyers from the logistical burden of managing physical files. Judges also have the option to retrieve court documents from the convenience of their home to prepare and research for trials via a secure remote access service.

To capitalise on the widespread popularity of mobile phones as an information delivery device, the Supreme Court introduced a Mobile Information Service (M-InfoSvcs) in August 2001. The service enables any mobile phone user to request for information on trials and hearings via SMS including the name of the judge and duty registrar, time and venue of the hearing. Other services include updates on the status of documents electronically filed to court, an alert service when applications and default judgments are filed to court, and a broadcast service informing subscribers of the release of the latest judicial decisions and other court-related information.

The Technology Courts is an advanced courtroom configured with video-conferencing and other audio-visual technology that enables lawyers to present their cases more effectively. The facilities allow evidence stored in a wide variety of media (eg videocassettes, digital video discs or video compact discs) and content format (eg audio and visual content like computer animations or three-dimensional graphics) to be tendered to court and to be played back and viewed from the various display devices (eg projection screen or liquid crystal display screen) in the courtroom. The use of electronic markings further relieves the need for repeated marking on all paper copies of the evidence and may also be recorded to form part of the court record. Through the use of video-conferencing, evidence may be given from a separate witness room or anywhere else in the world with the appropriate equipment.

Launched in January 2002, Justice Online (JOL) is web-based video conferencing system that enables lawyers to conduct multi-party court hearings from their offices instead of going down to the courts. It currently supports a variety of civil, family, admiralty and criminal matters in the Subordinate Courts and Supreme Court. Law firms planning to use the service need to subscribe to a broadband service provider, acquire the relevant video-conferencing equipment and subscribe to one of the available JOL packages. The target is to get about 90 firms on-board by April 2003, representing a "critical mass" of about 25 per cent of the law firms in Singapore who conduct litigation. It is estimated that JOL could save the legal industry up to S$ 20 million in billable hours in one year, for administrative non-contentious hearings in the Subordinate Courts alone. There are plans to expand the service to accommodate contentious issues. JOL stations have recently been installed in prisons to enable inmates to be interviewed by officers from the Attorney-General's Chambers.

Pay-per-Use Electronic Toll Booths

With the commissioning of the Electronic Road Pricing (ERP) system in 1998, Singapore became the first nation in the world to electronically charge for access to certain key areas of the city on a per-use basis. Designed to replace the labour intensive paper-based road pricing scheme (Area Licensing Scheme) introduced in 1975, the ERP is also able to offer differentiated charges based on time of travel, level of congestion and actual road usage. Used in conjunction with an electronic cash card, the flexibility of the system allows for the charges to vary according to prevailing road conditions. These are monitored by the Land Transport Authority and charges are revised every 3 months, if necessary.

Besides shifting more of the transport costs from ownership-based to usage-based, motorists are also spared the hassles of purchasing daily and monthly licenses. By not requiring human enforcement personnel at the gantries, the automated system helps to remove the potential for human error.

Originally conceived to better manage the demand for road use and keep congestion to a minimum, the ERP system has since been deployed for other transport related facilities such as deduction of parking tariffs at various government and private-operator managed carparks.

The Next Lap

Over the last twenty years, Singapore has made tremendous strides in exploiting IT in its bid to remain competitive in the challenging regional and global arenas. Led by the government, the nation prides itself as a reference model for showcasing how technology can be successfully assimilated into the daily lives of the population. The progressive and meticulously crafted national ICT programmes have established a strong foundation as Singapore leaps into new frontiers while embracing emerging technologies.

The journey has not been without its shares of bumps and potholes. Among the successes were also a number of failed experiments and initiatives.

Ambitious projects such as deploying public kiosks throughout the island fell short due mainly to the high penetration of computers and Internet access in homes. The establishment of a vibrant PKI community was hampered by the complexity, deployment issues and the state of the technology at the time. Attempts to promote a smart national ID did not take root probably due to the lack of compelling applications.

However, these projects did provide valuable feedback and were instrumental in helping shape the design and implementation of subsequent programmes and e-services.

Under Connected Singapore, the next phase of the e-Government Action Plan is expected to be launched in July 2003. The focus would be to further enhance the effectiveness and efficiency of the public service through exploitation of ICT and to fully encompass the "Many Agencies, One Government" vision.

A DIALOGUE WITH MS TAN SWEE HUA, DIRECTOR,
Electronic Services Division/Central Services Cluster,
Infocomm Development Authority of Singapore

IDA Office, Singapore

Ms Tan Swee Hua is currently Director, Electronic Services Division, Government Chief Information Office, Infocomm Development Authority of Singapore (IDA). The Division is responsible for conceptualising innovative and strategic IT initiatives and also provides project management support for strategic IT systems for the public sector. The Division works in close partnership with the various government agencies on the service-wide IT initiatives. Some of the major initiatives include the eCitizen portal, a one-stop virtual portal for delivery of public services, Government Electronic Business (GeBIZ) for electronic procurement of goods and services by government agencies, the central Public Services Infrastructure (PSi) for rapid development and delivery of electronic public services and Government to Employees initiative for public servants.

The author (JY) had the opportunity of a dialogue with Ms Tan (TSH) on 14 October 2002.

JY : **It would be very useful if we could begin with some general information on the status of Singapore's e-Government programme, and the role of your division in this programme.**

TSH : The e-Government Action Plan was launched in June 2000 by Deputy Prime Minister Tony Tan. The Plan sets the direction for the Singapore Public Sector to be a leading e-Government to better serve the nation in the Digital Economy. It supports the concept of "Many Agencies, One Government". That means, where the public is concerned, we want the government to be viewed as a single entity rather than many agencies.

The e-Government Action Plan, other than having a strong leadership, is governed and managed with different levels of accountability. At the highest level, the e-Government Policy Committee, chaired by Head of the Civil Service, sets the overall direction, reviews and approves policies. The Committee also establishes targets for e-Government deployment on a year-to-year basis and track the developments. The Ministry of Finance (MOF) is the overall owner of the Plan and its related programmes. The Infocomm Development Authority (IDA) is responsible for managing the programmes, and we work in close partnership with all government agencies to ensure successful implementation of the programmes. Their participation and support are critical to achieving our desired goals especially in the area of integration of processes across agencies.

The e-Government Action Plan is supported by a framework which focuses on the three critical relationships: Government-to-Citizens, Government-to-Businesses and Government-to-Employees.

In the area of Government and Citizens, we conceptualised the provision of a single window (the eCitizen portal) to government information and services. The intention is to realize the concept of "Many Agencies, One Government", through streamlining the citizen's interaction with the government and minimising the need to visit multiple websites of many government agencies. The same concept has been adopted for interactions between Government and Businesses, particularly when they apply for licences to start a business. We should not be organising information and services according to how we are structured internally but rather, based on the needs of members of the public.

With the eCitizen portal, information and services are presented as events in the "life journey" of individuals at different stages, eg registering a birth, getting married, looking for job and other lifetime activities. To realise this concept, we need the co-operation and collaboration of all agencies. We organise the major events into TOWNS, each relating to a different category of need (examples are education, healthcare, recreation or other aspects of interaction with the government). We had 8-9 TOWNS in the initial stage and for each TOWN, we appoint a lead agency as a "Town Owner" to conceptualise, plan and develop the TOWN. The lead agency's key role is to integrate information and services into meaningful service packages for users. We now have a comprehensive offering of information and services through 15 TOWNS. An e-service can appear under more than one TOWN, as it depends on how the public views it. The portal serves our purpose in terms of providing a single window to the public. Some of the e-services are already available in the respective agencies' websites but members of the public will need to know which website to go to for a specific e-service. If they need to interact with more than one agency, the portal provides a one-stop access to the information and services and this makes it more convenient for them to interact with the government.

JY : **In making the transition from a more agency-based structure to e-Citizen which is more customer centric, what were some of the challenges?**

TSH : Naturally, we faced challenges in implementing the eCitizen concept because that's not how agencies are organised. With this concept, agencies have to work together and collaborate under the respective TOWNS, eg under the Business Town, the Ministry of Trade & Industry being appointed Town Owner, has to conceptualise and bring together a number of related agencies to plan and develop the Town. They need to consider the major interactions businesses have with the government — starting a business, looking for business opportunities, staying in business, applying for schemes/grants, etc.

A phased approach has been adopted in delivering the e-services through the portal. As a first step, we work with agencies to deliver service packages which include all information and steps that the public has to undergo to complete a specific event. All related e-services are also listed there.

At the second stage, our focus is on achieving greater integration across agencies where applicable. This is most relevant in the area of Government to Businesses, eg starting a business for public entertainment requires application of licences from at least 5–6 agencies. The focus is thus on integrating the processes so that there will be seamless delivery of services to the business community. The objective is to allow a single application form to be submitted online and all related applications are initiated and routed to the respective agencies for processing. Besides reducing the hassle to the applicant, the processing turnaround of the application was reduced from 8 weeks to 2 weeks.

JY : **e-Government, in general has dual purpose, one is to make more efficient the governmental processes and the other is to serve the public — does this both achieve their objectives?**

TSH : Yes, when the public goes online, there will be shorter queues at the counters and the agency will reap benefits in terms of not needing the same number of counters to serve them. For the public, as with any online application provided on the Internet, the service is available almost around the clock and the public can access it anytime, rather than be confined to the operational hours of the counters. They can also access it from the comfort and convenience of their homes too.

JY   : **How does the Singapore Government promote e-Government services not just to IT literate but non-IT literate as well ?**

TSH : It is part of IDA's charter to encourage Singaporeans to adopt an e-lifestyle (under Infocomm 21). IDA's eLifestyle Marketing Department promotes the adoption of infocomm technology amongst the general public, especially those who are non-IT literate. Once they're shown the benefits of IT, we proceed to introduce government e-services to them in addition to other online services relating to shopping, entertainment, education, etc. We adopt a multi-pronged approach and address the issue of physical accessibility as well. Although our PC penetration rate is high, there will still be those who are unable to have access to the internet. We (MOF and IDA) provide physical access through community centres and introduce the PC help scheme to assist the lower income families to own a PC.

Next, we encourage them to go online. Besides conducting courses to show them how to use the Internet and access online services, we (MOF and IDA) have established an eCitizen help service at community centres where the public can go to for assistance to access government e-services.

There are many different ways in which we can change behaviour to transact with government online. Various agencies have organised promotional events to create awareness and encourage the public to use the online mode. MOF and IDA have also organised roadshows and published media stories to create general awareness. Specific stories/articles have also been published on how members of the public can explore and perform task online with the government, be it under healthcare, business, education, etc.

JY   : **In general, on the area of marketing and promoting e-Government, what are the key challenges that you have to handle?**

TSH : The challenges with government services are different from those of the private sector in that the private sector are free to choose their customers whereas the government can't. Similarly, for some of the services, the public can choose whether to use but they cannot do so for those that are governed by regulatory requirements. Therefore, our promotion has to be broad-based to reach out to the wide spectrum of public users.

On another front, we try to present our information and services as user-friendly (easy to use) and to simplify the processes so that it's simple to transact online with the government.

JY : **Let's talk about the Public Service Infrastructure (PSi) — which I understand is handled by your Division. Maybe you could give me some background.**

TSH : The key objective of PSi is to provide a robust, central infrastructure for rapid development and delivery of e-services. With the e-Government direction to put government services online, agencies were faced with the challenge to do so quickly. Instead of each agency developing its infrastructure individually, we decided to develop a central infrastructure (known as PSi) which all agencies could leverage. Other than ensuring that it is robust, scalable and secured, we have also implemented services that most agencies will require. For example, there is an e-payment service which agencies can use to rapidly deploy e-services which involve payment. Another tool called "e-service generator" can be used to develop e-services rapidly. PSi also provides the infrastructure to host the e-services.

In the area of authentication, we have set up a service for single-factor authentication with a common ID and Password (based on the CPF PAL Pin) which all agencies can use. For members of the public, it means that when they access agencies' e-services which require authentication, they only need to remember one ID and Password. This brings convenience to them.

PSi provides different "security authentication system" which agencies can use, depending on their requirements. In most instances, eg where the e-service is simply for making payments, authentication is really not required. We should make it convenient and authenticate only when necessary. In the event where identification is required and single-factor authentication is sufficient, this common ID and Password can be used for that purpose.

For highly secured transactions where there is a need to authenticate the individuals, eg medical-related e-services, agencies can use the PKI authentication service which is also provided under PSi.

JY   : **You have been involved in e-Government in Singapore for sometime and have observed how other nations, especially US, Europe have done it. In your view, are there any different challenges that faced implementation of e-Government in Singapore viz-a-viz that of western countries?**

TSH : First on the differences — Singapore is small compared to other countries (as mentioned above) and in most instances, these countries are likely to have different levels of government while we only have one. They have the federal, state and local governments, and in that sense, the challenges are much greater. Whatever the situation, a critical aspect of successful e-Government implementation lies in having strong "leadership" to drive e-Government. This would encompass appropriate governance and management to bring everybody together and work towards a common vision.

Having a high-level strategy is inadequate. The challenge is in the implementation. In this respect, we (MOF and IDA) have defined specific programmes and set targets for each year. To assist the agencies in achieving the targets, we facilitate and provide assistance/advice along the way. These can be in the form of creating opportunities for information sharing, coordination and collaboration or providing central infrastructure and services.

JY   : **e-Government, at the end of the day is part of overall government. My question is basically: how does e-Government help to better government or does e-Government lead to better government, in the first place?**

TSH : e-Government is not just putting our services online. There is also a need to focus on governance in the digital economy, which is different from governance in the traditional environment. The challenge lies in the ability to adapt or change existing policies, rules and regulations to better meet the needs of the new economy. As part of the process of putting their services online, agencies are encouraged to review their work processes and policies/rules/ regulations.

There must also be consideration on how we can provide better services to the public and enhance the government-citizen relationship.

Endnotes

1   Year 2002 figures from Singapore Department of Statistics.

2   Severe Acute Respiratory Syndrome, an atypical pneumonia, spread by a highly contagious virus.

3   NCB, *"Annual Report"* (1991).

4   Geographic Information System — used to manipulate and analyse geographically referenced data or geospatial data to support decision-making for planning and management of land use, natural resources, environment, transportation and urban facilities.

5   NCB, *"IT 2000 Report"* (1992).

6   Soh, Natalie, *"More Internet users here taking to surfing at speed"*, *The Straits Times*, 17 April 2003.

7   Asymmetric Digital Subscriber Line: a technology that utilises the standard telephone infrastructure for high-speed broadband access.

8   Broadband access through the national cable TV network.

9   Comprises mobile technology like GPRS and wireless LAN.

10 Dedicated high-speed fibre-optic to the broadband backbone via 1-Net corporate broadband services.

11 iDA, *"Connect Singapore — A New Blue Print for Infocomm Development"*, March 2003.

12 A certification body for issuance of digital certificates required for identification and authentication of PKI based transactions.

13 iDA statistics on Telecom Services for 2003.

14 Raju Chellam, *"More Reaching for Broadband"*, BizIT, *Business Times*, 21 April 2003.

15 Public wireless LAN access points based on the industry 802.11 standards.

16 iDA, *"Singapore's eCitizen Wins Prestigious Stockholm Challenge Award"*, press release October 2002.

17 Short Message Service.

18 A non-profit initiative of the City of Stockholm recognising pioneering IT projects which positively impact individuals and society.

Refereces

1   Hioe, William, *"Infocomm Policy and Development in Singapore"* presentation, Infocomm Development Authority of Singapore (2002).

2   Koh, Lim, Hui, Rao and Chng (eds), *"Singapore Economy in the 21st Century"*, McGraw-Hill (2002).

3   Chun Wei Choo, *"IT 2000: Singapore's Vision of an Intelligent Island"*, chapter in *"Intelligent Environments"*, Droege, Peter (ed), North-Holland (1997).

4   Toh Mun Heng, *"Singapore as a Regional Information Technology Hub"*, in *"Information Technology in Asia: New Development Paradigms"* (edited by Chia and Lim), ISEAS, 2002.

5   Chia Siow Yue and Jamus Jerome Lim, *"Singapore: A Regional Hub in ICT"*, in *"Towards a Knowledge-based Economy: East Asia's Changing Industrial Geography"* (edited by Masuyama and Vendenbrink), ISEAS/NRI, 2003.

6   Teng, Fang Yih, *"Politically Dot Correct"*, CIO Asia, December 2001.

7   Low, Linda (ed), *"Singapore – Towards a Developed Status"*, Oxford University Press (1999).

Useful Websites

www.gov.sg	Official website of the Government of Singapore
www.egov.gov.sg	Official website for information on the e-Government Action Plan
www.mof.gov.sg	Official website of the Ministry of Finance, Singapore
www.ida.gov.sg	Official website of the Infocomm Development Authority of Singapore
www.ecitizen.gov.sg	eCitizen portal aggregating government-to-citizen e-services
www.itsc.org.sg	Official website of the Information Technology Standards Committee
www.s-one.net.sg	Website showcasing broadband multimedia applications on SingaporeONE

CHAPTER 10

Digital Taiwan — Towards a Green Silicon Island

James SL Yong

▲▼▲▼▲▼▲▼

By finding a balance between environmental protection and economic development, we will develop Taiwan into a green silicon island.

Chen Shui-Bian,
Taiwan President,
inaugural address (2000)

▲▼▲▼▲▼▲▼

BACKGROUND

History

In the late 16th Century, when an early Portuguese ship sailed close to the island, a navigator onboard exclaimed "Ilha Formosa" (meaning "beautiful island"), and this became the name of the island for the next four centuries. Formosa was occupied by the Dutch between 1624 and 1662. The Dutch established a fortress on the *Tayouan* peninsula on the southwestern coast of the island. This was later evolved into *Taiwan*, and eventually came to be the name for the whole island. In 1662, the Dutch were defeated by Cheng Cheng-kung (Koxinga), a Ming loyalist. Cheng's son took over when he died, but in 1683, this last remnant of the Ming Dynasty was defeated by the Manchus.

The new Manchu emperors, being "inland" people not attuned to naval warfare, were not eager to extend their rule over the island. In the subsequent years, immigration to the island from the coastal provinces of China increased, as people fled the wars and famines on the mainland. Taiwan thus remained a loose-lying area for the next 200 years. At times, the Manchu attempted to extend their control over the unruly inhabitants, but time and again the islanders fought back.

In 1895, the Japanese defeated the Manchus in the Sino-Japanese War, and China was forced to cede Taiwan to Japan in perpetuity. Despite the harsh years of Japanese rule, notable progress was achieved on the island. The educational system was built up to the Japanese model and infrastructure and industry were developed extensively.

During World War II, the Allied Powers agreed with Chiang Kai-Shek's request that Taiwan be "returned to (Nationalist) China", which happened when the War ended in 1945. Following the Communist victory on the mainland in 1949, some two million Nationalists fled to the island of Taiwan and established a government there using the 1947 constitution drawn up for all of China. Over the next five decades, the ruling authorities gradually democratised and incorporated the native population within its governing structure. Throughout this period, the island prospered to become one of East Asia's economic "Tigers".

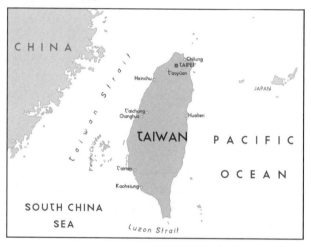

Economy and Geography

Today, Taiwan has a dynamic capitalist economy with a GDP of US$ 310 billion (in 2000). Real growth in GDP has averaged 7–8 percent during the past three decades. Exports have grown even faster and have provided the primary impetus for industrialisation. Inflation and unemployment are low; the trade surplus is substantial and foreign reserves are the world's fourth largest. Agriculture accounts for a mere 3 percent of GDP. Traditional labour-intensive industries are steadily being moved offshore and replaced with more capital and technology-intensive industries. The main industries are machinery, electrical and electronics equipment, computer products, textiles and clothing. Major trading partners are USA, Japan and China (via Hong Kong). Taiwan has also become a major investor in China, Thailand, Indonesia, the Philippines, Malaysia, and Vietnam.

Taiwan has a population of over 22 million people (84 percent Taiwanese, 14 percent Chinese and 2 percent Aboriginal). The capital city is Taipei on the northern part of the island. Other major cities are Kaohsiung, Tainan and Taitung. While urban life is fast-paced, hectic and often polluted, rural Taiwan still boasts of scenic mountains, lakes and countryside.

Government

Over the past five decades, Taiwan's governmental system has evolved from authoritarian military rule into a more representative democracy. Since 1949, it has been single-party rule by the Kuomintang (KMT) or the Nationalist party. In 2000, the opposition Democratic Progressive Party (DPP) was elected into power, installing Chen Shui-Bian as President. Yu Shyi-Kun was appointed Premier in February 2002.

Taiwan's national government is made up of five branches or Yuan: the Executive, Legislative, Judicial, Control and Examination Yuan.

The Executive Yuan has three arms: the ministries and commissions; the subordinate administrative organs of state; and the top policy-making body the Executive Yuan Council. There are eight ministries within the Executive Yuan: Education, Interior, Economic Affairs, Justice, Foreign Affairs, National Defense, Finance, and Transportation and Communications. In addition, there are various commissions, councils and subordinate organisations.

The elected Legislative Yuan handles all legislation. It is involved in policy debate and development, and has assumed the responsibility for initiating constitutional amendments. The Judicial Yuan, which is directly appointed by the President, serves as the highest judicial authority. The Control Yuan is in charge of censorship and other political matters such as censure and impeachment. The Examination Yuan supervises examinations for government positions.

At the local government level, a series of local councils operate, carrying out mainly administrative functions.

The dominant political issue continues to be the tug-of-war relationship between Taiwan and mainland China and the question of eventual reunification. The role of the private sector as an intermediary between the two sides has also been suggested as an alternative to official dialogue.

CHALLENGE 2008: THE NATIONAL DEVELOPMENT PLAN

In early 2002, Taiwan's Premier announced an ambitious national development plan called "Challenge 2008", launching an estimated NT$ 2.6 trillion (about US$ 75 billion) six-year programme aimed at transforming the economic and social environment of Taiwan into what has been called a "Green Silicon Island". The plan called for the government to put up two-thirds of the investment, with the rest coming from the private sector.[1]

In meeting the challenges Taiwan faced, the Executive Yuan conceived three major reforms and four major investments in the plan. The reforms were focused on government, banking and finance. The investments included cultivating talent, R&D and innovation, international logistics and a higher-quality living environment. There are ten major components in the national development plan:

(1)   **Cultivating talent for the e-generation**
This is essentially about creating an environment for internationalising learning. It emphasises the development of English language and IT skills (especially the use of the Internet) to meet the challenges of globalisation. Education in culture, art, sports and civility were also mentioned as important foundational goals.

(2)   **Developing the cultural creativity industry**
In addition to high-tech development, Taiwan must strive to build a more flexible organisational system to increase its competitiveness in the knowledge-based economy. The focus is on innovative design in production, especially artistic and aesthetic creation. The plan mentions three areas:
- cultural arts (eg performing arts, visual arts and traditional folk arts)
- design industry (ie application of cultural arts, such as popular music, costume design, multimedia production, broadcasting, game software design)
- peripheral industries that support the first two (eg management of exhibition activities, publishing, advertising and pop culture packaging).

(3)   **Developing an international base for R&D and innovation**
The government will encourage national R&D expenditures to reach 3 percent of GDP in six years, with the aim of making Taiwan the ideal Asian base for research, development and innovation. Specific initiatives would include encouraging businesses and academia to increase R&D activities, developing supportive government policies, attracting global R&D talent, and increasing emphasis on the application of semiconductors and the demand for digital content. Key industries identified for special research programmes included biotechnology, nanotechnology, system-on-chip (SoC) design and telecommunications.

(4)   **Increasing value-added production**
This was about establishing Taiwan as a production and supply centre for high value-added products, in the face of rising competition from cheap labour from China and parts of Southeast Asia. Government efforts would be directed in five areas: raising venture capital funds, helping industries develop core technologies, promoting key industries, encouraging businesses to invest in international marketing channels and promoting local brands development, and constructing industrial parks.

(5)   **Doubling the number of tourists visiting Taiwan**
Having long identified tourism as a major area of support for Taiwan's domestic economy, the plan relies on innovations to develop, grow and attract visitors to the island. The target set is 5 million foreign visitors by 2008. The present tourism traffic is around 1 million per year (2001 figures). To implement the plan, areas of industry focus identified were "client-orientation" and "target management".

(6)   **Developing "Digital Taiwan" or "e-Taiwan"**
This aspect of Challenge 2008 will be covered in the later part of the chapter. In a nutshell, the plan to develop Digital Taiwan uses ICT to quickly move Taiwan into the new knowledge-based economy, upgrade the competitive edge of local industries, establish a highly efficient government and promote a high quality information society. Five key thrusts are highlighted: e-Business, e-Government, e-Transportation, e-Life and the boosting of broadband usage to six million by 2008.

(7)   **Developing Taiwan as an Operations Headquarters**
This calls for investment in local infrastructure to make Taiwan an ideal location for Taiwan businesses and multinational corporations to establish regional or global operations headquarters. Some of the initiatives identified include: integrating land, sea and air links, simplifying customs processes, helping businesses strengthen their supply chain management, using tax incentives to encourage Taiwan businesses to conduct R&D, design and sales within Taiwan, and establishing a free trade shipping zone to speed up flow of goods and facilitate business activities.

(8)   **Improving the Transportation Infrastructure**
In response to changes in the domestic environment, this includes a set of island-wide highway and railway construction plans, which together form an integrated transportation framework for the island. Such an interconnected network will better serve the industrial sector and the general public, bringing Taiwan much closer to its objective of becoming a global logistics centre.

(9)   **Conserving water resources and the ecology**
This component of Challenge 2008 focuses on balancing rapid economic growth with environmental efforts to revitalise the land. Included are plans to rehabilitate forests, riverbanks and seacoasts, proper sewage treatment and effective water conservation. Comprehensive land use planning will be employed to reform the urban landscape and revive Taiwan's natural beauty.

(10)   **Building new hometown communities**
To retain talent, this is a societal-focused initiative that strives to provide a high-quality living environment (including facilities, cultural traditions, citizen participation and community concern). The "new hometown and new tribe movements" plan will integrate community development through self-reliance, community pride, common recreation and other goals.

THE DIGITAL TAIWAN PROJECT

The Digital Taiwan or "e-Taiwan" project plan, one of the key components of Challenge 2008, has the explicit goal of making Taiwan "fully digital" by 2008. This plan calls for an investment of more than NT$ 36 billion (over US$ 1 billion) over six years, and through implementing this plan, the leaders hope to shape Taiwan into the most "e-oriented" economy in Asia.

The project has evolved over a number of years. Past plans have included the National Information Infrastructure (NII) development programme in 1994, the intermediate range NII programme in 1997, the e-Government programme in 1998 and the National Information and Communication Initiative (NICI) in 2001.

In a move to stimulate private sector investment, Taiwan's premier also announced an NT$ 1.6 billion (US$ 46.3 million) investment in global logistics, operation and engineering. The success of the e-Taiwan project requires public-private sector collaboration.

Key Agencies

In early 2001, the government consolidated several committees into the NICI steering committee. NICI, headed by minister Dr Tsai Ching-Yen, was tasked to develop a blueprint for transforming Taiwan into a knowledge-based economy, and in December 2001 they submitted the "National Information and Communication Promotion Strategies" report with the vision of developing "e-Taiwan".

Another influential agency is the Research, Development and Evaluation Commission (RDEC). RDEC, under the leadership of chairman Dr Lin Chia-Cheng, is one of the major think tanks of the Executive Yuan with a status on par with the other ministries. It is responsible for policy research, planning, control and evaluation of policy implementation, information systems management and government publications. The RDEC is the key agency which spearheads Taiwan's e-Government programme. It has a Central Taiwan Division to assist county and city governments in their research and evaluation tasks. Each year RDEC recommends to the Premier research projects of importance to the country's development. Those eventually selected are assigned to appropriate agencies for execution. RDEC also integrates the expertise of the academia, government, and the industry sectors, as well as increase the coordination and interaction between the general public and the different agencies.

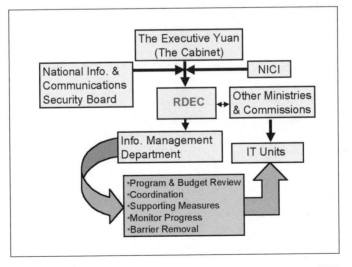

Source: RDEC (2002)

Figure 10-1: Agencies involved in e-Government

Key Projects and Frameworks

Based on the development of "e-Infrastructure" as its foundation, e-Taiwan will be implemented through three major projects, ie e-Government, e-Industry and e-Society, aimed at establishing Taiwan into an advanced, high-quality information society.

The e-Taiwan Project features five major development frameworks: e-Life, e-Business, e-Government, e-Transportation, and Broadband Access for 6 million households.

The Office of the e-Taiwan Project anticipates that by 2008 when most of these items will have been implemented, more than 20,000 job opportunities will be created, and business turnover from digital service-related industries will have topped NT\$ 100 billion. Another NT\$ 100 billion is expected to be saved from government household registry and land affairs systems as a result of computerisation.

e-Life

This sub-programme is geared to nurture an "e-Life" rich in cultural information, raise the quality of e-learning and eliminate a perceived digital divide. In addition, the media industry will be encouraged to produce digital motion pictures portraying a "Taiwan spirit". Currently, most digital products are mostly Western in content, and the Taiwanese desire is to see their own culture being portrayed in entertainment products.

e-Business

Integration of "e-markets" and "e-standardisation" is necessary if Taiwan is to join international supply chains. Moreover, multinational customer service models are crucial if Taiwan is to become a product design centre. Government assistance will be provided to industries such as electronics, semiconductors, telecommunications, opto-electronics, textiles and precision instruments in order to establish a system to coordinate design.

e-Government

Many government bureaucracies were transformed into "electronic windows" where the public would be able to access information on complex administrative procedures at anytime. The electronic system will make it easier for the public to pay taxes, apply for documents and get official information. Hundreds of different document types would become paperless in the project.

e-Transportation

The Intelligent Transportation System — the centre of integrated transportation information for bus, taxi, airline or train services — offers assistance to county governments to build intelligent urban transportation control system, and will help solve traffic problems by offering the public real-time transportation information. IC cards will be used on buses, trains and mass rapid transit systems as well as in parking lots.

Broadband access

By 2009, it is expected that half of Taiwan's population will be regular computer users, while 70 percent of the island's Internet surfers will be broadband subscribers. The target for broadband users is 6 million by 2008.

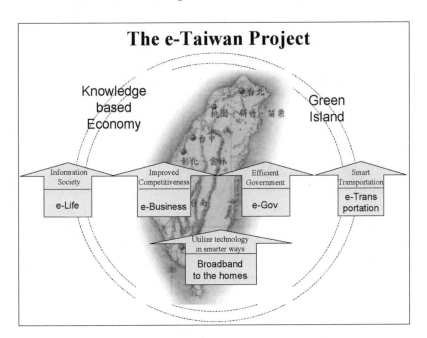

Figure 10-2: Major Development Frameworks of the e-Taiwan Project

ICT MATURITY INDICATORS

Observers[2] believe Taiwan is well-positioned to achieve its stated goals, given the strong technological foundation and open Internet environment.

Teledensity

According to ITU, at end-2002, Taiwan's teledensity (both fixed and mobile) was among the highest in Asia at 154 percent.[3] Taiwan's cellular phone penetration rate was reported to have passed the 100 percent mark in 2002.[4, 5] With some 22.6 million cellphones in use on the island, and a total population of 22.3 million, the penetration level reached 100.7 percent by April 2002. Considering that over 20 percent of the population is below the age of 14, a fair number of Taiwanese must have more than one phone each.

Landline penetration is around 55 percent, indicating that a large percentage of the Taiwanese population has a cellphone, but no landline phone.

Internet

By September 2002, Taiwan's Internet penetration reached 41 percent, representing some 9.5 million Internet users. More than 52 percent of households are connected to the Internet.[6] However, for Taiwan companies Internet connection usage was still at a relatively low 26 percent in 2002.[7] Cybercafes have also become very profitable businesses in cities.

Broadband usage

There were about 1.8 million broadband users by early 2003, of which 1.6 million were on ADSL and most of the rest on cable modem. Worldwide, Taiwan ranked 4th in terms of broadband usage level, after South Korea, Hong Kong and Canada. It is also envisaged that by the end of 2007, the island's main north-south broadband infrastructure will reach 1,150 gigabytes per second (gbps), and the international undersea cable, 1,000 gbps.[8] A clear target set in the e-Taiwan Project is to reach 6 million broadband users by 2008.

Wireless

Taiwan also makes extensive use of wireless technologies to reach the parts where it is difficult for cables to penetrate. In 2002, the government issued 5 licenses for 3G mobile service providers.

THE E-GOVERNMENT PROGRAMME

e-Government is one of the five major development frameworks of the Digital Taiwan project. Although the Taiwan public administration had been applying computers in their operations for many years, a concerted effort to the realisation of e-Government only began in 1997. RDEC, the key agency coordinating e-Government in Taiwan, defines the "e-Government concept" as

> the application of information and communications technology by government to link networks and deploy a variety of service infrastructure, including voice telephony, ATMs, the Internet, and information kiosks, for the purpose of providing extensive, proactive services not subject to the constraints of time or geographical location.

For Taiwan, it has been said that the key driving factors for e-Government are public expectations, national security and public safety, and global competition. Firstly, the citizens have elevated expectations of what information and services the government should be providing them. This stems from the Taiwanese experience of what commercial entities provide by way of online services, as well as from observations of other nations' online government initiatives. Secondly, governments were compelled to do more in terms of national security and public safety after witnessing the terrorist attacks on the US. Thirdly, there is a conviction that e-Government can make the economy more competitive.

Taiwan's stated e-Government vision spans three areas:

(1) To employ ICT in support of government reengineering, provision of innovative services, administrative efficiency improvement, and raising the quality of public services.

(2) To reform civil servants' operating procedures and reengineer the handling of public business so as to take advantage of modern ICT, thereby making government agencies more flexible and responsive, accelerating service speed, extending service time, broadening geographical service scope, enriching service options, and lowering costs.

(3) To enable government agencies, businesses and the public to conveniently obtain a variety of government services via a broad range of channels at any time and place, and to provide integrated, innovative inter-departmental services.

In line with this vision, measures were taken at four levels: strengthening infrastructure, improving information applications, enhancement of government information dissemination, sharing and integration, and implementation of government online services. Doing these will help achieve the aims of improving service effectiveness, enhancing clerical efficiency, and improving decision-making quality.

Mid-term e-Government Implementation Plan (1997–2000)

In November 1997, the RDEC was assigned the task of drafting a "Mid-term e-Government Implementation Plan (1997–2000)". This plan focused on the attainment of several key goals:

- full-scale deployment of a government backbone network;
- development of online public services and administrative applications;
- acceleration of a government information interchange; and
- establishment of electronic certification and network security mechanisms.

According to plan, an extensive inter-connection of government networks, the Government Service Network (GSN), was launched in 1997. The GSN provided government agencies at all levels with a common platform for the development of public service systems.

In 1998, RDEC established a Government Certificate Authority (GCA) to help in the creation of a reliable, secure and trusted network transaction environment. There was widespread establishment of government websites and promotion of online government information and services. Many areas of government administration were reengineered as well.[9]

e-Government Action Programme (2001–2004)

In April 2001, RDEC issued the "e-Government Action Programme (2001–2004)" aimed at enhancing the depth and breadth of government online applications during the 4-year term of this plan. The key goal of the programme was to enhance national competitiveness by promoting Internet applications throughout society and industry. The specific performance targets were:

- to implement electronic official document exchange at all levels of government within 1 year;
- to enable all levels of government organisations to build websites and provide Internet based services within 2 years;

- to nurture the government workforce to make use of the Internet within 3 years; and
- to deploy 1,500 Internet-based government services in 4 years.

Implementation Strategies

There seem to be three primary phases in Taiwan's e-Government programme:

(1) infrastructure development and penetration;
(2) online services development; and
(3) mobile government.

The overall programme focuses on the following implementation strategies:

- provision of GSN services to all agencies;
- acceleration of information infrastructure development;
- enhancement of information applications, and development of GIS applications;
- development of flagship projects;
- enrichment of government online services, including an integrated government portal;
- elimination of the digital divide by focusing on remote areas and "info-underprivileged" groups;
- making good use of private resources and expanding outsourcing;
- respecting human rights and promoting humane values, strengthening e-learning for civil servants, enshrining correct behavior and values, and encouraging innovation and vigor.

STATUS OF KEY INITIATIVES

Building on the foundation of government computerisation and public service automation accomplished over many years, Taiwan's e-Government programme is taking advantage of the Internet and other ICT by further integrating systems and deploying online applications.

The following sampling of key initiatives give a sense of the progress of the e-Government programme in Taiwan:

Government Service Network (GSN)

GSN (www.gsn.gov.tw), the backbone network and Internet service linking all government departments and agencies island-wide, is a fundamental piece of Taiwan's e-Government infrastructure. The backbone is linked directly to three major domestic networks. The GSN system began operating in July 1997. By the end of 2001, the users (ie government departments and agencies) were connected to the GSN by about 1,000 fixed lines, 3,000 ADSL lines, and nearly 10,000 dial-up connections. Total bandwidth exceeded 1,000 Mbps.

The GSN system is in the process of evolving into a second generation infrastructure — GSN II. By the end of 2002, 97 percent of government organisations were connected to the Internet, with 55 percent on broadband.

It is targeted that by end 2004, all government agencies will be connected to the GSN via the broadband network (GSN II).

Government Service Network

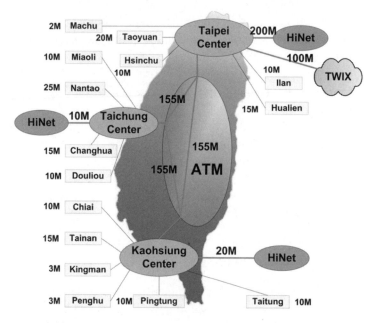

Figure 10-3: Taiwan's Government Service Network (GSN)

Government agency websites

Some 2,800 government agency websites were established by the end of 2001. By the end of 2002, RDEC reported that 85 percent of government agencies were providing services on websites. To encourage the agencies to enrich government website content and improve service quality, RDEC organises annual website evaluation and award contests.

Nationwide Internet access/service points

There are thousands of small villages and neighbourhoods in Taiwan. In order to encourage citizens all over the island to use computers and the Internet, the government set up Internet access/service points islandwide. Among the more successful schemes launched was the "e-Village Service" project, which aims to give Taiwan's rural people the same Internet privileges enjoyed by their urban counterparts.

The government has helped more than 6,500 villages and neighbourhoods to create their own "village websites" (http://village.gov.tw), and has established more than 170 "community information kiosks" in remote areas as of mid-2002. There is also a focus on getting the elderly and the disabled to make use of computers.

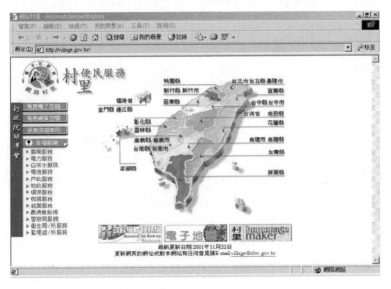

Figure 10-4: e-Village Services

All these activities are part of a programme to bridge the digital divide — between rich and less-affluent, urban and rural, young and old, able-bodied and disabled.

Central government portal

The administration has set up a government portal site (http://www.gov.tw) to integrate all online government services and information. This site provides search engine queries, webpage searches, agency directories, public opinion mailboxes, personal webpages, and real-time government news. Five hundred application forms were available for downloading and 100 online application services were offered as of March 2002. In addition, the government portal site also provides general basic service for government agencies, including electronic certificates, payment methods, form generators, and work flow utilities to speed up the development of online application services.

By end 2002, it was reported that about 10 per cent of all government services were accessible online through this portal.

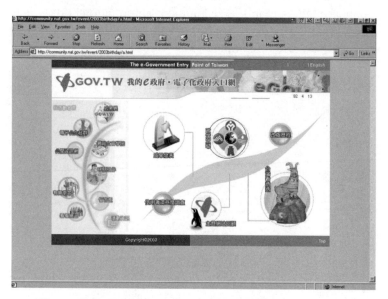

Figure 10-5: Taiwan's government portal (www.gov.tw)

Certificate Authority

To establish a secure and reliable network transaction environment, a Government Certificate Authority (GCA) was set up in early 1998. This facility provides online identity authentication and network identification services to government agencies and the public. By the end of 2001, the GCA had issued more than 200,000 digital certificates and had begun providing certification services in connection with online tax reporting, motor vehicle registration, online disbursements, e-procurement and electronic official document exchange. These services provide the public and private agencies with a secure and error-free means of making online applications and transmitting data. The website is http://www.pki.gov.tw.

e-Government PKI
http://grca.nat.gov.tw/

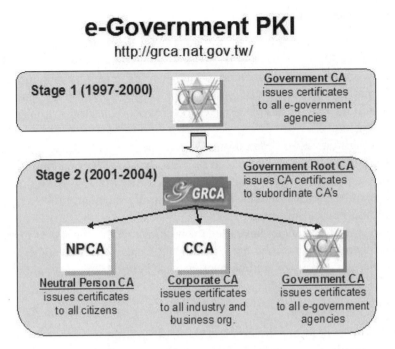

Figure 10-6: Government PKI

Intra-agency Administrative and Collaborative applications

Several initiatives have been implemented:

- The government has deployed an inter-departmental email system for all government departments and agencies. It is expected that this will sharply improve the efficiency of communications between government bodies.
- The electronic interchange of official documents began on a trial basis in July 2000 and today all ministries, local governments, and major agencies have implemented electronic official document interchange. This has sharply reduced document transmission time and raised the level of document computerisation.
- A national legal database has been compiled, providing online access to laws and regulations. This has greatly enhanced the transparency of information on laws and regulations.

Efficiency in other public administrative functions has improved through implementation of systems such as: online personnel, project management and government publication.

Online Procurement

The Public Construction Commission (PCC), Executive Yuan has been working on the development of online procurement for some years. The completion of an online procurement and government tender announcement information system, as well as an online catalogue, and price quotation and bidding systems has made government procurement more transparent, and efficient.

To facilitate online procurement, a domestic "Government Internet Purchasing Card" was introduced in 2002. This is a "virtual credit card", with only card numbers. There is no physical card. Use of the card is expected to decrease purchasing costs, simplify payment processes, and minimise purchasing fraud.

Government agencies have used the online procurement system to make more than 720,000 public tender announcements since November 2001. An average of 300,000 online queries were being received monthly.

Public e-Services

The number of online government services for Taiwan's constituents has been steadily rising. By end 2002, notable examples included:

- online tax reporting system (for both citizens and businesses);
- online motor vehicle oversight services system (which provides application and payment services, such as payment of traffic fines and auto fuel taxes, reporting of stolen motorcycles, and reporting of change of ownership or address);
- online database for employment services (ie vacancies and applicants);
- online public safety, business and industry, health care; and
- utilities service systems that provide convenient 24-hour public service.

Inter-departmental Gateway System

The government has also created a "Gateway System" to integrate inter-departmental information, reduce redundant copies of official documents, simplify related operating processes and generally improve the efficiency of administrative procedures. Examples include shared company and business registration information (which would enable the government to spare vendors the pain of repeatedly providing identical information to different agencies), inter-province land title transcript information, residential and conscription information, and online query systems for police, tax, legal affairs, immigration entry and exit, road management, fiscal administration, and healthcare or insurance information.

CHALLENGES AND HOPES FOR THE FUTURE

Taiwan has made significant strides since the launch of its e-Government programme in 1997. Most notably, the ICT infrastructure has been addressed, and various online services have been successfully launched. Within the government administration, progress has been made in providing civil servants with tools to enhance their efficiency and effectiveness. By end 2002, RDEC reported that 100 percent government agencies exchange official documents through the Internet and more than 10 percent of government application services were being provided on the Internet.[10]

However, the milestones of progress have also been accompanied by hurdles. This is only to be expected, and it is likely that new hurdles will arise and need to be overcome in order to benefit from the opportunities that lie ahead. The following section highlights some of the challenges faced.

Budgetary Constraints

Although Taiwan emerged from the Asian financial crisis of 1997 relatively unscathed, the worsening economic situation in the years following had a greater toll on the island's economy. Consequently the Taiwan government had to go through a period of rationalising and belt-tightening. Budget cuts have imposed sharp constraints on e-Government and many other national programmes. Selected projects have had to be reviewed. Despite this however, key programmes have been proceeding though creative deployment.

Systems Integration

e-Government is about integrating processes, structures and systems of various ministries and agencies. Many agencies still have their own computer systems; and work is still going on combining them.

Government staff, constituents unwilling to learn IT

Many older Taiwanese — both citizens as well as government employees — are reluctant to learn to use computers. With some of them in senior positions, this has been a hurdle for the rapid proliferation of IT in government and society.

Human rights groups resistance

In some areas, the e-Government push has also attracted the wrath of human rights groups, who view the administration's drive to aggregate information on its citizens with suspicion. One project which was stalled was a smart card that would combine information currently held on health and ID cards. Human rights organisations insisted that such data be kept separate.

Marketing e-Government

The RDEC has also had to persuade an often reluctant citizenry that conducting transactions online is not only convenient, but also safe and potentially rewarding. "We've put a lot of effort into marketing our applications," says Dr Lin Chia-Cheng of the Development and Evaluation Commission. "Our main idea is that when someone uses an e-Government service, for example e-tax, he gets rebates or similar incentives. The percentage of users is growing, and our goal is to have 80 per cent of the population satisfied with our online services in five years."

Getting enough high-tech workers

An ongoing problem facing Taiwan's e-Government implementation is the difficulty in recruiting adequate numbers of high-level computer specialists into the government. This challenge is not unique to Taiwan. To alleviate the difficulties, the government has turned to outsourcing an increasing proportion of its ICT projects to external parties.

Bilingualisation of websites

In a global world, the ability to exchange knowledge and information with other nations is an imperative to economic competitiveness and success. Given that English is the dominant language in the non-Chinese speaking world, it is important for Taiwan websites to be effectively bilingual. Since Taiwan's accession to the WTO, the urgency of using English as a tool for international communications and getting in sync with global commercial and social activities has become particularly apparent.

The challenge of effective bilingualisation of Taiwan's websites has become a subject of deep discussion. It has been noted that even in media websites, the "processing speed" of the Taiwanese media is fast with respect to the English-Chinese translation. Translations of statements by the President of the US, for example, can be found the next morning in all the major Chinese language newspapers. In contrast, the efficiency of the Chinese-English translation process is considerably slower.

Politics and the Civil Service — a blurring of lines

Political observers have commented that some of the early and to some extent, current, challenges faced in Taiwan's e-Government initiatives may be linked to the fact that Taiwan had only one major change in the ruling party for more than a half century. This was when the DPP took over from the KMT in 2000. This single event had a monumental impact on Taiwan's governmental structures, processes and systems. With any political change, there is invariably a ripple effect down the hierarchy where key civil servants are displaced. With this change comes some disruption, loss in continuity, and invariable inefficiencies as a result of the new team in charge having to learn the ropes as it were, of running the nation.

Taiwan is no strangers to challenges. It has always shown considerable pragmatism and resilience. In spite of many challenges to the e-Government programme, Taiwan continues to stride ahead in the unrelenting pursuit of Digital Taiwan — the Green Silicon Island.

PERSPECTIVES OF AN E-GOVERNMENT LEADER

Dr Lin Chia-Cheng,
Chairman of the Research, Development and Evaluation Commission,
Executive Yuan,
Taiwan ROC

Dr Lin Chia-Cheng is the Chairman of the Research, Development and Evaluation Commission (RDEC), and a member of the Executive Yuan (Taiwan's Cabinet).

Dr Lin received his Ph.D. in Political Science from the National Taiwan University in 1980. He then served as Professor of Political Science and Sociology at Soochow University, between 1981 and 1994. He was credited for introducing and widely promoting the application of leading edge political science research methodology throughout Taiwan's political science community, thus positioning him in the forefront of political science research in Taiwan.

Between 1994 and 1998, he served as Chairman of the Research, Development, and Evaluation Commission for the Taipei City Government (when Chen Shui-Bian took office as Taipei City Mayor). Dr Lin was also Deputy Mayor from 1997 to 1998. Between 1999 and 2000, Dr Lin continued as Professor, Department of Sociology at Soochow University, prior to assuming his present position.

The author (JY) had the opportunity of a dialogue with Dr Lin (LCC) in late 2002.

JY   : **Can you elaborate on the role of the Research, Development and Evaluation Commission (RDEC) in regard to the overall e-Government programme in Taiwan?**

LCC : RDEC has many different functions, of which e-Government is but one. I have multiple roles. I'm chairman of RDEC, and a member of the Taiwan Cabinet (Executive Yuan). I was also Deputy Mayor for the Taipei city government.

At the same time, I am on a high-level taskforce that looks at national ICT policy (focused on three main areas: e-Government, e-Business and e-Life).

JY   : **What are some of the key areas of focus in Taiwan's e-Government programme?**

LCC : A key area of focus in Taiwan's e-Government programme has been the development of infrastructure, eg provision of the Government Service Network (GSN) to government agencies and departments at all levels — both central and local government. By end 2001, users (ie government agencies) were connected to the GSN by some 1,000 fixed lines, 3,000 ADSL lines and 10,000 dial-up connections. All government units are expected to be online by end 2002, with an increasing percentage on broadband.

During the 1995 to 2000 period, a lot of infrastructure was developed. Also a large number of civil servants were trained to use computers. More than 90 percent of civil servants now have computers and make use of email, Web browsers and other office productivity software.

Another focus area is that of document exchange (especially for G to G) — to enhance the efficiency of inter-agency or inter-ministry information flow within the government. The Taiwan government strives to achieve a close to "paperless" situation. There is also a focus on knowledge management (KM).

The Taiwan government has set up a centralised portal site (www.gov.tw) which serves various functions:
- It acts as an information provision site — in terms of information to the people, government news as well as serving as a "data bank", eg it is an open website that contains all the government publications.

- It helps promote two-way dialogue or communication between government and the citizens. All government officials, even the Premier, have an email ID, and the people can write directly to him, and he will respond. This function is also used for survey questions.
- It provides basic online services — eg downloading of application forms, enabling online tax filing, etc. There are currently more than 500 application forms available for downloading and 100 online application services offered.

JY : **What are the key drivers or motivators of Taiwan's e-Government programme?**

LCC : The ICT industry is extremely important to Taiwan. For hardware development, Taiwan is probably number one in the world. For software, we are also very strong. So ICT is a major export. In general, there is a strong "engineer culture" in Taiwan.

The government supports by sponsoring research, setting up institutes, developing infrastructure, etc. Presently the telecoms company is also government owned.

All of these factors provide a good grounding for e-Government, as "e-technology" is no problem for a large part of the population.

Also, being a democratic state, the different political parties must compete in order to provide better services to the citizens. e-Government is one way to enhance such public service levels.

JY : **What do you see as some key challenges to the e-Government initiatives in Taiwan?**

LCC : Taiwan is an island, perhaps not very large, but we still have to address our "digital divide" problem. In addition to the normal divides, there is also a divide between North and South, East and West, etc. So that is one challenge.

Another problem facing Taiwan's e-Government implementation is the ability to recruit enough high-level computer specialists into the government. Perhaps some get higher compensations in private sector organisations. Whatever it is, this is an area that the government constantly needs to address.

All this leads to a concerted effort to try and outsource. But outsourcing also has its own problems, especially managing of outsourcing partners can be difficult. Our government agencies do have CIOs who can be the bridge between government requirements and the private company.

Then there is also the financial budget problem that the central government is facing. Also with regards to the budget, RDEC does not own the e-Government budget, but rather it belongs to the different ministries and agencies. Each of these entities tend to build their own applications and citizen interfaces.

There is an ongoing effort to break down or change the gateway used by citizens to reach the ministries or agencies. The government implemented a "Gateway System" to integrate inter-departmental information and simplify related operating processes. This is geared towards lessening the need for redundant copies of official documents and improving the efficiency of administrative processes. Web services is one technology being widely used in this effort to integrate the different agencies' websites.

JY   : **Some governments have mentioned that they need to go into e-Government because in the long run, there will be cost savings from the reduction in the number of manned counters, as more of the population can access online services. Comments?**

LCC : The cost savings from reduced counter operations cannot help the immediate budget problem. Furthermore the government would have a challenge in proposing cuts to counter services, which would necessitate the downsizing of staff numbers. Something like this needs to be done over a longer time frame.

Instead a big question for us is: how do we develop a good outsourcing process or system? Outsourcing is not easy to manage. The Taiwan government is accustomed to services provided by large global companies. But these are expensive. The local software companies are generally too small, relative to the global players. What would be ideal would be if the government could outsource some of the work to the local software companies — in that way, we solve two problems at once — we would have resources to implement e-Government services, as well as sustain the local software industry.

Another thing the government is considering is trying out "open source" software, eg Linux, Sun's StarOffice productivity tools.

JY : **How do you assess the readiness of Taiwan citizens to e-Government services?**

LCC : For the young people who are used to the Internet and online gaming, e-Government is certainly not a problem. In fact, it is more of an expectation. Over the years Taiwan has been actively trying to develop an "e-generation".

The usual issue is how to get the elderly, disabled, those in rural areas, etc. to be ready and willing to use e-Government services. There are special programmes to reduce the digital divide, eg training, special websites, providing public access points, etc.

Some public access points are being provided, eg in libraries. This has already started but is not yet pervasive. There are also initiatives in supermarkets, primary schools, etc.

It is important to have incentives to motivate the people to use computers and online services. For example, an idea relating to online tax filing is that we might even consider a slightly lower tax rate for those who file their returns online.

JY : **It has been reported in some countries that one of the biggest hurdles to e-Government deployment is internal to the government itself. For instance, realising e-Government often requires a graying of the lines between ministries and agencies. So implementing such initiatives may require shifts in areas of focus and control. In general, traditional government is organised in a vertical manner, whereas e-Government processes tends to cut horizontally. Any comments with regard to Taiwan?**

LCC : In Taiwan, the central Government, local Government situation is one of a vertical structure, with perceived clear divisions.

The Taiwan government is borrowing ideas from different places to try to make e-Government initiatives work, eg e-agriculture (an idea borrowed from India) — farm associations, easy connections with supermarket.

As part of government reform, we have reduced from 35 ministries and commissions down to 23.

The NICI taskforce at Cabinet level plays an important role in this area.

RDEC has a key role to play and also has the authority to push ministries to strive for greater efficiency as well as adopt e-Government practices. After all, "evaluation" is in RDEC's name and is part of its function.

JY : **What are some indicators of the success of your e-Government initiatives? How do you measure your progress?**

LCC : There are specific measures for different areas: improvement of service effectiveness, enhancing clerical efficiency and improving quality of decision-making. The measures are also at different levels, such as infrastructure, computerisation, information sharing and online services. Overall there are clear goals and strategies on how to attain key measurements.

JY : **Taiwan has obviously made significant strides in its e-Government programme. Do you have any concluding remarks on Taiwan's e-Government in general?**

LCC : We take a broader definition of e-Government to include role of government in the "e" environment, eg technology, business and society. The Taiwan government has an important role to play in each of these areas.

The Taiwan government has clearly taken many steps forward in its e-Government journey, and the future is one of building on these achievements.

The Taiwanese people have the attiitude and mindset of not being embarrassed to copy and learn from others in the space of e-Government (or any other domains). What Taiwan needs to do is to be a smart follower and to be able to do it fast.

Endnotes

1 Six Year National Development Plan (*"Challenge 2008"*) document, Government Information Office (GIO), Executive Yuan, Taiwan.

2 According to the Centre for International Development at Harvard University, Taiwan is rated "excellent" in Internet preparedness. The World Markets Research Centre has agreed with this assessment, observing that Taiwan government institutions provide top online services. The Centre for Public Policy at Brown University in a report *Global e-Government 2002* also ranked Taiwan's e-Government highest among 198 countries.

3   Asia-Pacific Telecommunication Indicators 2002 report, ITU (2002).

4   *"Innovating and Transforming Government through IT — Taiwan's Experience"* presentation by Dr Lin Chia-Cheng, RDEC, 30 November 2002.

5   *"Taiwan passes 100% cellular penetration level"*, Cellular News, posting on 20 June 2002. (www.cellular-news.com/story/6994.shtml).

6   Institute for Information Industry 2002.

7   *"Government outlines major transformation with 'e-Taiwan' plan"*, Taipei Journal, 16 July 2002.

8   Lin, Chia-Cheng, *"E-Government toward a Fair and Equitable Society — Lessons learnt in Taiwan"*, Research, Development and Evaluation Commission, Executive Yuan, Taiwan ROC, April 2002.

9   Hopfner, J, *"Beyond the Digital Push"*, MIS magazine (Asia), March 2003.

8   Chen, CK and Chang, CC, *"Developing a CRM-based E-Government Evaluation Model in The Changing Environment: Integrating Internal and External Customers in Public Services"*, 2003.

9   Lin, Yu-chuan, *"Transforming G2C Relationships—Taiwan's e-Government Experience"*, Research, Development and Evaluation Commission, Taiwan ROC, April 2002.

10   Hsiao, Naiyi, Huang, Tong-yi and Chen, Don-yun, *"Implementation Electronic Government in Taiwan: A Case Study of Taipei City Mayor's Email-box"*, paper presented at 2002 e-Government International Conference, Seoul, Korea, May 2002.

Useful Websites

www.rdec.gov.tw   Official website of the Research, Development and Evaluation Commission (RDEC), Executive Yuan, Taiwan.

www.gov.tw   Taiwan government portal

www.pki.gov.tw   Government Certification Authority.

village.gov.tw   Taiwan's Village Online project.

CHAPTER 11

Thailand: e-Government for Public Service Reform

James SL Yong and Poranee Phureesitr

▲ ▼ ▲ ▼ ▲ ▼ ▲ ▼

Make the welfare of your people your paramount concern.
Govern with integrity.

Buddha

▲ ▼ ▲ ▼ ▲ ▼ ▲ ▼

It was a sweltering Monday evening. Somchai fidgeted impatiently behind the wheel of his car. With him were his two children whom he had just picked up from school. The vehicle had hardly moved in the previous ten minutes. A train of stationary rear lights stretched down Silom Road for as far as he could see. Somchai muttered something incoherently.

"Dad, did you have a bad day at work?" asked his ten year old daughter, Pui, curiously.

"I'm just a little frustrated, kids." Somchai sighed as the car crawled a metre further. "I think we Thais have no choice but to waste so much of our time. It's like this traffic, we just can't seem to get things done quickly, especially when dealing with government offices. In fact, just before picking you up, I had to queue up for hours at the Revenue Department to file my income tax. I really wish the services of the Thai government could be comparable with those of the private companies."

"Dad, do you know that you can now use the Internet to file your income tax online?" Pom, his fourteen year old boy, joined in.

"Really?" Somchai was quite surprised. He felt that he was learning more and more from his children these days — especially when it came to IT and the Internet. "Well, I'm not so sure how complicated or reliable the system is."

Pom suggested "At least we can check out the information from the Revenue Department website and find out. My classmate Ton told me his father had started using this online tax filing, too."

Pui added enthusiastically, "Yes dad, I bet next time you'll be able to file your tax faster. When we get home, we'll show you how to get onto the website."

BACKGROUND

History[1, 2]

A unified Thai kingdom is said to have arisen in the mid-13th Century. It was known as Siam until 1939. Thailand is the only Southeast Asian country never to have been colonised. Indeed the word "Thai" means "Free", and "Thailand" means "Land of the Free".

Migrants from the north established the independent Thai kingdom of Sukhothai in 1238. Sukhothai flourished for nearly 200 years, before power shifted southward to Ayuthaya in the 14th Century. During the Ayuthaya kingdom, formal contacts between Siam and Europe were established. The first King of the present Chakri dynasty, Rama I, moved the capital to Bangkok in 1782. By opening their posts to European trade, by bringing in Western advisers, by strengthening the central administration against the hereditary provincial chieftains, and by playing off the British against the French, the Siamese managed to stay free.

The Westernisation of Siam took place largely under the absolute monarchy of King Mongkut (Rama IV) and his son, King Chulalongkorn (Rama V). During the reign of King Chulalongkorn, a proper code of law and education system was established, and the communication and transportation systems were modernised. King Chulalongkorn also carried out major administrative reform thus laying the foundation for today's modern system of government.

In 1932, a bloodless coup organised by young intellectuals educated abroad and imbued with the democratic ideals, turned the 800-year-old absolute monarchy into a constitutional one. Military government ruled the country more or less incessantly during the mid 20th Century. Thailand drafted its first five-yearly National Economic and Social Development Plan in 1961. This plan and its successors gave rise to changes in the Thai economic structure, gradually shifting from an agricultural-based to industrial-based economy.

In 1992, after an anti-government uprising, King Bhumibol Adulyadej appointed a civilian as interim prime minister. Over the past decade, multiparty coalitions have not proven very stable and the governments have changed several times, often without completing their full four-year term. A new constitution in September 1997 marked a major landmark for the political reform.

The government, led by Prime Minister Thaksin Shinawatra's Thai Rak Thai party, won the 2001 national election on a pro-poor, pro-rural, and pro-Thailand platform. This administration is the first to be elected to office under the new constitution. The government has put forward its medium-term strategies through the Ninth National Economic and Social Development Plan (2002–2006) which focuses on poverty reduction and balanced development.

Geography and Economy[3, 4]

Positioned in the middle of the Indochina region, Thailand borders Cambodia, Laos, Myanmar and Malaysia. It has a total area of 517,000 sq. km comprising a central plain, the Khorat Plateau in the northeast, and mountainous regions elsewhere. The rural area, which accounts for more than 70 percent of its population, is still agricultural based. The population is about 62 million (comprising 75 percent Thai, 14 percent Chinese, and 4 percent Malay). About 10 percent of the population live in the country's capital, Bangkok. The predominant religion is Buddhism.

The second-half of the 1980s and on into the 1990s was a prosperous time for the Thai economy. The average growth rate during the 1986–1990 period was 10 percent, and this continued until 1995, when the average growth was still strong at around 7.5 percent. At the same time, exports increased, and real estate prices surged tremendously. The heat of the Thai economy was, for some economists, a sign of the looming collapse of the economic bubble, and indeed the financial crisis struck in 1997.

In response, Thailand floated the exchange rate of the Thai baht and applied for aid from the International Monetary Fund (IMF). For the next few years, the trade and investment sectors were in poor shape because of a serious lack of liquidity, and imports slackened because of the global economic slowdown. However, under the strict rules of the IMF and the introduction of economic restoration measures in all areas, such as taxation, labour, state enterprises and investment, Thailand's economy gradually improved.

After contracting by 10 percent in 1998, Thailand's economy grew at over 4 percent in 1999 and 2000 — and stayed positive in 2001 and 2002, in spite of the global slowdown. Growth in 2003 is expected to be in the range of 3–3.5 percent.[5]

Government

The system of government for Thailand is that of a democratic constitutional monarchy. Although the King is the head of state, he does not govern the country directly but instead appoints the Prime Minister who is chosen by the House of Representatives. The national assembly consists of the Senate and the House of Representatives. At the provincial level, governors are appointed by the Ministry of Interior, with the exception of the Bangkok metropolis where the governor is chosen by popular vote. Beyond the provincial level, there is local administration for districts, tambons (groups of villages), and individual villages.

In addition to the office of the Prime Minister, the other ministries are: Defense, Finance, Foreign Affairs, Social Development and Human Security, Education, Tourism and Sports, Agriculture and Cooperatives, Transportation, Natural Resources and Environment, Information and Communications Technology, Energy, Commerce, Interior, Justice, Labour, Culture, Science and Technology, Public Health, Industry, and University Affairs.

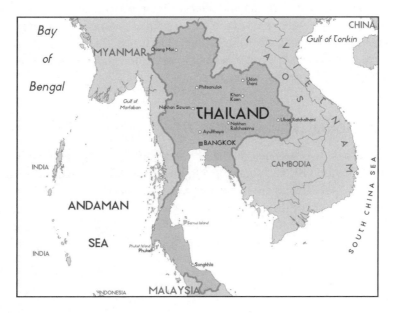

INFRASTRUCTURE OVERVIEW

As of June 2002, Thailand had 6.2 million fixed lines, a teledensity of 9.8 percent, and 12.6 million mobile phones. PC penetration was a mere 2.4 percent.[6]

Internet access was first introduced in Thailand in 1991 as an academic research network. By 2002, there were 18 commercial Internet service providers, 4 non-commercial Internet hubs, and 2 domestic Internet exchanges. Some service providers offer ADSL or cable modem options mostly for business users; however, most users connect via dial-up modems. The spread of broadband access was delayed by high costs that were partly related to the nature of the Thai telecommunications market due to an archaic regulation that forbade private enterprises from directly providing telecommunication infrastructure. As of 2002, it was estimated that there were only around 5,000 broadband subscribers in Bangkok metropolitan area.

The Internet user base in Thailand is approximately 3.5 million (or 6 percent of the total population). In fact, measuring the size of the Thai Internet market is not easy because of the widespread use of prepaid Internet accounts. It is believed that many subscribers have multiple prepaid cards and that they account for over half the market. Most of the users are in Bangkok. There are increasing numbers of Internet cafes emerging in major urban centres and other parts of the country. Internet access is also available at most secondary schools in the country. The move towards wireless LAN Internet access has emerged in a few private universities in Bangkok, but is still has limited public usage.

THE NATIONAL IT PROGRAMME

Over the past two decades, IT has been recognised as a key enabler for Thailand's economic and social development, and also a means to enhance Thailand's global competitiveness. During the 1980s, IT adoption surged in the private sector driven by business needs as the country experienced rapid economic growth. However, during the same period, IT usage in the public sector was slow by comparison.

Key Agencies

In 1992, the National Information Technology Committee (NITC) was initiated as a policy body to oversee the national IT policy direction in Thailand. This committee is led by the Prime Minister, and includes Ministers, Permanent Secretaries and other high-level officials from the public and private sectors.

To facilitate IT development in the country, the National Electronics and Computer Technology Centre (NECTEC) was established. NECTEC is a quasi-government body under the National Science and Technology Development Agency (NSTDA), within the Ministry of Science, Technology and Environment. NECTEC also performs the secretariat role for the NITC, as well as carries out research and development in the electronics and ICT areas.

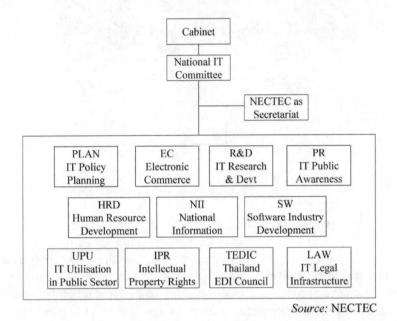

Source: NECTEC

Figure 11-1: Policy Body for Information Technology Development in Thailand

The IT 2000 Policy

Since their creation, both NITC and NECTEC have led a number of initiatives to address national issues in IT development. Despite budget constraints and issues of inconsistency in local government funding,[7] several milestones have been achieved.

One such milestone was the drafting of the IT 2000 National IT Policy in 1996. Three major areas were addressed in this first national IT Policy: building the national infrastructure, investing in IT-capable human resource development, and achieving good governance through the use of IT in rendering public services and government administration.

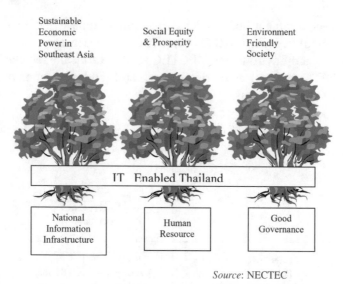

Source: NECTEC

Figure 11-2: Framework of the IT 2000 Policy

From the basis of the framework and recommendations proposed in IT 2000, several development projects were achieved as planned, while others fell short of targets. During the period, the country's economy and society had also changed rapidly, impacted by the financial crisis. There were also several external factors resulting from dynamic global changes such as borderless commerce, creation of new non-tariff barriers, as well as ICT advancement. By the turn of the millennium, Thai policy makers realised that there was a need to work on the next phase of the national policy to spearhead further, IT development in Thailand.

The IT 2010 Policy

A holistic approach was adopted in the development of the new IT policy. Several research projects were set up to assess the impact of and lessons learnt from the IT 2000 Policy, to analyse various situations in the IT industry in Thailand, to review IT utilisation in the private sector, and to study the national IT policy development in other countries. In addition, the policy makers had developed the new IT policy to align with the national development agenda specified in the Ninth National Economic and Social Development Plan. The national IT policy for the years 2001–2009, known as IT 2010, was proposed by NECTEC and approved by the Cabinet in March 2001.

The key objective of IT 2010 is to use IT to transform Thailand into a knowledge-based society. The focus is not on technological development per se. Rather, it is on the appropriate use of IT to drive balanced economic and social development progress in the context of a self-sufficient economy, to improve the quality of life of its major rural populations, and to reduce social disparity in Thai society to a minimum.

There are three specific goals for the IT 2010 policy.[8] The first is to raise the technological capability of Thailand (using the UN Technological Achievement Index as a benchmark) from being one of the "dynamic IT adopter" nations to being a "potential leader" in the region. Second is to strive to increase the proportion of knowledge workers in the country from 12 to 30 percent. And third is to increase the share of knowledge-based industries within the overall economy to 50 percent by the year 2010.

To achieve these goals, IT 2010 has identified five main flagships: e-Government, e-Education, e-Commerce, e-Society and e-Industry.

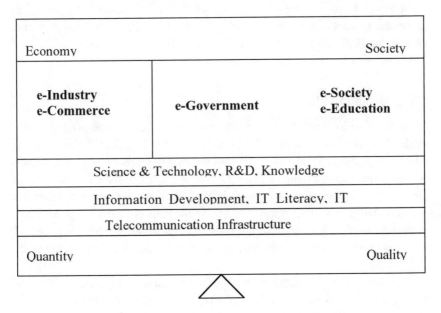

Source: NECTEC

**Figure 11-3: IT 2010 Policy Framework: Towards a
Balanced Development**

The National ICT Master Plan

The National ICT Master Plan (2002–2006) was conceived as policy implementation to complement the IT 2010 Framework. Following concerns that the ten year time frame was too long, and might hamper responsiveness to the latest technology developments, the five-year National ICT Master Plan was developed and approved by the Thai Cabinet in September 2002. The Master Plan is expected to be revised each year to keep up with the rapid pace of ICT development. It is also expected to have a follow-up five-year Master Plan in 2006.

The key objectives of the plan are to apply ICT to increase competitiveness, to develop a knowledge-based society, to apply ICT for sustainable development, and to develop businesses around the ICT industry. The Cabinet also agreed on the establishment of a new Ministry to oversee ICT development, and to be responsible for implementing the national ICT master-plan.

Subsequent to the approval of the national ICT master-plan, over 280 government agencies submitted their ICT operation plans to the Cabinet in December 2002. The integrated ICT operations plans were then put forward together with a proposal to set up an e-Government subcommittee.

The e-Thailand initiative

In addition to internal drivers, another initiative took shape after the third ASEAN informal summit in November 1999. The ASEAN Economic Ministers had endorsed an e-ASEAN proposal to enable ASEAN members to meet the rapid changes brought about by globalisation and the IT revolution, and to minimise the risk of the region being marginalised in the knowledge-based economy. Following the summit, the Thai government went on to actively deliberate the issues raised in the e-ASEAN proposal. As a result, the e-Thailand initiative was developed as a counterpart of the e-ASEAN initiative.

The goals for e-Thailand mirror that of the national IT plan, which were to exploit the potential of ICT to strengthen the country's economic competitiveness, reduce poverty, and achieve sustainable development. The framework for e-Thailand's development is: establishment of national information infrastructure, e-Commerce facilitation, liberalisation in trade, services and investment, e-Society, and e-Government. The e-Government initiative outlined in the ICT Master Plan was therefore integrated into the e-Thailand development agenda.

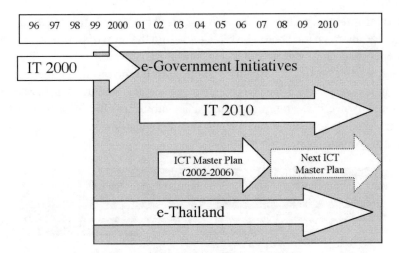

Figure 11-4: Timeline of the National IT Policies in Thailand

THE DRIVE TOWARDS E-GOVERNMENT

The promotion of IT usage in Thai public organisations dates back to 1994 when it was driven by a sub-committee of the NITC. Some measures implemented then included computer training courses for mid-level civil servants, IT equipment specifications for government agencies, appointments of Chief Information Officers (CIOs) in the public sector, as well as IT Master Planning for central (ministry) and local (provincial) administrations.

The ultimate aim of e-Government was to support the reform of public services by reducing paperwork and streamlining public services processes, thereby allowing citizens to access public services anytime and anyplace. The project mandate was to facilitate rendering good public services in what was dubbed the "4Rs campaign". This denotes Red-tape reduction toward one stop service, Rapid Response, Rural Coverage, and Round-the-clock service.

To achieve the e-Government vision, government agencies were ordered to provide at least one e-service to improve the public services on their websites. As a result of this directive, around 200 e-services for the public should be available by end 2003.

The e-Government initiatives received strong support from the central administration. The government stated publicly that new policies could be devised and new agencies established in order to support the e-Government initiatives. Prime Minister Thaksin committed that the e-Government vision should be realised within the term of his government. To encourage innovation and IT adoption, annual awards were given to recognise the best IT applications adopted in the government agencies.

Thai citizens' portal "www.Thaigov.net" was also initiated with a phased rollout of offerings, ranging from basic public service information for individuals and businesses to the publicising of electronic procurement for the government agencies.

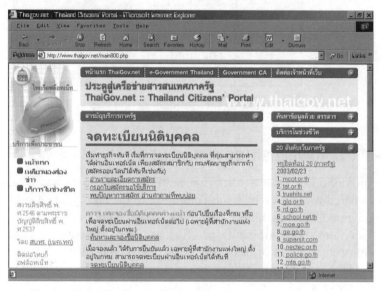

Figure 11-5: Thailand Citizens' portal "www.Thaigov.net"

In addition to the citizens' portal, there is also another portal called "Khonthai.com" (Khonthai means Thai people) set up by the Interior Ministry. This website contains several links to the websites of other public services, and provides free email accounts. Thai citizens can register for an email account at Khonthai.com by using their ID card number. Once their email account is registered, they will automatically get a Khonthai.com account and PIN code, which allows people to verify their registration data, including items contained in civil registrations, identification card details, change of name, address or marital status, and voting eligibility.

As for the citizen ID card issued by the Interior Ministry, more than 200 local administration districts have issued magnetic ID cards. These cards can also be used as ATM cards with certain banks, as well as student cards and social welfare cards. There is also a plan included in the national ICT policy to upgrade the magnetic cards to smart cards. Citizen information in the database of the Registration Administration Department can then be integrated with all other government databases.

The government has also expended efforts to promote greater IT adoption in the rural areas. Towards this end, the Telephone Organisation of Thailand and the Ministry of Interior carried out a project called Internet Tambon (www.tambon.khonthai.com) in 2000. A *tambon* is an administrative unit that groups around 10 villages. There are more than 7,000 tambons in Thailand. The project called for providing access to the Internet at government offices in each tambon. Some 4,000 tambons were to have access by the year 2002.

As for content development, the Community Development Department (Ministry of Interior), worked closely with the private sector in setting up a website called Thaitambon.com (www.Thaitambon.com), to promote Thai local products under the government's "One Tambon One Product" programme. The website provides comprehensive tambon information and serves as an e-Commerce storefront for local products from all tambon nationwide.

STRATEGIES AND KEY FOCUS AREAS

According to the ICT Ministry, the strategies for the implementation of e-Government initiatives were developed to align with those of the national IT plan. The following are some of the ways:

(1) A national "e-Government Plan" (complete with departmental action plans and budget allocations) is in place.

(2) An ongoing overhaul of public administration and public services delivery.

(3) A commitment to human resource development in public organisations.

(4) Technology transformation to cover both the back-office and front-office within public organisations.

(5) An ongoing development of computer and network infrastructure in the public sector.

(6) Continuing active citizen and private sector participation in e-Government deployment.

The time horizon is 10 years with the major deadlines of common back-office software platforms in 2004, and electronic service delivery to citizens by 2010.

To facilitate the implementation of the various e-Government projects, an umbrella project was set up. NECTEC was assigned to take responsibility for the coordination and facilitation of these e-Government efforts. The umbrella project spanned from March 2001 to March 2003. The main objective was to establish a framework, set up a standard, and determine guidelines for interoperability of e-Government services. As a result of this effort, it is hoped that there will be better collaboration and communication among the various government agencies.

The e-Government umbrella project, a multi-agency undertaking, comprises the following key contributors:

- NECTEC: main coordinator;
- Bank of Thailand: project sponsor and project team members; and
- CIOs of key related public agencies (eg Office of Civil Service Commission, Bureau of Budget, National Economic and Social Development Board and Office of Prime Minister): co-sponsors and project team members.

The project team first underwent various project management training courses and then delivered workshops for government CIOs, and officials; they also surveyed the readiness of Thai citizens to e-Government services; assessed the readiness of government officials; studied and analysed the existing public administration system; set up a framework for interoperability; established guidelines for project evaluation; coordinated the development agenda with the e-Thailand sub-committee; launched a website (www.egov.thaigov.net) as a public relations and information centre; and crafted certain e-Government efforts as pilot or model projects.

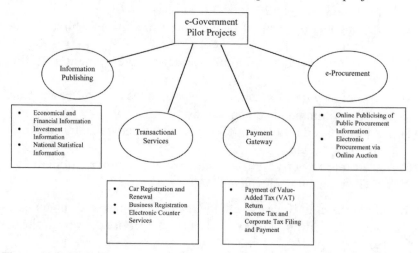

Figure 11-6: Four Tracks of the Pilot Projects for the e-Government initiatives

STATUS OF INITIATIVES

As a result of public administration reform and the national ICT policy, a Ministry of Information and Communication Technology was established in October 2002. Legal infrastructure required to support the national development of ICT was also initiated. A variety of sector and functional specific activities have been undertaken to address national issues including efforts to increase rural access and narrow the digital divide.

Addressing Human Resource issues

The IT Projects of Princess Maha Chakri Sirindhorn

The Thai princess has an active interest in the promotion of IT to tackle social issues. Since 1995, Princess Sirindhorn had spearheaded various IT projects, emphasising IT in education, raising the quality of life, and providing opportunities for the underprivileged. The five main programmes under the process/initiative were: IT for rural schools, IT for the disabled, IT for children suffering from chronic diseases, IT for cultural information dissemination, and computer training for prisoners.

The projects are funded by the Princess' Funds for the Development of Children and Youth, and carried out by NECTEC in coordination with relevant government agencies. The initiative, a precursor of several other national IT projects, significantly increased awareness of the benefits of IT in the development of Thai society.

SchoolNet Thailand

This initiative was launched in late 1995, the year the government had proclaimed as "Thailand Information Technology Year". SchoolNet aims to provide Internet access to all public secondary schools throughout the country. By using technology to improve the educational system, this project has tried to address the human resource development agenda. The project started out with 50 public secondary schools with computer hardware and software donated by the private sector. The Government provided free Internet dial-up connections and training for teachers.

At the end of 1997, NECTEC completed three crucial components as part of the educational reform programmes including IT literacy promotion, Thai-language content promotion, and the development of a nationwide school network. By February 2003, nine out of ten public secondary schools in the country had Internet access through SchoolNet.

Quick Quotes

During an interview with "Computer Today", Professor Dr. Pirash Thajchayapong, then President of the National Science and Technology Development Agency (NSTDA) mentioned "SchoolNet is the device we hope to lay out the foundation of IT education in Thailand. This pilot project is well under way and we hope that we can eventually transfer project ownership to the Ministry of Education. Anyway, one of the key success factors of this project is the limited budget allocated for the procurement of personal computers (PC) and other hardware, which could hamper the progress of the project."

"Personally, I would like to see more involvement from the private sector in the similar way Korea and Taiwan have done in the past. Given PC demands for all secondary schools in the country, we might as well be able to promote our PC manufacturing industry.", he noted.

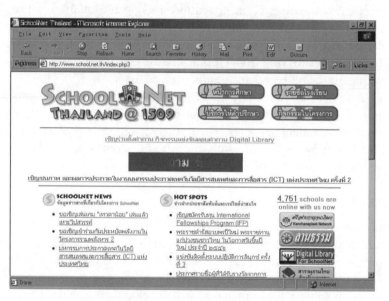

Figure 11-7: The SchoolNet website

The government CIOs programme

This was initiated in 1998. The idea was to increase IT knowledge within each government ministry and agency by appointing CIOs with in-depth IT training. CIOs attended a two-week training course organised by NECTEC and the Office of the Civil Service Commission (OCSC). The programme successfully raised levels of IT literacy with some 300 CIOs going through the training between 1999 and 2001.

The Cabinet also approved a related programme aimed at developing the IT vision of high-ranking government officials. The CEOs programme compelled the two highest-ranking officials within each government organisation to attend half-day training sessions organised by NECTEC and OCSC on the benefits of IT in public administration.

Infrastructure and Environment

Government Information Technology Services (GITS)

GITS is an effort to create a unified government network, and to support and expedite the computerisation of government agencies with IT applications, information exchange standards, and secured messaging infrastructure. The main GITS network service is a nationwide, high-capacity network called Government Information Network (GINet). By setting up a common infrastructure, the government avoids the extra costs and inefficiencies of uncoordinated and duplicated data networks that could arise if different agencies pursued their own connections.

GINet which runs on the existing Telephone Organisation of Thailand's network currently links the government headquarters in Bangkok with the provincial branches. As part of the network connection service, GITS provides various information services to the government officials such as daily newsclips, government directory services, and secure email.

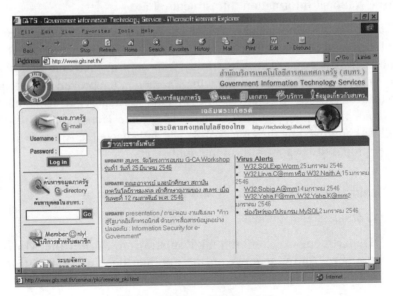

Figure 11-8: The GITS website

Public Internet Access

In August 2002, in an effort to provide more public Internet access points and promote the idea of e-Education, the Ministry of University Affairs set up e-Learning centres at several shopping plazas providing free Internet access. The shopping malls offered the Ministry free space while the computers were donated by private companies. The Ministry only had to fund daily operational expenses and the Internet connection fee.

The Cabinet also approved the establishment of a national e-Learning centre in Bangkok to be opened up in late 2003. The centre would showcase IT contests and exhibitions, as well as function as a science and technology museum.

IT Laws

Since 1999, Thailand has been developing an IT legal infrastructure through the legislation of six new laws via an IT Law Development Project. The laws are the:

(1)   Electronic Transaction Act;
(2)   Electronic Signature Law;
(3)   Computer Crime/Computer-Related Crime Law;
(4)   Data Protection Law;
(5)   Electronic Funds Transfer Law;
(6)   National Information Infrastructure Law.

With the launch of these new laws, the government aims to bring security and increased public confidence in the viability of online commercial and public transactions. The Electronic Transactions Act and Electronic Signature Law were submitted by the Cabinet and approved in principle, by the House of Representatives. The two laws were subsequently combined into one piece of legislation, called the Electronic Transactions Bill. This Bill was approved by the House of Senate and enacted in April 2002. The other proposed laws are still in the draft stage.

Achieving public sector reform and good governance

Online Business Registration

The Department of Commercial Registration, within the Ministry of Commerce, now accepts online applications for registration of companies in Thailand. The web-based application at the website www.thairegistration.com allows those who want to register their businesses to search through the database to find out whether their preferred business name is already taken. The users can then reserve and register their business name online.

Figure 11-9: The website of Department of Commercial Registration

Electronic Tax Filing and Payment

The Revenue Department has joined seven commercial banks in allowing taxpayers to pay for income taxes, corporate taxes, and value-added taxes (VAT) electronically. To pay taxes online, the taxpayers must first apply for the service at the website www.rd.go.th. The Revenue Department then verifies the taxpayer's identity in person before providing the user IDs and passwords.

To help promote the service, the Revenue Department provides an electronic manual with step-by-step procedures of how to use the programme. It also offers training for taxpayers at its computer centre. The Revenue Department has also upgraded its back-office systems to support the growth of online users.

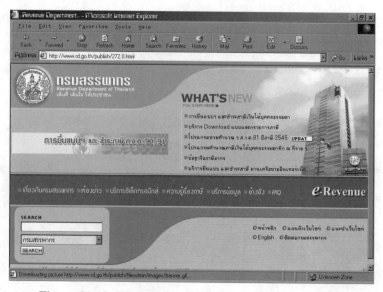

Figure 11-10: The website of the Revenue Department

Quick Quotes

Quoted in the Bangkok Post in June 2001, Ms Praomart Huntra, then Director of the Internet Tax Payment System Department, said that after closely monitoring VAT online payments for a month, they had found that lack of confidence in e-transaction security was not the problem, but rather a lack of basic computer skills of the taxpayer.

"This was because most taxpayers are accountants who are not familiar with operating computers. During the first month of the service, we had to teach them basic computer skills such as how to download a programme or how to choose fonts", said Ms Praomart.

"The hard part is to learn how to operate the programme the first time, but after taxpayers know how, they get used to it very quickly. The benefit is that our system can also help them check if they have filled out the right form or not. This can prevent errors while we can speed up our working process", she noted.

---

e-Procurement

In its efforts to improve transparency in the public procurement process, the Thai government mandated that each government agency improve its procurement process by taking part in the e-procurement project. A cross-agency e-procurement website (www.gprocurement.or.th) has been set up as a centre disseminating relevant information and facilitating the e-procurement process for the participating government agencies.

Private sector companies are encouraged to register their products in an e-catalogue at this website. When a purchasing official needs certain office equipment, she can review a list of suppliers in the e-catalogue and send the suppliers requests for proposals. After validating the specifications of the equipment in the proposals, the purchasing official then sends an invitation for bids to the selected suppliers. An online reverse auction then takes place during a predetermined time. Among the pioneers, Telephone Organisation of Thailand (TOT) started making use of this electronic procurement system in December 2002.

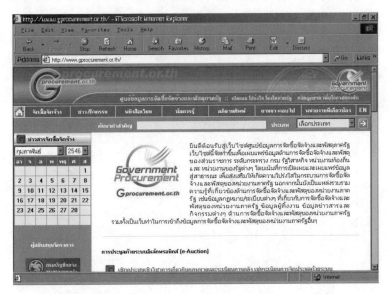

Figure 11-11: The government procurement website

CREATING THE FUTURE

Key Challenges

By the end of 2002, there were more than 200 e-Government project plans submitted — with expectations for completion by 2004. Given limited resources, the Thai government needs to prioritise its many programmes so as to maximise available financial resources and human capital.

Even if financial resources were adequate another major hurdle for the e-Government projects is the dire shortage of ICT skills, especially in the public sector. There is a perception that remuneration of ICT personnel in the government agencies is not comparable to those in the private sector. In 2001, there were only 20,000 ICT professionals from the total number of over 2.3 million government officers.[9, 10] As a result, many of these public sector agencies, especially those recently established as a result of the ongoing public administration reform, still do not have enough IT personnel to work on projects. Therefore, ability to maintain the progress of some of the e-Government initiatives is sometimes questionable.

The Thai government also needs to actively explore new relationships. This includes closer interaction among government agencies as well as innovative partnerships with private sector companies and non-governmental organisations (NGOs) so as to ensure quality and accessibility of e-Government information, services, and resources. Government agencies need to overcome the traditional reluctance to work with one another in order to leverage on economies of scale for e-Government and other projects.

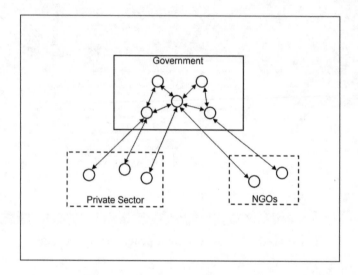

Figure 11-12: New Relationships

Private sector executives who are experienced in areas such as e-commerce, IT, marketing, and general management, and can play a part by giving feedback and advising government policymakers. The Thai government needs to find more ways to encourage the private sector to become active participants in public administration reform.

As for project management issues, the e-Government programme in Thailand seems to be somewhat bereft of centralised milestone reporting. There is no clear single point from which one can obtain a holistic picture of the overall progress. The relevant agencies may need to take the initiative for developing this overall project management plan.

Another hurdle that limits the potential of e-Government initiatives in Thailand is the level of overall readiness of Thai citizens to embrace this new channel of government services. Like many countries in the region, Thailand faces a digital divide problem — between urban and rural, young and old, and between rich and poor. Overall, 90 percent of Thai Internet users are the educated younger generation and white-collar workers in urban areas. One barrier to Internet penetration is the language problem. Even though the content in most government websites is Thai (with separate English pages in some cases) manoeuvring through the Internet requires some degree of English fluency and PC literacy. Unless this condition is met, there is a danger that many e-Government services could end up as "white elephants" — projects that serve only a minority of Thai citizens.

In summary, the development of e-Government initiatives in Thailand is still at a relatively early stage, as confirmed by a survey commissioned by NECTEC and conducted online on 10 local web sites.[11] Some 15,000 people took part in the survey between September and October 2002. Almost 70 percent of the respondents were less than satisfied with government websites. The top reasons for the low satisfaction rating were: inability to find the information needed, some information was not up-to-date, websites did not offer services that fit their needs, and presence of dead links.

Building on Key Achievements

Thailand has done relatively well in the development of the infrastructure for e-Government services. For instance, the common e-Government IT infrastructure — GITS and GINet — has been put in place. However, it is necessary for the relevant ICT agencies to ensure that ongoing development is coherent and integrated. Another positive development is the inclusion of an educational component in the e-Government project, such as the development of the infrastructure for the SchoolNet project. This endeavor potentially paves the way for further development of educational applications and the build-up of stronger IT-capable human resources in the country.

The creation of an ICT Ministry in 2002 is a clear indication of the strong commitment of the Thai government to leverage on ICT development, including e-Government and e-Business, as a driving force for sustainable economic growth and social development. Currently however, the e-Government initiatives in Thailand seem to lack adequate measurable goals for each e-Government project. It is not entirely clear who is overseeing the overall e-Government project implementation. Despite well-intentioned plans and strategies, without is a designated office with sufficient budget and recognised authority, supported by other relevant agencies and departments, the e-Government programmes may prove ineffectual when it comes to implementation. This designated office needs to conduct periodic audits to ensure that progress is being made to achieve stated goals and measurements are being reviewed regularly.

As for socio-economic concerns, there is a chance of marginalising groups in rural areas, or even the poor in urban areas, who are unable to make use of the new channels of government services. The digital divide cannot be solved simply by installing telephone lines, equipping each district office with a PC, or putting up local information on the Internet. The gap can only be narrowed when the "have-nots" see the benefit of IT, actively participate in civic affairs, acquire the skills needed for the evolving economy, access information that can provide better economic opportunities, and ultimately enjoy a well-balanced social life. e-Government projects have the potential of either equalising access to government and its services, or raising barriers to participation. The Thai government needs to continue to ensure that those who are already well educated or have Internet access are not the only ones who benefit from e-Government. Such disparity could increase problems of social and economic injustice, something which e-Government was meant to address in the first place.

PERSPECTIVES OF AN E-GOVERNMENT LEADER

Dr Thaweesak Koanantakool,
Director, NECTEC and Secretariat to NITC,
Kingdom of Thailand

Dr Thaweesak Koanantakool is the Director of the National Electronic and Computer Technology Centre (NECTEC), the statutory organisation overseeing R&D development for IT in Thailand. He also serves as the Executive Secretary of the country's IT policy planning body: the National Information Technology Committee (NITC) during the outlining of the National ICT Master Plan (2002–2006).

Thaweesak received his Bachelor and Ph.D. degrees in Electrical Engineering from Imperial College of Science and Technology, London University, UK. He started his government service career in Thailand in 1981 first at the Prince of Songkla University and later at Thammasat University. In 1983, he co-founded Telbiz Company Limited, an innovation company specialised in Thai language system for computer and email. He also co-founded the Advanced Research Group Company Ltd, a major publisher that conducts business research on IT subjects in Thailand, in 1987.

Thaweesak joined NECTEC in 1994 as a Deputy Director of NECTEC leading the Network/ Software Technology laboratories. The Network lab pioneered the Internet in Thailand by developing the largest academic and research network known as ThaiSarn. In 1995, he co-established the first ISP, Internet Thailand Company Limited, which is now the largest in Thailand. Thaweesak also led the SchoolNet Thailand project.

In 2000, Thaweesak received the Thai Royal insignia: The Companion of the Most Illustrious Order of Chula Chom Klao from His Majesty the King. Thaweesak has published more than 12 books and 150 papers and articles.

In February 2003, the author (JY) caught up with Dr Thaweesak (TK) in the midst of the Director's hectic schedule.

JY : **Thailand has a number of policies and plans relating to its overall ICT development. There were the IT 2000 and IT 2010 policies, the National ICT Master Plan, e-Thailand and so on. How do all these fit together?**

TK : Let me give you the whole perspective in brief. Previously we had the IT 2000 policy for the years 1996 to 2001. Under this plan we had some key pillars of development. Towards the end of IT 2000, there was an e-ASEAN initiative, and we then set up e-Thailand as a counterpart of the e-ASEAN initiative. This was a big drive to complete our IT 2010 policy framework. The IT 2010 policy can be summarised into 5 strategies: on the economic side (e-industry and e-commerce) social side (e-education and e-society). And in the middle, we have e-Government as a pivot which would be expanded into effective drives towards a knowledge society.

The National ICT Master Plan (2002–2006) comes after the IT 2010 framework. It is a policy implementation that goes hand-in-hand with the framework. What happened was that as we completed the IT 2010 draft, we actually coordinated with the Economic and Social Development Board to make sure that it was in synchronisation with the Ninth National Economic and Social Development Plan. So one could say that the heart of IT 2010 was in the Ninth National Economic and Social Development Plan. A few months later, the full-fledged report on IT 2010 was approved by the government. So, IT 2010 was born in March 2001 while the Ninth Plan was born in the previous year.

After IT 2010, which is a ten-year vision, the government asked NECTEC to develop the National ICT Master Plan, covering 4–5 years. So we earmarked the first ICT Master Plan to cover 2002 to 2006, and we expect to have a follow-up ICT Master Plan after 2006.

So with the process of converting the IT 2010 policy framework into National ICT Master Plan, it is not only the plan that matters, but also the process of developing the plan that educates all of the stakeholders in Thailand — to get involved and drive the whole plan together. In fact, it was the first Master Plan jointly written between the private sector and public sector. In the process, there were many public consultation meetings, involving thousands of people.

The actual Plan was released in February 2002 as a draft, to get people — especially businesses — ready for it. The Plan was finally approved by the government and officially launched on 25 September 2002. This was only five days before we launched a big government administrative reform (in October 2002) in Thailand. With the reform, a new ministry was formed — the Ministry of ICT — and this ministry was born with a ready-made Master Plan!

JY : **In the implementation of the various initiatives under the e-Government plan, what did you feel were some of the critical success factors?**

TK : We think a Critical Success Factor (CSF) is the leadership commitment, and in fact, once the draft of the e-Government Plan had been tabled, we have been assured by the Prime Minister that he is very interested in e-Government, and he has set a few deadlines for the e-Government implementation. The Prime Minister is still the Chairman of the NITC, and actually chairs the meetings himself. The commitment on setting up a new ministry (of ICT) is also added motivation that e-Government can be pushed to success.

JY : **Since we are talking about the new ministry, let me move onto organisation structures relating to e-Government. How do the NITC, NECTEC, and the new ICT Ministry link to one another?**

TK : In the past, before the Ministry of ICT, there was the National IT Committee (NITC) — which is just a committee, ie the members were part-time. We had NECTEC as Secretariat to NITC, to work full-time to support the work of NITC. As NECTEC has many diverse activities, when we had the Ministry of ICT, we feel a lot better because we know that there is an organisation set up to take care of the cooperation among the partners involved in the ICT development. NECTEC itself was originated as a technology organisation but we have been "enlarged" so much. We hope that our extension part is now well taken care of by a good organisation, and NECTEC itself will support the technology development in a stronger way.

NECTEC is a statutory organisation under Ministry of Science. We don't work for either normal Ministry or department, so we can support any other public agencies easily. The law covering us is very flexible. So right now we are fully supporting the ICT Ministry.

JY : **Let's talk about the implementation issues of e-Government, especially about the measurement of successful implementation. Does NECTEC get involved in that? Do you set any sort of benchmarks or measurements or indicators?**

TK : Yes, we put down a few benchmarks. For example, every Ministry should be able to link and exchange data completely by 2006. And each department will have at least one online interactive service by the end of 2003.

JY : **In the implementation of e-Government in Thailand based on your experience, I'd like to find out if you have noticed any significant difference between e-Government implementation in an Asian country like Thailand vis-à-vis in the Western countries?**

TK : Yes, I think that here, our country is somewhat less organised than some western countries where they have better infrastructure. For example, even before the e-Government project launch, most government departments in Thailand had websites but none of these websites shared common standards. Many are in the learning process — some are really good while the rest are beginners. Once we have systematised the e-Government development, we do expect a systematic government portal and basic shared services to be available at all government agencies. Government online services would have to follow certain standards, and right now, for example, every agency should have a privacy policy stated on its website, and they should share common engine so that the citizen who is looking for a service will not get lost. Common engines, as in search engine, directory service, help service, including the news exchange — the news that each government agency wants to publish to the public. We have completed the news exchange service so that the government agencies can upload their news into a news pool where the news agency can easily access the information from the government. We also invite the news agency to join the same project so that every government agency can put up a very comprehensive news headline in their website with top stories related to their agency. Therefore, this shared engine is very valuable for us and it's based on web services and XML. A simple example of the standardisation of how the government agency shares the information.

JY : **Going on to the use of services by the citizens or business, how would you describe the level of usage of the government services that have been put up so far?**

TK : We have a web-monitoring tool called "truehits.net" which allows every agency to monitor their website and put up their web statistics into global view. Unfortunately, we learnt that out of all the people who click into Thai websites (including entertainment, news, services, education and government), less than 5 percent of the clicks go to the government website.

We also conducted a survey to ask the people how often they visit the website, especially the government websites, and if they don't like it, what are the main reasons. We received a lot of interesting feedback.

The first answer is that they cannot find the service or information that they want. Secondly, they cannot remember the URL. This feedback, in our view, is quite reasonable. At least we know that our current websites have weaknesses and to solve the problem, we have designed a government portal that is easily navigated by the people. In other words it is more citizen-orientated.

We should also introduce easy navigation to government agency websites through search engine and pull-down menus, so that no one would have to remember the name of the URL or website. In Thailand, the official language is Thai but the URLs are in Roman characters. One does not expect the majority of the Thais to speak as good English as, say in Singapore. Therefore, this is our local problem and we have to solve it.

We have then introduced some key words in our URL and by typing any Thai word, it will link into the common website properly. We distribute free tool bar to the web browser, just like the Google bar. This tool bar will lead to the right place of government service or you go to the pull-down menu and select the website of each Ministry. There is also a directory service, ie LDAP, where you can key in the government agency and get the directory of the government officers who are publicly responsible. All these features are in place.

JY : **In your survey of the usage of the websites, were you be able to determine which government services are popular?**

TK : *(laughing)* The most popular website is the "lottery". The next most popular one is the website of the Revenue Department — ie the Tax Return form.

The Thai Income Tax submission is fully online now. Everyone can file their returns online as well as make tax payment. For payment transaction, the website of the Revenue Department will switch to the SSL services of the commercial banks, and once the payment is settled, the bank will return the credit code back to the website of the Revenue Department.

JY : **Moving on to the area of security — what considerations have been given to the data security, integrity and privacy issues in the implementation of e-Government solutions?**

TK : The security issue is given high priority. Every government agency is required to implement a security system for their Internet service. Most of them will have to put all their Intranet information behind a security firewall. During the process, we also distribute a standard security policy for all government officials who handle online service.

We also have an organisation called ThaiCERT — "Thai Computer Emergency Response Team". It does more than just emergency work as it also drafts the policy standards together with the National Security Office. ThaiCERT also provides security training.

In the area of privacy, we have completed the draft of the "Data Protection Law" and it has been approved by the National IT Committee (NITC). It is now in the process of submission to the Cabinet and then to Parliament.

JY : **Overall, in the implementation of e-Government, what do you see as some of the key challenges preventing Thailand from moving as fast as you would like to?**

TK : I think the key challenge is the speed at which we implement the "Electronics Transaction Act" for government agencies. Another key challenge is to provide basic secured core integration system to every government agencies and to work with the private sectors, so that the citizens and companies can also enjoy the secured authentication.

I would say that we need a fair amount of time to make sure that our society understands how to use Public Key Infrastructure (PKI). They not only have to understand what "PKI" is, but there must be some simple solutions so that PKI could be implemented where necessary and basic authentication could be used for those who does not need that much security.

JY : **You mentioned earlier that based on your survey, people have problems navigating or finding the URL. Does "Thaigov.net" help?**

TK : Yes, it does help to resolve the issues of remembering complicated URLs. In time, all the e-Government services from various Ministries will be channeled through ThaiGov.net. In April 2003, we are going to publicise the government portal. We hope that the Thai people can eliminate their online problems by keying the name "ThaiGov.net" or whatever other names on the Citizen portal. Just one URL to remember.

JY : **Are there any key messages that you would like to convey to readers about Thailand's e-Government programme?**

TK : In general, I think the key purpose of e-Government should be well balanced among the three sub-purposes: efficiency, transparency and democracy. And with these three, we have many things to touch on.

For example, for transparency, we also have to consider the privacy part of it. We must make sure that we do not have a digital divide for the users. In the remote areas, people do not have the Internet and the government has to provide some public Internet access or service over the counter.

As for democracy, we hope that the electronic implementation of government will help people to speak out and not just have the government doing it one way — we need a good feedback channel.

With this channel, we hope the government officers would care more about improving their services. Less money and time will be then wasted in public services. These are the key issues that our government officers who implement e-Government have to bear in mind.

Endnotes

1 Jessy, JS, *"History of Southeast Asia (1824-1965)"*, Penerbitan Darulaman (1985).

2 Mason, C, *"A Short History of Asia"*, Macmillan Press (2000).

3 US Library of Congress, *"Thailand: A Country Study"* (2003).

4 The World Bank Group, *"Thailand: Country Brief"* (2002).

5 GDP, National Economic and Social Development Board (NESDB) February 2003, http://www.nesdb.go.th.

6 Internet Index of Thailand, Internet Information Research Centre (IIRC) February 2003, http://ntl.nectec.or.th.

7 Internet Information Research Centre (IIRC). *"The Internet Index of Thailand"*. Bangkok (2003), National Electronics and Computer Technology Centre.

8 Koanantakool, Thaweesak, *"Struggling Towards a Knowledge-based Society"* paper for the International Symposium on IT and Development Corporation, July 2000.

9 Koanantakool, Thaweesak and Thuvasethakul Chadamas, *"National ICT Policy in Thailand"* paper for Africa-Asia Workshop, March 2002.

10 National Information Technology Committee (NITC), *"Demand of IT Manpower in Thailand Research Project"*, October 2001.

11 National Information Technology Committee (NITC), *"Internet User Profile 2002"*: Bangkok (2003) http://www.nitc.go.th/internetuser/survey2002.html.

10 National Information Technology Committee (NITC), *e-Thailand Initiative*. NITC Secretariat, Bangkok (2000) http://www.nitc.go.th/eThailand.

11 Tubtimhin, Jirapon, *"Frequently Asked Questions on E-Government in Thailand"* Bangkok (2001) http://www.egov.thaigov.net.

12 International Telecommunication Union, *"Bits and Bahts: Thailand Internet Case Study"* Switzerland (2002).

13 Various issues of the following periodicals were also used in the preparation of this chapter: *Bangkok Post, The Nation,* and *Computer Today* (Thai edition).

Useful Websites

www.nitc.go.th	National Information Technology Committee Secretariat (in Thai)
www.nectec.or.th	Website of the National Electronics and Computer Technology Centre (in Thai & English)
www.egov.thaigov.net	Government project information centre (in Thai & English)
www.thaigov.net	e-Government portal site for Thai citizen (in Thai)
www.khonthai.com	Portal site for Thai citizen developed by the Interior Ministry (in Thai)
www.tambon.khonthai.com	Website of the Internet Tambon project (in Thai)
www.rd.go.th	Website of the Revenue Department for online income and corporate tax filing (in Thai)
www.gprocurement.or.th	Website for the online procurement system for Thai government agencies (in Thai)

Perspective

CHAPTER 12

The e-Services Portal — Doorway to e-Government

James SL Yong and Lim Hiap Koon

▲ ▼ ▲ ▼ ▲ ▼ ▲ ▼

The doors we open and close each day,
decide the lives we live.

Flora Whittemore

▲ ▼ ▲ ▼ ▲ ▼ ▲ ▼

BEYOND WEBSITES

The earliest portals of the Internet world were Yahoo!, Lycos, Alta Vista and Excite, which appeared in the late 1990s as search sites and began to tack on various other services — from free email and forums to news, games and online shopping. Their value creation strategies centred around aggregating "eyeballs" and achieving "stickiness" in order to benefit from advertising, licensing and transaction fees. Although many of the commercial portals did not survive, a small number have achieved global success and sustainability.

When the enterprise portal market exploded a few years ago, there was a plethora of solutions offering the benefits of popular consumer-type portal models along with new functionalities geared toward enterprise deployment. For a time "portal mania" took hold of the virtual world and challenged the foundations of traditional websites which featured content on specific topics or domains without allowing for any user customisation for specific needs or preferences. During that period, the push for portal adoption was so fast and furious that simply keeping pace with available solution offerings and their capabilities was challenging. But exactly what defines a portal and what promises does it really offer?

The word portal is said to have derived from the Latin *porta* meaning "a gate". Middle English and Old French also have a word *portle*, meaning "city gate". In the Internet world, a portal denotes a special doorway, entrance or window into a website. The web pages forming a portal are not completely self-referential[1] anymore, but allow for personalisation, workflow, notification, knowledge management and groupware. They should possess infrastructure functionality, and integrate information and applications across an organisation. The core idea behind a portal is to aggregate information from different sources and create a single point of access to that information. It embodies the idea of a personalised filter into a library of categorised content.

According to Dataquest (part of the Gartner Group), "a portal enables a joint, personalised access to data, expertise, and applications." IBM's working portal definition elaborates: "Portals provide a secure, single point of interaction with diverse information, business processes and people, personalised to a user's needs and responsibilities." Another definition from Merrill Lynch defined Enterprise Information Portals as "applications that enable companies to unlock internally and externally stored information, and provide users a single gateway to personalised information needed to make informed business decisions."

With all the unbridled optimism about portals, it is sometimes difficult to see beyond the hype and truly appreciate their potential role and application. Yet, rapidly emerging portal concepts and technologies are making it increasingly important to understand the situations under which portals will work best.

As the hype subsides, true capabilities and enterprise benefits of the portal platform are beginning to take shape. Large and mid-sized companies have turned their attention to the portal platform to achieve a variety of goals: get closer to customers, enable more accurate decision-making, improve speed-to-market, streamline interactions with partners, and achieve operating efficiencies.

THE VALUE OF PORTALS IN THE PUBLIC SECTOR

Many public sector leaders have realised that they share many of the goals of e-Business leaders. Government agencies are moving beyond offering information-only websites to setting up full-service Internet portals. It no longer means putting up static web pages that reproduce the bureaucracies that leave citizens waiting in long lines or on hold for hours. As governments move services access to mere mouse clicks away for citizens, they find themselves with a spectrum of innovative business models to adopt. One of which is the portal model.

Typical objectives of a government Internet portal are:

(1)   To give people and businesses access to information and services provided by the websites of individual government ministries and agencies

(2)   To include guidance about how to find information and services that are not available via the Internet

This has led to what has been called "portal government". That is a way of developing smarter and more intuitive ways to organise, discover and connect constituents with the government information and services when they need to get something done quickly and easily.[2]

Public sector leaders tend to think of e-Government in terms of the value it could bring to both the constituent and to the government itself. Much of this value can be delivered and realised by offering services through a portal. In the context of public services delivery, portals offer single points of entry to multiple agencies and accord citizens or businesses the opportunity to interact easily and seamlessly with several agencies. It has now been generally accepted that Internet portals are becoming the way governments will present their information and service offerings.

Value is what encourages and retains citizen usage of portal services. It is what justifies continuing investment in Internet capabilities, and ultimately, what will drive governments to apply the portal as a catalyst for enterprise transformation.

To implement successful e-Governments, public sector leaders will need to innovatively organise and manage the processes, resources and organisational changes necessary to thrive in the new models of e-Governance. Thus, portals are not merely convenient platforms for customers to access government information and service; portals offer a whole new paradigm of operation for the continual excellence of new governance.

PORTALS IN ASIAN PUBLIC SECTOR TRANSFORMATION

The current state of development of e-Government solutions in parts of Asia no longer lags behind their Western counterparts. Some studies[3] have ranked Asian economies, such as Singapore and Hong Kong, among the most mature in e-Government development.

In particular, government portals are growing in importance, and many leading Asian countries have begun to consolidate their online service delivery into this next generation of government web presence. In Asia, the decision by e-Government leaders to use portal technology opens up new rules of electronic interaction with citizens, businesses, vendors, governments themselves and their employees. The portal becomes the medium through which each entity can be united.

For the rest of this chapter, we will consider recent advances in portal capabilities from four different angles: portal organisation, content and services, service support, and portal management.

The following examples showcase some Asian governments that have achieved significant progress in offering e-services via portals. These public administrative bodies have overhauled their processes and systems, turning them from being agency-centric to constituent-facing systems that span organisational silos.

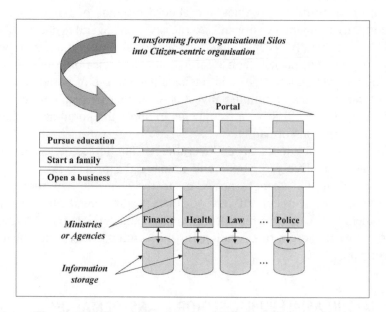

Figure 12-1: From Organisational Silos to Citizen-centric

Portal Organisation

Early government websites tended to be stand-alone web pages presented like a directory or menu, listing available information and services alphabetically or by some other classification system. While such an approach was fine for establishing web presence, it often fell short in the area of useability. The sequences of links users needed to navigate across the website were often long and non-intuitive.

The portal approach organises content in an entirely different manner. Instead of focusing on what agencies intend to deliver, the government now focuses on what citizens intend to achieve. Content is formatted or presented from the citizen's perspective. This provides for more intuitive navigation and allows citizens to customise their view of the portal to their individual needs.

The following is an example of a citizen-centric portal.

Example 1: The eCitizen Portal (Singapore)

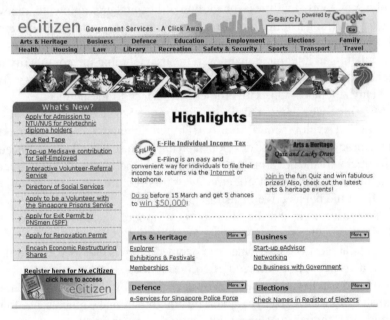

Figure 12-2: eCitizen portal (Singapore)

In 1999, the Singapore government embarked on a project to create a one-stop government-to-citizen (G-to-C) portal for their various government services. This portal, called eCitizen (www.ecitizen.gov.sg) is a highly targeted, e-services portal for citizens (and other residents) of Singapore. The eCitizen portal brings together online information and transaction services from many government agencies into a single window on the Internet. An independent report by the Stockholm Challenge[4] revealed that some 70 percent of the Government's online services available are at "interact" level (meaning part of the transaction can be completed online) or "transact" level (meaning the entire transaction can be completed online).

The eCitizen portal is owned by the Ministry of Finance (MOF) and managed by the Infocomm Development Authority of Singapore (IDA). The customer's needs and interests determine the organisation and service delivery principles for eCitizen. The contents of the portal are intuitively presented under 16 "Towns" that mirror the needs of an individual along a life journey. The Towns or content categories include: Arts and Heritage, Business, Defence, Education, Elections, Employment, Family, Health, Housing, Law, Library, Recreation, Safety and Security, Sports, Transport and Travel. The comprehensive range of online services offered include booking of sports facilities, scheduling of hospital appointments, renewal of road tax, filing a notice of marriage, moving house, setting up a business, filing of income tax and paying fines. These online public services are presented in an integrated manner to the users, hiding the complexity and agency-centric operations of conventional counter services, and projecting a "Many Agencies, One Government" interface to the public.

Ms Tan Swee Hua, Director, Electronic Services Division at the Infocomm Development Authority (IDA) in Singapore, explained that the "life journey" concept was developed on the premise that all citizens needed to interact with the government at some point in their lives. The government recognised that the most effective way to structure the services offered was from the perspective of its citizens.

Prior to deciding on the "life journey" model, the IDA had explored other options. One way was simply to list out all services and information and not categorise them. That was deemed inadvisable as it would have created more confusion and inconvenience. Another way that was considered was to categorise them by agencies, ie by Ministry of Education, Ministry of Finance, etc. However, this might not make much sense to the public even though that was really how the government machinery was internally structured.

Ms Tan added, "Our approach was to apply ourselves as citizens in such a situation — so as to arrive at the appropriate portal design, rather than design according to how government is organized. That is the meaning of being citizen-centric rather than agency-centric."

For many government agencies, the transition from being agency-centric to customer-centric was not always a smooth journey. For each Town, a lead agency was appointed as the "Town Owner" to conceptualise, plan and develop the Town. There were a lot of challenges because the agencies themselves were not always organised in a customer-centric manner at that juncture. Now, they would have to work together and collaborate to fulfill the Town concept.

In the case of say, the Business Town, the appointed Town Owner, the Ministry of Trade and Industry, had to bring together multiple related agencies to plan for the town. They had to make sure that they did not miss out on any context-specific life events such as starting a business or looking for business opportunities. They then had to review the processes needed to fulfill each event and try to achieve greater integration across agencies where applicable. For example, starting a business for public entertainment requires licenses from at least 5–6 agencies. The challenge was to integrate the processes such that it would be seamless to users. This issue was addressed by simplifying the process so that only a single application form needed to be submitted via a single interface. Besides minimising the hassle for the applicant the processing turnaround of the application was reduced from 8 weeks to 2 weeks.

By September 2002, monthly hit rates for the eCitizen portal has risen to 4.2 million from 240,000 the previous year. The government also implemented "My eCitizen", a personalised version of eCitizen. Rather than logging onto the generic portal and going through hundreds of services, citizens were able to customise the staggering 1,600 e-services available to suit their preferences.

In addition to creating service groupings based on life events, the government has incorporated a new approach by packaging services based on constituent demographics to present information and services. Citizens were offered choices from five categories: student, homemaker, working adult, business people and senior citizen — to gain instant access to a set of pre-determined e-services they were most likely to use. For example, a working adult would be able to access employment related services such as those offered by the Central Provident Fund,[5] or tax information on his personalised "My eCitizen" page.

Content and Services

Since governments adopted the Internet as a service channel, citizens have continued to expect more and better services from their governments. From the days of a basic web presence, the range and depth of services available on portals have since expanded dramatically, along with citizen expectations of greater value.

Around the world, governments are pursuing the vision of replicating all traditional services through their portals so as to achieve true one-stop access. However, the question from citizens has been, "What more can we do?"

In Asia, while some governments are still very much on their journey of bringing traditional counter services online, other more progressive governments are now experimenting with ideas to provide services beyond the traditional web browser. The term mobile-Government (m-Government) has been coined to mean further replication of content and services onto mobile devices such as mobile phones and Personal Digital Assistants (PDAs). Below are some examples of the cutting-edge innovations in content and services.

Example 2: One-Stop Information Delivery: GOV.TW (Taiwan)

Figure 12-3: The GOV.TW website

As one of its major flagship projects for e-Government, the Taiwanese government established a centralised government portal (http://www.gov.tw) to integrate all online government services and information.

The provision of an integrated information portal was deemed especially important since regional governments and their respective agencies were developing their own web initiatives. As a result, the organisation of content and channels of communication were not consistent and unambiguous.

Now centrally managed by the government, the GOV.TW portal has an extensive system of information delivery via the Internet. It contains information from national statistics, policy papers, agency phone books and real-time news updates. The portal also provides all the information in English to reach out to an international audience. To promote interaction with the public, the contact information of the head office is presented clearly on the opening page. All agencies' sites, although still not uniform in aesthetics, show the same amount of information.

Up until March 2002, five hundred application forms had been made available for download with 100 online application services being offered. In addition, the government portal also provides basic service for government agencies, including electronic certificates, payment methods, form generators, and work flow utility systems to speed the development of online application services.

Example 3: One-Stop Procurement: Electronic Tendering System (Hong Kong)

Figure 12-4: Hong Kong SAR's Electronic Tendering System (ETS)

The Electronic Tendering System or ETS (http://www.ets.com.hk), is a flagship project under the Hong Kong SAR's e-Government strategy to lead by example in the adoption of electronic transactions with the public and businesses. The government also desires to use an Internet-based system to extend its supplier base and to get closer to their overseas suppliers.

Developed and operated by GO-Business, ETS is an Internet-based electronic tendering system for the Government Supplies Department (GSD), which is the central purchasing, storage and supplies organisation serving over 80 government departments and public bodies in Hong Kong.

To encourage supplier use, ETS allows suppliers to personalise the website so that information can be proactively sent to them via e-alerts. They can specify the categories that they would like to get information about by departments within the government, or by the nature of the procurement, the kind of products, etc.

In addition, ETS has a workgroup-type feature on the site where suppliers can set up calendars, to-do lists, and distribution lists. If there is an opportunity they may be interested in, the system will update their calendars and send the relevant information to contacts on their distribution list. For example, information like the tender open and close dates can be sent to the suppliers sales departments and senior management.

As of 2000, the GSD has procured around US$ 570 million worth of supplies. In July 2001, ETS moved a significant step forward through enhancements in terms of its coverage and features. The HKSAR has planned to extend the ETS to all other government procurements, with a goal of transferring 80 percent of all procurement tenders online by the end of 2003. This involves providing direct connectivity between the ETS platform and all government departments via an end-to-end online tendering system to meet each department's procurement needs.

This step marks the importance of ETS in transforming the traditional paper-based tendering process to a robust Government-to-Business (G2B) e-Commerce application platform. This has strong impact on other government departments, quasi-government organisations and commercial sectors in adopting new procurement practices and hence accelerates the pace of e-Commerce adoption in Hong Kong.

The government is also considering building an Electronic Marketplace System (EMS) for small value purchases. Initial work has been towards integrating the two systems to achieve a "Total Procurement Solution".

Example 4: Single Password for Online Transactions with All Government Agencies — the SingPass system (Singapore)

More than half of the Internet users in Singapore transact with the government online, chalking up some 40 million transactions a year. Within this e-Government environment, more than 40 government agencies issue their own passwords for online transactions. For instance, the user passwords for the Housing Development Board, Sports Council and Central Provident Fund (CPF) Board are all separately issued.

Given the depth and magnitude of online public service delivery in Singapore currently where there are more than 400 government e-services that require the user to enter an ID and password to gain access, many citizens are finding it inconvenient and cumbersome to remember so many passwords.

In early 2003, the government implemented a more elegant log-in system with a single password. Called SingPass which stands for "Singapore Personal Access", it is set to become the only password a citizen will need for government websites.

With the aim of converting the entire suite of 400 e-Services to be authenticated via SingPass by the end of 2003, 2.4 million citizens who are CPF account holders will be given the option to make their current CPF password, their SingPass password. Another 400,000 people who are not CPF account holders can apply for SingPass either at the eCitizen portal, or at post offices and Community Development Councils.

Service Support

For governments to be able to provide more comprehensive public services through their portals, they will need to build capabilities behind their public front. This means that at the back-end, the portal requires strong levels of inter-agency cooperation and coordinated service delivery. Often this can only be achieved with large-scale agency restructuring, or even mergers in order to create a new interface to the constituents. In the final analysis, the services aggregated on the portal need to be linked to the physical agencies in a way that is transparent and seamless to the user. It is precisely because of this complexity that there are relatively few examples where such inter-agency cooperation have been successful.

Example 5: G4C e-Service Centre (South Korea)

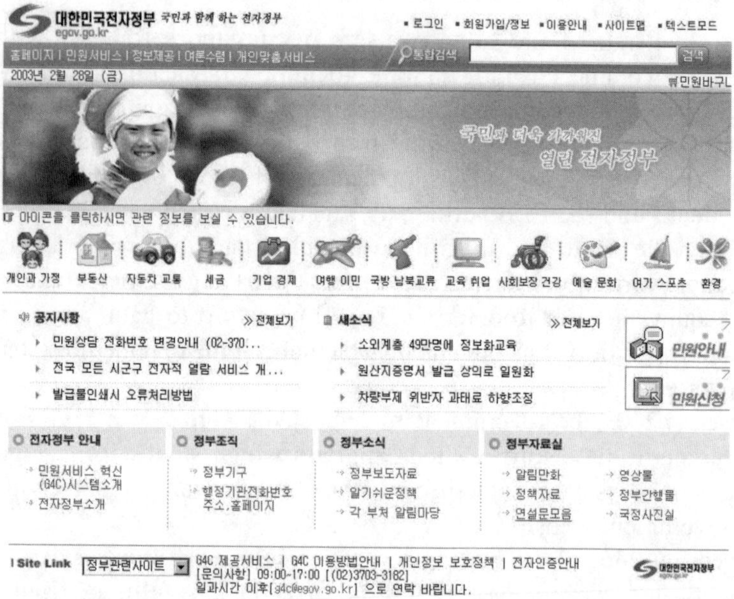

Figure 12-5: Korea Government e-Service Centre in Korea

In South Korea, the Government e-Service Centre (www.egov.go.kr) is an integrated portal where citizens can transact with the government on the Internet. Inter-agency efforts and collaboration have been key enablers in the implementation of this government portal. Specifically, this G4C (Government for Citizen) portal was co-initiated by three key ministries: the Ministry of Government Administration and Home Affairs, the Ministry of Planning and Budget, and the Ministry of Information and Communications.

To realise the goal of a "one-stop shop" for government information and public services, five national database systems regarding resident registration, land and property, motor vehicle and licensing, taxation, and corporation are interconnected across ministries and departments. In addition, the online public service map which covers more than 4,200 public services, provides information on procedures, e-forms, regional contact points, and other details for each service.

To support interconnectivity across ministries, the Korean government adopted enterprise-serving technologies and processes to break down the silo structure between physical government agencies. At the same time these tend to bolster communication and cooperation between related entities.

In particular, back-office development and support for the portal in terms of transactions and payments have been deemed as one of the most challenging and difficult tasks facing the government in its quest for success in achieving end-to-end electronic fulfillment in all services. To overcome these challenges, the government started on initiatives to establish a robust support infrastructure:

- **e-Document**
  The e-document application enables electronic creation, delivery, storage, and retrieval of government documents and records. The application is expected to radically speed up the delivery of official documents among the government ministries and agencies, as well as between the central and local governments. This streamlines the process of data communication and cuts down the costs of maintaining physical records and archives.

- **Digital Signature and e-Seal**
  Legally binding electronic documents with digital signatures and e-Seals enable government agencies and their customers to conduct online transactions securely and confidentially. Once registered with the system, each user is issued a digital certificate that provides access to a variety of online government services. This digital certificate can be used with various governmental agencies, eliminating the need for multiple pin numbers, passwords, or encryption keys.

- **Local Government Information System**
  In addition to interconnecting ministries of the central government, the Local Government Information System interconnects 21 database systems managed by local governments. Through the system, most of the services relevant to resident registration, land and property, motor vehicles, water and sewage, disaster management, regional development, road planning, forest management and others have been made accessible and available at any time.

Portal Management

A portal is an additional service delivery channel that requires active management. Resources are required to maintain operations, provide customer support and manage the portal. The issue of how to fund and manage these portals remains a pressing challenge for almost every country.

In recent years, governments have been outsourcing increasing amounts of their operations and technology management to the private sector where a growing class of Application Service Providers (ASPs) is offering services ranging from transaction processing to full portal hosting and management.

In terms of funding, some governments have steered away from the traditional source of funding from tax dollars to pay for portal management costs. Instead, these public service providers are engaging in commercial activities such as employing onsite advertising or charging user fees. Still, there are criticisms on the risks of funding e-Government with profit-oriented models. Commercial advertising creates potential conflicts of interest for government agencies if their websites have to become dependent on commercial revenues; charging a user free creates a disadvantage for people of more limited means and widens the digital divide between the rich and the poor.

The following case highlights an example of establishing private sector partnerships to manage and administer an e-Government portal.

Example 6: The ESDlife Portal (Hong Kong SAR)

Figure 12-6: Hong Kong's ESDLife portal

A major challenge to the Hong Kong SAR Government is to be able to deliver round-the-clock public services to 7 million residents, and to reduce the cost of service delivery at the same time. The government's goal is to broaden its reach to the residents of Hong Kong in an effective and efficient manner, without compromising the quality of public services

The solution came in the form of the world's first bilingual public and commercial services portal for the community, ESDLife (www.esdlife.com), which was developed under an innovative public-private sector partnership between the Hong Kong SAR Government and a commercial entity ESD Services Limited.[6]

ESD Services Limited is focused on implementing the core initiatives of the Hong Kong SAR Government's "Electronic Service Delivery" scheme. The government has adopted an innovative business model with a high level of private sector involvement in developing the project. Public and commercial services are provided under the same one-stop portal, so that citizens, businesses and tourists can obtain a full range of public and commercial services in a seamless and convenient manner.

To date, the portal covers a wide range of over 110 types of electronic public services provided by over 40 government departments and public agencies. Examples of public services include filing of tax returns, renewal of licences, application for business registration, payment of government bills, voter registration, and job searches. All are accessible through just a few clicks of the mouse. Kiosks were also set up around the city to provide convenient access for the population. (See Figure 12-7.)

Selected through an open tendering process, the private sector operator is responsible for the development, operation and management of the ESD information infrastructure. The government pays neither for the capital investment nor the recurrent operational and maintenance costs. Instead, it will only start to pay for each chargeable transaction made through the system after the number of cumulative chargeable transactions has reached an agreed volume. The operator is allowed to make use of the system to provide advertisements and revenue-generating private sector e-Commerce services (eg sale of event tickets, registration for educational courses, etc.) via the same portal website. This provides an additional income stream to the operator.

Managing the large number of parties involved in the project effectively is a key challenge highlighted by many members of the development team. The portal operator has to manage over twenty sub-contractors and business partners, including financial institutions, technology solution providers and kiosk landlords, while about thirty government departments and agencies were involved in providing electronic services. Communication, coordination and collaboration were essential to the success of the project. However, the impact of the public-private partnership on the development and management of the ESDLife portal was positive once the key challenges were overcome.

The adoption of a business model that involves private sector operators in portal management has substantially shortened the implementation timeframe. Under the public-private partnership, the business risk of the government is kept to the minimum while the charge-by-transaction model provides an incentive for the operator to drive public acceptance of e-Government services, continuously invest resources to implement sophisticated technology infrastructure and incorporate commercial e-services into the portal.

It is important to note that such rapport with the private sector is not established overnight. The Hong Kong government has an established track record on working with the private sector. Public-private partnerships have been around for decades and public sector leaders have become so accustomed to them that such partnerships have become part of the organisational culture.

"We try to outsource and use private sector resources as far as possible. Therefore the government's unique relationship with the private sector has to be leveraged on, in order to reap positive benefits," said Ms Joyce Tam, who is Principal Assistant Secretary, EG Division of Hong Kong's Commerce, Industry and Technology Bureau (CITB).

Considering the value creation activities that such collaboration will bring to residents, Ms Tam hopes that partnership between the government and private sector will be further enhanced through the ESD scheme, "We have to take one more step beyond simply involving the private sector. We want them to be the "real partners" to the government".

Indeed, if the case of Hong Kong's ESDLife is any indication, establishing win-win partnerships between government and the private sector today can significantly improve the way governments fulfill the "real needs" of the community for the long term.

Figure 12-7: Public kiosk in a Hong Kong shopping mall

LESSONS LEARNT IN PORTAL DEPLOYMENT

Government officials and IT professionals who have been involved in the design and implementation of portals in the public service generally report rich learning experiences in carrying out these projects. The following are some lessons gleaned while speaking to some of them.

The Tip of the Iceberg

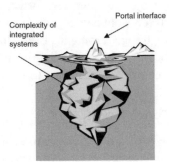

When embarking on e-Government programmes, a common misconception is to treat government portals as stand-alone applications. It is simplistic to look at some other government's seemingly successful portal and then make plans to transplant it into one's own environment.

The smart-looking portal interface that one usually sees is like the tip of the iceberg that is visible above the water level. There is a lot of complexity beneath the surface. Successful government portals are usually the culmination of years of effort in integrating disparate systems within and between agencies. It is only when the links between systems and agencies approach a degree of seamlessness that it is practical to consider planning for a government-wide portal.

The User View

Time and again portal architects have told us that a key design consideration is to see it from the viewpoint of the potential users of the portal. These users could be citizens, residents, visitors, or businesses. However, unless portal designers put themselves in the shoes of each of these categories of users, the portal interface will not be very effective.

A "Standard" Look-and-Feel

It was noted that left to their own devices, different government ministries and agencies will develop their websites according to individual styles and preferences. Some officials shared that their integrated portal initiative gave them the rare opportunity to come together to get an agreement of the "look-and-feel" of the website interfaces. This allowed them to achieve a more consistent (but not necessarily identical) theme that reflected a unity of purpose across the public sector.

Agency Ownership

Another key factor to portal success is clear demarcation of ownership. Creating seamless portals often requires some redrawing of the lines in terms of data, application and even service ownership. Strong leadership and clear vision are important to ensure that operationally there is no ambiguity in these areas, as it would lead to disagreements between agencies once the portal is launched.

In some countries, for various reasons it is not possible for all agencies to come onboard at the same time. Some may not be ready before the launch of the government portal. In such situations, a launch is still possible; however it is important to note that there needs to be a critical mass of agencies contributing to the portal if the project is to be successful.

Portal Security

While most Asian government portals allow open access to most functionalities, specific services may require the user to provide a unique ID, a national registration number being a common choice. In some portal projects, eg in Singapore, a single sign-on approach has been adopted to simplify the user experience. In other countries, specific services require additional validation with smart ID cards.

Portal Maintenance Issues

Ongoing management and maintenance of government portals are not trivial. It involves in-depth planning of resources and schedules. Typical processes for website and content management apply, except in the case of portals, the situation is probably many times more complex. Questions such as the following can be useful pointers to developing a sound portal maintenance strategy.

- Who creates content?
- Who approves content?
- Who maintains individual communities?
- What is the process for managing user feedback and queries?
- How should content be structured (taxonomy)?

CLOSING THOUGHTS

The digital economy presents new challenges as well as new opportunities for public service delivery. Some governments have chosen to meet these challenges by harnessing the portal technology and focusing on what citizens need and want, rather than on how agencies are structured, or the services they deliver.

Indeed, the experience of many Asian governments that have taken the integrated portal route is that an intentions-based portal makes it easier for governments, citizens and businesses to connect. This is especially evident where the portals have transformed the government-to-citizen and government-to-business interfaces. By providing aggregated content, user search for information and services can be streamlined. The ability to personalise content has also allowed visitors to customise the "look and feel" of their individual space on the portal, and predetermine the services that they commonly access.

Going forward, governments will continue to build new and innovative applications into their own portals, as well as deliver the content and services through new channels, eg wireless Internet connections. In addition, in line with the growing trend towards outsourcing, many governments will adopt new business models and embark on creative public-private sector partnerships to achieve their portal ambitions.

In Asia, we are seeing many signs of how e-services portals are reshaping governments. Evolving from disparate websites that serve customers of discrete government agencies, the advent of the portal concept has made seamless integrated public service delivery an achievable goal for many governments.

Endnotes

1   "Self-referential" websites are typically static and have little connectivity with other sites. Their pages only refer to themselves and are not connected by any means to other applications and external pages.

2   *"Transforming the purpose, practice, and performance of Government"*, Cisco Public Services Summit @ Nobel Week 2002.

3   Notably the US General Services Administration, World Market Research Center and Accenture.

4   The Stockholm Challenge is an awards programme for pioneering IT projects worldwide. The programme is run by the City of Stockholm in cooperation with the European Commission. The Challenge focuses on the positive effects of today's information society, and the benefit ICT can bring to people and society.

5   Singapore set up the Central Provident Fund (CPF) in 1955 to provide financial security for workers in their retirement or when they are no longer able to work. Over the years, CPF has evolved into a comprehensive social-security savings scheme, which not only takes care of a member's retirement, home ownership and healthcare needs, but also provides financial protection to CPF members and their families through its insurance schemes.

6   ESD Services Ltd is joint-venture between between Compaq, Hutchison Whampoa and Asia Global Crossing.

CHAPTER 13

Knowledge Management in the Public Sector

Praba Nair

▲ ▼ ▲ ▼ ▲ ▼ ▲ ▼

I not only use all the brains that I have,
but all that I can borrow.

Woodrow Wilson

▲ ▼ ▲ ▼ ▲ ▼ ▲ ▼

The 21st Century is undoubtedly the age of the knowledge worker. The foundations of the economies in Asia have gradually shifted from an industrial base to a service and knowledge base. In most developed nations, over 70 percent of workers are already engaged in knowledge work.[1] Increasingly, in these countries, the sources of wealth are derived more from information and knowledge resources and less from natural and physical resources. Knowledge has therefore, always been at the core of wealth creation and is a key source of economic growth.

Although knowledge management (KM) itself is a relatively new concept, organisations have long employed processes that can be classified under knowledge management practices in order to make decisions, produce goods and deliver services. No organisation can survive without creating, acquiring and transferring knowledge to its employees. What has changed however is the relative importance of knowledge as a source of wealth-creation compared to other factors of production. In an economy driven by the production of goods and services intensive in intangible capital; ideas, information and renewal of skills and competencies, are immensely more important.

The knowledge-intensive economy is characterised by the rapid creation and destruction of knowledge. It reflects an acceleration of change, enabled by new information and communication technologies. It also requires organisations to increase their capacity to adapt to rapidly changing circumstances. Furthermore, information technology has enabled easier access to information at lower cost. At the core of this accelerated change is a shift in emphasis on ways of learning. This shift in learning is from "known sources of education" to "learning from experience". In other words, knowledge is increasingly produced in the context of application and use.

KNOWLEDGE MANAGEMENT DEFINED

Knowledge can exist in many forms in an organisation. It can be found in explicit forms such as in written documents and procedures, and organisational systems and processes, or in forms intrinsic to an individual such as skills and experiences. Organisational knowledge may be embedded in products, processes or systems in various forms.

Most definitions of KM revolve around the concepts of organisational knowledge and the knowledge conversion processes. The American Productivity and Quality Center defines KM as "The strategies and processes of identifying, capturing and leveraging knowledge to enhance competitiveness." Gartner defines it as "... an emerging discipline that stresses a formalised, integrated approach to managing an enterprise's tangible and intangible information assets. ... Knowledge management is a coordinated attempt to tap the unrealised potential for sharing and reuse that lies in an enterprise's collective consciousness."

Thomas Stewart, the editor of the Harvard Business Review, defines KM as "the management or improvement of intellectual capital. Intellectual capital is the sum of everything the people of the organisation know which gives a competitive advantage." Larry Prusak, a leading proponent of KM, feels that "The only thing that gives an organisation a competitive edge — the only thing that is sustainable — is what it knows, how it uses what it knows, and how fast it can know something new."

While there are numerous subtly different definitions of KM, they all share three common features. Firstly, KM is an orgnisational strategy to enhance its competitiveness. Secondly, it is a systematic process of leveraging the organisation's intellectual assets. And thirdly it involves the process of identifying, capturing, sharing and creating knowledge. In essence, KM is a strategic organisational discipline that enables individuals to acquire, share, apply and create knowledge. In the process KM converts individual knowledge into corporate knowledge to enhance the organisation's capabilities.

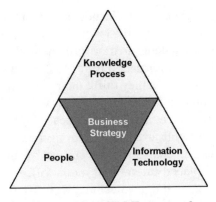

Figure 13-1: KM Framework

In order for KM initiatives to achieve any results, they must be aligned with the business objectives. KM programs that are not tied to specific business strategies and goals of the organisation have the highest risk of failure. Knowledge management involves integrating three key elements: process, people and technology (Figure 13-1). This trio has to come together to derive synergy. To leverage the knowledge asset, the organisation has to have in place dynamic processes that enable the right knowledge to get to the right person at the right time, so that it can be applied to create value for the organisation. Effective management of these processes requires a combination of technology and people — the information processing capability of IT and the expertise and willingness to share of the individuals. This interaction brings about knowledge flow within the organisation. Hence these three critical components need to be managed to achieve synergy: the knowledge processes that lead to value-creation; the people who learn and apply knowledge; and the technology which enables the knowledge processes.

PUBLIC SECTOR CHALLENGES

The power that governments wield — as employers, as buyers and as agents for economic growth — is enormous. As we enter the knowledge era and a period of incessant change, the impact of this influence takes on new dimensions. Donald Tapscott in his book, *The Digital Economy*, wrote, "… governments are central players in the new economy. They set the climate for wealth creation. They can act as a deadening hand on change or be a catalyst for creativity. They can cause economic stagnation through runaway deficits, or they can set a climate for growth." [2]

Governments at all levels face tremendous pressure to reduce spending and to maintain, or even increase the level of service provided to citizens. They are faced with the challenge to transform themselves. They recognise the value of an improved information infrastructure and see ICT as a key engine for revolutionising how they fulfill their basic mission — to deliver healthcare and education, stimulate economic growth, develop and maintain infrastructure, ensure justice, and maintain peace.

New technologies are only an enabler of stronger network relations. They cannot replace a deeper change in the culture of knowledge-sharing. Emphasis has to be placed on valuing more soft, informal and public knowledge; and strengthening connections with external parties such as private firms and research institutes. All these sources of knowledge have often been undervalued by traditional public sector organisations.

Increasing Public Demands

Even before the advent of the knowledge economy, citizens were expecting the same level of service from government agencies that they were receiving from the private sector. Making government "customer friendly" is but one of many challenges facing public administrators. All too often citizens complain that they wait too long in lines, get bounced around from office to office, and find government offices closed during the hours most convenient to the public. Improving the delivery of government services and information is an objective of most governments. Rightly or wrongly, they are expected to be a model for efficiency, innovation and service quality.

The following statement from the Commonwealth of Australia's Framework and Strategies for Information Technologies reflects the challenge shared by many government agencies:

> The public will expect government services to be comparable with the best services available from the private sector in terms of quality, accuracy, timeliness and user-friendliness. Clients will no longer tolerate delays, bureaucratic mistakes or excessively time-consuming and difficult procedures. They will expect to be treated individually and to have a range of options available to them, enabling them to select the best combination for their needs.[3]

Increasingly citizens demand individualised solutions. Policy-making and service delivery have been made more complex as the public sector now needs to work with more partners. This has created new demands on governments to obtain and integrate individualised knowledge for customising policies and services.

Governments are increasingly measured by their ability to sense and respond to the environment, formulate sound policies and execute on decisions. Policies and national decisions usually cannot be made without feedback from the public. Public policies and major policy adjustments need the support of multiple stakeholders who often have different views of what should be done.

The knowledge-intensive economy demands faster adaptation to an accelerated change in the environment of public policies and service delivery, as well as customised public policies and service delivery. Governments will therefore have to be more proactive and deliver services closer to the customer. The mindset of "one size fits all" is no longer valid. All this will have inevitable consequences on traditional hierarchies, which have been designed in part to keep service delivery and policies uniform.

Effect on Government Bureaucracies

The government bureaucracies that are often encountered by citizens did not develop overnight. The complexities prevalent in the service delivery networks of most governments evolved through necessity over time. As governments were asked to do more for a growing population and as the revenues and expenditures of governments increased, so too did the elaborate network of rules, regulations, processes and controls to prevent abuse and safeguard the common interests of the people.

In tandem with this growth came layers of staff and the development of hierarchical organisations within government bodies. Narrowly defined specialities flourished within vertically integrated departments and agencies. Dedicated information processing systems and networks evolved as a result. While the technology changed from mainframe-based systems to the networked-based systems of today, these separate information processing systems continued to support unique sets of forms, processes and procedures — rarely providing cross-agency function or support.

This technology legacy has only served to strengthen the walls that exist between many government agencies. Sometimes called the "stovepipe effect", this often results in the average citizen needing to go to multiple government offices to make a simple address change, and elevates the level of difficulty one encounters in getting a problem resolved, especially one that involves more than one department, agency or ministry.

KM is about using management tools in a way that systematically promotes knowledge-sharing, including improving intellectual capital by flattening rigid hierarchies and opening up bureaucratic divisions to promote horizontal knowledge-sharing; linking performance, pay and promotion to knowledge-sharing; and building communities of practice.

Breakdown of Government Monopolies

In the past, the authority of most governments was based on a monopoly of services. Over the past decade, many public monopolies have been opened to competition, notably in the infrastructure, education, communications and utility sectors. However the most significant breakdown of monopoly is going to be global and virtual — with increased competition from hospitals, schools and universities (to mention but a few examples) all over the world. If another country has higher standards or more differentiated services, there will soon be a demand for the same services.

With the globalisation of information, and increased internationalisation of people and capital mobility, traditional public service monopolies are increasingly in competition with foreign organisations delivering similar public services. For example, universities compete globally to attract the most endowments, the best students and the most qualified professors while research institutions compete to attract the best researchers and the most funding. Even in countries which traditionally have a public system of education, private entities have increasing influence on the education and training of citizens through distance learning, coaching, information and courses on the Internet.

There is no doubt that private firms are producing a greater share of goods and services that are increasingly intensive in intangible capital, directly competing with the public sector for the delivery of goods and services such as education, science, security and access to knowledge. Public policies are also being compared internationally, and citizens and lobby groups exert some amount of pressure on governments to live up to international standards. At the national level, decentralisation of processes and services has also increased competition among government agencies.

The traditional authority based on a monopoly of knowledge will also disappear. Governments no longer have a monopoly of knowledge in their field as information about policies and service delivery become much more available to citizens, lobby groups, and users. To keep citizens' confidence, governments need to increase the knowledge base of their activities and keep track of, and integrate, new knowledge as rapidly as it is produced.

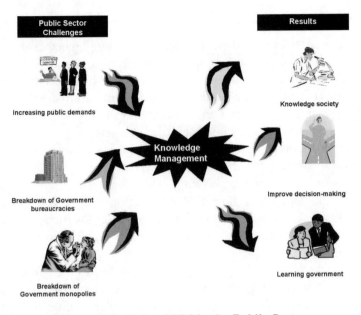

Figure 13-2: Role of KM in the Public Sector

THE CASE FOR KNOWLEDGE MANAGEMENT IN THE PUBLIC SECTOR

KM has always been at the core of government tasks — inseparable from strategy, planning, consultation, and implementation. The government has traditionally had a unique capacity to bring together the public and private sectors, as well as different strata of society to share knowledge around policy issues or about service delivery. The question is thus not whether governments have ever managed knowledge or whether they should, but rather how they can improve their practices to better adapt to the new knowledge-intensive economy.

The public sector will see a relatively large number of retirements and turnover within the next few years. This will make recruitment and retention extremely important in every government institution. The key to recruitment and retention in the public sector will be its ability to attract the younger generation into the public sector with a clear mission, strong leadership and modern approach to management. This situation will require good KM systems to compensate for the loss of public servants with years of experience who today represent the core of institutional memory. Higher rates of staff turnover have replaced the culture of lifelong employment, and challenge the traditional ways of maintaining corporate memory.

Improved decision-making

The core process of government is decision making; whether it is about policy, budget, or determination and provision of services. All of the inherently government functions are characterized by a decision. Quality of decisions depends on the quality and quantity of information. Decisions are also typically made along an information value chain. From a citizen or business standpoint, they give their data or money to government, then government seems to spend a lot of time and resources processing the information. When a citizen comes to get the information or a service, he or she hopes to get what is needed quickly and without error or hassle. The outcome depends on how well information is collected, processed, and analysed. Knowledge management can help government agencies improve decisions, leading to better service that is delivered faster and at lower cost.

Two events of 2001 dramatically illustrated the cost of ignorance: the collapse of new economy business models and the terrorist attacks on the United States. Both share a common trait — the failure to effectively exploit information that would have provided for better decision-making. According to leading market research firms, government spending on information exploitation will start to have a major impact on the soft technologies associated with collecting information and building knowledge, which will lead to a boom similar to prior phases of government investment in infrastructure and hardware.[4] New economy business failures, led by dot-coms and culminating with the collapse of Enron illustrate that, when intangibles are the primary source of shareholder value, transparency of information and effective management of intellectual assets are all the more essential.

Promoting a healthy knowledge society

For the public sector, the issue of KM should not be considered merely as an internal management and governance challenge. The public sector has a unique role to play in promoting the production, use, and transfer of knowledge which in many ways is a crucial public good. There is also a role to play in the provision of free basic knowledge.

Building stakeholder (citizens, users, private firms, lobby groups) capital by obtaining the right knowledge from all stakeholders and involving stakeholders in the decision-making process is an integral role of government. The pursuit of wealth has become the pursuit and packaging of information and knowledge. The successful government will be the one that enables its business community to most effectively obtain the best information, and apply it in a timely manner to the creation or sale of goods and services.

The public sector needs to review its role in the provision of knowledge that cannot be provided for by private firms, e.g. research on rare diseases, long-term environmental trends, etc. Public policies should set the basic rules of knowledge production, transfer and use in order to find the right balance between the necessity of promoting both innovation and equal access to knowledge. However, the intermediate goals of public policies are not always clear-cut. They tend to change depending on trends in the environment, making it difficult to determine the knowledge to be sought. The public sector should strengthen its connections with private firms, research institutes and universities. This will enable the government not only to keep abreast of current issues and emerging trends, but also make informed decisions on policy matters.

A Learning Government

Governments need to continually learn in order to remain relevant to the constituents they serve. Anticipating, learning and communicating policy outcomes will be at the core of the transformation of public organisations into learning organisations. A learning government is a government continuously learning from its successes and failures, capable of constantly reforming its structure, processes and policies to reflect new knowledge and insights. For example, governments need to respond to changes in the demographics of the country by making changes to policies. If governments postpone their decision to make changes, it will undermine the success of future reforms. In contrast, private firms only have a limited amount of time to transform knowledge into action. They need to quickly identify and introduce new services and products in response to changes in the environment — this is the private sector's "time to market".

KNOWLEDGE BASED ECONOMIES

All economies are knowledge-based. What is different today, however, is that rapidly growing economies depend more on the creation, acquisition, distribution, and use of knowledge. The effective use of knowledge is becoming the most important factor for international competitiveness and for creating wealth.

Singapore is already in high gear in moving towards a knowledge-based economy. People are the most important resource in Singapore's economy since there are few other natural resources. Investing in their long-term development benefits the country, as much as the individual. Singapore's national agenda requires employees who are motivated, innovative and enterprising for it to succeed. Citizens need to acquire new skills and knowledge to remain employable. Professionals and managers make up almost 25 percent of Singapore's labour force. And those with tertiary education make up 27.6 percent of the workforce in Singapore.[5]

In Malaysia, almost 50 percent of Malaysians are employed in the service sector followed by 28 percent in manufacturing. As Malaysia moves into a knowledge-based economy, two important observations can be made. The first is that the percentage employed in agriculture and manufacturing sectors will dwindle, while the service sector will grow. Secondly, the unemployment rate will grow as the country moves towards a knowledge-based economy.[6] Structural unemployment as a result of the economy shift is a challenge that many governments will need to manage.

The Malaysian Government has adopted several initiatives aimed at developing Malaysia into a knowledge-based economy. Of significance was the establishment of the Multimedia Super Corridor (MSC) in 1996, to foster the development of high technology and innovations for local and foreign companies in Malaysia through the provision of world-class multimedia facilities. The MSC was designed to be an engine of economic growth for the 21st Century as well as propel Malaysia towards a knowledge-based economy.[7] To attract knowledge workers, the Knowledge Worker Exchange (KWX) portal was set up. With more than 36,000 knowledge workers needed for the MSC, KWX assists clients and candidates create and maintain high performing work environments through the provision of contemporary and creative recruitment and related services.[8]

Hong Kong is also striving towards a knowledge-based economy. Ideas, creativity and knowledge workers are now the driving forces of Hong Kong's economy. In the past ten years the unemployment rate has jumped from around 1–2 percent to about 5.5 percent Among those currently unemployed, few are knowledge workers.[9] Owing to a structural shift in employment during the past decade, the service sector now employs over nine times as many workers as the manufacturing sector.[10] This is a stark illustration of the swing in Hong Kong towards a knowledge-based economy.

ERA OF CONTINUOUS LEARNING

One important feature of the knowledge-based economy is the introduction of new rules for countries, organisations and individuals. Specifically these new rules deal with the process of continuous learning and capability building.

From the 1950s through the 1980s, the formula for developing countries was to invest in education and training (refer to Endnote 6). Earnings of workers were commensurate with the level of education. In the 1990s, the rules changed when graduates started losing jobs because of the economic downturn. The notion of lifetime employment became a thing of the past. Many big technology companies such as Lucent Technologies, Motorola, Cisco Systems and Creative Technologies started to cut staff during the economic downturn. Creative Technologies, a globally renowned Singaporean company that makes the Sound Blaster PC cards, followed other multinationals and cut its global workforce by 10 percent.[11] These are some of the many examples that demonstrate in no uncertain terms that the days of lifetime employment are over. The way forward now is for employees to be willing to continuously learn to remain economically relevant in a knowledge-based economy. Peter Drucker puts it best when he said "continuous learning during one's working life will increasingly be a requirement for any knowledge worker".[12] He adds in his book, *The New Realities*, that "engineers ten years out of school are already facing obsolescence if they have not refreshed their knowledge again and again".[13]

The knowledge-based economy is dynamic and requires constant upgrading of skills to stay competitive, hence the need for continuous learning. Knowledge workers, their ideas and new discoveries are the most valuable assets that an organisation can have in a knowledge-based economy. The process of continuous learning and cross-training helps employees to conceive and develop new ideas. A recent buzz phrase in human resource circles is "ownership of learning". This marks the first step towards a paradigm shift in learning attitudes — that of the individual playing an active role in his own learning and development.

GROWTH OF KNOWLEDGE MANAGEMENT INITIATIVES

In Western economies, the private sector generally takes the lead in KM initiatives. In Asia, the reverse seems to be more common. Government bodies such as in Malaysia and Singapore have been taking the lead in implementing KM initiatives at the agency level. Consequently, many organisations, in the public sector, have incorporated KM as a core element of their organisational strategy. Knowledge and innovation are the key competitive factors in these economies.

Early Adopters in Asia

In Singapore, the public sector is the key driver of KM initiatives. One of the reasons could be the Government's emphasis on the Knowledge Economy. To encourage and support the government agencies to embark on Knowledge Management initiatives, the Infocomm Development Authority of Singapore (IDA) provides financial grants to public sector agencies who pilot KM projects.

Some organisations have been studying and exploring KM since the late 1990s. The interest in KM grew towards the turn of the century. Some institutions also started offering the public KM seminars at that time. Interest in the discipline has soared, particularly in the wake of the KM Asia series of combined exhibitions and conferences in July 2001 which attracted well over 1,000 visitors. A significant number of government bodies in Singapore have established dedicated KM positions and divisions.

The Hong Kong Police Force is one government agency actively implementing KM initiatives. One such initiative is the development and implementation of a Forensic Pathology Database in their Knowledge Management System. In Hong Kong, police officers are responsible for conducting death investigations on behalf of the coroner. The investigating officer is an essential component in the multi-disciplinary investigation of sudden, unexpected and unnatural deaths. According to the Hong Kong Police Force, KM has helped to improve both the quality and standard of the death investigation process.[14] It has helped to provide sufficient and accurate background knowledge and has improved communication between personnel involved in such investigations.

Generally companies in Hong Kong recognise the importance of human resources to the profitability and growth of their companies, but are less certain about how it may be integrated into the overall business model. Business leaders accept that KM requires long-term investment, and that high returns can only realistically be expected with time. The Hong Kong Productivity Council (HKPC) and the Knowledge Management Development Community (KMDC) have shouldered the responsibility for spearheading the KM cause in Hong Kong (refer to Endnote 9). The KMDC was set up to promote the awareness and to advance the practice of KM in Hong Kong.

In Malaysia, the National IT Agenda and the Governance Agenda incorporate the smart partnership model/concept in Malaysia's drive towards achieving a Values-Based Knowledge Society. The goal is to forge a smart partnership between the public and private sectors under the Malaysian Inc. Model of Governance, and work towards a Convergence Model of Governance for the Information Age. Hence, integrating and converging the public, private and community interests sectors. A knowledge-based development strategy in Malaysia includes an institutional framework to promote and encourage tri-sectoral smart partnerships. One of the strategic thrusts outlined in the Knowledge-based economy Strategic Plan is to develop the public sector into a knowledge-based civil service (refer to Endnote 7).

Focus of KM activities

When KM first started taking root in Singapore, the focus was mainly on developing IT systems for capturing knowledge. Knowledge management was regarded as a technology-centric discipline, largely because it was usually the IT departments in those organisations which had first determined to explore KM and to champion the emerging discipline. More recently, there has been a growing interest in the deployment of corporate portals as a KM tool, especially so when KM vendors started introducing and repackaging their solutions as KM portals.

The most common focus of organisations implementing KM initiatives is on operational activities. These would include the documentation of processes and capturing of project lessons upon completion of projects. The most common KM projects in the government sector are access to critical knowledge and after action reviews.[15] The objectives of which are to facilitate orientation and training.

Studies in Hong Kong show that of those organisations that have addressed KM, the vast majority have adopted a product-based approach to the discipline. In this approach, knowledge is perceived as a physical object which is captured, distributed and measured. The process approach which primarily sees KM as a social communication process is generally being ignored (refer to Endnote 9). Knowledge is generally seen as best practices which can be captured and shared. The Hong Kong Productivity Council founded the Asian Benchmarking Clearinghouse in October 1998 to promote benchmarking through the development of best practices. Through benchmarking, organisations reported being able to transfer these best practices into their units and divisions to improve overall productivity and efficiency.

KM activities that focus on operational processes have fewer barriers to implementation as the users see the direct benefits of such projects. Only a few companies have taken their KM programmes to the next level and focused more on the cultural issues that sit at the heart of contemporary understanding of current-generation KM. One of the reasons is that KM activities that focus on the people issues face more resistance, as tangible outcomes are more difficult to identify.

Although culture is the principal determinant of KM success, it is also the principal challenge. KM initiatives that focus on technical solutions are easier to implement. Many organisations espouse knowledge creation, sharing, learning and innovation, but in reality cultural barriers to KM govern individual and organisational behaviour. Some employees simply were not ready, willing, or able to share knowledge. Sometimes, the organisational structures prevented them from doing so. Some perceived barriers to nurturing a KM culture are a lack of incentives to share knowledge, and that employees do not always see knowledge creation or sharing as part of their job. According to a survey conducted by Straits Knowledge among Singapore organisations, actual practice is ahead of managers' beliefs in Knowledge Management.[16]

The economic downturn has forced a number of private sector firms to cut back on their budgets. Since KM was not seen to be generating any immediate results to the bottom line, it often did not rank as high in the priority lists of senior management. However, some knowledge-based foreign companies have transferred some of their KM practices from their headquarters when they set up operations in Asia.

The Singapore government's constant emphasis and support for the knowledge economy would certainly help to drive the KM movement in Singapore, at least for the public sector for the next few years. In addition to KM, the government has also been emphasising the importance of innovation. For example, a new multi-million dollar fund known as The Enterprise Challenge (TEC), helps to sponsor innovative proposals that have the potential to create new value or significant improvements to the delivery of public services. The purpose of TEC is to encourage creativity and innovative initiatives for the Public Service. As TEC has proved to be successful, the government decided to extend the TEC scheme with additional funding.[17]

CHALLENGES

There is little doubt that the increasing role of knowledge in policy-making, process innovation and service delivery can help improve public sector governance. The effectiveness and efficiency of the public sector can be directly enhanced by increasing the knowledge-base and transparency of public service activities. Challenges created by the knowledge-intensive economy necessitate the review of institutional arrangements for the provision of data and statistics on public services and policies.

Governments are increasingly required to make decisions on complex issues leading to debates about what governments know, or should know. Government decision-making around new and complex issues will invariably raise more questions about the effective governance of this decision-making. Government officials will be increasingly asked to provide the source of their information and ensure that bodies providing information, and government's relations with them, follow good governance rules. There needs to be a review of institutional arrangements and relations between providers of knowledge and decision-makers.

A vital metric of a society's success is knowledge. That which its citizens possess, that which is made available to its public servants, and that which is embedded in structural and other intellectual assets that can be leveraged upon. The challenge facing governments is not only to make the information available but also help communities think together. This would require creating an environment where communities truly value knowledge sharing.

THE WAY FORWARD

A holistic KM strategy is needed to avoid the mistake of investing in IT to increase data and information that would in turn require additional IT investments. This danger commonly arises when organisations have vague or non-existent strategies or definitions of what they want to achieve with their IT investments. The biggest misconception that IT leaders make is that KM is about technology. One of the reasons for this misconception is because KM vendors have been focusing on and promoting the "KM richness" of their products. The KM initiative has almost become synonymous with the implementation of the KM IT system. Information technology is but one part of a good KM strategy. It will be of very limited use if IT investments and changes have not been thought through — with due regard for staff incentive structures, human resources management, the type of information to be made available, ways to obtain and organise data, and staff interactions. The danger for organisations thus stems from the tendency to embark on KM initiatives without understanding how it will create value for the organisation.

Software houses and consulting firms are pushing on ahead of mature perspectives on KM. Given that the software houses are selling sophisticated

KM products and organisations are experimenting with KM before the discipline has been properly developed, we can expect large numbers of failures before many organisations will be able to point to successful knowledge-based strategies and practices.

Knowledge management is not as simple as it appears. Without proper preparation, it can be overwhelming. To ensure success, organisations need to take a big picture view by first defining KM in terms of a business objective. Once that challenge is met, the organisation will be in a much better position to determine which of its intellectual assets are worth organizing, managing and sharing.

To develop a KM strategy, the organisation must predefine the strategic business need for KM. If KM is not tied to a business goal, the organisation could end up with an expensive system that takes up server space but has no real purpose or return on investments. Unfortunately, this first step is one that many organisations fail to take. The organisation must articulate what KM really means to it. It can range from retention of best practices and providing virtual collaborative workspaces, to encouraging innovation. Then, it is necessary to decide whether the current process of dealing with corporate knowledge is effective, and if the corporate culture is ready for procedural changes. Knowledge management is not so much a "systems solution" as it is a "people solution". It is therefore important to take a look at the people and processes that will be affected by KM and address the relevant issues accordingly. Once these issues have been resolved, the organisation can then evaluate the existing technology infrastructure to determine whether it's adequate for KM. This can be done by matching the required KM capabilities against the existing technology. The decision can subsequently be made as to whether any additional systems are required.

If governments in developing countries want their economies to benefit from a knowledge-based economy, they must develop policies that will embrace such an economy. The individual policies that governments undertake are entirely up to them. They should develop policies with their socio-cultural, economic and political environments in mind. It is important to remember that government bureaucracy will determine the pace at which it accepts and implements KM.

Knowledge management could certainly help governments to be effective in the fulfillment of their mission. It could play a key role in government functions. The public sector has a unique responsibility in bringing together the public and private sectors, as well as different communities in society to share knowledge around policy issues and service delivery. The ability of the government to effectively exploit information would enhance their decision-making capability. If KM is going to help governments transform themselves, it will require a change in the way the government acquires, captures and disseminates knowledge. The value of KM is not in itself but in the realisation of the results that flow through it.

Endnotes

1   Skyrme, DJ, Knowledge Economy Conference, Beijing, 1999.

2   Tapscott, D, *"The Digital Economy"*, McGraw Hill, New York (1996).

3   *"Framework and Strategies for Information Technologies in the Commonwealth of Australia – Exposure Draft"*, Office of Government Information Technology, Canberra, Australia, 1996.

4   Caldwell, F, Gilbert, M, Hayward, S, Logan, D, Lundy, J, *"New Focus on Knowledge and Collaboration Begin in 2002"*, Gartner, 7 January 2002.

5   Labour Force Survey, Manpower Research and Statistics Department, Singapore, November 2002.

6   Abdulai, David, *"The Process of Continuous Learning and Training: The New Rule for Malaysian Workers in the Knowledge-based Economy"*, *Malaysia and the k-economy: Challenges, Solutions and the Road Ahead* edited by DN Abdulai, Pelanduk (2001).

7   Knowledge Based Economy Master Plan, Institute of Strategic and International Studies, September 2002.

8   http://web.kwx.com.my/kwx/asp/aboutkwx02.asp.

9   Liu, T, *"Towards a knowledge-based economy"*, *KM Magazine*, Jul/Aug 2002.

10 Hong Kong Yearbook 2001.

11 *"Creative Technologies to close US plant"*, *Financial Times*, 21 March 2001, p 21.

12 Drucker, PF *"Managing in a Time of Great Change"*, New York: Truman Tally/Dutton.(1995).

13 Drucker, PF, *" The New Realities"*, New York: Harper and Row (1989).

14 http://www.info.gov.hk/police/aa-home/offbeat.

15 Azzman, M, Report of the Global Knowledge Forum Proceedings, March 2000.

16 *"Knowledge Management in Singapore organisations"*, Straits Knowledge, July 2002.

17 Keynote Address by BG (NS) Yam Ah Mee, Deputy Secretary (Development), *"The Education Technology Seminar"*, Singapore, 8 February 2002.

CHAPTER 14

e-Government and the Security Challenge

Jeffery BH Tan and Edwin LC Ang

▲ ▼ ▲ ▼ ▲ ▼ ▲ ▼

On the Internet, no one knows you're a dog.

**A quote from a Peter Steiner comic
in the New Yorker in the early 1990s**

▲ ▼ ▲ ▼ ▲ ▼ ▲ ▼

In late 2002, there was a high-profile case involving a New York based identity theft ring that reportedly absconded with sensitive financial information of more than 30,000 US citizens. This breach cast a shadow over the security measures of supposedly tightly controlled financial systems of credit bureaus. Once regarded as the benchmark for enforcing rigorous security practices, such bureaus are now under scrutiny for potential loopholes in security practices, particularly those relating to external access via public networks like the Internet.

It was later discovered that an ex-employee of the technology company that provided the systems had started the scam. The perpetrator had access to passwords and codes of customers that were used to retrieve the information. With the easy availability of access via public infrastructure, he continued his criminal activities long after having left the company.

This example highlights both the technological and procedural challenges facing those providing electronic services dealing with sensitive information and who are required to make the services freely available to the general masses. A big part of e-Government fundamentally involves integrating islands of disparate systems to offer a rich variety of government services via electronic channels. These services usually require the exchange of sensitive personal and corporate data and are potential sources of security breaches. Governments will need to ensure that adequate safeguards are in place to minimise possible outbreaks and yet keep the e-services useable for the general masses.

IN A NUTSHELL

Most e-Government initiatives start out with agencies building electronic relationships with each other or with selected external groups such as government suppliers or subcontractors. The cost savings and efficiency boosts related to systems like electronic procurement are potentially enormous. As such, the next wave of e-Government is to extend the transactional relationship that has been established between agencies to reach out to the constituents at large. The security concerns for such mass deployment are no different from those faced by commercial enterprises offering web based services. In fact, given the potential sensitivity and criticality of some government services, public sector systems security might need to be even more rigorous.

Programmes like the Inland Revenue Authority of Singapore's Online Filing[1] (e-Filing) of personal income taxes has shown how convenient and efficient the future can be for the citizen. Furthermore the potential cost savings simply spiral into orders of magnitude as entire methods of processing are moved from torturous paper based processes into instant electronic completion.

Public trust and confidence are vital to all government services. With an almost daily stream of stories about cyber crimes and security breaches, there are inevitable public concerns about whether existing and future e-Government services are adequately secured. Those involved in developing the systems need to adopt appropriate measures and best practices to minimise the possibility of security breaches. Such efforts should also be complemented with adequate legislation and policies to deter violations and provide effective means to respond to any security compromise.

The growing numbers of electronic transactions that are conducted behind a faceless public network are vulnerable to a myriad of security issues. Beyond the more readily recognisable system and technology-related threats, there is now also a concern for the safeguard of the massive stores of information generated by these transactions. Besides preventing deliberate rogue attacks, e-Government service providers need to also consider the possibility of unsolicited compromises or accidental violations.

Following the events of September 11 and the foreboding threat of cyber terrorism, IT security has become a major concern to governments and businesses alike. In a world heavily reliant on computers, a cyber terrorist can conceivably wreak more havoc to public and government IT infrastructure in a fraction of a second than a terrorist with explosives. This presents a renewed urgency to review existing security practices and ensure their relevance in the face of these imminent threats.

In this chapter, we will be looking at the major security issues, the technology and emerging policies that addresses those concerns and how various countries approach the challenges. We also delve into the topic of

Information Assurance, an emerging IT discipline centred on information protection and how to maintain trustworthiness in an electronic realm laden with security concerns.

WHAT'S AT STAKE?

While we are preoccupied with the threats of malicious viruses that seem to capture the attention of the media, there is a plethora of other potential security compromises[2] that could just as easily cripple and malign an e-Government service.

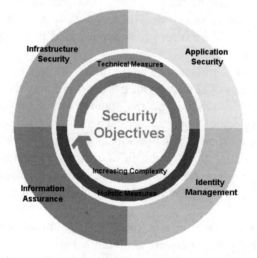

Figure 14-1: The Security Quadrants

Most security concerns can be classified under four broad categories:

(1)   **Infrastructure Security** — Government data networks provide the core infrastructure for timely interactions between agencies and the various constituents. Establishing and maintaining a high level of network security are key to ensuring the availability of the computing infrastructure on which all other information services rely. It also ensures the integrity of the information managed by the government.

(2)   **Application Security** — Governments have traditionally been proponents of applying rigorous application security. However, given the broader public access requirements of e-Government services, the vulnerabilities have to be reassessed to balance the potential risk impact with appropriate security measures.

(3) **Identity Management** — With the rise in the number of faceless electronic transactions, governments need to address the challenges of managing identifiable access to information and applications scattered across a variety of internal and external computing systems. Furthermore, they have to cater to a growing number of public users who demand uncomplicated access mechanisms, without compromising security or inadvertently allowing access to sensitive information.

(4) **Information Assurance** — Governments must be responsible custodians for the huge amounts of personal information they are entrusted with. Software programs, websites and services must provide adequate protection against illegitimate access and have to ensure they live up to data protection and privacy best practices. Sharing of information between agencies should also be conducted with adequate care to prevent any infringement on the use of information away from the source.

These broadly defined security categories can increase in both complexity and scope. In the old days of purely intra-government exchange of information, infrastructure and application security were adequate, as the environments were proprietary and highly controlled. With the increasing use of public networks for e-Government portals, the need to manage remote and faceless identities, as well as privacy considerations has made security issues more fluid and demanding, and pushed the boundaries of information security beyond technology.

Besides sound technical solutions, adequate legislation and enforceable policies are required to ensure that those perpetrating errant and indiscriminate actions can be held accountable. Many countries have now enacted laws dictating acceptable levels of online etiquette and recognising the authenticity of electronic transactions. National level privacy policies are also being reviewed or considered for relevance in managing the imminent threats of information being utilised for unscrupulous gains.

Another growing area of acceptance is the certification of security practices according to established global standards. Just as ISO 9000 provides the standard for quality management systems, information security management standards such as ISO 17799 serve to provide a benchmark for assessing security risks, and offer guidelines for mitigating and reducing such risks. Compliance with these standards could help reduce business damage by preventing and minimising the impact of security incidents. Although governments typically already have stringent compliance requirements, these could be enhanced by incorporating best practices advocated by such certification bodies.

INFRASTRUCTURE SECURITY

With the proliferation of e-Government services, the public network infrastructure is now becoming the mainstream medium for disseminating government information and providing an efficient means of transactions within government, between agencies and with citizens and businesses. Moreover, this network also supports critical infrastructure such as finance, transportation and energy. As a result of this increased interconnectivity, information systems and networks are now exposed to a growing and wider array of threats and vulnerabilities. As the nature, volume and sensitivity of the information increase, so do the consequences in the event of a breach in the security of the network.

All these raise significant issues for the network and information security of e-Government. The OECD advocates the need for greater awareness and understanding of security issues and suggests the need to develop "a culture of security".[3] Such a culture would make security an inherent consideration when designing, developing and deploying systems on a network, and not as an afterthought. It would involve all stakeholders that are party to the deployment of the system, making them aware of the security risks, consider appropriate preventive measures and assume a responsibility to enhance the security of the information and networks.

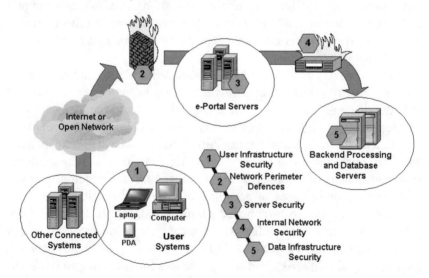

Figure 14-2: Typical Infrastructure Security Components

In every form of security, one must analyse the risks, and attempt to mitigate those risks. It is always a fine balancing act. Understanding what the risks are in relation to what we are protecting, allows us to make better judgements about the precautions we need to take. This is necessary because there is a cost for every security measure put in place. For any given system infrastructure, the basic security considerations include:

• allowing only legitimate and authorised access to the network, data and services;
• maintaining the integrity and secrecy of the data while in transit;
• maintaining the integrity and confidentiality of information stored on the network;
• ensuring the availability and usability of the systems and network;
• monitoring the network for undesirable traffic, malicious codes (like viruses) and potential intrusions (hacking by unauthorised persons), and taking the appropriate corrective measures before extensive damage occurs;
• enacting the proper security policies associated with the use of the infrastructure, including policies governing security devices (such as firewalls), systems access, and strictly enforcing these at all times; and
• reviewing the systems (via audit logs and vulnerability assessment and testing) regularly.

Threats to a network can be either deliberate (eg hacker penetration) or accidental (eg a confidential message being sent to the wrong recipient). Deliberate threats can be further subdivided into passive (eg monitoring but not alteration of information) and active (eg deliberately changing the value of a transaction). Network and infrastructure security involve putting in place relevant safeguards against such potential compromises. These safeguards comprise not only technological solutions but also adequate physical and procedural measures to prevent unwarranted violations.

Network security measures such as firewall and virus detection solutions are already a common feature in most e-Government systems. The more sophisticated technology of network intrusion detection and enhanced cryptography are starting to find their way in as these technologies mature.

Besides the myriad of technological solutions and corresponding policies, the key to maintaining adequate levels of security is the diligent application of security audits. By scanning networks, servers and even applications for security bugs and holes, security audits check for weaknesses that could be exploited in order to gain unauthorised access to proprietary data and launch attacks on the network. System audits also ensure that the security of the computing systems is kept up-to-date, as new threats and vulnerabilities emerge, with correspondingly new ways to deal with them.

The key challenge facing e-Government service providers is the need to maintain a consistent, and yet compartmentalised network and infrastructure security across multiple agencies. As more services are integrated via a unified e-Government portal, the ability to ensure the accessibility and usability of the services without comprising the security of the individual systems is a critical concern. Existing differences in the agencies' networks pose a challenge in attempting to interconnect systems securely due to their proprietary and sometimes incompatible security functions. Coupled with the need to ensure ease of public access, it is imperative that a compromise in one subsystem does not bring down interconnected systems.

In Singapore, the Public Service Infrastructure (PSi) provides a complete end-to-end platform for government agencies to develop, deploy and operate e-services efficiently.[4] It comprises several components that collectively provide a comprehensive environment for the rapid and secure deployment of e-services. Besides a secure network infrastructure with intrusion detection capabilities, PSi also provides support for integration with databases and legacy systems of government agencies. Designed as a multi tier infrastructure, it is capable of allowing upgrades to the components without affecting the e-services that are already deployed.

Malaysia is looking into establishing a national ICT security policy to provide a comprehensive framework that ensures secure information systems and network infrastructures within all sectors in the country.[5] Spearheaded by multiple agencies, including the Ministry of Energy, Communications and Multimedia and the Malaysian Administrative Modernisation and Management Planning Unit (MAMPU), the effort focuses on preventing leaks and safeguarding confidential data. The policy also complements the Malaysian Public Sector Management of ICT Security Handbook (MyMis) released by MAMPU.[6]

APPLICATION SECURITY

An application cannot evolve with the business it supports if its security relies on the last-minute addition of a firewall, ad hoc encryption of communications, or simply using stronger authentication mechanisms. To boost confidence in the robustness of an application, security needs to be designed into the architecture. An understanding of the risk of each application is critical to defining what level of precaution is appropriate. The various cross-agency linkages that require the exchange of information present a security challenge due to the often independent and inconsistent security practices being applied to software applications.

Adequate infrastructure security protects data from potential attacks by effectively creating a fortress around the data source. The deployment of firewalls and other network infrastructure elements provides the necessary network defences against potential compromises from perpetrators at a generic level. Beyond these perimeter safeguards, the software applications that service the users could themselves pose a security loophole as they are sometimes overlooked, as with the New York identity theft ring case described at the beginning of this chapter.

Application security provides authentication, authorisation, confidentiality and non-repudiation services at a finer layer of granularity not accorded by the more general security services of the network and infrastructure layer. In particular, the focus is on user authentication and authorisation mechanisms to access application functionality, selective encryption services to protect sensitive data (such as passwords and others), as well as confidentiality and non-repudiation services to secure transactions where appropriate.

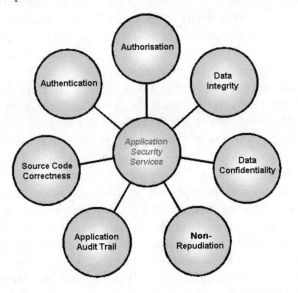

Figure 14-3: Major Application Layer Security Services

Security services provided at the application layer include the following:

- authentication — verifying the legitimacy of the user to access the application and its associated services;
- access control — managing the level of access and services to within the authorised capacity of the user;

- data confidentiality — ensure data is not retrieved by unauthorised personnel or applications;
- data integrity — maintaining data consistency and preventing unsolicited manipulation; and
- non-repudiation — prevents denial of validity of transactions.

It also includes the provision of logging and audit trails for all application activities performed, safeguarding against the introduction of malicious or unintended code, amongst others. e-Government implementers are embracing industry accepted software development methodologies that advocate secure application development practices and code transparency. This is in contrast to previous "black-box" approaches where security features are treated as components that get "plugged" into applications without minimal regards for coding flaws that might expose the application to security breaches.

Application security faces two primary challenges. The first is making sure the security required by an application's business objectives is met without hampering the usability of the system. The second is making sure combinations of custom applications with off-the-shelf and open source components are properly integrated and configured in a way that does not expose the environment to undue risk.

Application security services, unfortunately, do have constraints, particularly in terms of performance and usability. Some security mechanisms exert more trade-offs than others. For instance, cryptographic implementation will have more performance implications, than authentication or authorisation services. But authentication affects usability more because users are required to identify themselves to the various subsystems. Yet each mechanism has a part to play towards overall security.

While many, if not all, government e-services are expected to have been built around stringent application security requirements, most were developed as standalone systems for access within their respective agencies. With the advent of e-Government and the one-stop service paradigm, the need to integrate across agencies so as to present a more consistent interface to users could potentially introduce security gaps not adequately addressed by existing security deployment.

Some of the governments in the region have resorted to defining and implementing national application infrastructure to consolidate the security requirements of agencies and also make it easier for new services to be incorporated. In the case of Singapore's PSi, there is a set of application services that were built with configurable security implementation depending on the application's security requirements (refer to Endnote 4).

IDENTITY MANAGEMENT

Recent world events, particularly the 9/11 tragedy, have re-emphasised the critical importance of identity management. The ease with which the terrorists conducted their activities have led the US Government to reconsider applying a nationwide identity programme for citizens and other "high-risk" groups. The emphasis is probably not so much focused on keeping an eye on citizens but more to monitor for any signs for potential compromise in national security.

While most e-Government services today provide basic user authentication via a pseudo identity and password scheme, such verification is not sufficient for certain transactions of a more sensitive and private nature, or those involving services that might result in catastrophic outcome if no proper accountability can be enforced. The term "identity management" is used here to refer to the positive identification and authentication of users across interconnected systems in a consistent manner. The difficulty of balancing security and simplicity, coupled with the management of multiple versions of user identities across multiple systems and agencies makes the task even more daunting.

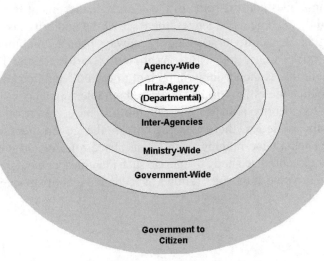

Figure 14-4: Scope and Complexity of Identity Management[7]

Authentication technologies form the basis of identity management and can be classified into three types: knowledge-based (what you know), possession-based (what you have), and biometrics-based (what you are). Knowledge-based solutions use a shared secret between the sender and the receiver. It is the most widely implemented mechanism in use today in the form of passwords and PINs,[8] and has been employed since the time of Julius Caesar in 50 BC, because of the simplicity in its implementation. Possession-based solutions use the presence of physical devices as a basis for authentication. These include physical keys, passes, tokens[9] and smart cards. Biometric-based solutions depend on a variety of unique human characteristics for authentication, and this includes fingerprints, voice, facial, retina, iris and even typing or writing patterns. However, as each method has various strengths and weaknesses, they are often combined for added security. This is commonly referred to as multi-factor authentication.

The technology capable of identifying unambiguously the parties partaking in an electronic transaction has been available for some time, in the form of public-key cryptography[10] found in Public-Key Infrastructure (PKI) solutions. The challenge has mainly been in deployment. These measures tend to be rather costly to implement and are often perceived as cumbersome. In addition, due to the proliferation of web-based solutions, the web-based Single Sign-On (SSO) technology (discussed further in the "The Road Ahead" section below) has sprung up to allow a more centralised view of user profiles, and better operational management of the users access rights to protected government web resources at the backend. Together these technologies address some of the identity management issues.

Beyond the technical challenges, the issue of the authority responsible for managing the validity of identities has always been a stumbling block, one that raises many questions. Who will coordinate the identity management that is increasingly important to both the public and private sectors? Which identities will be considered reliable, and who will set the standards for identity issuance and reliability? These are "trust" issues, and in some societies, there is sensitivity if the government were to undertake such a wide-ranging, highly centralised role. Would it even be practical for a centralised body to manage such identities, or would a trusted network of separate authorities (known as federated identity management) be preferred?

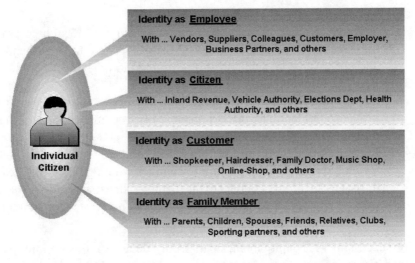

Figure 14-5: Various Realms of Identity — Who should manage?

The Role of PKI

Public-key infrastructure (PKI) is the combination of software, encryption technologies, and services that enables secure communications and business transactions on a public network. A typical PKI encompasses the issuance of digital certificates to individual users and other entities such as servers. These digital certificates are a means to determine the identity of the transacting parties and to ensure the legitimacy of the transaction. With tools to manage the entire life cycle of the digital certificates (ie creation, renewal, revocation, and key management), together with related services and stringent procedures (such as proper verification of users and entities), PKI provides a viable infrastructure for secure and non-repudiation of transactions.

PKI provides information security and identity management in several essential ways:

(1)   **Authenticate identity of transacting parties**
        Digital certificates with the associated cryptographic keys, issued as part of PKI allow individual users, organisations, and website operators to mutually and confidently validate the identity of each party in a transaction.

(2)   **Verify integrity of transaction**
Through the use of hashing techniques (in digital signatures), messages or documents exchanged can be verified to be authentic and not to have been changed or corrupted in transit.

(3)   **Provide information privacy**
Since PKI incorporates cryptographic keys, it can also be used to provide confidentiality protection, possibly from interception during transmission.

(4)   **Ensure non-repudiation of messages**
By employing digital signature techniques with digital certificates, messages are tightly coupled to the identity of the transacting parties, thereby ensuring that transactions cannot be repudiated, or claimed to have been forged.

For successful PKI deployment, apart from adequate infrastructure and procedures to manage digital certificates, applications also need to be PKI-enabled. Digital certificates by themselves cannot provide full PKI benefits unless the corresponding applications are designed to exploit them. An example would be the Secure Sockets Layer (SSL) applications used by a majority of websites. Most SSL implementations are so called "server-side SSL" which can authenticate the server and secure the transmission from browsers, but are not capable of ensuring non-repudiation.

Smart Cards — Panacea or a Fading Promise?

Smart cards are typically plastic cards with embedded microprocessors (smart chips) that can be programmed to perform computational tasks or securely store information in hardware. Most smart cards deployed for e-services are used in conjunction with PKI to provide the secure key generation and/or storage of the signing cryptographic keys,[11] that are required to guarantee the authenticity of signed messages in PKI transactions.

After the 9/11 attacks in 2001, numerous nations around the world were prompted to actively explore the use of the smart card as a national digital identity card. Many countries already use identity cards for various government interactions but without the smart chip. The use of the smart card would logically extend the use of the national card to support digital transactions both for individual-to-government transactions, as well as possibly for other commercial transactions as well.

Figure 14-6: Smart Cards

However, adoption of the smart card has been hampered in some countries by the need for mass distribution of these cards, and the signing keys to every user. Adding to this is the need for smart card readers on the personal computers of users for secure transactions. To increase user convenience, some government agencies are looking into the possible use of USB tokens as a direct substitute for smart cards. These would be used purely for certain e-Government digital transactions. The USB token is for all intents and purposes, digitally identical to a smart card, but can be connected to the USB port of a computer without the need for a separate reader device.

A number of Asian countries have embarked on projects to introduce national identity card based on smart card technology. Malaysia, Hong Kong, Thailand, Japan, Korea and even China have announced ambitious projects to equip the population with such electronic identities.

Malaysia in particular has been credited for being the first nation in the world to rollout a multipurpose national smart card intended for nationwide deployment by 2007.[12] The Government Multipurpose Card (GMPC) project is one of the seven flagship applications under the highly publicised Multimedia Super Corridor (MSC) initiative. Labelled as MyKad, the smart card replaces the identification card and driving licence with four other applications: supplementary passport information, medical information, electronic cash, and digital certificates for secure PKI-based transactions. Despite the potential advantages of such an infrastructure to the digital lifestyle of Malaysians, some have expressed concerns about the adequacy of its security features and the handling of sensitive personal information. In response to these concerns, the government is looking to introduce a data protection bill to ensure secrecy of information stored on these cards.[13]

In Hong Kong the Multi-Application Smart Identity Card is a smart card for storing personal information and photographs as found on existing identity cards, and other immigration related data. It will also incorporate thumbprint storage for biometrics authentication and support other value-added applications such as a driving licence, library card, and digital certificate for secure PKI-based transactions. The card is expected to be launched in the second half of 2003 and the target is to complete the identity cards replacement exercise within 4 years.[14] As in the case of Malaysia, similar concerns about security and privacy of data have been raised.[15, 16]

Thailand has also approved a proposal for mandatory cards containing social security and health records. The Thai government plans to start issuing the "e-citizen" identity cards from the second half of 2003.[17] Japan also has plans to introduce an optional smart ID containing the cardholder's signature, photograph and address. A cornerstone of their system is the introduction of a national ID network in August 2002. This has since drawn widespread opposition due to the lack of adequate privacy protection.[18, 19]

In China, the National ID Card project, which started in 2002, targets to replace the existing ID cards of more than 800 million citizens (over 18 years old) within a ten-year period.[20] The new smart card ID will also have biometrics capabilities for enhanced security to reduce fraud and counterfeiting. Unlike the Malaysian and Hong Kong approaches, the contactless cards are intended only to be a legal document to identify residents. Other multi-application functions such as e-cash and medical information are considered extraneous for identification purposes, and are optional.

Biometrics

Biometrics refers to the measure and use of human physiological or behavioural characteristics to verify the identity of a person. This includes fingerprints, retinal and iris scanning, hand geometry, voice patterns, facial recognition and many others. Some techniques are more advanced in terms of accuracy or speed of scanning, than others.

As biometrics technology matures, it is increasingly used either in place of other authentication mechanisms, or in conjunction with those mechanisms, for added security. Biometrics has some unique properties and advantages:

- the person to be identified has to be physically present at the point of identification, thereby making it difficult to masquerade as someone else;

- there is no longer a need to remember passwords or PINs, nor a need to carry any security tokens. Apart from convenience, password disclosures or loss of token devices is no longer a security issue with biometrics; and
- it can also be used for identification by matching a database of user profiles. This in addition to merely authenticating that the individual is who he claims to be.

Since biometrics rely on human characteristics, it is possible to encounter deviations from the norm. For example, when a person has a bad cold or loses his voice temporarily, then that person's voice signature would be altered, and the authentication may fail. Therefore, for extremely secure requirements, multiple biometrics features such as, fingerprint and facial characteristics, and even multi-factor authentication would be needed.

Under the US Enhanced Border Security and Visa Entry Reform Act, the US National Institute of Standards and Technology (NIST) is working on updating the existing US immigration visa system with one based on both facial and fingerprint biometrics. This is to be fully implemented by 2004. Approved countries wishing to have continued visa waiver for their citizens for entry into the US would also be required to have similar systems in place by 2004.

INFORMATION ASSURANCE

> *Information Assurance is the ability to provide the right person*
> *with the right information at the right time on whatever device*
> *that's relevant. IA is also the ability to make sure the wrong*
> *person — the hacker, the terrorist, the thief, the virus creator, the*
> *mischief maker — is kept out of the loop.*
>
> **Sean Finnegan, a federal security manager with Microsoft Corp.**

Information Assurance (IA) is an emerging field in IT, born out of the increasing dependence on information systems in our everyday lives. It goes beyond the security of information. It requires a comprehensive approach that considers the business processes, policies and cultures, as well as access to appropriate technical tools and adequate user education.

Figure 14-7: Inputs to Information Assurance

Although there is as yet no universally accepted definition of IA, it is essentially about a holistic approach to providing the safeguards and measures to build the trust and confidence that is vital to preserve the integrity of e-services. As governments embrace the Internet to deliver information and services to citizens and businesses like never before, ensuring the integrity of the government infrastructure is more critical than ever.

While much progress has been made in the area of security, providers of e-services need to be aware of the evolving threats. They will thus need to continually evolve measures to adequately counter them. The IEEE Computer Society Task Force on Information Assurance (IEEE TIFA) asserts that IT is advancing more rapidly than IA technology. This creates an increasingly imbalanced environment in which to enforce IA.

Current emphasis on the security aspects of IA focuses on the detection of, and response to, vulnerabilities and events relating to cyber attacks. Known as intrusion detection systems, these monitor data traffic and server events against a database (known as "signatures"), to identify an attack. The problem is that there is a great dependence on such signatures being up-to-date. Often these are too general in nature for individual IT infrastructure, leading to false alerts. Although these can be fine-tuned to be very specific, the effort involved to tune and maintain the rules can be substantial.

For IA to succeed, there are many underlying areas in IT that need to simultaneously address their vulnerabilities in order to create a credible holistic defence. In the narrow focus of threat of cyber attacks, for example, the best cryptography will not ensure IA success if the software engineering does not avoid buffer overruns and memory leaks[21] in the creation of applications. More broadly, if the mechanisms to deliver information are inadequate, then the resulting failures will have similar effects to cyber attacks.

There are currently various efforts underway (eg IEEE TFIA) to examine the full nature of IA beyond reacting to intrusions and patching vulnerabilities. One of the key objectives is to inculcate a growing appreciation for the need to better define the technologies underlying IA, and of the possible product liabilities in marketing "buggy" software and systems designed without care for vulnerabilities.

Besides security, privacy is widely acknowledged as one of the key concerns of IA today. Privacy of personal information is becoming a highly debated topic, especially with regards to e-Government services. Studies conducted by various government agencies and advocacy groups show that personal information is bandied around the technological and communication networks of the world. The vast amount of personal information collected and stored by government and corporate organisations not only provides an enticing proposition to would-be perpetrators for deliberate exploitation, but also presents a source for unintentional compromises. At any given time, highly computer-literate people, in both the public sector and segments of the private sector, can, within seconds, know everything about an individual by using these sophisticated technologies. It is no longer a question of whether the potential to gather such information is out there, but rather how extensive it is and what measures can be taken to protect the interests of the information provider.

It is generally recognised that certain privacy rights might have to be given up in the new digital realm in order to effectively combat the new threat of international terrorism. However, there is also an expectation that fundamental privacy values are maintained and not unconditionally ignored as secondary, while attempting to collect more personal information on citizens to be put into large databases.

Government services require secure, accurate transactions with its constituents online, with particular attention paid to privacy and security concerns. A survey done by Taylor Nelson Sofres[22] in 2002 of 27 countries (including 8 from the Asia Pacific), indicated a substantial level of concern among the sample population when providing personal information via e-Government services. Other surveys in Canada and the US clearly show that many individuals perceive that their personal information is used in cyberspace in very cavalier ways.

These perceptions could have consequences for the further development of e-Government programmes as they rely on the willingness of the citizen to interact and transact with governments on-line. To create the necessary climate of trust and confidence amongst the public, governments need to provide adequate safeguards that any personal information shared with them will be kept confidential and not subject to unmoderated sharing between departments, except in applicable legal circumstances in the interests of the state, and for the overall public good. More advanced mechanisms would include clear statements about privacy and data protection measures as legislated policies. There are also some who advocate that governments should apply similar standards of practice as are imposed on most commercial sites with regard to soliciting consent from the individual to use his or her personal data. For these advocates, consent of the individual is considered the bedrock principle of privacy. However, given the nature of governments and their role in upholding national interest over the individual, such ideals are difficult to maintain.

The growth of privacy and data protection practices around the world reflects government response to citizens' concerns about their privacy. However, since 9/11 more governments have amended once strong privacy laws to enable agencies and departments to amass and share personal information of their citizens in the growing effort to combat terrorism. These can be observed in developments in the European Union and the US, in which agencies are being given greater exemptions to collect and share personal information in the current fight against terrorism. All these result in the creation of a new tension of opposing forces — the right to privacy versus the growing philosophy in many countries for the need by governments to have access to large amount of personal information for a variety of reasons.

BEYOND TECHNOLOGY: LEGISLATION AND POLICIES

Regulations in information security cover many areas including data protection, data privacy, computer misuse, legal recognition of electronic transactions, official controls on cryptography, copyright of digital materials, security audits, standards and certification of security practices. All these regulations are intended to protect the rights of all parties with particular consideration for national security, conformance with public policies, encouraging adoption of electronic transaction among the business community, and ensuring compatibility with international practices.

National security generally deals with preventing activities that would have a detrimental effect on a nation's well-being. This could cover aspects of economic (eg money laundering), social (eg anti-drugs, anti-terrorist) and political safeguards to curtail any threats to the independence and sovereignty of a nation. Public policies deal with individual, industry and various constituents interest to provide the necessary protection against unfair and unscrupulous practices. The business community requires legislation to legitimise electronic form of transaction with appropriate enforcement policies. To facilitate cross-border trade involving electronic data exchange, countries need to adopt adequate security practices deemed comparable to that of their trading partners.

With the proliferation of electronic transactions and the use of computers as mainstream business tools, many nations have enacted relevant legislations to provide the environment for such transactions to become legally binding. These legislations have also been extended to encompass security concerns to address the growing threats of hacking and other computer related crimes. Mostly, such legislations work as a form of deterrent to the perpetrators while allowing the victims recourse in the event of an unfortunate attack.

An area that has garnered much attention lately is that of data privacy protection. This widely debated topic is concerned about the relative ease of collating information about individuals from multiple electronic sources. As our personal identities and behaviours are captured by the electronic systems that we interact with daily, it is conceivable that there may be many repositories of such data. These present a potential breach of individual privacy. Unscrupulous data collectors could also abuse the information for personal gain. Another fear is the possibility of making confidential information known to unauthorised parties. This might have adverse consequences to the individual involved (eg the disclosure of personal information that might result in discriminatory practices against the individual).

The European Union is by far, the most advanced in privacy laws (contrary to the common belief that the United States leads in this field) and has instituted stringent legislation in its member countries. Such legislation could impose that similar measures are available before electronic exchanges can take place between two countries. The implication is that countries desiring to maintain trading relationships with the EU, would at some point need to enact appropriate and adequate privacy protection schemes that meet the standards as defined by the EU. Some countries like Hong Kong and Australia have adopted similar practices, while others in the region are expected to follow with their own variants.

The following are some relevant legislation and codes of practice for some countries in Asia:

Hong Kong
- Computer Crime Ordinance
- Electronic Transaction Ordinance
- Personal Data Privacy Ordinance
- Copyright Ordinance

Malaysia
- Copyright Amendment Act (1997)
  - Computer Crime Act
  - Digital Signature Act
  - Telemedicine Act
- Communications and Multimedia Act
- Proposed Personal Data Protection Act

Philippines
- Electronic Commerce Act

Singapore
- Computer Misuse Act
- Electronic Transactions Act
- Data Protection Code

Thailand
- Proposed Personal Data Protection Bill

EMERGING IT SECURITY TRENDS

Governments are leveraging commercial solutions and delivery channels to deploy e-Government services to reach out to the public in a timely and efficient manner. This makes e-Government services vulnerable to growing security threats confronting any commercial e-service delivered via public networks. Government agencies and their service providers will need to keep abreast of security trends in the industry. Some of these are described in this section.

Single Sign-On (SSO) Issues

SSO has always been touted as the holy grail of the Internet. It is absolutely desirable for identity management but often impractical to implement. Realistically, true SSO is difficult if at all possible to achieve because of the deployment of disparate network devices, systems components, and a typical mix of off-the-shelf and custom-built applications. In response, the IT security industry coined a new term "Reduced Sign-On" (RSO), towards achieving a realistic level of implementation. Therefore, for cost-effectiveness SSO service should only be provided for subsystems that support such integration, largely for web related access control (Web-SSO). Otherwise, the cost of SSO far exceeds the benefit that would be derived in trying to integrate existing devices and legacy applications. An inherent threat of SSO is the possibility that someone with illegitimate access (eg stolen ID and password) to a subsystem could have unimpeded access to all interconnected systems without being subsequently challenged. RSO is increasingly being accepted as a practical alternative to SSO for overall systems access control. The Liberty Alliance Project is a global consortium comprising private and public sector companies, that is developing an open, interoperable standard for network identity. The consortium released its initial specifications in mid January 2003.[23]

Web Services Security[24]

The introduction of web services technology in the application infrastructure arena substantially broadens the scope and security risk. This extends identity management beyond people to other non-person entities such as networks and servers. e-Government security solutions must hence evolve from intra-site to cross-site, and across multiple open networks. In this way, transparent logons and redirections (today via web-based SSO) can give way to the seamless transfer of these authenticated attributes and privileges to interconnected systems safely. This is the trend the IT industry is moving towards, and it is unlikely that e-Government portals will be able to ignore this in future.

Enhanced Application Security

General purpose infrastructure security such as firewalls, intrusion detection and content filtering solutions are increasingly inadequate for protecting against application specific attacks and vulnerabilities as these application targeted hacks bypass those defences easily. For instance, web-enabled servers essentially provide unimpeded path for HTTP traffic, straight through well-configured firewalls. This could allow intruder access not just to web and applications servers, but potentially to connected internal database servers. Hackers will increasingly exploit weaknesses in web applications and portal servers to gain other internal access. This is a progression from web defacement attacks common today (even against government websites) to more insidious attacks on internal networks. The need for additional application-level security becomes crucial. These could include selective encryption of data, stringent activity loggings digitally signed and collated, and enhanced regular vulnerability assessments and reviews.

Integrating Wired and Wireless Security

With advances in portable devices such as handhelds (eg personal digital assistants or PDAs) and intelligent mobile devices such as smart phones, the demand for e-services through wireless channels is likely to arise. This may be particularly relevant to public emergency services agencies, such as the Ambulance, Fire and Police, serving the public in situations where physical agility is important. The provision of wireless services will come with the need for associated wireless security. Although the fundamental threats to wireless security are no different than wired security, the challenges are different by virtue of the "physical disconnect" that wireless technology allows. Traditional methods of physical data entry points no longer apply, and the need to integrate wireless to wired security seamlessly will be critical should wireless e-services be embarked upon. This matter is further compounded by the fact that many existing wireless technologies were not built with adequate security in place. The widely deployed wireless LAN (IEEE 802.11) standards are being revised to incorporate the necessary security features.

Outsourcing of Government Security

As IT systems and their corresponding security requirements become more complex, it will become less cost-effective for non-critical government systems to be maintained in-house. Some of these systems could in fact, be outsourced to specialised security providers to support, monitor and maintain. Conventional thinking is that government services ought not to be outsourced so as to maintain secrecy. However, it has been shown that it is possible to outsource selective e-Government services, under stringent controls, to reputable private organisations. Although this is more evident in North America and Europe, it is also gaining ground in Asia.

IT Security Insurance

A new development in the industry is IT Security Insurance. There is a growing number of insurance companies that provide niche insurance cover, and offer monetary compensation in the event of damage due to hacker attacks against an organisation. This form of coverage requires that adequate security measures are already be put in place before insurers will underwrite the risks.

Auditable Commercial Software

There has been growing concern in some public administrations that many e-Government systems are running on a few key software platforms which are delivered as finished products with proprietary and "closed" codes. This prevents users from being able to assess the adequacy of the built-in security features. Some have even speculated on the possibility that software companies may take national interests over that of their customers' interests. For example, a recent report speculated that operating systems with potential backdoor access could be used to exploit other governments' national security. Such concerns have prompted the industry to look into avenues that would permit a closer scrutiny of source codes for eligible customers. Known as the "open source model", these practices essentially extend software licensing to include certain aspects of the source code. The purpose of which is to be more transparent with the actual implementation details of the product. Governments all around the world are prime motivators for such services due to the need to ensure adequate security in every aspect of their e-Government services.

Certified IT Security Professionals

Increasingly, the most valuable assets of organisations are being stored in computer databases and digital repositories in data centres. There has been a noticeable rise in incidences of illegal intrusion and malicious acts targeted at computer systems, which is hardly surprising given the higher stakes. One of the key challenges in managing security risks is the ability to recruit qualified personnel.

Many are turning to a new breed of IT security professionals who have attained relevant credentials, such as the Certified Information Systems Security Professional (CISSP),[25] to substantiate their competencies and skills. A certified IT security practitioner is also expected to better uphold the high standards demanded of the profession.

THE ROAD AHEAD

In February 2003, a report about a malicious hack on a credit card processing facility that could have compromised up to eight million credit card accounts worldwide came to light. e-Government systems with repositories containing valuable details of citizens could equally have been the target of the perpetrators. Imagine the political and social backlash if unauthorised persons were to gain access to sensitive personal details of citizens from the government. Unlike the credit card companies that can replace the exposed accounts with new ones, there is no clear recourse for the government, which could potentially be held at ransom.

The implementation of e-Government services has heralded a new era in the way government interacts with its constituents. Information technology has allowed new levels of intimacy and transparency that were not previously conceivable. Some have even advocated that current developments are leading towards the evolution of e-democracy,[25] where the constituents are partners to the government.

Conversely, the advancement in IT has also provided perpetrators and criminals with increasingly sophisticated tools to "ply their trade". The new breeds of cyber criminals are also capitalising on the promise of these new technologies to pose an even greater threat. Capable of launching attacks anonymously from possibly anywhere, the task of curtailing them has moved beyond traditional surveillance and investigative methods. Enforcement agencies all over the world are turning to new crime fighting techniques (like digital forensics) to counter against these faceless criminals. Likewise, preventive security measures also need to be continuously updated to keep pace with the evolving threats.

Such security threats are a bane to e-Government if not appropriately addressed. The e-revolution is expected to persist unabated, which would require e-Government service providers to proactively raise the barriers high enough to keep the hackers and criminals at bay while ensuring unencumbered access to legitimate users.

Endnotes

1   www.iras.gov.sg.

2   *"2002 CSI / FBI Computer Crime and Security Survey"*, Computer Security Institute in conjunction with the Federal Bureau of Investigation.

3   *"Guidelines for the Security of Information Systems and Networks: Towards a Culture of Security"*, Organisation for Economic Cooperation and Development, 2002.

4   *"Overview of Public Service Infrastructure"*, Infocomm Development Authority of Singapore, 2002.

5   Rozana Sani, *"National Security Policy"* , *Computimes*, January 2003.

6   *"Malaysian Public Sector ICT Management Security Handbook"*, MAMPU, January 2002.

7   *"Identity Management"*, White paper presented at Annual Conference (December 2002) by the National Electronic Commerce Coordinating Council.

8   Personal Identification Number.

9   A physical device with identity related information.

10 Encryption technology that utilises key pairs; one to encode and the other for decoding.

11 Cryptography key used to generate electronic signature, unique for each user.

12 Sreejit Pillai, *"20 Million Malaysians to Get Smart Cards"*, Malaysia.CNET.com, September 2001.

13 *"Bill to Protect Personal Data Being Formulated"*, Bernama, Malaysia.CNET.com May 2001.

14 *"LegCo Panel on Security: The Hong Kong Special Administrative Region Identity Card Project"*, Legislative Council Hong Kong, 2002.

15 *"'Smart' ID Card Worries Hong Kong"* , *Associated Press*, March 2002.

16 Alfred Hermida, *"Smart Cards Head for Hong Kong"* , BBC News Online, April 2002.

17 *"E-citizen Cards Due Next Year"*, *The Nation*, December 2002.

18 Gohsuke Takama, *"Japan's National ID Network Has Gone Live Already"*, 31 July 2002.

19 *"Japan Launches National ID Network"* , *Reuters*, August 2002.

20 Bin Li, *"Smart Cards in China: An Overview"*, Card Forum Intl., July/August Vol.6 No. 5.

21 Known applications vulnerabilities susceptible to being exploited.

22 *"Government Online: An International Perspective"*, TNS Consultants, December 2002.

23 *"Liberty Architecture Overview: Version 1.1"*, Liberty Alliance Project, January 2003.

24 Stephen H Sigmond and Vikram Kaura, *"Safe and Sound: A Treatise on Internet Security"*, RBC Capital Markets.

25   CISSP is offered by the International Information Systems Security
     Certification Consortium, a not-for-profit industry consortium dedicated to
     training and certifying information systems security professionals and
     practitioners worldwide.

26   Thomas B Riley, Executive Director and Chair, Commonwealth Centre for
     Electronic Governance, *"eDemocracy in a Changing World"*.

Useful Web Sites

www.ida.gov.sg	Official website for the Infocomm Development Authority of Singapore.
www.mampu.gov.my	Official website for the Malaysian Administrative Modernisation and Management Planning Unit (MAMPU).
www.jpn.gov.my/gmpc/main_menu.htm	Website for MyKad, the Malaysian Government Multipurpose Card.
www.niser.org.my	The website of the National ICT Security and Emergency Response Centre in Malaysia.
www.itsd.gov.hk/itsd/index.htm	Website for Hong Kong SAR's Information Technology Services Department.
www.nitc.go.th	Website for Thailand's National Information Technology Committee (NITC), the body that oversees national IT policy.
www.nectec.or.th/home	Website for Thailand's National Electronics and Computer Technology Centre (NECTEC), the secretariat office for NITC.
www.meti.go.jp	Website for Japan's Ministry of Economy, Trade and Industry, comprising the Commence and Information Policy Bureau.

www.npa.go.jp/hightech   Website for Japan's National Police
Agency on Security for Information
Systems (in Japanese).

www.egov.vic.gov.au/International/AsiathePacific/asiapacific.htm
Website of e-Government Resource
Centre based in Australia with useful
links to information on IT news of
government initiatives in the region.

www.kablenet.com   Website of Kable Ltd, a leading and
independent publisher of e-government,
public service IT and telecoms news.

www.projectliberty.org   Official website of the Liberty Alliance
Project, formed to provide a federated
identity management solution for the
Internet.

www.electronicgov.net   Website of the Commonwealth Centre
for Electronic Governance, focusing on
e-democracy and e-governance.

www.securegov.org   Website focusing on security in
government systems.

www.infosecuritymag.com   Website of the Information Security
Magazine, a leading publication on IT
security and division of TruSecure
Corporation.

www.gocsi.com   Official website of the Computer
Security Institute (CSI).

www.cdt.org   Website of the Centre for Democracy
and Technology.

www.privacyinternational.org   Website of Privacy International, a
human rights group focused on
surveillance by government and
corporate groups.

CHAPTER 15

Making e-Governance Happen — A Practitioner's Perspective

Bok Hai Suan

▲ ▼ ▲ ▼ ▲ ▼ ▲ ▼

The leader has to be practical and a realist,
yet must talk the language of the visionary and the idealist.

Eric Hoffer

▲ ▼ ▲ ▼ ▲ ▼ ▲ ▼

BEYOND THE VISION

There is no shortage of visionary, ambitious and well-articulated national e-Government plans drawn up by enthusiastic executives from public administrations all over the world. However, exemplary implementation of e-Government are as yet few and far between. e-Government is not simply a technology deployment project. It is a response by the public service to the economic and social implications of an information society and a knowledge-based economy.[1] It has significant long-term impact on society, economy and politics. Such a programme also requires considerable time, effort and money. Its development has been found to closely correlate with a country's social, political and economic composition. However, in many countries the legal and cultural systems, as well as institutions, lag the revolutionary changes presented by technological innovation. Implementing e-Government would be extremely challenging within such an environment. It is interesting to learn from the lessons of early adopters of e-Government — the challenges they faced, and their responses to those challenges. This chapter is the result of extensive reviews of e-Government reports and interviews with senior executives who have been closely involved in e-Government projects in Asia.

A recent UN study showed that of the 190 member states surveyed, 169 (90 percent) had a government website[2] (Figure 15-1). Yet out of the five stages illustrated (ie Emerging, Enhanced, Interactive, Transactional and Seamless), only 10 percent of all the e-Government projects had reached the Transactional stage. None had attained the Seamless stage. The reality for most countries is that there is still a long journey ahead as they strive to realise their dream of e-Governance.

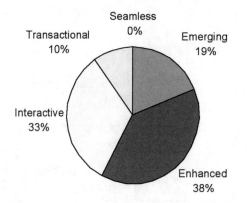

Notes:　•　Emerging: web presence with limited and static information
　　　　•　Enhanced: web presence with dynamic contents
　　　　•　Interactive: capabilities to download information and interact with government electronically
　　　　•　Transactional: capabilities to activate financial transactions such as making payments
　　　　•　Seamless: full integration of e-Government processes across government agencies

Figure 15-1: Stages of e-Government Development

The same study uses an e-Government index to track the progress of e-Governments among UN members. This index measures different aspects of the e-Government environment, such as web presence, telecommunications infrastructure, and human capital.

The e-Government global index is 1.62 compared with 1.37 for Asia/Oceania. Asia/Oceania fares consistently below the global index in all ten measures (Figure 15-2). However, not all countries in this region fare badly. Five countries score 2.0 and above, the highest being 2.60. At the other end of the scale, eight countries score 1.0 and below. The lowest score is 0.67. This disparity suggests that countries in the region are at different stages of e-Government development. More e-Government development activities in this region can be expected.

According to IDC, IT spending by Asian governments will have exceeded US$9 billion in 2002. The growth in e-Government spending ranges from 13 percent in Hong Kong, 20 percent in Singapore and an impressive 40 percent in China.

Indicators	Global	Asia/Oceania	Indicators	Global	Asia/Oceania
Web Presence Measure	2.6	2.46	Mobile Phones/100	15.3	11.1
PCs/100	10.17	7.07	TVs/1000	288.49	227.87
Internet Hosts/10000	215.39	96.77	Human Development Index	0.731	0.709
% of POP online	11.25	8.89	Information Access Index	0.646	0.446
Tele lines/100	21.44	14.55	Urban as % of Total Population	61.9	47.3

Notes: Asia/Oceania includes Armenia, Australia, Azerbaijan, Bangladesh, Brunei, Cambodia, China, Georgia, India, Indonesia, Iran, Japan, Kazakhstan, Kyrgyzstan, Laos, Malaysia, Maldives, Mongolia, Nepal, New Zealand, Pakistan, Philippines, Republic of Korea, Samoa (Western), Singapore, Sri Lanka, Tajikistan, Tajikistan, Thailand, Turkmenistan, Uzbekistan, and Vietnam.

Figure 15-2: e-Government Index for Asia/Oceania

Not only is e-Government implementation a complex undertaking, it does not always produce positive results. While it enhances quality of information, boosts productivity, and improves effectiveness of certain decisions, inconclusive results are found in the areas of improving coordination and cooperation, citizen-government relationships, and organisational power and control. Negative effects may also have been experienced in the areas of privacy, legal rights and job satisfaction.[3] To maximise the positive impact of e-Government and mitigate the negatives require a sound understanding of the contexts within which e-Government operates, the challenges faced, and the possible strategic responses (Figure 15-3).

Different contexts pose different challenges to e-Government implementation, which in turn demands different responses. It is noteworthy that the contexts and associated challenges are not static. Governments have to review implementation strategies regularly as the context and challenges do change even while deployment is in progress.

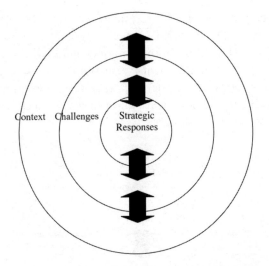

Figure 15-3: e-Government Delivery Challenges

E-GOVERNMENT CONTEXT

As indicated earlier, contexts pose challenges to e-Government implementation. For instance, the way in which e-Business is implemented in the commercial world cannot be directly replicated to online government projects. Generally e-Business is market-driven, customer-focused and profit- motivated. In contrast, e-Government needs to be guided by economic and social objectives, citizen-focus, and political vision. Further, the impact of e-Government is wider, deeper and usually longer. The scale of investment and implementation is typically much larger than that of commercial e-Business. All these introduce different challenges, and hence different strategies will have to be considered.

We can view e-Government as operating within five inter-related contexts: political, public service, economic, technological and social. These contexts are shaped by both past and present policies, culture, structures and processes. Different countries operate within different contexts. For instance, larger countries like China, India, Korea and Malaysia have much larger public bases to serve than small economies like Singapore, Hong Kong or Brunei. Those driving their e-Government initiatives need to consider not only the population size, but also how to manage multi-level strategies, say at national, provincial and local levels.

Different perspectives of e-Government have also been expressed by various academics and consultants. Whether broadly represented by three components (formal politics, administration and civil society),[4] or two environments:[5] policy environment (security/privacy, innovation, digital divide and technology standards) and societal environment (political, economic, social and technological), all of these perspectives are covered by the five contexts discussed here.

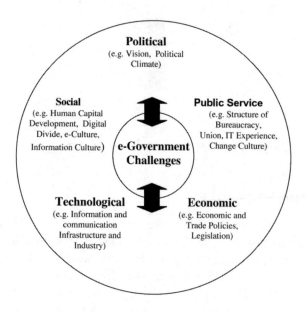

Figure 15-4: e-Government Context

Political Context

Political leadership is key to e-Government success. It provides vision, impetus, and commitment of resources for e-Government implementation. Typically, e-Government programmes extend beyond a single term of elected government to complete. A strong, well-endorsed and committed leadership would go a long way in providing sustainable support and building on earlier foundations. Further, political leaders need to define and communicate the drivers for e-Government. Some of these drivers may be: responding to a shrinking public service workforce; high expectations of citizens and the business community for more accessible, convenient and responsive public services; economic diversification; or a vision to promote participative governance. All these drivers define the focus and priorities of e-Government.

As Haji Mahmud bin Haji Mohd Daud, a senior official in the Brunei Darussalam Government, noted: "We have developed our e-Government directions by strongly emphasising and tightly linking our programme to economic and business drivers."[6]

Public Service Context

The vision of e-Government needs to be realised through the public service, the largest bureaucracy in most countries. Complete with their intricate policies and processes, many such bureaucracies have existed as long as the country itself. With the new capabilities and possibilities presented by e-Government solutions, discontinuities may arise within existing policies, processes, jobs and skills. A public service with a culture of being forward-looking, service-oriented, innovative, and committed to continuous learning, will be a valuable asset to e-Government implementation.

Positive relationship between the public service organisation, its staff and the union can be a key success factor to e-Government implementation. A powerful union typically has a strong and direct influence over the acceptance and pace of changes in the public service. A union that is receptive to the idea of e-Government can help accelerate the adoption process and increase the chances of success. Conversely, a union that is cynical of the motives and benefits of e-Government may impede or derail the entire programme.

ICT literacy and experience play an important role in e-Government. A public service attuned to the use of IT will take less time, resources and effort to implement e-Government. Most of the e-Government leaders today have had a long history of computerisation. Many had their first taste of computerisation back in the 1960s or 1970s. However, late starters may not be gravely disadvantaged as Internet technology (the backbone of many e-Governments) matured only in early 1990s. The real challenge lies in effectively leveraging ICT in the public service.

Economic Context

e-Government typically involves hefty national investments. Sustainable economic growth is required to fund its implementation over an extended period of time. Economies badly hit by downturns such as the Asian financial crisis in 1997, or the 9/11 tragedy in 2001 would have no choice but to scale back, review their priorities and take stock of their funding capability for their e-Government programmes.

Legal frameworks and trade policies of an economy play a vital part in promoting e-Business. A legal framework that is capable of handling e-Business related issues like computer abuse, fraud, and cross-border e-Business would protect the interests of e-service providers and consumers, and promote the use of e-Government. In the area of trade, economies with trade policies and practices that make it cheap and easy to import and use new technologies would have an edge over others.

Lastly, an economy that is heading towards becoming information and knowledge-based will be conducive to e-Government implementation for three reasons. Firstly, public awareness of IT in these economies is likely to be higher, making them more receptive to e-Government. Secondly, the ready supply of skilled IT manpower, and IT product and services help jumpstart the development. Finally, IT spending in e-Government has spin-off effects on these economies in terms of economic activities. For instance, in the area of government IT expenditure, the government alone represents 20–40 percent of its GDP in member countries of the Organisation for Economic Co-operation and Development (OECD).

Technological Context

A stable nationwide ICT infrastructure is a precondition for effective e-Government implementation. The state of information and communications infrastructure in the country is an indicative measure of IT and Internet use. Although the presence of a sophisticated infrastructure does not automatically imply high usage, the lack of it is certainly a barrier to e-services. Without such an infrastructure, e-Government can benefit only a small population, most likely the affluent, educated, urban dwellers.

The existence of a vibrant ICT industry in the economy contributes to e-Government in terms of cost-efficiency, expertise, and technology. Government cannot deliver e-Government on its own without being diverted from its core responsibilities. Neither can it depend entirely on foreign companies to deliver e-Government for them because key parts of the programme are likely to be interwined with national competitiveness and security.

Social Context

The Human Capital Development Index of a country also reflects its government's maturity. Developed by the United Nations Development Programme (UNDP), it measures the economic, social, and cultural progress of a country. A country with a poor economic climate, particularly when a large part of the population cannot even afford basic goods and services, will find implementing e-Government particularly challenging. For such countries, priority has to be in improving economic conditions rather than convincing their people that they need e-Government.

The digital divide in a country is another factor affecting e-Government. According to the World Economic Forum, 88 percent of all Internet users come from industrialised countries, which have only 15 percent of the world's population. At the global level, the problem of the digital divide is real although the situation seems to be improving. The digital divide also exists in most countries where the elderly, the less privileged, and the less able do not have easy access to IT and the Internet. In Hong Kong, for instance, PC and Internet usage are closely correlated to monthly household income and educational attainment, but negatively correlated with age group.[7] A similar pattern is repeated in many economies. People who do not have access to PCs and the Internet will be at an increasing disadvantage — they are less able to participate in an economy and society that is increasingly e-enabled. This may result in wider income gap, weaker social fabric, and poorer acceptance of e-Government.

The higher the general awareness and acceptance of electronic gadgets and services in the society, the easier it is for the government to introduce e-Government. Lessons from the implementation of electronic data interchange (EDI), an early form of e-Government, demonstrate the importance of preparing a society to accept a new technology. A study of EDI in seven countries concludes that the diffusion of EDI needs to be stimulated, in this case through government interventions.[8] These interventions include knowledge building, economic incentives, policy and legislation, and organisation management. And it takes time for the society to accept the technology. Unlike EDI, which focuses on a smaller trading community, e-Government usually involves large populations of users. Changing an individual's attitude towards transacting electronically with government will often be many times more demanding.

e-Government is about improving information processing with IT. It requires a suitable information culture to optimise its use. In this respect, information culture refers to the openness of the government to share information with its citizen, and its keenness to engage in frequent dialog with its people. In countries where information transparency is highly valued and widely practiced, e-Government is a useful tool that the government has never had at its disposal previously. Disseminating and collecting information quickly would no longer be a mammoth task. In these countries, e-Government will be well-received. In countries where the culture is to withhold information, they are likely to receive less enthusiastic public support.

Lastly, in societies where individual privacy is closely guarded, e-Government may be received with some suspicion. Theoretically every piece of information or detail of transaction is traceable in e-Government, and it enables government agencies to share individual's information more easily. The extent to which the public trust that their government will handle their personal information in an appropriate manner, will influence their receptiveness of e-Government.

KEY CHALLENGES IN REALISING AN E-GOVERNMENT VISION

A number of common themes emerge from lessons learned from e-Government implementation.[9] These include: top leadership, government transformation, programme management, change management, resource management, learning and innovation culture, and marketing. They represent the key challenges faced by governments when attempting to transform their e-Government visions into reality.

Public Service Reform

Reinventing the public service to meet the increasing expectations and demands of citizens, and facing up to the challenges of national economic competition are the main drivers of most e-Government programmes. One of the most formidable challenges in e-Government implementation involves re-examining existing models and underlying mindsets, policies, processes, rules and regulations in public administration. Many of them have been deeply entrenched for decades, intertwined with many levels of government policies and legislation, and operated within an often extraordinarily complex political context. Further, it involves a great number of actors or institutions, each with different objectives and interests.[10]

Public service transformation or reform is not new. Other than movements like total quality management and re-engineering, public service has been restructuring through means such as deregulation, outsourcing and competition.[11] While it is common to find e-Government programmes featuring technology as its central theme, technology alone is inadequate to drive significant changes in the public service. While technology may render existing assumptions invalid, provide new options, and vary the relative importance of different factors; it requires sheer political will, strong leadership and muscle to unfreeze existing practices and remould them.

One common objective of e-Government is to provide single visit and efficient services to the public. A common response to this objective is to redesign and integrate service delivery processes across agencies to improve service quality and turnaround time. This often results in "turf fight"[12] as it involves breaking down territorial walls between agencies and linking them into a common value chain. Power and responsibilities of agencies may expand or contract, move upstream or downstream across agencies as a result of integration and redesign. Workload may be redistributed. Legislation may be changed to provide for relocating responsibilities and sharing of information across agencies. Information systems across agencies may be modified to link them together. These changes will not occur easily without some conflict among the affected agencies to protect their own interests. Often deadlocks occur, and they have to be resolved by higher authority in the government.

Long-term Commitment

Implementing a full range of e-Government services across a country is a long-term affair. While the implementation of IT systems may be faster today due to the rapid advancement and maturing of technologies, the time needed to initiate and embrace changes brought on by e-Government to institutions and people cannot be compressed drastically. Change is a transition, and transition from one stage to another takes time. Changes brought by e-Government are large-scale that takes a long time to complete. It cannot succeed without sustainable commitment.

e-Government requires large financial investments. It has to compete with other government programmes such as social welfare, infrastructure development, and economic restructuring for funding. The level of e-Government funding determines the pace of its implementation. The ability to pursue an e-Government vision through continuing and generous funding beyond one elected term of government is a major challenge to most governments.

Transparency and Accountability

e-Government creates greater transparency in efficiency, information and decision-making. Regardless of whether this would lead to clearer accountability, the government will face a more informed population. Some believe that the transparency brought upon by e-Government is an insurance against graft and incompetence in the government. This is an unexpected challenge to some governments.

Transparency in efficiency

Electronic transaction in e-Government is traceable and turn-around time can be objectively measured. Setting and measuring of service levels will be more open and precise. The government will face challenges to meet the service levels it promises to its citizens and business communities.

Transparency in information

IT enables information to be disseminated accurately and speedily. Once published on the Internet, it becomes information in the public domain. It is less possible to hold back, filter, or distort information. Some governments post their agenda and minutes of county meetings and policy changes on Internet to promote transparency and speed of information dissemination. Government may be expected to be more transparent and forthcoming in information dissemination with the newly acquired capabilities offered by e-Government.

Transparency in decision-making criteria and procedure

Decision logic and process flows programmed in e-Government systems are formalised and visible. The handling of routine transactions is no longer the prerogative of individual public service officers. Consequently, the public gets to understand the public service decision-making criteria and process of the government better. They are also more aware of their rightful benefits and expect to receive fair and equal treatment from the government and its personnel. The may result in a generation of more informed and demanding public.

Active Public Participation

Some e-Government researchers believe that the use of electronic services in polling and on-line forums could lead to changes in the democratic process of a country. The term e-democracy describes the new opportunities presented by e-Government to actively involving people in governance. In particular, the use of the Internet in e-Government allows the government to present and collect information on the same platform. It creates a direct channel between the government and the people. The challenge for the public service officers is to engage the people openly and productively, and to win support for the government and its policies while gathering useful input from the ground.

Just as e-Government enables citizens to reach a wide plethora of information and people, e-antigovernment, on the other hand, is expected to create pressure on government. While people can freely express their opinions about the government, public service officers need to be knowledgeable and eloquent in explaining and defending government policies and procedures.

High Public Expectation

As discussed above, electronic services make service delivery time more predictable and visible. It reduces latency in turnaround time, and the number of decisions and action steps taken by human operators. This brings about new expectations. Studies show that the public tends to compare the service level of government e-services with that of the commercial organisations. Such comparison can be in terms of systems response time and processing time. Citizens expect a narrow gap between e-services provided by government and those of commercial organisations.

One executive related an incident whereby a member of the public working in a bank challenged a government agency to process payment as quickly as his bank. He even offered to "teach" the agency how to improve its processing time. Pampered by the efficiency and convenience offered by competitive profit-driven commercial e-services, an incident like this would not be the last.

Massive Change

While commercial enterprises may choose to focus on niche markets or specific customer groups, e-Government is meant for every citizen. Getting millions of citizens ready for e-Government is a gargantuan task. The diversity of the populace in terms of education, attitude, social class, and geographic location adds to the complexity of the exercise. Such massive changes require careful planning and strategising, and the commitment of adequate resources.

Working with staff and unions to embrace the changes brought by e-Government is challenging in most countries. These changes may include job redesign, responsibility changes, retraining, and in some instances even job loss. Failure to manage these issues equitably may result in low staff morale, low productivity, industrial action, resentment and resistance against e-Government. Such problems could impair the successful implementation of e-Government, and affect overall public confidence.

High Profile

e-Government is large scale, high impact and high profile. It impacts many aspects of a society — political, social, and economic. It is highly visible inside and outside the country because of its sheer size. A success story in e-Government is a powerful testimony of a competent government and its leadership. On the other hand, large-scale failure may cast doubt on the credibility of a government. The publicity generated by e-Government may influence the investment decision of prospective foreign investors looking for a country with an efficient and competent government. The highly visible public profile of e-Government is echoed by one executive who related his recent experience: "As the usage of this system is high and nationwide, system problems will be reported to helpdesk by public, commented on by VIPs or even highlighted in the press ... we must have the mechanisms to monitor system's availability and measure performance so that we can detect it before it is felt by the public. Responsiveness to problems and queries is extremely crucial." This comment draws attention to one important aspect of e-Government implementation. That is other than good design and sound technology, the ability to plan and orchestrate, to anticipate and manage initial teething problems during e-Government implementation is important in managing public perception and receptivity.

Policy and Legislation

While it is common knowledge that a local ICT industry brings cost efficiency to e-Government development and implementation, the challenge to the government is to create a favorable and attractive environment to nurture the industry. This includes putting in place attractive fiscal and administrative incentives to attract direct foreign investment, technology transfer, product development, and skills building that are strategic to e-Government implementation. In addition, policies that make the import of ICT equipment and expertise easy and at low cost through the lowering of tariffs and reduction in administrative red tape.

Relevant and effective legislations must be in place to support e-Government electronic services provided over the Internet. At the least, electronic records and digital signatures must have the same legal status as paper-based documents. In addition, the legislative framework must be ready to handle e-Business issues such as fraud, resale and theft of data, and tax issues on cross-border transactions. Beyond these, governments must build capabilities to investigate misuse and fraud cases to ensure that the integrity of e-Government will not be compromised.

The New Digital Frontier

The application of new technology is a key trait of e-Government. Most e-Government plans feature the latest technologies like biometrics, wireless, PDA, and digital-TV as their selling points. While there are legitimate reasons to leverage on the new capabilities offered by these new technologies, it is important to avoid being overly enamoured with fancy technology innovation and instead focus on creating real value for the government and its constituents. It is also important to manage the high risks of deploying untested technologies.

One common example of putting technology above business needs is the use of smart card technology. It is common to find organisations eagerly replacing their plastic cards with smart cards and yet not knowing how to make use of the chip on the smart card. A new technology like the smart card opens up new opportunities. The challenge is for governments to turn the opportunities into real value. New technology comes with risks that must not be underestimated.

As aptly summarised by one e-Government executive who has experienced the pains of using untested new technology: "Knowing that the software is new to the market, the project team has to make numerous conferences to the R&D department [of the software vendor] in order to get problems resolved ... substantial amount of time was spent in chasing vendors to resolve unknown problems ... I was personally involved in the technical discussion to ensure all problems were resolved and there was no impact to the overall project schedule." There are many IT project failures traced to mismanagement of the technology risks, in particular those concerning new and untested technology. The ability to accurately access a technology and to work around technological constraints is a key challenge to e-Government executives.

Making e-Government accessible countrywide is a big task. e-Japan, for instance, targets to provide high-speed access network to 30 million households, and ultra-high speed access to 10 million households by 2005.[13] Such a vision is ambitious but necessary. It requires meticulous planning, abundant financial resource, and a large pool of skilled e-Business and ICT trained expertise. The infrastructure must also be highly scalable to handle peak volume transactions. Poor performance of e-Government systems may breed reluctance and resistance to use of the system. Most countries do not have such technology and expertise locally. Attracting foreign expertise and investments will thus be necessary to speed up implementation.

Privacy and Security

The ability of the government to collect and retrieve data on the behavior of individuals is a primary concern about the potential violation of personal privacy in some countries. It is a conflict between information needed by the government to provide better service and the individual's right to privacy. The challenge is for the government to provide sufficient technical or legal protection against the collection and use of such data for increased control, and to ensure privacy rights are not violated.

Safeguarding the integrity of personal information and guarding against deliberate attacks are essential to instilling confidence and acceptance of e-Government. Strict legislation, monitoring and enforcement must be in place to ward off security threats. These threats may originate from attacks to client platforms, transmissions, and servers by hackers or internally malicious users.[14] In recent years, cyber warfare is becoming a real concern with more essential government services being put on-line. Hacking of government websites by local and foreign dissidents is not new. Such hacking can create serious negative consequences to essential public services, and shake the confidence of the public in e-Government.

STRATEGIC RESPONSES

While different governments respond to their challenges differently, there are common lessons which can be gleaned from their e-Government implementation strategies (Figure 15-5). One key theme emerging from these strategies is that realising e-Government involves a multifaceted balancing of needs and priorities. These competing priorities may be between meeting the needs of the business community and that of citizens, between different geographical areas or operational areas, or even between different design considerations.

The ten strategic responses discussed below are inter-related, and often inter-dependent. A strategy chosen for one area may impact the strategy for another. For instance, funding strategies may influence the deployment approach.

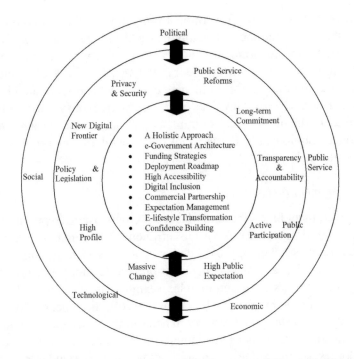

Figure 15-5: e-Government Context, Challenges and Strategic Responses

(1) A Holistic Approach

e-Government has to be managed as a government programme rather than as an IT project. This is because e-Government is really a multipurpose, social engineering strategic instrument that can bring about political, economic, and social returns.[15] It is, however, more widely recognised for its contributions to efficiency, in terms of speed and cost savings of moving goods, services, raw materials, machinery and human resources across or within the economy. The power of e-Government to shape the social and political arenas is less known and seldom exploited.

There are two advantages in taking a holistic approach. Firstly, the e-Government vision tends to be better aligned with the development goals of the nation. Consequently, securing top leadership attention, support and funding for e-Government programmes would be less of a problem. Secondly, by addressing the multifaceted issues like other government programmes, the political, economic, legal and social issues would be addressed simultaneously with technology issues. Such a holistic approach is more likely to produce substantial and sustainable changes. It is also more effective than reacting to unanticipated and undesirable effects after implementation.

Most countries set up e-Government programme offices or committees to steer their e-Government development and implementation activities. Chaired by senior government officials, they work with the government agencies to implement e-Government initiatives. The office or committee typically has the mandate to influence, coordinate and facilitate changes across agencies, whether it involves policies, processes or systems. It studies and addresses the implications of implementation, ensures the adoption of common technology standards, tracks the development progress, and obtains feedback.

(2) e-Government Architecture

An e-Government blueprint or model is extremely useful in providing the map and building blocks for e-Government.[16] It guides the building sequence, defines technology and technical standards, identifies information sharing protocols, facilitates concurrent project development, minimises overlapping sub-systems, and enables seamless integration. It helps to identify common e-Government functions like collection agent, information centre, citizen interfaces and services. It determines the technologies needed (eg broadband, EDI, digital TV, telemetry for remote sensing and signaling technologies, smart card, etc.) and defines technology standards that will guide interoperability between existing and new systems and technologies. Adopting internationally recognised standards such as ISO and IEEE is a common practice. In a nutshell, a well-defined architecture with a long-term perspective promotes integration, saves cost, guides technology acquisitions, enables reuse, and helps to develop e-Government faster.

There are many types of architecture: enterprise, business, application, software, technology and operational. Not all are ICT-related. For example, enterprise architecture comprises vision, principles, process, people, technology and standards.[17] It links strategic objectives to data, applications, and technology infrastructure. There are also different approaches in developing these architectures. Some define security and inter-organisational architectures. Other architectures may depict linkages between people, linking people to information, linking people to financial transactions (eg payment, purchase) and resources (eg booking, requisition). Architectures can also be defined as a government's relationship with three entities[18] — Government to Employees (G2E), Government to Businesses (G2B), and Government to Citizens (G2C). There is thus no single architecture for e-Government. Different architectural approaches serve different purposes. The acid test is that it must meet the specific objectives of the e-Government programme.

Development architecture is key to developing an open, flexible and scalable technology platform for e-Government. Distributed object technologies and meta-language are two important developments at this moment. Distributed object technologies include Java distributed object model and Enterprise Java Beans (EJB) architecture, and the Common Object Request Broker Architecture (CORBA). The main attraction of these approaches is that the objects created can be easily reused in multiple applications across different platforms. Meta-language like Extensible Markup Language (XML) provides open and flexible data structures that can be understood by different applications. It permits user definitions of the vocabulary and grammar. Different communities have a specific set of definitions developed for them. For instance, RosettaNet is designed to implement a common supply chain on the Internet, while Microsoft Biztalk is a generic framework to support online trading. Where practical, adopting suitable industry standards helps to jumpstart the development process. Ultimately, the success of e-Government depends on sound architecture, right technology and good people. As one executive put it: "New technologies such as Java and J2EE are still evolving. We need to keep track of their rapid changes. Skill-sets in managing these are still scarce in the job market. This is further complicated by the use of Open Source technology platforms ... [We] need to have a seeder team with superior technical skills in the technologies to kick-start the skills level, a few strong technical people to play the evangelist role for technologies, and have a strong foundation for the architecture and design framework."

(3) Funding Strategies

Securing e-Government funding requires first securing the commitment of the political leadership. A number of funding strategies have been considered. One strategy is to redirect part of the existing budget to e-Government. Instead of expanding the manpower budget, for instance, the additional budget may be channeled to automate some of the existing workload. Another strategy is to fund e-Government projects from the savings of earlier projects. A third strategy is to fund projects based on the progress made, rather than a one-time release of funds. Other funding strategies include commercial partnerships and sponsorships. In maximizing the use of allocated funds, it is common for governments to employ joint procurement with these partners and sponsors so as to achieve economies of scale and to reduce duplication of effort. Some governments also channel part of their research grants to e-Government related initiatives.

(4) Deployment Roadmap

Where to begin is an important question. Depending on the priority of a government and the circumstances in the country, a number of strategies may be considered. One strategy is process and system (architecture) driven. A process approach starts with the upstream activities before the downstream activities. A building block approach starts with building common systems and components first so that they can be reused later to construct other parts of the system. Although this strategy optimises on cost, it does take a long time to see concrete results.

The second strategy is experimentation and learning-driven. This strategy starts with building simple and basic services first (like web publishing), before moving on to interactive and transactional services (like payment). It is useful in situations where there are limited skills and experience in e-Business development and operations.

A third strategy is outcome-driven. The driving force can be criticality of service, speed of implementation, target community, geographical area, or e-readiness. Alternatively, it accords priority to areas that are critical to the government. These areas include citizen networks, payment services, job matching, education loans, opinion polling and others. Alternatively, its priority may be to implement something quickly so as to build up the acceptance and momentum of e-Government. It could also target at a specific community like the import-export business community. This strategy does lead to quick results but the total implementation cost is likely to be high.

A combination of these strategies may be adopted at different stages of e-Government development. Clearly, learning from the implementation experiences of other successful e-Government programmes will short cut the learning curve. However, one must tailor the experience of other governments to suit local conditions, and there may be areas that governments want to invent their own wheel to make a difference.

(5) High Accessibility

Good access to e-Government services is key to the success of e-Government. A highly scalable and reliable, nationwide information infrastructure is the backbone for e-Government service delivery. Contrary to general perception, e-Government comprises not only the technology infrastructure like servers, networks, client workstations, and smart cards, but also physical infrastructure like one-stop centres, and authentication infrastructure like the e-Government ID and password. One common strategy adopted by many countries is to increase the number of public access points, and place them at convenient locations such as public libraries, shopping centres, government offices, hospitals, subway stations, and clubs. These convenient and free public access points help to increase public awareness, acceptance and usage of e-Government.

Most governments undertake the development of the national information infrastructure for use by all their government agencies (eg Public Service Infrastructure in Singapore). Beyond this, they set policies to accelerate the infrastructure development in the country like ensuring all new buildings are installed with cable ducting and deregulating the use of wireless equipment. Other commonly used measures include fiscal, competition and tax measures to reduce the cost of network access and PC ownership. Working with the private sector to set up data centres, cyber cafes, application service providers, and Internet service providers is also a practical way to develop the ICT industry to propagate the awareness of e-services in the country.

(6) Digital Inclusion

Fiscal and policy measures can be used to assist the less privileged, the needy, and the elderly to plug into the digital economy. These measures may be in the form of direct financial assistance, low interest loans, inexpensive Internet access, subsidised basic IT facilities, incentives for commercial and not-for-profit organisations to provide affordable IT products and services, and even allow the use of "pension funds" for ICT-related purchases. Other forms of assistance can include refurbishing of old computers for the needy, setting up free Internet kiosks in public places and funding research into new information appliances for the disabled. Even with all these measures in place, it will take many years to bridge the digital divide in a country. Before a society becomes digital inclusive, the government must continue to provide personal services for those not digitally connected, while it introduces electronic services.

While most studies on the digital divide focus at the population level, the divide can also occur at the industry and enterprise levels. For instance, industries like agriculture are less likely to use much IT compared with service industries such as finance and banking. Some industries may not have the IT infrastructure to enjoy the benefits of e-Government. At the enterprise level, small businesses are likely to use IT less extensively than larger enterprises. As a result, they may not be able to plug into e-Government. Special assistance like IT grants and technical assistance schemes can hence assist specific sectors of the economy.

(7) Commercial Partnership

A number of e-Government plans[19] (eg Japan, India, Hong Kong) identify the private sector as key partners in implementation. This is especially true in four areas: resource, technology, buy-in and commercial practice. These plans identify outsourcing as a key strategy to enlarge the delivery capacity of the government, and to accelerate the delivery of e-Government. This is practical as most e-Government systems use commercially available technologies. The government can draw on the ready expertise and the resources of the commercial sector. In Hong Kong, up to 80 percent of new government IT projects are outsourced.

Government could also collaborate with IT user communities, academia and research bodies to explore how new technologies like biometrics and wireless can be used in e-Government. They can jointly set up development, testing and education centres in technology areas that are strategic to the country's e-Government programme. Testing of the practicality of concepts in the laboratories can be done, thus reducing the risks of technology exploration during e-Government development.

In the area of promoting e-Government buy-ins, government can leverage on commercial, not-for-profit, professional and voluntary organisations to reach different groups of people in the country. It can work with professional bodies like the medical association and the law society to encourage their members to use specific e-Government services. It can reach the under-privileged and needy through working with charity and voluntary organisations.

The promise of e-Government — of making public services more dynamic, efficient, and citizen orientated — has led to smaller gaps between the services from e-Government and those of the commercial world. In this respect, some governments study and adopt applicable best practices from the commercial sector to improve areas like customer service, process design, and IT systems design.

(8) Expectation Management

The high profile and huge budget of e-Government inevitably attracts public attention to what e-Government delivers. Exposed to commercial IT marketing advertisements, the public may have an inflated expectation of what IT can do, or how quickly results can be realised. However, the implementation cycle of a mega scale programme like e-Government is long. It is not unusual for an e-Government sub-system to undergo major revisions over a few years before it achieves its objectives. In addition, changes in policies and processes that come with e-Government will not please all sectors of an economy. Critics of e-Government will exploit hiccups in its initial implementation to discredit it. e-Government programme managers need to walk a tight rope of marketing the benefits of e-Government, and managing the high expectations of the public. Putting a system on pilot implementation to gather feedback from focus groups is one effective way to manage expectations. Providing ample time for the public to see, feel and adapt to the system before full-scale implementation will certainly help to reduce initial surprises and anxiety.

(9) e-Lifestyle Transformation

e-Government is geared towards transforming a society into an e-society over time. This transformation is however likely to be evolutionary rather than revolutionary because of its large scope, scale and complexity, the profound changes to public service, and the readiness of the large user base.[20] National level awareness programmes is an approach gaining popularity. Some countries use road shows, the media, IT exhibitions, IT ambassador, newsletters, and national IT events to create awareness and a favourable perception of e-Government. The purpose of these awareness programmes is to reach all echelons of society, in particular those who are not familiar with IT.

Promotional techniques such as advertisements, lucky draws, contests, etc. have been employed by various public administrations (eg Singapore and Taiwan). This is especially useful in highly commercialised societies where citizens are used to commercial promotions to attract their attention. In a way, governments have to compete with commercial enterprises for public attention. However, unlike commercial enterprises, public administrations do need to be moderate in their approach as they draw on public funds.

Involving citizens actively and early in e-Government development and deployment is vital. Citizens are not only consumers of government services, but they are also partners in the governance process.[21] Their involvement helps to create systems that benefit them and attain greater buy-in. At the same time, it creates better understanding of government policies and processes among citizens. Their inputs may even make the government re-think the basis of some of the existing current policies and processes. A number of studies have highlighted the importance for the public service to obtain direct public inputs rather than assuming that they understand their needs. One executive shared his experience of having a fully developed, adequately tested, ready to implement system rejected by industry users. They did not think the system met their needs and hence did not want to use the system. In the end, the system had to be modified before it was deployed.

Change programmes can be segmented to target a community or sector to address their specific concerns. A "one-size-fits-all" approach may not go down well in countries where there is significant social and cultural diversity. Considering that e-Government is a long-term program, many governments adopt the strategy of starting the changes in schools. This is to prepare a future generation of e-citizens. The introduction of the smart card, e-learning, e-purse, and the Internet in school not only prepares the young for an e-society tomorrow, they serve as IT evangelists in their homes today.

(10) Confidence Building

Public confidence in e-Government can sometimes take years to nurture, but it takes only a few lapses in privacy or security to shake the confidence built. Privacy and security are issues that must be taken seriously and tackled at the policy, technology and establishment level. Governments must develop the capability to prevent or deter acts of sabotage on e-Government foundations. At the policy level, governments must put in place effective legal framework to safeguard privacy and security. This includes the enactment of various laws to handle cybercrimes, computer fraud, intellectual property rights, cross-border transactions, dispute resolution, authentication, cross-border treaties and other issues. At the technology level, standards and infrastructure must be developed to provide adequate protection. This includes employing technologies and techniques like encryption, two-factor authentication, smart cards, digital certificates, etc. At the establishment level, some governments have set up independent agencies to conduct independent audits on privacy and security of e-Government, and to build trust.

SUMMARY

e-Government should not be mere political rhetoric, but neither should it be merely technology exploitation. It is part of a nation's development programme targeted at improving citizens quality of life and national economic competitiveness through the use of relevant enabling technologies. We have seen that e-Government has wide-ranging and long-term economic, social, and political implications. These need to be carefully addressed during implementation. Operating within often tumultuous political corridors, the sheer size and complexity of e-Government makes its implementation an arduous challenge to most administrations. The risk of failure is also high. The impact of a failed e-Government programme can be high-profile and extensive. Fortunately, these difficulties are not insurmountable. While demanding nothing less than a thorough understanding of the contexts, in-depth appraisal of the challenges, well-formulated implementation strategies, strong political leadership and long-term commitment, some nations have shown that e-Government visions can be turned into reality.

Endnotes

1   Eileen M Milner (2002), *"Delivering the vision: where are we going?"* in Eileen M Milner (eds), *Delivering the Vision: Public services for the information society and knowledge economy*, Routledge: London, pp 172–174.

2   *"Benchmarking e-Government: A Global Perspective"*, UN Division for Public Economics and Public Administration and American Society for Public Administration, May 2002.

3   Kim Vibory Andersen and James N. Danziger (1995), *"Impact of IT on Capabilities, Interactions, Orientations and Values"*, in KV Andersen, *Information Systems in the Political World: Implementation, Use and Implications of Economic Modelling*, IOS Press: Ohmsha.

4   Ake Gronlund, *"Introduction"*, in *Electronic Government: Design, Application and Management*, Idea Group Publishing (2001), pp 1–22.

5   Frederick Loomis and Charles Gerhards, *"e-Government: An Executive Road Map to the Digital Frontier"* in *Pushing the Digital Frontier*, edited by Nirmal Pal and Judith M Ray, AMACOM (2001), pp 283–305.

6   Dialogue between James Yong and Awang Haji Mahmud bin Haji Mohd Daud, Director of the IT and State Stores Dept., and Secretariat to BIT Council, Brunei Darussalam (14 December 2002).

7   *"Building a Digitally Inclusive Society"*, IT Services Department, Hong Kong SAR, February 2002.

8   Kim Viborg Andersen (1998), *"Conclusions: An Analysis of the Contributions on EDI and Data Networking in the Public Sector"*, Kim Viborg Andersen (eds), *EDI and Data Networking in the Public Sector*, Klwer Academic Publishers, pp 303–318.

9   a. Mark A Abramson and Grady E Means, *"The Challenge of e-Government: Initial Lessons Learned from the 'Early Days'"*, Mark A Abramson and Grade E Means, *e-Government 2001*, Rowan and Littlefield Publishers (2001), pp 1–8.
    b. UN Report, ibid.
    c. Genie NL Stowers, *"Commerce Comes to Government on the Desktop: e-Commerce Applications in the Public Sector"*, Mark A Abramson and Grade E Means, *e-Government 2001*, Rowan and Littlefield Publishers (2001), pp 44–84.

10 Dr JB Kristiadi, Deputy Minister, State Ministry for Administrative Reform, *"Administrative Reform in Indonesia"*, the BICA Conference, 12 March 2001, Jakarta.

11 Ake Gronlund, *"Electronic Government — Efficiency, Service Quality and Democracy"*, in Ake Gronlund, *Electronic Government: Design, Application and Management*, Idea Group Publishing (2002), pp 23–50.

12 In a dialogue between James Yong and Datuk Dr Mohammad Rais bin Abdul Karim, Director-General, MAMPU, Malaysia on 4 October 2002, the latter mentioned to changes brought about by e-Government sometimes led to "turf fights" over data sharing and new responsibilities.

13 e-Japan Priority Policy Program, IT Strategic Headquarters, 29 March 2001.

14 Andreu Riera, Jordi Sanchez, and Laia Torras, *"Internet Voting: Embracing Technology in Electoral Process"*, in Ake Gronlund, *Electronic Government: Design, Application and Management*, Idea Group Publishing (2002), pp 78–98.

15 Eileen Milner, *"Electronic Government: More than just a 'good thing'? A question of 'Access'"*, Barry N Hague and Brian D Loader (eds), *Digital Democracy: Discourse and Decision-making in the Information Age*, Routledge: London (1999), pp 63–72.

16 a. Electronic Government Flagship Application: Electronic Government Information Technology Policy and Standards, Malaysian Administrative Modernisation and Management Planning Unit (MAMPU), Prime Minister's Department, Malaysia, 1 July 1997.
    b. Electronic Government Flagship Application: Blueprint for Electronic Government Implementation, Malaysian Administrative Modernisation and Management Planning Unit (MAMPU), Prime Minister's Department, Malaysia, 1997.

17 Hemant K Bargrava and Jun Lee, *"Managing the Emerging Technology"*, in *Pushing the Digital Frontier*, edited by Nirmal Pal and Judith M Ray, AMACOM (2001), pp 135–153.

18 *"e-Government 2001: Accelerating, Integrating, Transforming Public Services"*, Managing for Excellence, Ministry of Finance and Government Chief Information Office, Infocomm Development Authority of Singapore.

19 a. *"Report of The Working Group on Convergence and e-Governance for The Tenth Five Year Plan"*, Government of India Planning Commission, November 2001.

   b. e-Japan, ibid.

   c. HK Report, ibid.

20 Elieen M Milner (2002), ibid.

21 Elisabeth Richard, *"Tools of Governance"*, Barry N Hague and Brian D Loader (eds), *Digital Democracy: Discourse and Decision-making in the Information Age*, Routledge: London (1999), pp 73–86.

CHAPTER 16

The Future of e-Government — Perspectives and Possibilities

Lee Kwok Cheong and James SL Yong

▲ ▼ ▲ ▼ ▲ ▼ ▲ ▼

The best way to predict the future is to create it.

Alan Kay

▲ ▼ ▲ ▼ ▲ ▼ ▲ ▼

INTRODUCTION

e-Government has been high on the list of priorities for most nations the world over. Much effort and resources have been directed at e-Government initiatives at different levels. Infrastructure have been developed, policies crafted, legislation enacted, ambitious applications rolled out — all part of the evolutionary progress of the state into the knowledge economy.

The Internet is here to stay. While some people are still feeling the pain after the dotcom fallout of 2000, the whole episode of market over-exuberance and "start-up mania" is not without its positive lessons. The silver lining in this cloud is that many business models, processes, structures and probably most significantly management mindsets will never be quite the same again. All changed, we believe, for the better.

Dotcoms may or may not regain their former glory,[1] but dot govs are just beginning to get into stride. Astute government policy makers and planners have benefited from the lessons of the e-Business pioneers. Many government administrations now offer interactive, transaction-oriented websites, increasingly shifting toward more customer-centric, and service-oriented models. On the other side, the bar of public expectation has risen after having experienced the possibilities offered by e-Business companies.

In this chapter, we take a step back from individual e-Government projects and go back to the fundamental roles and influences of e-Government. We reflect on what e-Government means or can mean in different contexts and from different perspectives. As the e-Government arena becomes more complex and encompasses more areas, we will attempt to do this through a series of metaphors that aid in capturing the essence of e-Government. In so doing, we will touch on several themes likely to impact how e-Government will continue to evolve, particularly in Asia.

EIGHT PERSPECTIVES OF E-GOVERNMENT[2]

Katsushika Hokusai (1760–1849) was a talented Japanese painter and wood engraver well-known for his "Thirty-six Views of Mount Fuji" series of woodblock paintings. These views show very different perspectives of the famous mountain between the Yamanashi and Shizuoka Prefectures of Japan. Hokusai's life philosophy, reflected in his autobiographical notes, shows a man never satisfied with superficiality. He was always changing his lifestyle to explore different facets of art and life, looking for the deeper meaning of things, and pursuing ever-greater understanding.

Figure 16-1: Hokusai's "Great Wave off Kanagawa"

Just as with the different faces of Mount Fuji, our research and observations into what we term as "e-Government" reveal that we are dealing with a complex and multi-faceted discipline. Any effort to develop a deeper appreciation should consider the subject from different perspectives or contextual viewpoints. We may not have as many perspectives as artist Hokusai had of Fuji, but we do offer eight, which we believe underlie key insights. Also, to help illustrate these perspectives, we have employed a metaphorical approach to reflect different roles of e-Government. We have selected eight metaphors — simple, easily recognisable objects that can carry deeper meanings when applied to the field of e-Government (see Figure 16-2).

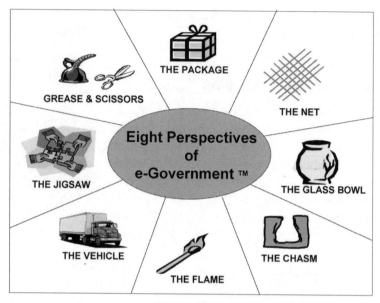

Figure 16-2

Perspective #1: Grease and Scissors

The "grease and scissors" metaphor underscores a role that e-Government, indeed organisational ICT in general, has long been associated with — that of productivity improvement.

The "can of grease" imagery conveys a sense of lubrication, smoothening or streamlining of processes, procedures or even politics. It has been said that the "e" in "e-Government" is broader than just "electronic". It could stand for "enabling". A true implementation of e-Government should encompass administrative streamlining before any technology deployment is even considered. Just as with the can of grease, e-Government should first of all help the government machinery move faster, in the right direction and against reduced resistance.

A complementary aspect of productivity improvement is embodied in the metaphor of the "scissors", which suggests the need to overcome unhelpful or irrelevant bureaucratic procedures and restrictive structures;

in other words, cutting through the "red tape". This also encompasses initiatives for reengineering public administration.

Whether greasing or cutting, the key objective is to be able to reduce the overall costs needed to carry out government operations and services, while preserving the quality, efficiency and integrity of the overall system.

This aspect is well understood by most of the government administrations we have spoken to. Certainly in Hong Kong, the EG Division of the Commerce, Industry and Technology Bureau (CITB), which coordinates the e-Government programme, urges all agencies and departments to carry out business process reengineering (BPR) prior to implementing any e-Government solutions. The same goes for Bruneian projects, such as TAFIS, where process reengineering is an integral part of project phases. Similar observations have been made in Singapore and Malaysia.

Perspective #2: The Jigsaw

The picture of inter-linking jigsaw puzzle pieces is used to depict the role of e-Government solutions in connecting or linking together different ministries, agencies and departments to form a more cohesive and integrated government.

Traditionally, government agencies tended to work independently and often in isolation. Each agency might be very efficient in its own functional area, but because of the lack of coordination across agencies, unintended results can occur, such as the duplication of efforts, or even conflict in procedures. From the constituents (ie citizen or business) standpoint, this can create much frustration on the part of the individual who often has to visit multiple agencies in order to get something done. Even worse, basic information needs to be repeated to multiple parties in different agencies because there is little centralised data sharing. Ownership is also weak when a particular process cuts across multiple areas.

Leaders of e-Government projects need to clearly convey to all agencies and individuals involved the importance of integration. They need to ensure clarity of roles, encourage subjugation of "turf protection" tendencies and recognise willingness to share data. The situation is self-reinforcing. Good e-Government solutions can only be developed when underlying "silo issues" are resolved. In turn, well-designed e-Government solutions make it easier for different government ministries and agencies to work in closer collaboration. In Singapore, it is this drive for integration that underlies the "many agencies, one government" vision of the civil service.

The jigsaw metaphor can be extended even to cross-border collaboration. Neighbouring economies or regional blocks would benefit from closer synergistic relationships, so as to avoid having to reinvent the wheel in core government solutions. Real G-to-G collaboration, anchored on trust and interdependence, allows for information sharing on regional issues, eg control of terrorism, managing the outbreak of diseases or dealing with common economic challenges.

Perspective #3: The Vehicle

e-Government can also be represented by a "vehicle" — a truck or van that can "support" or "carry" other industry sectors forward. This is an indirect way for e-Government initiatives to contribute positively to the growth of the economy. This is done when key e-Government projects provide the impetus for development in certain industries.

An obvious, but not necessarily the only example, is the ICT sector of the economy. Deployment of e-Government projects will require a wide variety of products (hardware and software) and services to be provided. In some countries, e-Government flagships or projects help to nurture related local industries and the people who work in these. The projects may provide local vendors and professionals the opportunity to build up their businesses, skills and experience. Often it will give them the opportunity to work alongside international players, further accelerating learning and technology transfer.

In some economies, for instance Hong Kong, Taiwan, or Singapore, there is a deliberate effort to develop public-private sector partnerships, through outsourcing and other models. These are clear cases where the private sector will be able to grow on the back of the e-Government vehicle.

e-Government can also give a boost to e-Commerce or e-Business. The introduction of online public services will invariably get the public more attuned to interacting and transacting online. Most issues of access points, infrastructure and devices would have been resolved. People would have gained experience and familiarity with common online applications such as search engines, portals, email and perhaps even payment methods.

 Perspective #4: The Flame

Plutarch (45–125AD), a priest of the Temple of Apollo in Greece, is remembered as having said " The mind is not a vessel to be filled, but a fire to be kindled". We would like to borrow this metaphor of the flame. e-Government should not be viewed simply as technology but rather, as a wide-ranging programme with the potential to transform public administration by leveraging on the creativity and innovativeness of public sector officials and their partners.

A good e-Government programme should provoke and challenge. It should urge stakeholders to review time-honoured practices, conceptualise new service models, overhaul operations and find creative applications of relevant technologies. In short, e-Government should play the role of the flame that kindles the imagination of the public sector. A term that aptly captures what often needs to be done is "creative destruction".

A quick scan of modern history reveals that government programmes have had a strong track record of leading to innovative spinoffs and commercial successes. For instance, it is commonly known that research efforts of the 1960s into distributed computer communications carried out by the US Defence's Advanced Research Project Agency (ARPA) led to the development of ARPANET, which evolved into the Internet as we know it today. Similarly NASA's early technological experiments leading to landing the first man on the moon have led to numerous innovations, including the microchip. In the same vein, might not the e-Government endeavours of today give rise to the innovations of tomorrow? We believe this to be a very plausible scenario.

Innovation is essential to sustainable competitiveness. Competitiveness guru, Professor Michael Porter of Harvard Business School has on several occasions advised Asian leaders to heed where their economies are, and whether they have planned sufficiently for economic transition. Many nations have made the transition from a factor-driven economy to an investment-driven one; others may be ready to move from an investment-driven to an innovation-driven economy.

Perspective #5: The Chasm

A pressing concern in all the Asian economies is that of the digital divide — often represented by a gorge or a chasm — between the information "haves" and "have-nots". It is feared that this digital divide will continue to widen, despite various initiatives being undertaken to bridge it. Modern technology moves so quickly that even those in urban areas (who usually have greater access to technology) need to keep running just to be up-to-date. Those in rural areas often face huge challenges.

The digital divide typically falls along old fault lines in Asian societies: male versus female, urban versus rural, and especially income level. And the gap is growing. The poorest in society are multiplying much faster than new technologies can reach them. Meanwhile, advances are boosting productivity in the higher social strata at an even faster pace, adding affluence to the already well-off.

Bringing the poor and disadvantaged up to speed has become critical, not simply for moral reasons but for economic ones, and ultimately for the political payoff. The poor are often too marginalised to participate in politics. Raising their standard of living will surely increase democracy.

There have been increasing efforts to bridge the digital divide. The aim is to spread knowledge and bring relevant information to the rural communities. Once the villages are wired, job opportunities are expected to be opened up. A good example is the private sector driven Drishtee project[3] in rural India. This is a kiosk-based e-Government initiative, which encompasses web-based services provided by local villagers at kiosks, normally set up at roadsides or by village bus stations. Village entrepreneurs own these kiosks by financing them through a government-sponsored scheme. The availability of the services ranges from getting a land record for a loan, applying for an identity card, checking out the latest crop prices or local weather news, or just filing a complaint about a rut in the road.

The kiosk operators need basic computer skills as the software is largely menu-driven. The unit revenue earned by the kiosk owner is a few cents per transaction, but the volume of the operations and the demand enable viability very early in the operation. This initiative has interested local businessmen to act as channel partners and invest in the operational cost using a tiered franchise model. Villagers save on the opportunity cost of travelling and the time spent for receiving these services in person at the district offices, not to mention the cost of bribery and the freedom from worrying how long they would be at the mercy of errant bureaucrats.

Even in an industrialised economy like Taiwan, the government faces the problem of the digital divide between leading edge urban cities and the rural areas. Amidst the spread of the IT revolution that modernises the country's high-tech industries, a clear dividing line can be drawn between individuals capable of making use of IT for greater economic benefit and individuals who do not have this capability. For young people, people with higher education, and people in the higher income brackets, IT literacy is a stepping stone to achieving a high income and a good career. Those who are too old to try using a computer or too poor to afford one, invariably get left out in the new economy.

Taiwan's approach to bridging the divide anchors on advocating lifelong e-learning.[4] This involves establishing cyber learning spaces and promoting distance learning. Taipei invested large amounts of capital in e-learning for its whole community. A rural primary school in a small mining town (Rui-Gan) outside Taipei city offers an example of this strategy. The city provided the school with modern computers, software, and Internet access. The school curriculum was thematically based and students at all levels were expected to search for information related to the various themes on the Internet. In addition, parents were encouraged to be involved in some of the student projects. Parents could access the Internet at school for business and other purposes. Such activities encourage the adults to also engage in the lifelong learning experience together with their children.

Despite all these efforts, we do see the digital divide situation in Asia worsening, rather than improving, in the next five years. Unless some radical way can be found to uplift millions of people and bring them into the digital community, the divide may be a timebomb that may generate social upheaval. A national strategy will help to ensure coordinated efforts and widely dispersed benefits. While many distinct efforts are presently under way, piecemeal efforts most likely would do little to alleviate this complex problem. The other essential element is the community involvement in the use of IT tools to solve existing community's problems. Thus, bridging the digital divide requires both the top-down mandate of the government and the bottom-up involvement of its citizens.

Perspective #6: The Glass Bowl

A Korean civil servant once explained to us why he thought good government should aim to be like a glass bowl. He likened the contents of the bowl to the government and its glass walls to transparency. The clarity of the walls should reflect the transparency of public service procedures and processes.

James D Wolfensohn, President of the World Bank, said: "We see that in today's global economy countries can move towards a market economy, can privatize, can break up state monopolies, can reduce state subsidies, but if they do not fight corruption and put in place good governance ... their development is endangered and will not last."

Wolfensohn's sentiments reiterate that transparency (or more accurately, the lack of transparency) is still an issue in some Asian countries. Although the overall situation has improved compared to a decade earlier; when conducting business in this part of the world, one still comes across a "You scratch my back, and I'll scratch yours" mentality. Inter-personal relationships continue to play a prominent role in business or government dealings.

The fact that the remuneration of civil servants is often lower than their private sector counterparts, and that public administration usually takes longer time with burdensome rules and procedures, provides ample opportunities when bribery can help expedite the process. Rooting out corruption, therefore, continues to be one of the major governance challenges in this region.

Among the many approaches applied to fight corruption, e-Government, in particular, the use of ICT like the Internet and wireless technology, has been singled out as an effective method. Although e-Government services were originally conceived mainly to boost efficiency and convenience, the reduction of corruption opportunities has surfaced as a side benefit.

Government transparency should be embedded in the design of e-Government processes and systems. Citizens rarely have a clear picture how government decisions are made. This lack of transparency prevents the public from actively participating in government, raising questions, or protesting unfair decisions. e-Government can play an essential role in revealing to the public the policies their government adopt or the actions taken. It can also help reduce the number of bribes and incidents of collusion among corrupt bureaucrats if the officials involved could be held personally accountable for their actions. There are many Asian examples of how e-Government programmes address the transparency issue head-on.

In South Korea, the OPEN (Online Procedures Enhancement for Civil Applications) system enables the Korean public to track online the progress of their applications for services. In 1998, the mayor of Seoul Municipality launched a campaign to battle corruption. As part of a concerted effort to bring transparency to government functions such as licensing and permit approval, government reformers not only streamlined the complex regulatory rules which had provided ample opportunities for extorting bribes, they also created an online monitoring system to track the progress of government applications. Today, citizens can find out at anytime where precisely their applications stand in the evaluation process, thwarting corrupt bureaucrats who in the past demanded bribes to expedite applications or even to tell a citizen of the status of an application. (http://www.metro.seoul.kr)

In Gujarat state in India, a system of Computerized Interstate Checkpoints has sharply reduced corruption at the state border through the use of computers and electronic devices at ten remote interstate border checkposts. The project encompasses the automation of the highway toll and fine collection system. The old checkpost system was arbitrary and time consuming, with manual processes needed for verifying documents, estimating penalty amounts, and collecting fines. Often, the fine itself was illegally negotiated. In the computerised process, all checkposts are centrally monitored using video cameras installed to digitally capture the registration number of vehicles passing through. An electronic weighbridge ascertains the weight and the system automatically issues a demand note for fines, if any. Most drivers use a stored value card for payments.

Another Indian effort to propagate the idea of "zero tolerance" for corruption came from the Central Vigilance Commission (CVC), which has begun to share with citizens a large amount of information related to corruption. The CVC website (http://cvc.nic.in) publishes the names of officers from the administrative and revenue services against whom investigations have been ordered, or penalties imposed for corruption. Citizens can also submit information against public officers about possession of "black money" or assets, believed to be disproportionate to known sources of income. The commission would then scrutinize the information received and carry out detailed investigations if needed.

Perspective #7: The Net

Another important facet of e-Government concerns its impact on the "net" of relationships of public administrations. Specifically, e-Government has the potential of transforming the public sector's relationship with citizens, businesses, and as other societal organisations.

e-Government presents an opportunity for government to effectively tailor services to each citizen and business. Citizens interact widely with government to pay their taxes, apply for official documents, receive benefits and so on. Many of these activities generate a great deal of paperwork for both sides, taking up tremendous human resources and time. Businesses also have a great deal of interaction with government, such as applying for permits and licences, paying taxes or applying for grants. For these purposes, it is often necessary to deal with multiple departments and agencies. Creating a single point of contact, perhaps through e-Government portals, and leveraging on different channels made possible by technology — PCs, mobile devices, public kiosks, interactive TV, etc — could simplify these services and enable greater access and self-service by the different constituents. For government, there is opportunity to redirect resources from purely administrative activities to focusing on helping customers with complex queries, or to improving services to people from more vulnerable segments of society. It will not be an easy journey but the potential benefits will make it worthwhile.

The CRM Approach

The discipline of Customer Relationship Management (CRM) has been widely applied in business. CRM refers to the use of technology and redefined processes in order to enhance the quality of the organisation's relationship with its customers. Such benefits are becoming more important to public sector agencies. Governments face an increasingly urgent need to improve relationships with citizens who are becoming accustomed to better customer relationships with commercial entities.

Although government agencies are mission-driven and commercial enterprises are profit-driven, both types of organisations serve their customers in similar ways. Like commercial organisations, every public agency is under tremendous pressure to increase operational effectiveness. CRM solutions typically help government agencies improve communication and response time to constituents, trim operating costs, empower employees with data for decision-making, and satisfy a growing demand for instant access to organisation-wide data.

Some of the greatest challenges in using CRM approaches to bring government and citizens closer together are not technological, but rather human and cultural. Knowledge-sharing, rather than knowledge-hoarding, must become the norm. Indeed some market-watch groups observe that some public sector entities have begun looking beyond "citizen-centric" government to trying to become "citizen-led" government.[5] To achieve this, government:

- must learn to relate to citizens as individuals and as groups in ways, that enhance successful collaboration;
- needs to realise that if peer-to-peer networking software takes off, a citizen's permission will be required to participate in his or her world of completely private networks; and
- needs to collaborate with responsible citizens groups in ways that would make peer-to-peer collaboration networks want to include the government as a trusted third party.

Privacy Concerns

With the growth of online services, users are increasingly concerned about privacy issues. In dealing with the government many want those responsible for government websites to tell them what the personal information they give will be used for. Many government websites thus have privacy statements to assure visitors and users of the website, either that their data is not being shared or if it is being shared, the circumstances.

e-Government services present a new mode of communication and interaction between the government and the people where there should, as far as possible, be transparency in terms of the nature and extent of information-sharing. This will ensure that concerns over personal privacy do not become a barrier to the adoption of such services by the public.

e-Democracy

An important aspect of e-Government relates to the area of "e-Democracy". The origin of the word "democracy" is telling. The Greek word *demos* means exercised by the people, and *kratos* is power. Together the words define a government by the people exercised directly or through elected representatives. But what is the meaning of "e-Democracy" and what's the key difference between democracy with an *e* and without?

The area of e-Democracy has to do with creating two-way communication in order to improve governance and enhance quality of feedback. It is about taking full advantage of ICT to enable open dialogue between policymakers and civil society. Traditionally, citizens participate through voting and other constitutionally permitted means. With e-Democracy, not only can citizens provide feedback, they can also interact through discussions, negotiations, and other methods that would have normally required a physical presence. Online discussion groups, forums, chats and the, like can help to support the democratic process by facilitating, broadening and deepening participation in the process.[6]

It has been said that e-Democracy can bring about two key benefits. Firstly, as public administrations post information and policies online, citizens' awareness of public affairs increases. Secondly, as awareness of public affairs increases, so does the ability of citizens to make better choices and decisions when participating in the democratic process. In this way, the society as a whole moves closer to achieving the ideals of a true democracy.

Take for example, an e-Democracy system that the Thai government has tried to put in place. The country adopts the check and balances system similar to that of the Western democracies. In addition to the traditional feedback channel such as in-person appeals or letters posted to government representatives, a website called *Rakang* (http://www.rakang.thaigov.go.th) was set up to allow Thais to file online complaints about government services directly to the Prime Minister. The word *Rakang* in the Thai language means *Bell*. It symbolises the idea that the government pays personal attention to each citizen, allowing anyone to come to the door of the government office to ring the bell and voice one's troubles. Bell-ringing was a traditional way in which the citizen made an appeal to the ruler during the paternalistic monarchy of the ancient Sukhothai kingdom. The *Rakang* website also provides links for the citizen who would like to tipoff the authorities about any misconduct, or file specific complaints to the police department or the office of the local administration. Nevertheless, this feedback channel is largely seen as something that would only appeal to Thais who are both interested in politics and comfortable with the Internet.

Another area related to e-Democracy is the experimental effort geared towards the e-Voting ideal. Broadly, e-Voting is about utilising ICT to provide new methods of casting votes in elections or other ballots under statutory control. It also covers activities that underpin the electoral process, such as registration and absent voter application. At present, however, e-Voting appears to be still too premature and is heavily debated even in the European countries and the United States. Voting over the Internet still has technical and logistical obstacles such as authentication, security, privacy and audibility. Nevertheless, if such a system becomes practicable, it will surely alleviate the problem facing Asian countries such as India, where elections usually span over many days, with over 600 million voters and some 800,000 polling stations.

Perspective #8: The Package

Increasingly, e-Government is being seen as something that can be "exported". This is represented as a "package" comprising knowledge, skills, competencies, experiences, intellectual property, and even "modules" (applications, software, hardware, infrastructure, etc).

In many economies, we have observed a shift to the next phase of e-Government. In this new phase, more government administrations will need to make a strong case for directly linking e-Government solutions to national competitiveness. Rather than focusing solely on the aspects of public sector productivity and the introduction of new service channels, as was the case in the earlier phase, there will be a drive towards using e-Government to help "boost the bottom line" of the national economy. This trend has surfaced not as a result of an academic exercise, but is driven instead, by severe economic challenges and concerns, especially in Asia.

Who moved my cheese?[7] was a management bestseller in the early 2000s. It is also an apt reminder of the perceived threat facing many Asian nations grappling with how to respond to the China economic juggernaut that has gobbled up much of their "cheese" or past economic opportunities. Even since the Asian financial crisis in 1997, China has turned in annual growth rates of 7–8 percent. In 2002, Chinese exports in 2002 surged 21 percent to US$ 322 billion, making it the largest exporter of goods to the US. At the same time, China's economy seemed to shrug off the global economic slowdown, pulling in almost US$ 50 billion in new foreign direct investment (FDI), more than the rest of Asia combined. Some market watchers have warned that this may be just the beginning. So far, some 80 percent of China's export capacity is concentrated in only six provinces[8] along its eastern coast, with the vast interior of the country still relatively untapped.

The challenge of the maturing China economy is never far from the minds of Asian leaders, both in public and private sectors. With China's entry into WTO, the issue becomes even more immediate. The different Asian economies have been impacted in differing ways, and have developed their own responses, as the sample below shows:

- In Malaysia, investment in Penang, the nation's largest manufacturing centre, has slowed. A number of factories have closed down as multinationals decide to relocate operations to cheaper plants in China. Malaysia's Multimedia Super Corridor (MSC) will have a harder time attracting investors, as much capital gets sucked up by China.
- Thailand faces similar problems with manufacturing, but the Thais are trying to compensate for weaker US demand by redirecting exports to China and boosting domestic consumption.
- Government planners in Singapore are trying to steer the economy into knowledge-intensive industries further up the value chain, increasing the intensity of focus in areas like biotechnology, design and software development. Singapore has also signed a Free Trade Agreements (FTA) with the US and other developed nations, a move that may pave the way for others in ASEAN to do the same.
- Further north, the Taiwanese face a dilemma. Politically they want their identity separate from the mainland's, but economically they are becoming more and more entwined. Taiwan needs China — the mainland now absorbs 25 percent of Taiwan's exports — but fears being over-reliant. Despite various government-imposed restrictions on direct investments in mainland China, an exodus of skills and money continues. Almost half a million Taiwanese have taken up residence in Shanghai alone.
- The container ports in Hong Kong are threatened by cheaper terminals in Xiamen, Shenzhen and Shanghai, which are also closer to where the goods are going to and from. The city's financial sector is likely to be challenged by Shanghai as China liberalizes its financial system.

What does all this have to do with e-Government? Primarily, the various economic imperatives will increasingly drive national leaders in Asia (and indeed the world over) to look to e-Government programmes as direct contributors to national economic competitiveness, development and growth. This is a departure from the earlier days of e-Government, where it was merely viewed as as an internal productivity initiative, then later as a added channel for delivering public services.

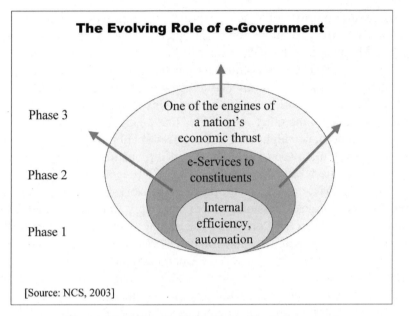

Figure 16-3: The Evolving Role of e-Government

THOUGHTS ON THE E-GOVERNMENT EVOLUTION

It is probably safe to say that the "novelty" of e-Government has worn off. In the early years, some government administrations may have thought that e-Government was the fashionable thing to do, and went ahead with their initiatives on that basis. After all, everybody else was going in the same direction. After several years of massive investments in time and money, most now have a better appreciation of the value of their e-Government undertakings.

Couple this with a tough economic environment and intense fiscal pressures, and it is not surprising that many of the projects that do not bring clear value have been reprioritised, rescheduled or even dropped. In many economies today, there is little room for "nice to have" projects. Projects that are pursued need to show their benefits and relevance to the progress of the state.

How e-Government will evolve from here depends largely on how seriously different government leaderships take some of the various perspectives we have described.

A base scenario would see governments employing e-Government primarily at the operational level, in order to benefit from productivity gains. The practice of government will be largely unchanged, just made more efficient. There is nothing wrong in pursuing this strategy. It is certainly a sound step for any administration. Standing still while others are progressing would be to fall behind. This strategy however may not fully leverage on the other possibilities that e-Government can offer.

Another scenario might be to use e-Government to focus on enhancing the relationship between government and its constituents. Depending on the degree to which approaches like CRM (citizen relationship management?) is adopted, and the pervasiveness of e-Government (through mobile and wireless technologies perhaps), this can lead to significant changes in G2C, G2B, or even G2E. Some researchers point to "u-Government", or ubiquitous government, as the wave after e-Government.

An extreme scenario would see e-Democracy taken to such an extent that government administration becomes bogged down by citizen participation at every step, with e-Voting on all significant issues. By definition, that would be total democracy, but one has to wonder if it is necessarily a step forward.

One should not forget that e-Government, with all its wide-ranging possibilities, is simply a tool. It is one of the many tools that could help bring about the elusive state we call "good government". At the end of the day, it is up to the nation's leaders and the public administrators to decide how they will make use of the tool.

Confucius was once asked what he thought were the essentials of good government. He replied,

> The ruler should esteem five excellences and avoid four evils. The five excellences are: plenitude without extravagance; taxation without exciting discontent; desire without covetousness; dignity without haughtiness; majesty without fierceness. The four evils to be avoided are: without instruction in the law, to inflict punishment — that is tyranny; without proper warning to expect perfect adherence — that is oppression; late in giving orders and expecting early obedience — that is robbery; to tax and to spend in a stingy manner — that is a misuse of government function.

The wise words of the sage are as true today in the 21st Century as they were in 500 BC.

Endnotes

1   Mullaney, TJ, *"The Web is finally catching profits"*, *Businessweek*, 17 February 2003.

2   The *"Eight Perspectives of e-Government"* is a framework and consulting approach introduced by NCS Pte Ltd.

3   Mishra, Satyan, *"Connecting India village by village"*, India: The Drishtee Project. Offers mobile, kiosk-based e-Government for rural India. http://www.iicd.org/base/story_read?id=4956.

4   Higgins, Andrew, *"E-learning's role"* (2002).

5   Wylie, J, *"e-Government is next big opportunity for CRM vendors"*, *Trend Monitor*, May 2001.

6   Office of the e-Envoy, UK government, *"Report of the e-democracy"*, 2003 www.edemocracy.gov.uk.

7   Johnson, S, *"Who moved my cheese?"*, Vermilion (1998).

8   Guangdong, Fujian, Zhejiang, Jiangsu, Shandong and Liaoning.

INDEX